Mendelssohn, the Organ, and the Music of the Past

Eastman Studies in Music

Ralph P. Locke, Senior Editor
Eastman School of Music

Additional Titles of Interest

Anton Heiller: Organist, Composer, Conductor
Peter Planyavsky
Translated by Christa Rumsey

Bach and the Pedal Clavichord: An Organist's Guide
Joel Speerstra

Dieterich Buxtehude: Organist in Lübeck
Kerala J. Snyder

French Organ Music from the Revolution to Franck and Widor
Edited by Lawrence Archbold and William J. Peterson

Maurice Duruflé: The Man and His Music
James E. Frazier

*Mendelssohn, Goethe, and the Walpurgis Night:
The Heathen Muse in European Culture, 1700–1850*
John Michael Cooper

Pierre Cochereau: Organist of Notre-Dame
Anthony Hammond

Sacred Song and the Pennsylvania Dutch
Daniel Jay Grimminger

Schumann's Piano Cycles and the Novels of Jean Paul
Erika Reiman

Widor: A Life beyond the Toccata
John R. Near

A complete list of titles in the Eastman Studies in Music series
may be found on our website, www.urpress.com.

Mendelssohn, the Organ, and the Music of the Past

Constructing Historical Legacies

Edited by Jürgen Thym

UNIVERSITY OF ROCHESTER PRESS

First published 2014

University of Rochester Press
668 Mt. Hope Avenue, Rochester, NY 14620, USA
www.urpress.com
and Boydell & Brewer Limited
PO Box 9, Woodbridge, Suffolk IP12 3DF, UK
www.boydellandbrewer.com

ISBN-13: 978-1-58046-474-1
ISSN: 1071-9989

Library of Congress Cataloging-in-Publication Data

Mendelssohn, the organ, and the music of the past : constructing historical legacies / edited by Jürgen Thym.
pages cm — (Eastman studies in music, ISSN 1071-9989 ; v. 118)
Includes bibliographical references and index.
ISBN 978-1-58046-474-1 — ISBN 1-58046-474-2 1. Mendelssohn—Bartholdy, Felix, 1809–1847. 2. Organ music—Germany—19th century—History and criticism. I. Thym, Jürgen, 1943– editor. II. Series: Eastman studies in music ; v. 118.
ML410.M5M635 2014
780.92—dc23   2014028712

A catalogue record for this title is available from the British Library.

This publication is printed on acid-free paper.
Printed in the United States of America.

In memory of Russell Saunders (1921–92)
and David Craighead (1924–2012)

Contents

Acknowledgments

This book is deeply informed by the confluence and synergism of performance and musical scholarship. Initially, and in part, it owes its existence to a 2009 conference organized by the Eastman Rochester Organ Initiative (EROI) entitled "Mendelssohn and the Contrapuntal Tradition" and masterminded by Hans Davidsson with his colleagues David Higgs and William Porter in the Department of Organ, Sacred Music, and Historical Keyboards of the University of Rochester's Eastman School of Music. And the "three professors" are present in a performance reconstructing Mendelssohn's organ recital in Leipzig in 1840—available by way of an enclosed internet link given below. Hans Davidsson also contributed an essay on Mendelssohn's organ sonatas that, taking its cue from the Craighead-Saunders Organ in Christ Church in Rochester, New York, brings together organ construction, performance practice, and music criticism. My first thank-you therefore goes to Eastman's organ department with a tradition, extending for nearly a century, of combining instruction, performance, and scholarship on the highest level. Appropriately the book is dedicated to the memory of two distinguished organ professors, David Craighead (1924– 2012) and Russell Saunders (1921–92), whose teaching inspired generations of Eastman students and who lend their names to the Craighead-Saunders Organ that, since 2008, has stood at the center of the EROI conferences.

I am grateful to the contributors to this volume, some of whom had to wait for a long time to see their essays in print: Celia Applegate, John Michael Cooper, Hans Davidsson, Wm. A. Little, Peter Mercer-Taylor, Siegwart Reichwald, Glenn Stanley, Russell Stinson, Benedict Taylor, Nicholas Thistlethwaite, R. Larry Todd, and Christoph Wolff. They all set time aside, often on short notice, to help the editor in the process of finalizing their contributions for publication. R. Larry Todd and John Michael Cooper were particularly helpful when it was decided to enlist additional contributors to the volume, thereby expanding and enriching the topic of that EROI conference. In this context, I also need to thank several anonymous prepublication reviewers for their guidance informed by constructive criticism. Persuaded by John Michael Cooper, one of the sages of Mendelssohn scholarship, I decided to add MWV numbers to Mendelssohn's compositions at the first mentioning of the work within the chapter. (The splendid accomplishment of Ralph Wehner, he argued, should be given its proper due.)

I gratefully acknowledge the help of Ralph P. Locke, senior editor of the Eastman Studies in Music series, as well as of Suzanne Guiod and Sonia Kane, former and current editorial directors of University of Rochester Press. Their interest in the project, patience, and faith that the book would finally be completed sustained me on the long road to the finish line.

I received administrative and logistical support along the way from John Allegar, Marc Bollmann, Kathy Buechel, David Higgs, Naomi Gregory, Wm. A. Little, Andrea Mace, Cornelia Thierbach, and several others, and beg forgiveness in case I have forgotten someone else who was particularly helpful.

Therese Malhame was a superb copyeditor, whose eye for consistency of style was particularly welcome in view of a most diverse group of contributors, each with his or her own style traditions. In the final phase of production, Julia Cook, Tracey Engel, and Ryan Peterson skillfully navigated the project through the usual obstacle course. Michael Hager of Museum Photographics in Rochester, New York, performed small miracles in improving some of the visual images.

Some publishers and institutions gave permission to include musical examples and illustrations or cite extended passages. I acknowledge them here with gratitude: Alte Pinakothek, Munich (Gabriele Göbl); Bach-Archiv, Leipzig (Peter Wollny); Bild und Heimat Verlag, Reichenbach/Vogtland (Inge Weber); Stadtgeschichtliches Museum Leipzig (Christoph Kaufmann); Oxford University Press (Suzanne Ryan).

Jürgen Thym
May 2014

Introduction

Of Statues and Monuments

Jürgen Thym

Felix Mendelssohn grew up in an era and in a region of Europe—namely the German-speaking lands—that liked statues and monuments, not so much for their own sake as because they reflected a deep awareness of history. In fact, he contributed to such monuments—aural, semistaged, and in stone—throughout his life, calling attention to, indeed constructing, historical legacies through his activities. He even confessed his fondness for such monuments in England, when he proposed, perhaps in jest, that Dr. Henry John Gauntlett, an influential figure in British organ reform in the nineteenth century, "ought to have a statue."[1]

Profuse numbers of statues and monuments were installed in the German states of Europe following the Wars of Liberation 1813–15, and, more prominently, after the foundation of the German Empire in 1871. Celebrating victories in wars and casting them as triumphs in stone had, of course, been a practice since ancient times. (One only needs to walk among Rome's archaeological sites to encounter triumphal arches and columns that reformulated military successes as icons of heroism and greatness for current and future generations.) Just a few years after Mendelssohn was born, the German-speaking people shook off the yoke of Napoleonic empire building and expressed their military victories—albeit accomplished with considerable foreign help, especially from the British and from tsarist Russia—in monuments throughout much of the nineteenth century and well into the twentieth century. Beethoven had participated in such celebrations early on with ephemeral works such as *Wellingtons Sieg, oder die Schlacht bei Vittoria*, op. 91 (Wellington's victory, or The Battle of Vitoria) and the cantata *Der glorreiche Augenblick*, op. 136 (The glorious moment), both performed at the Congress of Vienna in 1814–15.[2] Perhaps to atone for his reluctant participation in Napoleon's wars against Prussia and Russia when he was a crown prince, Ludwig I of Bavaria, once he ascended to the throne, would not be outdone in manifesting his Teutonic credentials in marble and granite. The Befreiungshalle (Hall of Liberation) in Kelheim near Regensburg celebrated the military success of the German people in the Wars of Liberation against Napoleon. Conceived in the 1830s, it was inaugurated on the fiftieth anniversary of the Battle of Leipzig in 1863. Not to be outdone by the Bavarians, the Germans—now united under Prussian hegemony—commemorated the same victory in the Völkerschlachtdenkmal or Battle of the Nations monument near Leipzig at the centennial of the event, just a few months before another international war put an end to the "long" nineteenth century, to the European world order, and to civilization as it had been known. There were other victories to be celebrated and cast in stone: The Siegessäule (Triumph column) in Berlin's Tiergarten proudly announced Prussian military successes in several wars leading up to the unification of the German states. And when current military events did not suffice, there were battles in the past—even in the very distant past—that could be remembered in monument-worthy projects invoking the "common" history of the German people: The Hermannsdenkmal near Detmold, begun in 1841 and completed in 1875, celebrated Arminius the Cheruscan, a Germanic tribal chieftain, whose cunning military genius trapped several Roman legions in the swamps near the Teutoburger Wald in 9 CE, dealing a severe blow to the Roman Empire and—one might also argue—delaying the process of civilization that Roman occupation and influence would have meant for the lands east of the Rhine.

The liberation wars against Napoleon made German-speaking people realize that, in addition to language, they had a common history and culture. They imagined that they were a community in the sense that Benedict Anderson and other recent cultural theorists have used the term.[3] The fractured state of the situation around 1815—the Habsburg Empire and Prussia, both conceived or evolved as multinational and multiethnic entities, as well as an agglomeration of medium-size and smaller states, all of them ethnically more homogeneous than the two major players—and the equally problematic religious divide between Catholics and Protestants among Germans made a political solution to the "German question" nearly impossible. But in the *Vormärz* period— the era before the 1848 revolution that defines Mendelssohn's lifetime as an adult—other icons of nationhood, furthering the imagined community (and, by and large, of a less belligerent nature), stood ready to be found. And were. Mendelssohn was indeed a key player in their "discovery."

We can begin to traverse Mendelssohn's accomplishments in celebrating national icons in 1840, because that year made the Germans again collide with the French: the so-called *Rheinkrise* (Rhine crisis)—manufactured by the French government to distract attention from the miscalculations of its foreign policy in the Eastern Mediterranean—pitted French and German political and national aspirations against each other, with the rhetoric on both sides reaching fever pitch. Mendelssohn's civic nationalism should be distinguished from the more jingoistic and shrill expressions of nationhood that were characteristic on both sides of the Rhine.[4]

In June of that year the citizens of Leipzig celebrated the four-hundredth anniversary of the invention of the printing press with a three-day festival. Even though Johannes Gutenberg, its inventor, was born and lived most of his life in Mainz, Leipzig—being the center of printing and publishing in German-speaking lands—considered that it had a civic duty to commemorate a man whose technological advances had enriched the community and contributed immeasurably to the spread of literacy, enlightenment, and Luther's Reformation to distant shores. The highpoint of the festival was the premiere of Mendelssohn's Symphony no. 2 ("Lobgesang" [MWV A18, op. 52]), with Mendelssohn conducting the Gewandhaus Orchestra, on June 25. This "Große Musik für Leipzig,"[5] a symphony cantata mixing purely instrumental and choral movements and thereby harking back to Beethoven's Ninth, gathered the various strands of the festival into a celebration of the triumph of light over darkness, of enlightenment over ignorance, and thereby confirming the Beethovenian symphonic narrative "per aspera ad astra" (literally: "through hardship to the stars," a pattern often seen by commentators as embodied in Beethoven's Fifth Symphony). The "Lobgesang" was to become one of his most popular compositions during his lifetime, though it quickly lost favor soon after his death and is rarely performed today. (For a Kierkegaardian interpretation of the symphony-cantata, see chapter 11.)

A somewhat more nationalistic subtext, it should be admitted, was not absent during these days of civic celebration. A day before the "Lobgesang" premiere, a statue of Gutenberg was unveiled (probably a replica of the one in Mainz) at the market place in Leipzig, with Raimund Härtel, co-owner of the music publishing company Breitkopf und Härtel, comparing Johannes Gutenberg (yes, it was St. John's Day or *Johannistag*) with St. John the Baptist, who, like Gutenberg, had prepared the way for someone greater coming after him—Gutenberg's printing press indeed had led to Luther's translation of the Bible, which had allowed the German people to read the Word of the Lord in their native language and in turn fostered Luther's Reformation. A *Festgesang* (MWV D4) for male chorus and brass composed by Mendelssohn sounded at the unveiling: "Vaterland, in deinen Gauen / Brach der gold'ne Tag einst an" (Fatherland, the golden day burst forth long ago in your regions). A year later, in 1841, it served to accompany another, rather different unveiling: that of the aforementioned Hermannsdenkmal near Detmold.[6] The English-speaking world, though, is familiar with this tune in an even more sharply different context: after it was discovered that the melody perfectly matched a preexisting Christmas text by Charles Wesley, the melody was disseminated through hymnals as the carol "Hark, the Herald Angels Sing"— quite devoid of any politico-national implications.

A little more than a month after the Gutenberg celebration, the citizens of Leipzig were invited to a concert given for the benefit of another civic purpose.

Mendelssohn had decided that Johann Sebastian Bach, the most illustrious musician who had ever resided in Leipzig, deserved to be commemorated with a monument near St. Thomas Church. The composer added to his already strenuous schedule by setting time aside to practice the organ (his pedal technique, especially, needed considerable improvement) in preparation for a full-length organ recital at St. Thomas, a fundraiser, featuring works of Bach and framed by two improvisations at the beginning and at the end. The latter would feature a fugue with the pitches B♭, A, C, and B♮ (spelling the name of BACH) interwoven in a variety of textures. The concert on August 6 was favorably reviewed by Robert Schumann in the *Neue Zeitschrift für Musik*.[7]

Indeed, the event brought in enough money to proceed with the project. In 1841 Mendelssohn asked his friend, the painter Eduard Bendemann in Dresden, to provide him with a sketch of what the monument might look like;[8] Hermann Knaur in Leipzig and Friedrich Moritz Hiller in turn were asked to finish it: a column in the neo-Gothic style (vaguely reminiscent of cemetery art) that included some relief sculptures, including a bust of J. S. Bach. The commemorative column was inaugurated, in the presence of Bach's last surviving grandson, in Leipzig on April 23, 1843.[9] Today a different and more ostentatious monument of Bach—presenting him as if he were a Fifth Evangelist and model Lutheran—greets the visitor at the south entrance to St. Thomas Church; it was designed by Carl Scheffner and erected in 1908. Mendelssohn's Bach monument can still be found, but now hidden in a park nearby. A comparison of the iconography of these two Bach monuments for Leipzig might prove instructive.

Mendelssohn's connections with J. S. Bach were manifold and, in a way, preceded the younger composer's birth (see chapter 8). A veritable Bach cult can be discerned in the family of his maternal grandparents, the Itzigs—a reverence nurtured by keyboard lessons and music-theory instruction provided by none other than Bach's student Johann Philipp Kirnberger. Felix's paternal grandfather, Moses Mendelssohn, the famous philosopher of the German Enlightenment, also took music lessons with Kirnberger. The composer's parents were members of the Berlin Sing-Akademie, where Bach's choral works were rehearsed; his father Abraham donated a substantial collection of music materials—by and large, works of Bach—to its library, and so did his great-aunt Sara Levy in later years. In addition to family links, there was a pedagogical lineage that linked Mendelssohn directly to Bach's teaching and the contrapuntal tradition (see chapter 1): Mendelssohn's teacher Carl Friedrich Zelter had been taught by two Bach students, Kirnberger and Johann Friedrich Fasch. (The latter was the founder of the Berlin Sing-Akademie in 1791, whom Zelter succeeded as conductor in 1800.) In other words, ancestry and teachers imbued Mendelssohn's outlook with a definite Bachian orientation that, rather than being a burden, spurred him on to preserve the legacy of the distant master in his own compositions as well as performances and acts of civic commemoration.

The Bach commemorations in Leipzig in 1840 and 1843 seem like faint reverberations of an earlier event that Mendelssohn spearheaded as a twenty-year-old conductor (and that put him forever on the map of musical historicism): the first modern performance, in 1829, of Bach's *St. Matthew Passion* with the Berlin Sing-Akademie. Even though rooted in the Bach tradition of previous decades, the performance, given ample publicity in Berlin as well as in other German cities, was a major milestone in the revival of earlier music in general and Bach's music in particular. It was the most powerful sign of musical historicism in the nineteenth century, a monument or statue cast in sound rather than stone. It foreshadowed nothing less than a paradigmatic shift in musical culture—with repercussions far beyond Berlin and other musical centers in Germany. The revival of early music was to change concert life in the next hundred years; it turned the concert hall into a museum for the performance of musical artworks of the past rather than (as in, say, Beethoven's day) almost entirely of the present.[10]

Mendelssohn grew up in Berlin, which in comparison with Dresden, Munich, and Vienna was perhaps a cultural backwater. Still, the Prussian capital was eager to catch up with other European capitals in terms of arts and sciences, especially as a result of the reforms instituted after the devastating military defeat in 1806 at the hands of Napoleon. Family connections and influential teachers and friends may have helped as well in Mendelssohn's being considered to participate in the organization and artistic direction of official events. He indeed became a public figure quite early on. In 1828, he was asked to write the music for a cantata commemorating Albrecht Dürer at the tercentenary of the artist's death (see chapter 9). The somewhat amateurish poetry by Konrad Levezow may not have interested the few elder statesmen among the composers in Berlin (and there were very few to begin with), but Mendelssohn's teacher Zelter, claiming advanced age and other responsibilities to avoid the challenge, used his personal influence in favor of his prodigy student. For the nineteen-year-old youngster, it certainly was tempting to contribute music for a state occasion, and he accepted. Johann Gottfried Schadow and Karl Friedrich Schinkel, Berlin's most distinguished sculptor and architect, respectively, were both involved; royalty was present; and, of course, a statue of Dürer was unveiled at an appropriate moment during the festivities. True, Mendelssohn had composed better pieces a few years earlier, such as the *Midsummer Night's Dream* overture (MWV P3, op. 21) and the Octet (MWV R20, op. 20), but the *Festmusik* ("Dürer Festmusik," MWV D1) prompted the royal family, government officials, and Berlin's artistic and intellectual elite to take notice of him in a major public event.

Rehearsals for the performance of Bach's *St. Matthew Passion* were fully under way early in 1829, when Mendelssohn had already contemplated his next move. The year following would be another anniversary, the tercentenary of the Augsburg Confession, a landmark in the consolidation of Protestantism in Germany and thus an event of civic commemoration (well, at least in some regions of the German Confederation, especially those parts of Prussia that were Lutheran or Reformed). Perhaps it was foolhardy for a composer with a Jewish name, even though baptized and thus Christian, to believe that he could employ his art to commemorate an event dear to Protestantism. In any case, the commission never quite materialized. Anti-Semitism, even though difficult to pinpoint, may have been involved.[11] After completing the work, now known as the "Reformation" Symphony (MWV N15, op. posth. 107), he began his grand tour, exploring different cultures and different musical traditions. The work remained a stepchild throughout his life: he revised it, conducted a rehearsal of it in Paris early in 1832 (not really a locale where Lutheranism was rampant), premiered it in Berlin later in that year (apparently without the positive reception he might have expected), then abandoned it altogether. It was published and given an opus number only after his death (see chapter 3). And he was never awarded the appointment he had hoped for in Berlin, starting his career instead in Düsseldorf in the Rhineland and then moving to Leipzig, a city whose musical culture he decisively shaped during his tenure as conductor of the Gewandhaus Orchestra and, during his lifetime and beyond, as founding director of the conservatory there.

Berlin beckoned again in the 1840s as a result of Friedrich Wilhelm IV's ascent to the throne. The aforementioned Rhine crisis of 1840 provided an impetus to the young monarch, who had just succeeded his father Friedrich Wilhelm III, aligning his state with German national aspirations. The Rhineland, a largely Catholic region, had become a Prussian province as a result of the treaties negotiated at the Congress of Vienna; any French ambitions of annexing that province would pit France against one of the two key-players in the German Confederation. At the beginning of his reign, the new king relaxed censorship, stopped the prosecution of so-called demagogues (i.e., political opponents), provided shelter to exiled artists and intellectuals, ameliorated tensions with the Catholics in his western provinces, and encouraged regional parliaments. His subjects had good reasons to hope that he would respond to political and social changes that, during the reign of his father, had built up but not been addressed. In short, Prussia was suffering from what in modern German parlance is known as a *Reformstau*: a pileup of needed reforms.

Alas, the king had rather antiquated ideas about his power being divinely ordained. While Felix was more guarded in his criticism, his sister Fanny, with refreshing irreverence, called some of the monarchical constructs "sentimental nonsense."[12] And she was right: when the Paulskirche Parliament, a constitutional assembly that had met in Frankfurt/Main for much of 1848–49, offered Friedrich Wilhelm IV the crown of the German Empire— in its "kleindeutsch" manifestation without the German-speaking regions of the Habsburg Empire—he refused: he would not accept any power that emanated from the street. As one historian has put it, the king would have liked "to do something great, something historical for 'Teutschland'; he vacillated between his ambition and his hatred for anything modern, liberal, democratic. The latter prevailed."[13]

Mendelssohn was to get an early preview of the monarch's indecision. Friedrich Wilhelm IV had great plans for making Berlin a center of the arts, comparable to Dresden, Munich, and Vienna. He wanted to attract the most illustrious artists and intellectuals to the shores of the Spree or Havel Rivers, and, quite early, Mendelssohn figured in his vision. Mendelssohn was cautious, even strongly reluctant to move to Berlin (he had been disappointed by Berlin before), but he finally relocated his family. (After all, being close to his mother and the Hensels—his sister's family—was tempting.) Defining his responsibilities as royal Kapellmeister proved difficult: he was supposed to head a new music institute, compose liturgical music at the command of the king, and perform large-scale works (meaning: oratorios). Mendelssohn was indeed on the verge of becoming the "Staatskomponist" of Prussia. Unfortunately, disentangling bureaucratic competencies and overcoming vanities and pettiness proved vexing and sapped the composer's energies. Even two audiences with the king did not advance things much further, except for the conferral of the title of GMD or Generalmusikdirektor. To no avail: the first state-funded conservatory in German lands opened its doors to musicians in Leipzig in 1843 (a full quarter century before Berlin was ready); the king of Saxony (where Leipzig was located) proved to be more skillful in cutting through red tape than his counterpart in Prussia.

In spite of the frustrations that Mendelssohn encountered with court and bureaucracy in Berlin, the fruits of his Berlin appointment are not insubstantial: the music for Sophocles's *Antigone* (MWV M12, op. 55, 1841), the incidental music for Shakespeare's *A Midsummer Night's Dream* (MWV M13, op. 61, 1843—beginning with the eponymous concert overture composed when he was seventeen), the music to Racine's *Athalie* and Sophocles's *Oedipus at Colonus* (MWV M16 and M14, respectively—both of 1845). By the time the latter works were performed in the Neues Palais in Potsdam with royalty attending, Mendelssohn could no longer tolerate life in Berlin. He had taken care not to sever his ties to Leipzig anyway and could therefore move his family back to a city that provided him with a more flexible framework for his artistry.

It is, of course, futile to speculate as to how Mendelssohn would have negotiated the turbulence of the Revolution of 1848–49, and, even more futile, about how he would have responded to Friedrich Wilhelm IV's rejection of the imperial crown, delaying the national and democratic aspirations of the German people, setting the stage for another decade of reactionary politics in Prussia, and dashing the high hopes in his reign once and for all. Mendelssohn died a few months before the revolution got its sputtering start in German lands. He most certainly sympathized with those demanding constitutional reform and the right of citizens to participate in government. But he would have abhorred the excesses of the events and taken issue with the more radical factions that emerged in their wake. His response to the nationalistic rhetoric emanating during the Rhine crisis of 1840 perhaps provides a clue. Famous and not-so-famous poets produced lots of jingoistic verses: *Lied der Deutschen* (Song of the Germans) beginning with the famous line "Deutschland, Deutschland über alles" (Hoffmann von Fallersleben), *Die Wacht am Rhein* (The guard on the Rhine: Max Schneckenburger), and *Rheinlied* (Rhine song: Nikolaus Becker). The latter, starting with the assertive lines "Sie sollen ihn nicht haben / Den freien, deutschen Rhein" (They shall not have it / The free German Rhine) was set to music no fewer than seventy times (by luminaries such as Robert Schumann, Konradin Kreutzer, and Heinrich Marschner) and stimulated a French reply by the renowned poet Alfred de Vigny: *Le Rhin allemand* (set to music by Félicien David). Sensing a successful business venture for his music publishing company, Raimund Härtel encouraged Mendelssohn to set it as well: it had the potential of being quite profitable. Mendelssohn declined. In a letter to his brother Paul in November 1840, he found the issue "childish."[14]

Mendelssohn died in 1847, at what was, even in those days, the early age of thirty-eight. In his short life, quite remarkably, he managed to commemorate at least four figures who later would be instrumental in defining German-ness: Dürer, Bach, Luther, and Gutenberg. Perhaps Beethoven should be added here as well, because both the "Reformation" Symphony and the "Lobgesang" Symphony invoke Beethoven as a point of reference (to say nothing about more subtle references to Beethoven in Mendelssohn's early string quartets). Goethe and Schiller may be missing from the list, but we could imagine a composer such as Mendelssohn—who was imbued with an obvious sense of official-dom and was apparently motivated in part by a need to assimilate and pay his dues to the culture that was also his[15]—being present at a Goethe centenary in 1849 (he met the old man in Weimar three times) or at a Schiller commemoration in 1855 or 1859, and composing music for such events. Mendelssohn's colleague Robert Schumann seems to have picked up, in or around 1849, the older composer's knack for commemorative events: the *Lieder aus Wilhelm Meister, Requiem für Mignon,* and *Szenen aus Goethes Faust* can be linked, more or less persuasively, to the Goethe centenary being celebrated throughout German lands during that year. The oratorio on Luther that Schumann contemplated around 1852 may have, if it had been completed, fulfilled a similar function of cultural-national commemoration.

Throughout his life Mendelssohn contributed greatly to German nation building, in that he lent his talent as a creative and performing artist to markers and reminders that encouraged the people to imagine themselves as a nation having a common history and culture. And yet, it is difficult to see in him a proponent of national fervor, even less of nationalistic fervor. He spoke several languages, was widely traveled, and thus knew different nations, traditions, and cultures. He was a cosmopolitan, and certainly as much so as his contemporary Franz Liszt. As a composer and conductor, Mendelssohn recognized and secured the legacy of non-German traditions: Palestrina (see chapters 1 and 2) and Handel's oratorios (see chapter 10). And he was instrumental in spurring on the initially mentioned Gauntlett in the English organ reform (see chapter 6).

While Dr. Gauntlett was never recognized with a statue for his accomplishments in the British Isles, Mendelssohn was honored after his death by the city that owed him so much: a monument in front of the Gewandhaus in Leipzig. Excesses of German nationalism, gaining the upper hand and, entwined with racial prejudice, becoming official politics in the 1930s, were the forces responsible for removing the statue from sight and site in 1936; the efforts to efface Mendelssohn's accomplishments and consign them to oblivion were, sadly, given the stamp of approval by certain German musicologists of the era.[16] The statue was not restored to its site until 2009 at the two-hundredth anniversary of the composer's birth.[17]

One concluding meditation on statues and monuments may be allowed here. When Ludwig I of Bavaria tried to make sure that he would not be outdone by any other monarch in proving his Teutonic credentials in the 1830s, he gave the order to build, near Regensburg, the Walhalla, a Greek-style temple on a high hill overlooking the Danube. The interior was conceived as a work in progress, having space for hundreds of plaques and busts commemorating the most illustrious figures of German history. Over the years, an odd collection of political, military, and cultural icons were honored with acceptance into Walhalla.[18] The editor of the volume at hand visited the place in May 2013 and was overwhelmed by the aura of the locale no less than by the problematic nature of the selection of iconic figures. Heinrich Heine was only recently admitted, so was Edith Stein, a Catholic nun of Jewish origin, who perished in Auschwitz. (Their inclusion was at least confirmed through an insert page in the official tourist brochure.) Mendelssohn, strangely enough, is still waiting to be recognized. But, then, why should he be added to that odd Pantheon of German-ness? His deeds constructed and celebrated the cultural legacies of German people in a civic form of nationalism whose positive influence is not often discerned in the statues and monuments that dot the lands of Central Europe.

‽

A number of chapters of this book were lectures at a conference of the Eastman Rochester Organ Initiative in 2009, focusing on Mendelssohn and the Contrapuntal Tradition. Additional chapters were commissioned from various scholars to flesh out the richness of the topic, leading, in turn, to a slightly different framework for the contributions, captured in the book's title.

Part 1 ("Composition and Tradition") explores some of the compositional traditions Mendelssohn made his own by training and travel, and by dint of his openness and curiosity to all things musical. R. Larry Todd, whose "Mendelssohn and the Contrapuntal Tradition" was originally the keynote lecture at the above-mentioned conference, lays out the richness of contrapuntal legacies Mendelssohn inherited. While J. S. Bach undoubtedly loomed large throughout the composer's life, Mendelssohn also drew on other sources of contrapuntal thought: from Palestrina to the *stile antico* to post-Bachian contrapuntalists such as Mozart and Beethoven. Zelter's teaching imbued Mendelssohn with a way of composing, performing, and thinking about music based on the conviction that music history is a living tradition that informs the present. Siegwart Reichwald continues with a detailed account of Mendelssohn's indebtedness to what he calls the "Catholic Tradition," discussing two works that originated—by and large—during the composer's Italian journey: the *Kirchen-Musik* (MWV B19–21, op. 23) and *Drei Motetten* (MWV B23, B24, and B30; op. 39). In his reading of Mendelssohn's "Reformation" Symphony (MWV N15, op. 107), Peter Mercer-Taylor adds another figure looming large in the composer's inherited legacies: Beethoven. While acknowledging the symphony's indebtedness to the contrapuntal traditions of Palestrina and Bach, he sees the work's narrative goal in the vocality, represented by the Lutheran chorale, of the finale, and thus as Mendelssohn's first essay in a symphony taking up the challenge of Beethoven's Ninth. (The "Lobgesang" would be another such symphony.)

Part 2 pays homage to "Mendelssohn and the Organ." As Wm. A. Little demonstrates in his contribution, Mendelssohn's connections with the "queen of instruments," as the Germans call it, were substantial and manifested themselves in a variety of activities—performing, composing, and editing works for organ—and in two countries: Germany and England. That Bach loomed large in these activities goes without saying: Russell Stinson shows how Mendelssohn's tribute to the Thomas-Kantor was given body in sound in a special organ recital in 1840 in Leipzig's St. Thomas Church with the purpose of gathering money for, and following up with, a tribute in stone a little later. (A reenactment of this famous recital, by three professors of organ at the Eastman School of Music, was made for use with this book and can be found at www.esm.rochester.edu/organ/ mendelssohn.) Mendelssohn brought his enthusiasm for all things Bachian to the British Isles, where he performed Bach's works on a variety of organs in churches and in concert halls: Nicholas Thistlethwaite makes a persuasive case for Mendelssohn's encounter with Henry Gauntlett in England as being significant for the latter's setting in motion, almost single-handedly, the English organ reform during the Victorian era. Hans Davidsson continues with an essay on performance practice, highlighting the special qualities of the Craighead-Saunders Organ in Christ Church in Rochester, New York, and exploring the kinds of organs Mendelssohn's organ works were written for, with particular emphasis on registration and tempo. He comes to the conclusion that Mendelssohn's Sonatas for Organ (MWV W56–61, op. 65) most likely were composed as a homage to Bach—in other words, constitute another *Denkmal* to the Thomas-Kantor.

Part 3 ("Mendelssohn's Inherited Legacies in Context") presents essays related to the book's title in widening concentric circles. Christoph Wolff explores the Bach tradition that flourished among members of Mendelssohn's maternal forebears, especially his great-aunt, Sara Levy, and his grandmother, Bella Salomon, as well as in his paternal lineage. Mendelssohn's early "Dürer" Cantata (MWV D1) is the focus of John Michael Cooper's essay. Rather than tossing it off as an inconsequential, occasional, and youthful composition, he accords it significance as a contribution to a large historical project that manifests itself in literature, the visual arts, and in music since the early nineteenth century: the discovery of a distinctly German cultural identity. Mendelssohn's performance practice in bringing to life Bach's *St. Matthew Passion* or Handel's oratorios may, nowadays, raise the eyebrows of those striving for authenticity; Glenn Stanley provides a historical context for the composer's Handel reception by comparing it with other restorative efforts in architecture and literature in the early nineteenth century. Benedict Taylor takes on the "two Mendelssohns" thesis with which critics, of the past as well as of more recent times, tried to separate works of undisputed originality from those denounced as tired imitations, espousing religious sentimentality, such as *St. Paul, Elijah*, and the symphony cantata "Lobgesang." Using philosophical thoughts from Kierkegaard's *Either/Or* as a filter, the author reads the latter work as a heroic attempt to reconcile religious art with secular art-religion. Celia Applegate unfolds a panorama of Protestantism in its various manifestations in Prussia and England and explores Mendelssohn's ability to negotiate religious tensions through his sacred music.

Taken together, the various chapters present a vivid picture of a serious yet frequently imaginative composer seeking to negotiate the interaction among and between a number of major principles and factors, including high-level musical creativity, national and religious identity, and the adaptive reuse of musical traditions from the recent and more distant past.

Notes

1   See the title of chapter 6 in this volume by Nicholas Thistlethwaite.
2   Oliver Korte and Albrecht Riethmüller, eds., *Beethovens Orchesterwerke und Konzerte: Das Handbuch* (Laaber: Laaber-Verlag, 2013), 58–59 (Stefan Weinzierl on concert life in Vienna, 1807–14) and 256–78 (Frédéric Döhl on *Wellingtons Sieg*); Nicholas Mathew, *Political Beethoven* (Cambridge: Cambridge University Press, 2013).
3   Benedict Anderson, *Imagined Communities: Reflections on the Origin and Spread of Nationalism* (London: Verso, 1983); see also the revised and expanded second edition of 1991 with a new preface.
4   On Mendelssohn's civic nationalism, see Richard Taruskin, *Music in the Nineteenth Century*, vol. 3 of *The Oxford History of Western Music* (New York: Oxford University Press, 2010), 166–77.

5   Christian Martin Schmidt, "*Lobgesang*—oder: Große Musik für Leipzig," in *Dem Stolz und der Zierde unserer Stadt: Felix Mendelssohn Bartholdy und Leipzig,* ed. Wilhelm Seidel (Leipzig: Edition Peters, 2004), 163–72.
6   A fuller account of the Gutenberg ceremonies in Leipzig in 1840 can be found in R. Larry Todd, *Mendelssohn: A Life in Music* (New York: Oxford University Press, 2003), 395–97.
7   Chapter 4 and, in greater detail, chapter 5 describe the event. Mendelssohn's organ recital was "reconstructed" in a performance on the Craighead-Saunders Organ in Christ Church in Rochester, New York, during the Eastman Rochester Organ Initiative (EROI) Festival in 2009 and, again, on the same instrument during the EROI Festival 2012 by Hans Davidsson, David Higgs, and William Porter in Rochester. The performance on September 27, 2012, was recorded and can be accessed through an internet link: www.esm.rochester.edu/organ/mendelssohn.
8   The book's cover shows Bendemann's drawing of the envisioned monument; another image can be found as figure 5.1 in Russell Stinson's chapter.
9   A fuller account can be found in Jürgen Ernst, Stefan Voerkel, and Christiane Schmidt, *Das Leipziger Mendelssohn-Denkmal* (Leipzig: Mendelssohn-Haus, 2009), 13–29.
10 Martin Geck, *Die Wiederentdeckung der Matthäuspassion im neunzehnten Jahrhundert* (Regensburg: Bosse, 1967); Celia Applegate, *Bach in Berlin* (Ithaca, NY: Cornell University Press, 2005); and also Lydia Goehr, *The Imaginary Museum of Musical Works: An Essay on the Philosophy of Music* (Oxford: Clarendon, 1992).
11 Judith K. Silber, "Mendelssohn and the *Reformation* Symphony: A Critical and Historical Study" (PhD diss., Yale University, 1987); and Silber, "Mendelssohn and His 'Reformation' Symphony," *Journal of the American Musicological Society* 40, no. 2 (1987): 324–31. See also Thomas Grey, "The Orchestral Music," in *The Mendelssohn Companion,* ed. Douglass Seaton (Westport, CT: Greenwood Press, 2001), 417.
12 Todd, *Mendelssohn: A Life in Music,* 87.
13 Golo Mann, *Deutsche Geschichte des 19. und 20. Jahrhunderts* (Frankfurt/Main: Fischer, 1992), 228: "Friedrich Wilhelm IV. hätte gern etwas Großes, Historisches für 'Teutschland' getan; er schwankte zwischen seinem Ehrgeiz und seinem Haß gegen alles Moderne, Liberale, Demokratische. Der letztere überwog." Translations are by the author unless otherwise indicated.
14 Todd, *Mendelssohn: A Life in Music,* 407.
15 Leon Botstein speaks of "the aesthetics of affirmation and assimilation." R. Larry Todd, *Mendelssohn and His World* (Princeton, NJ: Princeton University Press, 1991), 5–42. And Jeffrey Sposato devotes an entire monograph to the issue in *The Price of Assimilation* (New York: Oxford University Press, 2006).
16 See, for instance, the strategic omissions in Wolfgang Boetticher's writings about Robert Schumann after 1941, or the negative assessment of Mendelssohn in Gotthold Frotscher's *Die Geschichte des Orgelspiels und der Orgelkomposition* (Berlin: M. Hesse, 1935; 2nd ed., Berlin: Merseburger, 1959—the second edition is a reprint of the first).
17 Ernst, Voerkel, and Schmidt, *Das Leipziger Mendelssohn-Denkmal.*
18 See Albrecht Riethmüller's critical assessment of the Walhalla concept, as it pertains to musicians, *Die Walhalla und ihre Musiker* (Laaber: Laaber-Verlag, 1993).

Part One

Composition and Tradition

Chapter One

Mendelssohn and the Contrapuntal Tradition

R. Larry Todd

We might begin with a statement uncontroversial enough: in matters of counterpoint, Mendelssohn was preoccupied with the music of J. S. Bach. The evidence is formidable and irrefutable. It is not just that Mendelssohn was disposed to writing fugues and canons, or to insinuating into his music familiar Lutheran chorales in order to accumulate extra layers of complexity. More to the point, Mendelssohn took the trouble to emulate distinctly Bachian counterpoint—I am thinking here of his preference for rich, involved, chromatic part writing—that was for the time historically remote and learned. Thus, as early as 1827 he published an erudite fugue in A major as the fifth of the *Sieben Charakterstücke* for piano (MWV U60; op. 7, no. 5)—a mirror-inversion fugue laden with augmentation and diminution, as though, one weary reviewer from the Leipzig *Allgemeine musikalische Zeitung* reported, "the composer officially wished to demonstrate how diligently he had studied and mastered his subject through counterpoint."[1] In subsequent fugues Mendelssohn never exceeded the dense accumulations of special devices in this composition, but he did return to the esoteric technique of mirror inversion in the piano Fugue in B Minor (MWV U131; op. 35, no. 3 [1837]) and in the first movement of the Organ Sonata (MWV W56; op. 65, no. 1), and, perhaps most tellingly, incorporated a mirror-inversion fugue into the overture to *Elijah* (MWV A25, op. 70). There the inverted subject lends extra emphasis to the depiction of a world turned upside down by the calamitous seven-year drought, announced by the prophet in the opening recitative.

Presumably, Mendelssohn's attraction to Bachian counterpoint was what led Hector Berlioz, who viewed the strictures of fugal composition as an "unpardonable offense against musical expression,"[2] to aver that his colleague was "a little too fond of the dead."[3] (Berlioz also acknowledged, it should be added, that Mendelssohn possessed "une des capacités musicales les plus hautes de l'époque.")[4] Berlioz's rejection of traditional counterpoint reflected in no small way his student experiences at the Paris Conservatoire, where he encountered not so much the rigors of Bach as the annoying pedagogical habits of another scrupulous contrapuntist, Luigi Cherubini, who will briefly emerge later in this essay. Still, we must concede that Mendelssohn would have expended no little effort in refuting Berlioz's judgment, for Mendelssohn's engagement with Bach's music was certainly deep and enduring, and it began early, at least when the composer was only ten.

Writing to Goethe in 1819, Carl Friedrich Zelter relayed a remarkable anecdote about the prodigy's Bachian ruminations: "In the score of a magnificent concerto by Sebastian Bach the hawk eyes of my Felix, when he was ten years old, became aware of a succession of six pure fifths, which I perhaps never would have found, since I did not pay attention to them in larger works, and the passage is in six parts. But the handwriting is autograph, beautifully and clearly written, and the passage occurs twice. Now is that an oversight or a license?"[5] The work in question was the Brandenburg Concerto no. 5, in particular, measure 11 of the first movement, as Bach had notated it in the 1721 fair-copy holograph prepared for the Margrave of Brandenburg. As example 1.1 reveals, Bach here attempted to improve a series of hidden octaves between the viola and solo violin, only, according to Albert Schweitzer, "to fall out of the frying pan into the fire"[6] by inadvertently engendering between the viola and harpsichord dreaded parallel fifths.

Now just around this time, in the latter half of 1819, the young Mendelssohn was beginning to fill, under Zelter's supervision, a musical album with exercises in figured bass, followed the next year by chorale harmonizations, exercises in double counterpoint, and fugue and canon in two and three parts.[7] Our student then proceeded to four-part fugue in 1821 and produced twelve fugues for string quartet (several of them double fugues or chorale fugues),[8] which in turn gave way to choral, motet-like fugues in five voices.[9] He thus pursued a systematic course in increasing degrees of contrapuntal complexity, from two- to three-, four,- and five-part counterpoint. Taking a broad view, we might suggest that the culmination of this graduated method came in 1825, when the sixteen-year-old completed the finale of his Octet (MWV R20, op. 20), with its energetic, opening eight-part fugato and subsequent treatments of eight-part counterpoint. Mendelssohn's elder sister, Fanny, followed a somewhat similar course of instruction with Zelter, who revealed to Goethe in December 1824 that she had just completed her thirty-second fugue (regrettably, almost all are lost).[10] Thus, we must imagine a scenario in which two sibling prodigies together fathomed the cerebral tradition of high counterpoint, through which of course they deepened their musical relationships to Bach.

Zelter's tuition was in fact heavily indebted to the writings of two eighteenth-century Berlin theorists devoted to Bach—Johann Philipp Kirnberger and

Example 1.1. Bach, Brandenburg Concerto no. 5, mvt. 1, mm. 10–11

Friedrich Wilhelm Marpurg. With respect to Kirnberger, Zelter drew upon *Die Kunst des reinen Satzes in der Musik* (1771–79), an imposing treatment of figured bass, chorale harmonization, and double counterpoint based on the precepts of Kirnberger's teacher, J. S. Bach.[11] It was Kirnberger who, in response to Rameau's *basse fondamentale*, developed the *Grundbass* as an analytical tool for interpreting bass lines, an approach Zelter was still following in 1819, as revealed by Felix's exercises, several of which display an added, abstract bass line tracing the motion of the underlying *Grundbass*. With regard to Marpurg, Zelter drew upon the *Essay on Fugue* (Die Abhandlung von der Fuge, 1753–54), where he could have found some of the earliest analyses of Bach's *Art of Fugue* and thorough explications of the more esoteric forms of counterpoint, such as double counterpoint at the ninth and eleventh. Hyphen-like, Zelter thus effectively linked Felix to a distinctly eighteenth-century, Bachian approach to composition, a transmission of influence that we can conveniently summarize in a pedagogical tree connecting Bach to arguably his most devoted nineteenth-century follower (fig. 1.1). Mendelssohn's memories of his childhood studies

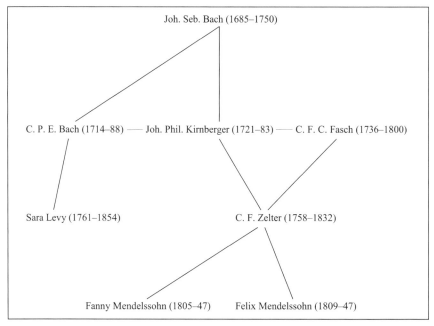

Figure 1.1. Pedagogical tree from Bach to the Mendelssohns.

still resonate years later when he confessed to Johann Christian Lobe, who in 1846 became the editor of the Leipzig *Allgemeine musikalische Zeitung*, his preference for "the finely woven voices, the polyphonic movement," and then added, "here my early studies in counterpoint with Zelter and my study of Bach may have had their principal impact."[12]

Marking Mendelssohn's life like recurring signposts are numerous events that reinforced his ties to Bach, of which we may briefly review just a few. First of all, there is the date Abraham and Lea chose for their son's baptism—March 21, 1816, coincidentally or not, the birthday of Bach. Knowing what we now know about the Bachian proclivities of the Mendelssohn family—the composer's mother, Lea, and elder sister, Fanny, made a habit of playing the *Well-Tempered Clavier*; his great aunt Sara Levy, a patroness of C. P. E. Bach and student of W. F. Bach, had performed the Fifth Brandenburg at the Berlin Sing-Akademie as early as 1805; and his father, Abraham, was actively involved in collecting Bach manuscripts—I am inclined to imagine that the date was no coincidence. Be that as it may, as early as 1821, the twelve-year-old Felix was reporting from Leipzig that he had visited the current Thomas-Kantor, Johann Gottfried Schicht, and readily connected him to the grand tradition: Schicht, Felix wrote, "sleeps in the same chamber in which Sebastian Bach lived, I have seen it, I have seen the little spot, where his Clavier stood, where he composed his immortal motets, where he (in Professor Zelter's expression) punished [*kuranzte*] his young charges, and hopefully I will bring along a drawing of this honorable house, in which Rosenmüller, Bach, Doles, Hiller, and Schicht worked and still work."[13] Just a few years later, Felix received from his maternal grandmother, Bella Salomon, a copy of the score of the *St. Matthew Passion.* Probing and absorbing its complex mysteries required several years before, at age twenty, the young composer gave the celebrated revival of the work in 1829 at the Berlin Sing-Akademie, the signal event that stirred the German musical consciousness and identified the *Neuchrist* Mendelssohn as an unabashed Bach disciple.

Mendelssohn's study of the Passion produced tangible results in his own music, including the extended series of chorale cantatas from the later 1820s and early 1830s, and of course his first oratorio, *St. Paul* (MWV A14, op. 36), brimming with fugues (four- and five-part), chorales, and involved, chromatic part writing. Yet another facet of his Bachian pursuits was on display in 1840, when he gave a monumental concert of Bach's organ music at the Leipzig Thomas-Kirche.[14] Robert Schumann informs us that Mendelssohn concluded with an improvisation on the chorale "O Haupt voll Blut und Wunden" (the Passion chorale that figures so prominently in the *St. Matthew Passion*), into which he wove a fugue on B–A–C–H. The purpose of the organ concert was to raise funds for a Bach statue, which was finally unveiled in 1843, incredibly enough the first modern remembrance of the composer. On April 13, 1843, Mendelssohn presented an all-Bach program at the Gewandhaus, and then reconvened with a select audience before the Thomasschule for the unveiling of the statue, a four-sided sandstone monument, adorned by a Gothic covering and cross, that featured on one side a colossal bust of Bach, and, on the other three, bas-reliefs symbolizing the Thomas-Kantor's work as organist, teacher, and composer. Attending the event was Wilhelm Friedrich Ernst Bach (1759–1845), J. S. Bach's last surviving grandson, a living link to what for most was an increasingly distant, receding tradition, though as far as Mendelssohn was concerned, a tradition that remained timelessly relevant. Writing to his mother, Mendelssohn expressed his satisfaction at the intricate design of the monument: "The many columns, little columns and scrollwork, above all the bas-reliefs and the old, splendid wig-adorned countenance shone freely in the sunlight, and gave me great joy. With its many decorative ornaments the whole really recalled the old Sebastian."[15]

Not surprisingly, Bachian allusions inform Mendelssohn's music on several levels, and not infrequently his reflections about Bach triggered contrapuntal responses. One example is the relatively little-known piano Fugue in E-flat Major (MWV U57) of September 1826, finished exactly one month after one of Mendelssohn's most un-Bachian creations, *A Midsummer Night's Dream* overture. The subject of the fugue, which describes a triadic descent from the fifth scale degree followed by an expressive ascending seventh and stepwise descending resolution, impresses as a contrapuntal gloss on the terse, chromatic recitative in the *St. Matthew Passion* in which Christ predicts his betrayal before the gathered disciples, "Wahrlich, ich sage Euch: Einer unter Euch wird mich verrathen" (exx. 1.2a and 1.2b). Suffused with chromatic dissonances, Bach's recitative pivots deceptively from E-flat major to C minor, a trace of which may be found in measures 5–6 of Mendelssohn's composition, with the entrance of the fugal answer, in which the harmony momentarily swerves toward C minor.

No less revealing is the subject of Mendelssohn's Fugue in D Major (MWV U105), the second of the Six Preludes and Fugues for Piano, op. 35, published in 1837. Here the composer took the trouble to disguise somewhat the source of the fugue, the D-Major Fugue from Book I of the *Well-Tempered Clavier* (exx. 1.3a and 1.3b), by removing the florid thirty-second notes and stately dotted rhythms of Bach's subject, leaving, as it were, a skeletal reduction. Bach's fugue had made a memorable impression on Mendelssohn in Switzerland in 1831, when he practiced it on an organ in the village of Sargans. From his close friend Eduard Rietz, Mendelssohn had learned that the Dresden organist Johann Gottlob Schneider had routinely played the subject of Bach's fugue in the bass voice in the pedals, an effect that Mendelssohn deemed unimaginable, until he tried the passage for himself, along with other organ works of Bach, and concluded, "Das war ein furchtbarer Cantor."[16] Recently Wm. A. Little has cast some doubt on the veracity of Mendelssohn's claim—it is unclear whether the Swiss organ could have accommodated Bach's subject in the pedals[17]— but in any event, by the time Mendelssohn finished his own D-Major Fugue in 1834, originally in a version for organ, Bach's subject was already transformed into the simplified form also used in the piano fugue that Mendelssohn ultimately published as op. 35, no. 2. The result, as Robert Schumann recognized, was a lyrical composition nearly mistakable for a *Lied ohne Worte*. Still, like its brethren in opus 35, the D-Major Fugue contained

> much of Sebastian, and might deceive the sharp-sighted reviewer, were it not for the melody, the finer bloom, which we recognize as modern; and here and there those little touches peculiar to Mendelssohn, which identify him among a hundred other composers. Whether reviewers agree or not, it remains certain that the artist did not write them for pastime, but rather to call the attention of pianoforte players once more to this masterly old form, and to accustom them to it again. That he has chosen the right means for succeeding in this—avoiding all useless imitations and artificialities, allowing the melody of the cantilena to predominate while holding fast to the Bach form—is very much like him.[18]

Of course, during the mid-1840s, Robert Schumann himself succumbed to *Bachmanie*. Together with his wife, Clara, he undertook a rigorous course in counterpoint that involved a close study of Bach's fugues, and the composition of three cycles—Robert's Six Fugues on B–A–C–H for Organ, op. 60, and Four Fugues for Pedal Piano, op. 72, and Clara's Three Preludes and Fugues for

Example 1.2a. Mendelssohn, Fugue in E-flat Major, subject

Example 1.2b. Bach, *St. Matthew Passion*, Recitative "Wahrlich ich sage euch"

Example 1.3a. Mendelssohn, Fugue in D Major, op. 35, no. 2, subject

Example 1.3b. Bach, *Well-Tempered Clavier* I, Fugue in D major, subject

Piano, op. 16, all from 1845. Presumably around this time Robert had a remarkable conversation with Mendelssohn that reinforced, albeit in an unusual way, his uncompromising devotion to Bach, a conversation that Robert later summarized in his *Erinnerungen an Felix Mendelssohn Bartholdy*, drafted in memoriam after the composer's death in November 1847.

What prompted this conversation was not a musical issue, but an advance in astronomy—the dramatic announcement of a powerful, new telescope known as the Leviathan of Parsonstown. In 1845 the third Earl of Rosse, William Parsons, successfully installed a seventy-two-inch reflecting telescope at Birr Castle in Ireland; it was the largest telescope in the world until 1917, when the one-hundred-inch Hooker telescope was inaugurated on Mount Wilson in California. Though Irish weather was not especially accommodating to nineteenth-century astronomers, Parsons's Leviathan facilitated the detection of previously unknown stars of the eighteenth magnitude and revealed for the first time spiral structures of certain galaxies. Schumann shared with

Mendelssohn the reaction of one awed commentator, who observed that if solar inhabitants were to peer down at the earth through such a device, earthlings would impress as nothing more than diminutive mites on a cheese. But Mendelssohn had an answer for this sobering thought, and brought Schumann back down to earth by unexpectedly invoking the Bachian sublime: "Yes," he replied, "but the *Well-Tempered Clavier* would certainly instill respect in them."[19]

Confirmed Bachian that he was, Mendelssohn was still cognizant of a broader contrapuntal tradition, of which Bach formed a central pillar. If Mendelssohn returned again and again to Bach as a wellspring of inspiration, he did not hesitate to explore and emulate a variety of historical models that epitomized the art of counterpoint. Because Mendelssohn's eclecticism as a contrapuntist is often overlooked in a literature that has privileged his role in the Bach Revival, I would like to consider a few examples of non-Bachian sources that figured in Mendelssohn's conception of counterpoint. For even if he preferred Bach, there was no shortage of other contrapuntists to pique his curiosity about the most learned and august of musical disciplines. His study of Bach was part of a larger project, to restore to modern European musical culture the relevance and immediacy of the contrapuntal tradition writ large.

Occasionally Mendelssohn's immersion in Bach in fact masked a deep knowledge of other eighteenth-century composers. A case in point is Mendelssohn's early setting of the *Magnificat* from 1822 (MWV A2), sometimes thought to have been inspired by Bach's *Magnificat* BWV 243. But as Ralf Wehner argued in 1997,[20] in the library of the Berlin Sing-Akademie Mendelssohn had available to him a setting of the *Magnificat* in D Major, Wq. 215 by C. P. E. Bach,[21] a composer whose mannered, eccentric style Mendelssohn had absorbed into several of his string symphonies of 1821 and 1822. Emanuel Bach's *Magnificat* attracted Mendelssohn's attention not so much for its *Empfindsamkeit* as for its closing double fugue in the Gloria on "Sicut erat." The challenge of taking up this text inspired Mendelssohn to go two steps further by creating a quadruple fugue on four subjects, the first of which bears striking resemblances to Emanuel Bach's opening subject (exx. 1.4a and 1.4b). The result attained a complexity worthy of J. S. Bach, though the impetus for the composition appears to have been the contrapuntal display of his son.

In a similar way, the fifth of Mendelssohn's twelve fugues for string quartet (MWV R1–8, R11–12, R14, R17), from April 1821, might initially impress as a studious double fugue in the Bachian mold. In C minor, it uses an ascending triadic subject that then moves chromatically from G to F♯, before tracing a stepwise descent to the tonic pitch (ex. 1.5a). Well into the fugue, after the entrance of the second subject, and after Mendelssohn begins combining the two, something remarkable happens, when the subject returns in the subdominant in measure 99 (ex. 1.5b). Here Mendelssohn, or possibly Zelter—the handwriting in the autograph is unclear—took the trouble to write out the pitches of the subject, which in German nomenclature spell F–As–C–H. Mendelssohn thus

Example 1.4a. Mendelssohn, *Magnificat*, fugal subjects

Example 1.4b. C. P. E. Bach, *Magnificat* in D Major, Wq. 215, subject

Example 1.5a. Mendelssohn, Fugue in C Minor, beginning

Example 1.5b. Mendelssohn, Fugue in C Minor, mm. 99–100

embedded into his exercise a clear, homage-like reference to Zelter's teacher, Carl Friedrich Christian Fasch, founder of the Berlin Sing-Akademie.

Appropriately, Fasch was one of the most dedicated contrapuntists of his age, as we learn from a biographical account of the composer published by Zelter in 1801, the year after Fasch's death.[22] There we read of his peculiar, obsessive habits: how he would expend a year or two constructing a playhouse out of cards, track the military maneuvers of the major powers in war- and peacetime, maintain detailed charts of seafaring vessels, notate thousands of figured-bass exercises for his students, and, in order to gauge his own inspiration for composition, multiply series of numbers. A successful effort would incline him toward composition; a miscalculation could banish his musical creativity for a day. According to Zelter, Fasch consumed little more effort in solving a contrapuntal conundrum than in dispatching a routine harmonization.[23] Fasch was especially drawn to designing complex canons, many of which he shared with the indomitable Kirnberger, whose usually grudging respect Fasch easily won. In particular, Zelter cited Fasch's imposing *Fünf-facher Canon*—a perpetual, quintuple canon for twenty-five parts—eventually published in the collected edition of Fasch's works released by the Sing-Akademie in 1839.[24] This labyrinthine riddle would have tested the patience of most musical enigmatologists: all told, it combines in a vertical array three four-part canons, and one each for six and seven voices. Not satisfied with this feat, Fasch was also able to infiltrate into the various parts liberal examples of inversion, diminution, augmentation, and stretto, so that, in Zelter's words, "with every note the eye fell upon a hidden artifice."[25]

Today Fasch's music is largely forgotten, but in the 1820s Felix was an avid student of it. The bulk of Fasch's surviving music comprised sacred works, including chorale arrangements and cantata-like psalm settings (one, titled *Mendelssohniana*, used the translation of Psalm 30 by Felix's grandfather, Moses Mendelssohn). The summit of Fasch's art, however, and the work that intrigued Felix, was a Mass for sixteen voices (four four-part choirs) and continuo from 1786; Felix's copy of the Kyrie survives in the Bodleian Library at Oxford.[26] Fasch had conceived this magnum opus after examining a sixteen-voice Mass by the seventeenth-century Roman composer Orazio Benevoli and finding its antiphonal effects monotonous and lacking in harmonic variety. The expansive scoring permitted Fasch to test various combinations of voices, now dividing the ensemble into four-part choirs or eight-part complements, and occasionally indulging in the most complex and demanding texture, that of sixteen-voice imitative polyphony, as in the fugal "Cum sancto spiritu" of the Gloria, which, according to Zelter, Fasch composed in just two days.[27]

In 1828, the nineteen-year-old Mendelssohn responded to Fasch's polychoral experiment by designing his own, the similarly scored motet *Hora est*, on two Office texts for Advent (MWV B18). Here Mendelssohn strove to observe Fasch's cardinal principle, that each four-part choir should be harmonically self-sufficient and "pure." But like Fasch, Mendelssohn could not resist the temptation to attempt sixteen-part polyphony, and in one stunning, radiant passage, to introduce the image of Christ appearing on a cloud with the hosts of saints, he contrived a passage with sixteen cascading entries (only six of them shown in ex. 1.6), thereby easily breaching the eight-part textures of the finale of the Octet.

If Mendelssohn received through Fasch's Mass the monumental style of seventeenth-century Italian polychoral music, another more remote source of the contrapuntal tradition was available to him in the *stile antico* associated with Palestrina. Most likely, Mendelssohn first became acquainted with the *stile antico* through J. S. Bach.[28] We know, for example, that earlier in the nineteenth century Zelter had begun rehearsing portions of the B-Minor Mass, and in that work Mendelssohn could have found ready examples in the framing movements of the Credo. Less clear is how early Mendelssohn had access to the music of Palestrina, who did not figure in Mendelssohn's correspondence until November 1830, during his Roman sojourn, when, safely settled in his lodging on the Piazza di Spagna, he reported to his family that he had a Viennese piano, and portraits and scores of Palestrina and Allegri.[29] Be that as it may, Mendelssohn first employed the *stile antico* three years earlier, in 1827, when he composed a large-scale motet for five-part chorus and orchestra on the archetypical Catholic text, *Tu es Petrus* (MWV A4; "Thou art Peter, and upon this rock I will build my church," Matthew 16:18), causing his friends, according to his sister Fanny, to "fear that he might have turned Roman Catholic."[30] Traveling to Heidelberg in November, Mendelssohn visited the jurist Anton Friedrich Justus Thibaut, author of *On Purity in Music* (Über Reinheit der Tonkunst, 1825) and an unabashed enthusiast for Palestrina. According to Mendelssohn, it was Thibaut who awakened his new passion for "die alt-Italienische Musik,"[31] by which he meant old Italian sacred polyphony. While Mendelssohn argued that everything converged in Bach, Thibaut offered as a counterweight Tomás

Example 1.6. Mendelssohn, *Hora est*, mm. 122–27

Luis de Victoria, a Spanish Renaissance composer closely allied stylistically with Palestrina, and suggested that the two new friends build their relationship on these two composers, like separated lovers who agreed to look at the moon and imagine that they were near each other.[32]

While in Heidelberg, Mendelssohn had access to Thibaut's extensive library, where he may have examined settings of *Tu es Petrus*, though whether he encountered any of Palestrina's motets on the text, including one for seven parts (ex. 1.7), remains unclear. Having returned to Berlin, Mendelssohn then

Example 1.7. Palestrina, *Tu es Petrus,* beginning

completed his own motet on November 4, 1827, in time to present it to Fanny
on her birthday ten days later. Impressed by the saturation of the orchestral
parts with the choral head motive, Fanny referred to the composition as "neun-
zehnstimmig," that is, for nineteen parts, among which she reckoned the
five-part chorus and fourteen instrumental parts (had she counted the three
trombones, which enter later into the motet, the tally would have increased
to twenty-two). Her brother's strategy indeed entailed joining a choral and
orchestral exposition of the head motive, comprising a descending fifth followed by ascending stepwise motion. Ruled in the archaic alla breve meter
requiring the use of obsolete breves, Mendelssohn's score bespeaks a new fascination with the *stile antico* and its remote historical age, but also, as in *Hora est,*
a striving for monumentality. And so, after a brief, chordal exordium for the
full ensemble, the chorus introduces a cappella the head motive in five-part
imitation (ex. 1.8), in the order of tenor, bass, alto, first soprano, and second
soprano, followed, without interruption, by a stream of instrumental entries in
the viola, second violin, first violin, flute, cello, and double bass, again the choral bass, trumpets, horns, timpani (limited to the descending fifth), and flutes
doubled by oboes. Mendelssohn's goal was to turn a Palestrinian point of imitation, with its transparent textures and carefully controlled dissonances, into
a seamless unfolding of texted and textless polyphony—to erect, as it were, a
cathedral of vocal and instrumental sound upon solid motivic bedrock.

Mendelssohn held such regard for his motet that he described it as his
most successful and best composition to his friends Karl Klingemann and the
Swedish musician Adolf Fredrik Lindblad; what is more, during his first visit

to London in 1829, the composer considered having the work performed at a music festival.[33] Thoughts then turned toward publication; Mendelssohn authorized Adolf Bernhard Marx to offer the work to Simrock in Bonn, and Mendelssohn himself entered into serious discussions with the Viennese firm of Pietro Mechetti to issue the work in full score, with a dedication to the pope, Gregory XVI.[34]

Nothing came of these efforts, however, and the composer set the motet aside until his visit to Paris in 1832, when he made the mistake of showing it to Luigi Cherubini. A stickler among contrapuntists, Cherubini singled out passages for revision, over which the two had an earnest discussion. Mendelssohn later recalled the incident in a letter to his parents: "Cherubini told me, when I showed him my *Tu es Petrus*, in his most grouchy [*höchst brummig*] way, 'but this has to be redone,' and I argued with him long and hard about it."[35] There are, in fact, several passages in the motet where the orchestral or choral parts momentarily rub against one another, producing a dissonant friction that has nothing to do with Palestrina and the *stile antico* but more with the density of the textures.[36] Be that as it may, Mendelssohn divulged to Ferdinand Hiller at least one contentious passage about which Cherubini caviled. "The old fellow is really too pedantic," Mendelssohn reported, "in one place I had a suspended third in two parts, and he wouldn't pass it on any condition."[37] Measures 37 and 38 indeed contain a passage in which a B in the tenor, suspended against a G♯ in the bass, moves through an A to a G♯ as the bass proceeds to a C♯ (ex. 1.9). In the wash of sound the suspended pitch is easily lost among the C-sharp seventh sonority of the measure; nevertheless, the voice leading offended Cherubini's sense of contrapuntal propriety, and Mendelssohn later yielded the point by conceding to Hiller, "The old man was right after all; one ought not to write them."[38]

The Palestrinian ideal also influenced Mendelssohn when he conceived the opening of his "Reformation" Symphony (MWV N15, op. posth. 107), finished in 1830. The slow introduction opposes two contrasting textures, a Palestrinian point of imitation to suggest Catholic polyphony (ex. 1.10), and a series of wind chords (not shown in the example) to intimate the strains of a homophonic chorale, and with them the incipient Lutheran faith, later to emerge in the triumphant appearance of "Ein' feste Burg" in the finale. The imitative passage unfolds a series of 4–3 suspensions treated in strict style, with entries rising by fifths, from D to A, E, and B. But more striking is the subject itself, familiar to Mendelssohn from J. S. Bach's treatment of it in a *stile antico* setting in the Fugue in E Major from the second volume of the *Well-Tempered Clavier*. Mendelssohn was also aware of this subject, an old Gregorian chant formula, from another composition, which brings us to another contrapuntist who figured significantly in Mendelssohn's conception of the discipline—Mozart.

En route to Weimar, where in 1821 Goethe compared Mendelssohn to a second Mozart, the twelve-year-old paused in Leipzig, and there heard a

Example 1.8. Mendelssohn, *Tu es Petrus*, beginning

performance of the Jupiter Symphony at the Gewandhaus. Impressed by the spectacular stretto of the finale, in which Mozart joined five subjects simultaneously rotating in quintuple counterpoint, Felix drafted a nine-measure stretto of his own on Mozart's first subject, the chant intonation, and sent it to Eduard Rietz in Berlin (ex. 1.11), to demonstrate what might be done with the four pitches.[39] Particularly striking about this sketch is its resemblance to an exercise in species counterpoint. Here Felix momentarily abandoned his Bachian leanings in order to engage with the Austrian tradition of counterpoint codified in

Example 1.9. Mendelssohn, *Tu es Petrus*, mm. 36–39

Example 1.10. Mendelssohn, "Reformation" Symphony, beginning

Example 1.11. Mendelssohn, Contrapuntal Sketch

the *Gradus ad Parnassum* (1725)—Johann Joseph Fux's celebrated attempt to systematize the counterpoint of Palestrina, and, of course, the treatise critical in the musical education of Haydn, Mozart, Beethoven, Schubert, and, considerably later in the nineteenth century, Anton Bruckner. Felix's sketch begins with an elementary note-against-note texture in whole notes (first species), and then proceeds to half notes against a whole note (second species, m. 5), and quarter notes against a whole note (third species, m. 6). Telling, too, is the *nota cambiata* in measure 6, almost as if he had at hand a copy of the *Gradus* for reference. But this relatively modest sketch was just a preamble to what followed in 1822, when Felix composed his eighth string Sinfonia (MWV N8), and then produced a second version with added winds and timpani, in effect realigning the limited ensemble of the North German string symphony with the familiar classical, double-wind orchestra of Mozart's scores.

Felix modeled the finale of his symphony on the Jupiter finale, and so, like Mozart, took up the challenge of embedding into a sonata-form movement four subjects that could be combined in various displays of invertible counterpoint (ex. 1.12). Like Mozart, too, Felix brought his finale to a culmination in a coda-like stretto; here he gradually accumulated simultaneous presentations of all four subjects, augmented by a newly fashioned fifth subject derived from a diminution of the fourth subject.[40] Example 1.13 presents a few measures that illustrate Felix's method, and his youthful attempt to match the studied elegance of Mozart's quintuple counterpoint.

Upon arriving in London in 1829, Mendelssohn may have had an opportunity to examine Mozart's approach to teaching counterpoint. Thomas Attwood, the organist of St. Paul's and a founding member of the Philharmonic, had studied with Mozart in Vienna from 1785 to 1787. Impressed by Mendelssohn's debut appearances as conductor, pianist, and organist, Attwood now developed a strong, fatherly affection for the young composer.[41] We do not know for sure, but it seems plausible that Attwood would have shared with Mendelssohn a prized possession from the 1780s, his composition exercises annotated by Mozart, where Mendelssohn could have examined in detail a systematic course of instruction in species counterpoint.

When in 1840 Robert Schumann labeled Mendelssohn the Mozart of the nineteenth century,[42] he was alluding to a certain classicizing strain in Mendelssohn's music, which often projects clarity of textures, formal balance, and symmetrical phrase structures. But Mendelssohn found in Mozart a formidable contrapuntist as well, more than capable of producing dense, involved part writing, and occasionally Mendelssohn responded to this facet of Mozart's genius. Admittedly, when Beethoven's patron Prince Radziwill asked Mendelssohn in 1822 to improvise on the subject of the Fugue in C Minor, K. 426 (ex. 1.14), the source was a learned, Bachian mirror-inversion fugue for two pianos that Mozart had composed in 1783, just as he was coming to terms with Bach's music. And so Mozart had chosen a subject not unlike that of *The Musical Offering*. But Mendelssohn's sharp eye also took note of the contrapuntal Mozart in less obvious contexts, as in the finale of the double Piano Concerto in E-flat Major, K. 365, a lighthearted rondo in the middle of which Mozart unexpectedly placed a miniature two-part canon (ex. 1.15a). Sixteen measures in length, this passage inspired Mendelssohn to conceive a two-part canon for the middle section of his Andante in D Major for Piano from 1826 (MWV U53), with a subject (ex. 1.15b) likely derived from Mozart's concerto. Mendelssohn chose to explore the canonic gambit more fully than Mozart, and so in the Andante rather persistently spun out the two voices in strict imitation

Example 1.12. Mendelssohn, Sinfonia no. 8 for Strings, finale, Subjects

Example 1.13. Mendelssohn, Sinfonia no. 8 for Strings, finale, mm. 460–66

Example 1.14. Mozart, Fugue in C Minor for 2 Pianos, K. 426, beginning

Example 1.15. (a) Mozart, Piano Concerto in E-flat Major, K. 365, finale, mm. 270–74; (b) Mendelssohn, Andante in D Major, mm. 33–36

for fully thirty-two measures. One good canon, it seemed, deserved another, even more elaborate.

If Mozart belonged to the eighteenth-century tradition so esteemed by Zelter, the figure of Beethoven, whose music had a dramatic influence on Mendelssohn from 1823 on, also impelled him to contemplate the learned forms of counterpoint. In particular, Mendelssohn came of age just as Beethoven was creating the final, monumental works of his transcendent late style, a defining feature of which was its withdrawal into a cerebral world of counterpoint. Much has been written about Mendelssohn's response in his strings quartets opuses 12 and 13 (MWV R25 and R22) to Beethoven's late string quartets, and Mendelssohn's Piano Sonata (MWV U54, op. 6) is often read as evincing a certain anxiety of influence over Beethoven's Piano Sonata op. 101. But the depth of Mendelssohn's relationship to Beethoven's counterpoint in the late style has attracted relatively little attention. There is, of course, the slow movement of the String Quartet op. 13, with its chromatic fugato closely related to the fugato in the slow movement of Beethoven's "Serioso" Quartet op. 95 (exx. 1.16a and 1.16b). But it is not widely known that Mendelssohn and his sister Fanny were among the first generation of pianists to essay the "Hammerklavier" Sonata, with its arcane fugal finale *con alcune licenze*, including that singular and most recherché device, presenting the florid, neo-Baroque subject in retrograde.[43] And it is not widely known that Mendelssohn was quite familiar with the *Missa Solemnis*, a copy of which was in his library by 1828.[44] Indeed, in 1830 Mendelssohn acquired from the Viennese autograph collector Aloys Fuchs the so-called Wittgenstein Sketchbook, filled with Beethoven's sketches for the Piano Sonata op. 109, Diabelli Variations, and the first three movements of the *Missa Solemnis*.

Mendelssohn never performed Beethoven's most unwieldy work, though he may have thought about the *Dona nobis pacem* and its sequential fugal subject when, early in 1835, he composed his Fugue in A-flat Major (MWV U108, op. 35, no. 4; exx. 1.17a and 1.17b). A more likely source here, though, was the fugal finale of Beethoven's Piano Sonata op. 110, in the same key (ex. 1.17c). As William Kinderman has emphasized, Beethoven worked on the *Missa Solemnis* and the Piano Sonata op. 110, concurrently, and there are clear enough ties between the two fugues. Mendelssohn's subject, which rises in a series of sequential fourths separated by compensating, descending stepwise motion, appears to combine features of the opus 110 and *Dona nobis pacem*. But by conceiving opus 35, no. 4 as an accelerando fugue—at the appearance of the second, faster subject the tempo shifts to *un poco animato*—Mendelssohn effectively acknowledged a primary debt to opus 110, which uses diminution, double diminution, and tempo changes to create an accelerando effect. As it happened, in 1834, his sister Fanny Hensel had composed a piano fugue in E-flat major that, like Beethoven's opus 110 finale, employed diminution to impel the music forward; what is more, Fanny's subject (ex. 1.17d) begins with

Example 1.16a. Mendelssohn, String Quartet, op. 13, mvt. 2, mm. 20–23

Example 1.16b. Beethoven, String Quartet, op. 95, mvt. 2, mm. 35–41

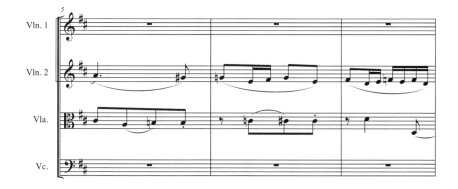

Example 1.17a. Mendelssohn, Fugue in A-flat Major, op. 35, no. 4, beginning

Example 1.17b. Beethoven, *Missa Solemnis*, Agnus Dei, mm. 107–10

Example 1.17c. Beethoven, Piano Sonata, op. 110, Fuga, beginning

Example 1.17d. Fanny Mendelssohn Hensel, Fugue in E-flat Major, beginning

an ascending fourth, another suggestion of her interest in Beethoven's opus 110.[45] Along with Hensel's fugue, Mendelssohn's opus 35, no. 4 may well have been a response to Beethoven, and part of his effort to "work through," as she put it, Beethoven's late style.[46]

As should now be clear enough, for Mendelssohn counterpoint was a constant companion throughout his career, an essential way of hearing that fundamentally informed how he composed, performed, and analyzed music. If he did not hesitate to count himself an ardent disciple of J. S. Bach, he also strove to contextualize Bach's achievements as a contrapuntist by relating and comparing them variously to the *stile antico* and to those of contrapuntally like-minded musicians who followed. So in 1830 Mendelssohn gladly exchanged canonic pleasantries in Vienna with Simon Sechter, to whom Schubert had turned at the end of his life in 1828 for instruction in fugue. And in 1836 Mendelssohn must have taken some satisfaction in receiving the dedication of Carl Czerny's *Die Schule des Fugenspiels*, op. 400, a cycle of twelve fugues. In an accompanying letter Czerny conceded that he had essayed a genre especially prized by Mendelssohn, and so asked for the composer's indulgence.[47] For Mendelssohn, music was the history of music, a living tradition that had endured over the centuries, and had reached summits again and again in the rarified world of counterpoint. Perhaps this was why Mendelssohn was a bit too fond of the musical past, and why we should be as well.

Notes

1   *Allgemeine musikalische Zeitung* 30 (1828): 63. Translations are by the author unless otherwise indicated.

2   Hector Berlioz, *The Memoirs of Hector Berlioz*, ed. and trans. David Cairns (New York: Norton, 1975), 74–75.

3   Ibid., 294.

4   Berlioz, *Correspondance générale*, ed. Pierre Citron (Paris: Flammarion, 1978), 1:441.

5   Zelter to Goethe, May 25, 1826, in *Briefwechsel zwischen Goethe und Zelter in den Jahren 1799 bis 1832*, ed. H.-G. Ottenberg and Edith Zehm (Munich: Carl Hanser Verlag, 1991) [= W. Goethe, *Sämtliche Werke nach Epochen seines Schaffens—Münchener Ausgabe*, vol. 20/1], 923.

6   Albert Schweitzer, *J. S. Bach*, trans. Ernest Newman (London: 1923), 1:405–6.

7   See R. Larry Todd, *Mendelssohn's Musical Education: A Study and Edition of His Exercises in Composition* (Cambridge: Cambridge University Press, 1983).

8   For an edition, see Felix Mendelssohn Bartholdy, *12 Fugen für Streichquartett (1821)*, ed. Klaus Bundies (Offenburg: Edition Offenburg, 2007).

9   Including *Tag für Tag sei Gott gepriesen*, *Gott, du bist unsre Zuversicht*, and *Die Himmel erzählen die Ehre Gottes*. For editions, see Felix Mendelssohn Bartholdy, *13 Psalmmotetten*, ed. Pietro Zappalà (Stuttgart: Carus, 1997).

10   Zelter to Goethe, December 10, 1824, in *Briefwechsel zwischen Goethe und Zelter*, 828.

11   Johann Philipp Kirnberger, *The Art of Strict Musical Composition*, trans. David Beach and Jürgen Thym (New Haven, CT: Yale University Press, 1982).

12   Johann Christian Lobe, "Conversations with Felix Mendelssohn," trans. Susan Gillespie, in *Mendelssohn and His World*, ed. R. Larry Todd (Princeton, NJ: Princeton University Press, 1991), 198.

13   Felix to his family in Berlin, November 1, 1821, in Felix Mendelssohn Bartholdy, *Sämtliche Briefe*, vol. 1, ed. Juliette Appold and Regina Back (Kassel: Bärenreiter, 2008), 73.

14   See chapters 4 and 5 in this volume as well as the link to the audio of the reconstructed 1840 recital.

15   Mendelssohn to Lea Mendelssohn Bartholdy, December 11, 1842, in Paul Mendelssohn Bartholdy, ed., *Letters of Felix Mendelssohn Bartholdy from 1833 to 1847* (London: Longman, Roberts and Green, 1863), 317 (translation modified).

16   Mendelssohn to his family in Berlin, September 3, 1831, in *Felix Mendelssohn Bartholdy, Sämtliche Briefe*, vol. 2, ed. Anja Morgenstern and Uta Wald (Kassel: Bärenreiter, 2009), 387.

17   Wm. A. Little, *Mendelssohn and the Organ* (New York: Oxford University Press, 2010), 109–10.

18   Robert Schumann, *On Music and Musicians*, ed. Konrad Wolf, trans. Paul Rosenfeld (New York: Pantheon, 1946), 214–15.

19   Robert Schumann, "Aufzeichnungen über Mendelssohn," in *Felix Mendelssohn Bartholdy*, ed. Heinz-Klaus Metzger and Rainer Riehn (Munich: Edition Text + Kritik, 1980), 103.

20   Introduction to Wehner's edition of the *Magnificat* in the *Leipziger Ausgabe der Werke Felix Mendelssohn Bartholdys*, series VI, vol. 5 (Wiesbaden: Breitkopf und Härtel, 1997), xvi.

21   See Wolfram Enßlin, *Die Bach-Quellen der Sing-Akademie zu Berlin: Katalog*, vol. 1 (Hildesheim: Olms, 2006), 62–67.

22   C. F. Zelter, *K. F. C. Fasch* (Berlin: J. F. Unger, 1801).

23   Ibid., 53.

24   *Sämtliche Werke von Karl Friedrich Christian Fasch*, 7 vols. (Berlin: T. Trautwein, 1839).

25   Zelter, *Fasch*, 18n.

26   Bodleian Library, M. Deneke Mendelssohn Collection, B. 5, fols. 155–61.

27   Zelter, *Fasch*, 26.

28   See further Christoph Wolff, "Bach and the Tradition of the Palestrina Style," in *Bach: Essays on His Life and Music* (Cambridge, MA: Harvard University Press, 1991), 84–104.

29   Letter of November 8, 1830, in Mendelssohn, *Sämtliche Briefe*, 2:126.

30   Sebastian Hensel, *The Mendelssohn Family*, trans. Karl Klingemann (London: Sampson, Low, Marston, Searle and Livington, 1882), 1:151.

31   Letter of September 20, 1827, in Mendelssohn, *Sämtliche Briefe*, 1:221.

32   Ibid.

33   Letters of February 5, 1828, to Klingemann, February 19, 1828, to Lindblad, and July 17, 1829, to Berlin, Mendelssohn, *Sämtliche Briefe*, 1:237, 242, and 340.

34   Letters of October 2, 1830, October 6, 1830, December 9, 1830, January 30, 1831, and March 21, 1831, in *Sämtliche Briefe* 2:96, 98, 158, 198, and 237.

35   Letter of March 23, 1835, in Mendelssohn Bartholdy, *Sämtliche Briefe*, vol. 4, ed. Lucia Schwiewitz and Sebastian Schmideler (Kassel: Bärenreiter, 2011), 197.

36   See, for instance, the first violins and first soprano in measure 89, and the bass and instrumental bass line in measures 100–101. For examples, see Rudolf Werner, "Felix Mendelssohn Bartholdy als Kirchenmusiker" (PhD diss., Universität Frankfurt/Main, 1930), 40.

37   Ferdinand Hiller, *Mendelssohn: Letters and Recollections*, trans. M. E. von Glehn (New York: Vienna House, 1972), 28.

38   Ibid.

39   Letter of November 4, 1821, in *Sämtliche Briefe* 1:74.

40   See further my "Mozart According to Mendelssohn: A Contribution to *Rezeptionsgeschichte*," in *Perspectives on Mozart Performance*, ed. Peter Williams and R. Larry Todd (Cambridge: Cambridge University Press, 1991), 163–70.

41   Letter of September 18, 1829, in *Sämtliche Briefe*, 1:404.

42   In a review of the Piano Trio no. 1 in D Minor, op. 49; *Neue Zeitschrift für Musik* 13 (1840): 198.

43   Mendelssohn performed the sonata at a private soirée in Stettin in 1827; see R. Larry Todd, *Mendelssohn: A Life in Music* (New York: Oxford University Press, 2005), 167. See also my *Fanny Hensel: The Other Mendelssohn* (New York: Oxford University Press, 2009), 88–89.

44   Letter of February 5, 1828, to Klingemann, in *Sämtliche Briefe*, 1:237.

45   See Todd, *Fanny Hensel*, 178.

46   Fanny Hensel to Mendelssohn, February 17, 1835, in Marcia Citron, ed., *The Letters of Fanny Hensel to Felix Mendelssohn* (Stuyvesant, NY: Pendragon, 1987), 174.

47   See R. Larry Todd, "*Me voilà perruqué*: Mendelssohn's Six Preludes and Fugues, op. 35 Reconsidered," in *Mendelssohn Essays* (New York: Taylor and Francis, 2008), 196–97.

Chapter Two

Mendelssohn and the Catholic Tradition

Roman Influences on His *Kirchen-Musik*, Op. 23 and *Drei Motetten*, Op. 39

Siegwart Reichwald

Introduction

"Mendelssohn is one of those open characters you don't often find; he believes firmly in his Lutheran religion, and several times I've seriously shocked him laughing at the Bible."[1] Berlioz seems to have stated the obvious about Mendelssohn's Lutheran faith. From his performance of the *St. Matthew Passion* and his countless remarks about the greatness of Bach's music to Mendelssohn's many chorale settings and Bach's obvious influence on *St. Paul* (MWV A14, op. 36), it seems a foregone conclusion that Mendelssohn was a Lutheran composer. Things are, however, never as simple as they seem. Consider, for example, that Mendelssohn's first published sacred works are his opus 23 (MWV B19–21), a diverse collection that includes an Ave Maria; in his second publication are three Latin motets (MWV B23, B24, and B30, op. 39), dedicated to the nuns at Trinità dei Monti. His first published large-scale sacred work is Psalm 115 "Non nobis Domine"/"Nicht unserm Namen, Herr" (MWV A9, op. 31), a work conceived in Latin and only later translated into German. At the end of his career, when Mendelssohn worked on *Elijah* (MWV A25, op. 70), he composed concurrently his largest Catholic composition, *Lauda Sion* (MWV A24).

A look at works published during Mendelssohn's lifetime presents an even more surprising picture. Mendelssohn decided to publish only nine (ten in England) of his sixty smaller sacred works: *Kirchen-Musik für Chor*, op. 23

(1832); *Drei Motetten für weibliche Stimmen mit Begleitung der Orgel*, op. 39 (MWV B24, B30, B23, 1838); and *Drei Motetten*, op. 69, consisting of *Jubilate* (MWV B58), joined by a *Te Deum for the Morning Service* (MWV B25, 1847), and *Magnificat et Nunc dimittis* (MWV B59–60, 1847). Of the nine published smaller works, seven have Latin texts and six are intricately connected to his Italian experience. Underscoring the importance of his Grand Tour of 1829–31 is Mendelssohn's decision not to publish any of his eighteen smaller choral works composed before this trip to Italy, thereby making his "Italian" opuses 23 and 39 the only public offerings of sacred motets for almost his entire career— until the publication of his opus 69 motets in 1847, composed initially for the Anglican Church. While Mendelssohn wrote twenty smaller works for the Domchor in Berlin as director of church music under Friedrich Wilhelm IV, none of them seemed to rise to Mendelssohn's high standard for publication. That leaves thirteen other unpublished occasional choral works, six of which are in English, four in Latin, only two in German, and one in French.

Besides his surprisingly ecumenical publication record, Mendelssohn's sacred music has been a hard nut to crack for musicologists. While he was arguably the most influential German composer of sacred music of his generation, music historians to this day are still grappling with the style, content, and function of his Psalm settings, motets, and other occasional pieces. Carl Dahlhaus, Georg Feder, and R. Larry Todd, among others, have wrestled with the dilemma of what Dahlhaus termed "imaginary church music," placing the majority of Mendelssohn's sacred music outside of the church walls.[2] With the decline in Protestant church music during the Enlightenment and the simplification of liturgy in the Prussian Union Church (Lutheran and Reformed congregations), Mendelssohn seemed to follow his teacher Carl Friedrich Zelter's footsteps in placing sacred works—contemporary and earlier works—in the broader context of *Volks-Bildung*.[3] His exposure to a wide range of styles from Palestrina to eighteenth-century Italian and German Baroque music—including the cantatas and oratorios of J. S. Bach—shaped the young composer's aesthetics in regard to both style and religious content, leaving the questions of purpose and function of sacred music in nineteenth-century Protestant Germany unanswered, as Mendelssohn's sacred compositions seem caught somewhere between the church and concert hall. Since a comprehensive study of Mendelssohn's sacred repertoire and its complex aesthetic issues warrants a complete volume devoted to this difficult task, this study will focus specifically on his two sets of "Roman" motets opuses 23 and 39 and their Catholic influences, as the composer's Italy experience was of great significance in his oeuvre of smaller sacred works. I hope to convey Mendelssohn's curiosity about and sensitivity to his Roman Catholic surroundings while, at the same time, he maintained a strong sense of self-identity. As his grand tour helped shape Mendelssohn's aesthetics, the young composer began to forge a path toward a new brand of sacred music for his own, Romantic age.

Mendelssohn and the Protestant Palestrina Revival

James Garratt's monograph, *Palestrina and the German Romantic Imagination*, has explored the various cultural agents in the Palestrina revival of the first half of the nineteenth century. Fascinatingly, Mendelssohn, more than any other composer, is directly linked to almost all important philosophers, theologians, artists, poets, and composers in this cultural movement, including Johann Wolfgang von Goethe, Arthur Schopenhauer, Georg Wilhelm Friedrich Hegel, Karl Friedrich Zelter, Karl Friedrich Schinkel, Anton Friedrich Justus Thibaut, Johann Nepomuk Schelble, Christian Karl Josias von Bunsen, and Giuseppe Baini. One central issue in post-Enlightenment thought was that of originality in art. While the philosopher Arthur Schopenhauer emphasized the artist as the creator of new art, Goethe saw the importance of historical models as part of the artistic process.[4] Mendelssohn's discussions with Goethe about music history, literature, art, and philosophy—specifically Hegel[5]—must have given the young composer much food for thought about his own path as a modern composer during a time of growing historicism.

Mendelssohn's musical upbringing, of course, placed him at one of the centers of neoclassicism with his studies under Karl Friedrich Zelter and the Sing-Akademie. Mendelssohn actually witnessed the building of the new home of the Sing-Akademie, a place Todd describes as the "new musical temple" and "a living musical museum."[6] This new building was designed by Karl Friedrich Schinkel, whose famous neoclassical design of the memorial cathedral from a decade earlier combined the ancient Egyptian, Greek, and Gothic styles, an aesthetic approach to which Garrat actually views Mendelssohn as the "musical analogue."[7] The other equally important German institution for the Palestrina revival was the Singverein in Heidelberg under the direction of Anton Friedrich Justus Thibaut, a strong proponent of the Old Italian school.[8] Mendelssohn had, of course, read Thibaut's *Über Reinheit der Tonkunst*, and the two had several long and interesting conversations during Mendelssohn's visit to Heidelberg in 1827.[9] A third important organization dedicated to sacred music (Catholic music and the oratorios of Handel) with which Mendelssohn was very familiar was the Cäcilienverein in Frankfurt, founded by Johann Nepomuk Schelble, whom Mendelssohn had known since childhood and whom he visited on his way to Italy.

Mendelssohn's eighteen unpublished pre-Italy works reflect his unusual upbringing, as the majority of them are studies that are based on historic models or explore specific contrapuntal styles. His *Jube Dom'ne—Ein Abendgebet* (MWV B10, 1822) and Kyrie (MWV B12, 1823) were written for the Cäcilienverein, while the *Te Deum* (MWV B15) and *Antiphona et Responsorium* "Hora Est" (MWV B18) were written in honor of the founder of the Berlin Sing-Akademie, Carl Friedrich Christian Fasch (1736–1800). Mendelssohn went to Italy with his eyes wide open in order to learn and discern what to do with the rich heritage of Renaissance and Baroque art. Studying and writing church music was an important aspect of his Italian journey. In numerous letters to his family and his teacher Zelter, Mendelssohn discussed liturgical chant, works by Palestrina, Allegri, and Baini, as well as paintings with sacred themes by Titian and Raphael, among others.

Mendelssohn's first employment upon his return from his grand tour meant further engagement with Catholic liturgy and church music, as it included the regular performance of church music in Catholic Düsseldorf. His summation of the concepts of Protestant and Catholic church music, written during the Düsseldorf years in a letter to Pastor Ernst Friedrich Bauer, accentuates the importance of his Italy experience in his aesthetics of church music:

> Real church music, that is, music for the Evangelical Church service, which could be introduced in the celebration of the service proper, seems to me impossible; and this not merely because I cannot see into which part of the public worship music could be introduced, but because on the whole I cannot imagine that such a part even exists. . . . As for actual church music, or if you like to call it so, music for public worship, I know none but the old Italian compositions for the Papal Chapel, where, however, music is a mere accompaniment, subordinate to the sacred functions, co-operating with the wax candles and the incense, etc.[10]

His opuses 23 and 39 are his most direct musical responses to what he learned about Catholic church music—and sacred music in general—during his formative grand tour.

Kirchen-Musik, Op. 23

Mendelssohn's opus 23 might be his most enigmatic publication, especially when considering the composer's notoriously high respect for published works. Just the title of the publication in itself is fascinating: *Kirchen-Musik für Chor* (Simrock, 1832), published as three separate pieces with a shared title page; the opus number was left off. Mendelssohn chose a range of compositions as his first sacred works that seem to have no connections of any kind. Yet, one might view these three pieces as quasi-liturgical pieces that offer "Kirchenmusik" in a Romantic sense, where Bach's music turns every room into a church.[11] The order of the three pieces does not seem arbitrary, as the composer started with a Lutheran composition, "Aus tiefer Not" (MWV B20), followed by the Catholic "Ave Maria" (MWV B19), and then offering "Mitten wir im Leben sind" (MWV B21) as a synthesis between the previous two.

The two chorales for opus 23 came from a group of chorales by Luther, which Mendelssohn had jotted down in Vienna. In a letter to Zelter, Mendelssohn wrote about the allure of the chorales: "Before my departure from Vienna an acquaintance gave me some of Luther's songs, and as I read them, they appeared to me in a new strength, and I plan on setting many of them this winter."[12] Mendelssohn's setting of "Aus tiefer Not" was actually composed after his "Ave Maria." He began the work on October 18, 1830, in Venice. On December 18, 1830, he sent a copy to his teacher Zelter, explaining some of the rationale for this composition:

> I am sending you some music. . . . It is a chorale, which I composed in Venice. . . . You once told me it was unfortunate for you and the Akademie that nothing was composed in four parts, but always for two choirs or eight parts, and since this piece fits the parameters you had given me, and since it might be according to your wishes, I therefore copied it for you. If you think it worthy to be sung by the Akademie, it would, of course, give me the greatest pleasure.[13]

The fact that Mendelssohn chose to send this particular piece to his teacher might say something about the value he placed on this composition, as there were other pieces he could have sent. One wonders if Mendelssohn had thought specifically about the Sing-Akademie before he even began writing the piece, since the work is far removed from his cultural surroundings. Writing a harmonically complex four-part piece literally in view of St. Mark's and its associated polychoral style seems odd. "Aus tiefer Not" is in many ways a typical Lutheran chorale motet/cantata, as the first and fifth movements frame the work with typical Bachian chorale settings. The three inner movements are extensive contrapuntal movements with nos. 2 and 4 as solo movements and a simple homophonic chorus as the centerpiece.

If "Aus tiefer Not" represents Mendelssohn's Lutheran heritage and the performance ideals of the Sing-Akademie, Mendelssohn's "Ave Maria" presents some of the compositional concepts that reflect his approach to and the influence of Catholic compositions. This work is unlike his earlier Catholic compositions, where Mendelssohn intentionally explores a particular style. Rather, Mendelssohn presents a nonliturgical "Ave Maria" that stands on its own contemporary compositional merits, which is presumably why the composer deemed it worthy of publication.

Because of the Ave Maria text, scholars have looked for Catholic stylistic models, especially since even Mendelssohn's father, Abraham, had pointed out the Catholic qualities of the work, albeit with a critical eye: "One major spot in the last [composition] in the middle, as well as the end, seemed to me too artificial and difficult for the simple pious and genuine Catholic style, which is the prominent feature elsewhere."[14] Interestingly, Mendelssohn actually composed the piece before his stay in Rome, beginning it in Vienna and finishing it in Venice.[15] Despite its Catholic text, whose liturgical function is underscored in the initial qualifying title in the autograph as *Offertorium*, Mendelssohn did not have a Catholic, liturgical performance in mind, but rather the German Chorverein. It is dedicated to Schelble and the Frankfurt Cäcilienverein, yet the inspiration for the solo part was his friend, the tenor Eduard Mantius, as can be gathered from a letter to his family, in which he explains the musical setting: "At the Ave, which is a salutation to Mary, a tenor (I was thinking about a disciple) is singing at first everything by himself before the choir enters. Since the whole piece is in A major and climbs pretty high at the words 'benedicta tu' he needs to get his high A prepared—it will sound beautiful."[16]

As suggested in the letter, his theatrical conception of the work becomes obvious right from the start with the responsorial opening. The eight-part chorus with its simple triadic sonorities references the consonant Venetian polychoral style without actually imitating it. The opening section functions as a salutation to Mary in a quasi-liturgical setting that is at the same time theatrical. In order to keep the "action" simple and focused Mendelssohn decided to leave out the phrase "et benedictus fructus ventris tui, Jesus" (and blessed is the fruit of your womb, Jesus), which would counteract the immediacy of the salutation.

As the words of the middle section become more specific with the plea for prayers for forgiveness of sin, the music offers another quasi-liturgical setting with the men approaching Mary in unison, while the upper voices articulate the plea for prayer in simple homophony. This responsorial plea is repeated three times, after which a much more complex eight-part counterpoint commences, which incorporates three motivic ideas—each on specific words: "pro nobis peccatoribus," which is a motivic continuation of the male unison "Sancta Maria"; "ora pro nobis," the earlier motive of the treble voices; and "Sancta Maria," an intensified distillation of the unison motive. The complex counterpoint and a much more chromatic language are what caused Abraham's observation that the music was too artificial and complex for the otherwise "simple pious and genuine Catholic" feel of the work. The counterpoint simplifies again in terms of diatonic language and homorhythmic text declamation with two mixed choirs for the last line of the prayer, "ora nunc et in hora mortis nostri."

Mendelssohn's dramatic approach becomes most obvious in the final section, which is a basic repeat of the opening salutation section with added pleas for help ("ora pro nobis") from the middle section—again a level of complexity that Felix's father felt to be counterproductive. From the overall ternary design, the varied use of contrapuntal techniques, the shifting harmonic language, and the carefully planned "action" of the composition, we can see that Mendelssohn does not emulate any particular Catholic style; rather, he employs various stylistic traits as reference points to present a musical narrative that is in its essence Romantic.

Even though "Mitten wir im Leben sind" was composed only a few days later than the "Ave Maria" and "Aus tiefer Not," they are compositionally worlds apart. Mendelssohn wrote about the composition first from Florence, and he completed it Rome. It is difficult to surmise how much the Roman environment influenced the work. Based on its style, one could assume a significant influence. During the first few weeks in Rome, Mendelssohn had begun exploring all the sights, including the Vatican and the Sistine Chapel. While the young composer had not yet spent much time with members of the papal choir or their director and Palestrina scholar Giuseppe Baini (1775–1844), he had inspected many Old Italian scores from the library of bibliophile Fortunato Santini (1778–1861). Mendelssohn had also spent considerable time with diplomat Baron Christian Karl Josias von Bunsen (1791–1860), who was a strong proponent of Palestrina's music. Bunsen would play an important role in Mendelssohn's appointment in 1842 as Generalmusikdirektor of German church music as part of the liturgical reforms under Friedrich Wilhelm IV.

What might at first glance seem an obvious Lutheran composition espouses, under closer inspection, many traits of the Old Italian style, as Mendelssohn takes a free approach to the use of the Lutheran chorale "Mitten wir im Leben sind," which is actually an adaptation of the sequence *Media vita in morte sumus.*[17] It should be assumed, however, that Mendelssohn was not aware of the original source of this chorale. Other than the opening line, "Mitten wir im Leben sind" is freely composed. Mendelssohn nevertheless followed the textual division of three stanzas and refrain in his three-part design: A–A′–A″. Mendelssohn's own concise musical description in a letter to his sisters covers the basic design for each stanza well: "I have once again a new chorale for the Sing-Akademie: 'In the midst of life we are surrounded by death, therefore we search for who can provide help to us poor people in the time of need?' That's asked by the male voices, and then enter the female voices *piano*: 'you alone, Lord, provide.' Then there is wicked noise and at the end 'Kyrie eleison.'"[18]

The first part—before the "wicked noise"—is a very simple antiphonal four-part homophonic setting much different from the typical chromatic Bachian settings Mendelssohn usually writes. Garratt suggests that, "the chorale portions of the work reflect not the style of Bach's harmonizations, but the nineteenth-century 'reformed' chorale, the return to the supposed simplicity and suitability for congregational singing of the chorales of the Reformation period advocated by Thibaut and, among others, Mendelssohn's organ teacher August Wilhelm Bach (1796–1869). There is a reciprocal relation between early nineteenth-century ideas on chorale reform and the idealization of old Italian homophony."[19] This viewpoint assumes a lot of specific thought on Mendelssohn's part concerning the state of modern church music. On the other extreme is Ulrich Wüster's suggestion that Mendelssohn was inspired by Titian's *Madonna with Child and Saints*, a painting Mendelssohn described in detail in a letter from Venice.[20] While the painting captures some overlapping sentiments, the opening male chorus sounds too much like a Weberian male chorus to suggest more direct, stylistic associations to the painting.

The most fascinating aspect found in this work is the contrast of styles—from the Männerchor and antiphonal ethereal female chorus to the eight-part chorus that contains at times powerful homophony, at times Palestrina-like stacked imitation, and then followed again by male-female antiphony. Mendelssohn's own words might be once again the best guide for locating the stylistic trends in this chorus. In all of his correspondence from Italy, Mendelssohn refers to "Mitten wir im Leben sind" as a chorale. In one letter he calls it "one of the best church music pieces I have produced, and it growls wickedly and whistles dark blue," pointing out the dark and intense character of the work.[21] Five days earlier he called it a "Lutheran chorale for eight parts a capella," a title that implies Mendelssohn's deviation from his typical chromatic four-part settings, replaced by a simpler, mostly consonant setting.[22] To his friend, pastor Julius Schubring, Mendelssohn writes, "I write you today only a few lines, since I have so little time these days, and I feel an inner urge, I write much church music, namely a chorale "Mitten wir im Leben sind" by Luther, which you would like, I think."[23] Mendelssohn uses language here that indicates extreme pleasure in the process of writing church music, presumably because he felt he had something important to say. The fact that opus 23 would become his first published sacred compositions, and that he titles them *Kirchen-Musik* underscores this assumption.

Mendelssohn explained part of his creative process to Klingemann:

> Your poems call for sound and thus real sound should not be missing. Since then I have experienced this need only once with the same high intensity and strangely enough, when writing for the [Sing]akademie, with the Lieder by Luther, which an acquaintance gave me in Vienna for my journey; I ask you, read them, or if you cannot access them, open a hymnbook to the following: "Mitten wir im Leben sind" or "Aus tiefer Not" or "Vom Himmel hoch, da komm ich her," "Ach, Gott vom Himmel sieh darein," "Mit Fried' und Freud," in short, all of them. How every word calls for music, how every stanza is a different piece, how one finds progression, movement, growth; it is just too wonderful, and so I work in the middle of Rome diligently on them and visit the cloister where he [Luther] lived and witnessed the mad spectacle of the clergymen.[24]

Mendelssohn equates Luther's chorales with Klingemann's poetry as texts that he is able to set to music with great immediacy. The composer seems to be less concerned about contrapuntal ideals or stylistic models; rather his focus is on expressing the words as directly as possible. It seems that the various stylistic strains are based more on intuition than on reflection or planning, which might be the reason that opus 23 is different from his earlier church music, as they no longer seem studies of historic styles. The styles have been internalized and have become part of his Romantic language. Another fascinating aspect is Mendelssohn's imagining of the heroic Luther experiencing the frivolities of religious culture at the geographic center of Catholicism—sentiments Mendelssohn shared.[25] It seems then that the emotional content of "Mitten wir im Leben sind" goes far beyond liturgical function and appropriate contrapuntal styles, as it captures Mendelssohn's vivid impressions of a new and strange place.

The three pieces in opus 23 are not liturgical pieces or even pieces intended for worship. Rather, Mendelssohn explores a wide range of Catholic and Lutheran styles with the goal of expressing texts that spoke to him during his journey into Catholic Italy—beginning in Vienna and ending in Rome. This music is less imaginary church music and more Romantic expression about Mendelssohn's Catholic experience. The use of the title *Kirchen-Musik* seems to be just a simple reference to the sacred nature of the text and the various stylistic reference points to Lutheran and Catholic church music. The fact that Mendelssohn wrote the pieces with the Sing-Akademie and the Cäcilienverein in mind underscores the secular nature of the composition, which should not call into question the sincerity with which Mendelssohn approached the text.

Drei Motetten für weibliche Stimmen mit Begleitung der Orgel, Op. 39

At first glance the three motets of opus 39 are closely related to his experiences in Rome, as these works are dedicated to the nuns at Trinità dei Monti. Mendelssohn writes in great detail about his inspiration in a letter from Rome:

> [I] work diligently until eleven, and from then until dark I do nothing but breathe the air. Yesterday we had nice weather for the first time in several days. After working in the morning on "Solomon" for a while, I went up to the Monte Pincio and spent the rest of the day there. . . . At the sound of the Ave Maria, one goes to the church of Trinità dei Monti; there the French nuns sing, and it is charming to hear them. I am becoming quite tolerant and listen to bad music with much devotion—but what is there to do? The compositions are laughable, the organ playing even more ridiculous; but it is twilight now, and the whole, small, colorful church full of kneeling people, lit up by the sinking sun as soon as the door opens. The two singing nuns have the sweetest voices in the world, touching and tender; and in particular when one of them sings the Responsorium with her sweet voice, rather than the rough, severe, and monotonous voice expected from a priest, it creates a sense of wonder. Knowing also that the singers are not allowed to be seen [during the service], I made a strange resolution; I will compose something for those voices, which are etched in my memory, and I will send it to them (there are various ways to do it). I know they will sing it. That will be something special, to hear my composition from people I have never seen, and they will sing it to the barbaro Tedesco, whom they have also never seen. I am excited about it; the text will be in Latin, a prayer to Mary. Do you like my idea?[26]

Only half of the music of opus 39, however, was composed in Rome, as one motet was replaced and several other movements were added more than six years later.

While Mendelssohn chose liturgical texts, it seems unrealistic that the nuns would actually incorporate these compositions into their services. And if they did, Mendelssohn would have to assume that he would not hear them performed, since his plan at that point was to leave Rome before Easter. Yet the first liturgical use is for the Tuesday after Easter, the second would be the Sunday after Pentecost, and the last not until Advent season of the following year. There are no further discussions or hints by the composer about the text choices. Nevertheless, more than six years later Mendelssohn published his opus 39 with a dedication to the nuns at Trinità dei Monte in Rome, thereby purposely linking all pieces gathered under this opus number with his experience at Monte Pincio—including the later composed "Laudate pueri" and the additional two movements of "Surrexit pastor."

Mendelssohn composed "O beata et benedicta" (MWV B22) and the first movement of "Surrexit pastor" (MWV B30) on December 30, 1830, and "Veni Domine" (MWV B24) the following day. Over six years later, in August 1837, he decided to add two movements to "Surrexit pastor," using the text that follows the Responsorium, as well as verse 7 of the Easter sequence. He also composed "Laudate pueri Dominum" (MWV B30) that same month while staying near his uncle's estate in Koblenz. The following year his published opus 39, *Drei Motetten*, omitted "O beata et benedicta" but included instead "Laudate pueri Dominum."

The rejected motet, "O beata et benedicta," is a much simpler composition than the other two movements composed during the last two days of 1830. It is therefore not surprising that Mendelssohn replaced this motet with the newly composed "Laudate pueri Dominum." The simplicity of this composition is in accordance with the composer's original idea to write music for performance by the nuns. The brief three-part motet is a simple homorhythmic setting that incorporates antiphonal singing—much in line with his description of the liturgy at Trinità dei Monti. The organ mostly doubles the vocal parts while adding a clear counterpoint in the bass. Harmonically, the setting is rich in consonances and is mostly diatonic. The appeal of the composition is found in the close scoring of the three vocal parts, emphasizing the sound of the "sweetest voices in the world, touching and tender."[27]

It is impossible to know why Mendelssohn chose this particular text. While a liturgical text fits Mendelssohn's aim to write for the cloistered nuns, the antiphon for Trinitatis was too far into the liturgical year for serious consideration of an actual liturgical performance by the nuns during his stay in Rome. There are, however, good musical reasons for his text choice. This general text about the triune God does not present complex interpretative challenges and thereby allows a simple musical setting; the emphasis can be on the sound itself. By framing the motet with the organ's introduction and closing (with alleluia) and unison singing on "Father, Son, and Holy Spirit" versus three-part texture on "O blessed Holy Trinity/Unity," Mendelssohn moves this composition into the realm of the simple timeless truth and beauty he describes in his liturgical experience at Trinità dei Monti.

A few months later Mendelssohn would write in great detail about his liturgical experiences during Holy Week as something that encompassed more than just music. He recognizes that in Catholic liturgy, worship is a process far beyond the aural, as it includes the various physical acts of the priests and the people—the aroma of incense and the spatial arrangement of all the participants. In short, all senses are involved, yet the music plays a subordinate role of a larger dramatic experience.[28] In a small sense, "O beata et benedicta" captures the limited role of music in that concept of liturgy as a dramatic yet timeless experience.

That Mendelssohn experienced Italy and Catholicism with his eyes wide open can be seen in his many descriptions of sacred art. I have argued elsewhere that Mendelssohn might have been directly or indirectly inspired by paintings of Titian and Raphael when writing these motets.[29] While these influences cannot be clearly proved, since the composer himself does not make these connections specifically, it nevertheless seems reasonable to assume that Mendelssohn wanted to capture a complex worship experience that expressed more than the meaning of any given text.

This broader quasi-liturgical experience might be part of the reason why Mendelssohn replaced "O beata et benedicta" with "Laudate pueri." A careful look at the texts of the other motets reveals that Mendelssohn's specific ordering of opus 39 actually creates an overarching, liturgical narrative on the life of Christ from Advent to Easter. "O beata et benedicta" is a text of an antiphon for the first Sunday after Pentecost, which does not fit into this narrative (see appendix 2.1). The three published motets explore the meaning of the life, death, and resurrection of Christ within the context of the broader biblical narrative through the use of three key liturgical texts. The first motet text from the third Sunday in Advent not only talks about the anticipation of the coming of Christ, but it places the plea for the arrival of the promised Messiah within the historical, inter-Testamental context of a scattered and oppressed Jewish people. The Jewish context of these motet texts is brought into sharper focus in the second motet with Mendelssohn's translation of "Laudate pueri" as "Ihr Kinder Israel"—a translation not found in the *Lutherbibel*. The opening verses from Psalm 113 are a call for Israel to praise the everlasting, eternal God, which, in light of the previous motet, would include Jesus the Messiah in this praise. Psalm 128 then talks about searching out God and following his laws, which are recurring themes in the life of Jesus. The last motet pulls together the concepts of Old Testament prophecy, searching for God, and keeping God's law with liturgical texts from the Tuesday after Easter that identify the risen Christ as the Good Shepherd who sacrificially died for his sheep. It seems reasonable to argue that Mendelssohn viewed opus 39 loosely as a liturgical motet cycle based on the life of Christ. As mentioned above, his vivid descriptions of the liturgy at St. Peter's in Rome shows an obvious awareness and understanding of the Roman Catholic liturgical year as a continuously unfolding drama.

While there is no obvious musical thread that connects the three motets motivically, it is nevertheless interesting that the key scheme of the motets supports a cyclical interpretation:

1. "Veni Domine": G minor
2. "Laudate pueri": E-flat major–A-flat major
3. "Surrexit pastor": G major–E minor–G major

Stylistically, the two $\frac{6}{8}$ movements of the first and third motets are in many ways cousins, which is not surprising, as both were composed in Rome on consecutive days on December 30 and 31, 1830.

"Veni Domine" is the only published motet that he composed in Rome in its entirety. It is the most compact of the three motets with four distinct but short sections. Throughout the motet, the organ part figures prominently. The first section is a brief question posed in unison in the voices with simple chordal accompaniment in the organ, invoking a quasi-liturgical setting. While the melody is not taken from a chant, it is nevertheless eerily similar to the opening line of Palestrina's setting of the same text (see exx. 2.1a and 2.1b).

If the ensuing $\frac{6}{8}$ section makes the opening part seem like a "slow introduction," it is no surprise that the other three sections are interdependent, creating a well-defined ABA′ design. This is obviously far removed from the paratactic contrapuntal style of the Italian Renaissance masters. Even within the A section Mendelssohn composes with clear structural syntax, in which each contrapuntal phrase has a specific formal function that also includes a clear key scheme: The first thirteen measures move from tonic G minor to dominant D major, the next eighteen measures actually modulate to D minor; the last twelve measures recapitulate the opening measures, staying in the dominant key, thereby incorporating sonata form principles in this "exposition." Within each phrase Mendelssohn employs several contrapuntal techniques. The first thirteen and corresponding last twelve measures of the A section are conceptually Palestrina-like, as the three vocal parts are in imitation with the organ parts over a slow moving bass line. The "transitional" section is responsorial in two four-measure phrases (2 + 2) followed by an imitative phrase that completes the modulation to D minor. Just within this A section Mendelssohn has synthesized various paratactic contrapuntal styles within a syntactical, quasi-exposition section.

The contrasting B section relies more directly on the organ as accompaniment, since the soprano 1 functions as a solo voice for the first ten measures,

Example 2.1a. Palestrina, "Veni Domine," opening

Example 2.1b. Mendelssohn, "Veni Domine," opening

which is then followed by a choral response with the same material with an added four-measure cadential extension. This section vacillates between G major and G minor, expressing the tension between the plea for help and the confidence in God's faithfulness. The A′ section completes the transformation from supplication in G minor to hopeful anticipation (Advent) in G major— another nineteenth-century formalistic tool that underscores Mendelssohn's ability to use a progressive movement design cloaked in contrapuntal procedures from the Renaissance.

The second motet in the set, "Laudate pueri," has no direct connection to Mendelssohn's compositional work in Rome. Yet contrapuntally Mendelssohn invokes Italian characteristics with an imitative opening at the unison and the fourth at irregular entrance points. A closer look, however, again shows a tightly composed piece that espouses Mendelssohn's nineteenth-century compositional ideals of contrast and resolution at the harmonic as well as thematic/contrapuntal levels. "Laudate pueri" consists of three sections. The first two sections have two distinct themes in third-related keys (E-flat major and G minor). Thematic, textural, and harmonic contrasts are then resolved over the course of the third section. Textually, the fugato theme is a call for thanksgiving and praise, while the homophonic section represents the act of praise. As these two texts merge, the children of Israel seemingly join in the praise of the everlasting God. Mendelssohn's expression of hesitation through the use of a deceptive cadence makes a very strong musical case, however, for a continued call rather than a joining of the "Kinder Israel," as the final cadence is delayed until the head motive with the words "Ihr Kinder Israel, dankt dem Herrn" is stated one last time.

Compositionally, Mendelssohn uses counterpoint on the surface level as well as structurally. The composer was trained in counterpoint since childhood, and composing polyphonic music was part of his musical identity. His training, however, did not follow any particular school, as Zelter devised his own curriculum based on various styles.[30] His contrapuntal language is also not limited to sacred works. The opening of the *Hebrides* overture (MWV P7, op. 26), for example, or the development section of the first movement of his "Italian" Symphony (MWV N16, op. posth. 90)—pieces he was working on in Rome—are just two of countless examples of the essential role counterpoint plays in Mendelssohn's style. As is the case in both orchestral works, his use of counterpoint is subordinated to a structural design. While Mendelssohn might choose counterpoint to synthesize various themes or motives and thereby makes counterpoint a process, he will also use counterpoint just as language, something he bemoaned during his revisions of the *Hebrides* overture.[31] In the case of this motet movement, Mendelssohn intentionally composes counterpoint with an "Italian accent," an accent that is very slight, since the underlying compositional procedures are more syntactic than seventeenth-century counterpoint would be.

The second movement of this motet, "Beati omnes," is an antiphonal work with alternation between three solo voices and the three-part chorus. This movement has a much simpler design and the consonant Italian sound quality of the displaced motet *O beata et benedicta*. Through simple homorhythmic, antiphonal statements of the text, the liturgical function of reflection is emphasized. The frequent repetition of the words "Blessed are" focuses on the promise of God's blessing, which could easily be interpreted as a reference back to Mendelssohn's lingering call to join in the praise of the eternal God of the previous movement. This reference to the continued call also underscores the possibility of an overall narrative, culminating in the text of the third motet, which points to the redemptive work of Christ as the reason for Christian worship.

Only the first of the four movements of "Surrexit pastor" (MWV B23) was actually composed in Rome, which might be one of the reasons why the last motet is different from the first two on several accounts. First, it is written for four voices, thereby changing the contrapuntal approach and the role of the organ accompaniment. Second, the four movements create a mini-cantata or a short operatic scene. Third, the two inner movements are the only two solo movements of the whole collection. And fourth, the last movement uses a completely different, Handelian vocal style.

The first movement of "Surrexit pastor" is, just like the opening motet, in $\frac{6}{8}$, and the key of G major strengthens the notion of viewing the three motets as cyclical. The fourteen-measure organ introduction uses motivic material from the opening theme, entering in measure 15. Four solo parts present the first line of text in a clear homophonic declamatory style. The fermata between "The good shepherd" and "who laid down his life" signifies a reluctance to bespeak the unfathomable sacrifice of Jesus as the Lamb of God. The second half of the phrase is a well-crafted line made up of a descending motive that is sequenced up by step three times, creating a strong sense of climax on the last part of the sentence on the word "sheep"—the object of Christ's love. After a four-measure organ interlude the choir answers antiphonally with the exact phrase the soloists sang, creating a quasi-liturgical effect. As has been the case in the organ introduction and interlude, the polyphonic construct has a constant upward motion, which might seem counterintuitive to the text about Christ's sacrificial death. It is, however, liturgically an Easter text, which becomes obvious in the next section. An eight-measure phrase sung homophonically by the soloists leads to another fermata. This time the pause denotes the end of the liturgical text, preparing the listener for the Alleluia, which confirms the Easter function of the text. The chorus again responds with the same phrase with an organ interlude before the Alleluia sung *forte*. The tension between the intensely dark text and the organ accompaniment and Alleluia comes to a head in the final Alleluia, which swells contrapuntally, as soloists and choir enter one-by-one, imitatively, yet singing in a hushed piano.

Other than the use of four parts instead of three in the other motets, this first movement matches on the surface the quasi-liturgical stylistic traits of the previous two motets. At the same time, the hushed ending prepares the listener for the ensuing movements, which are less liturgical and more dramatic in character. It becomes quickly evident that this last motet is more dramatically conceived then the previous two. The restless three-note offbeat motive in the organ at the beginning of the second movement is a musical descriptor of the panicked, breathless question about Christ's missing body. Mendelssohn creates an arch that crests in *forte* as the voices repeat the question in unison. The questions then slowly die down in resignation, as no answers are forthcoming. This movement seems situated far from a simple liturgical setting of the singing nuns at Trinità dei Monti.

The third movement, however, moves the motet back into the realm of an Easter setting, as it is a simple, short proclamation that Christ is risen. The final chorus is a mostly paratactic design, with the return of the opening eight-measure phrase at the dominant in measure 22. Mendelssohn uses typical sixteenth-century contrapuntal techniques such as voice pairing, close imitative entrances, and short homorhythmic phrases, albeit with "instrumental" Alleluia lines reminiscent of mature Baroque style. Despite the somewhat unusual juxtaposition of styles, the last movement functions as a climactic close of not only the third motet but of all of opus 39.

Mendelssohn's work offers a fascinating musical and spiritual journey of a searching soul that finds answers in the redemptive work of Jesus. While the texts are liturgical, none of the motets have a truly liturgical function. Yet together they offer part of the allure of the Catholic experience and the unfolding drama throughout the liturgical year. Mendelssohn's musical language reflects this complex approach through allusions to Catholic styles within a progressive, modern structural design.

Conclusion

Seen in their cultural and biographical context of Mendelssohn's Italy experience, opus 23 and opus 39 represent not only two thoughtful and thought-provoking musical reactions to Roman Catholic culture and liturgy, but they offer a broader quasi-liturgical Christian experience. While the *Kirchen-Musik* explores the differences and commonalities between the Lutheran chorale tradition and the Catholic religious experience, opus 39 captures a more complex liturgical practice that involves an experiential expression of Christology beyond just the aural senses. The tools he used were based neither on the "neoclassical" ideals of a Palestrina revival as suggested by Thibaut nor on the artistic amalgamation and eclecticism of Schinkel's memorial cathedral. Mendelssohn surely was fully aware that none of these six compositions could adequately fulfill a liturgical function in Catholic or Protestant services, because his goal was not to reform church music, which gave him the freedom to express religious content in an individualistic and unconventional manner. His target audience was not a congregation, and the performers he had in mind were not members of a church choir. In both cases, he presumably had the German Bürger in mind—Catholic or Protestant—with a level of sophistication and religious understanding where the dedication to the nuns at Trinità dei Monte of opus 39 would further an engaged performance or listening experience for spiritual edification and personal enjoyment. His musical language therefore did not have to adhere to specific traditions or exhibit certain contrapuntal traits. For Mendelssohn that meant the freedom to use his own musical language to express "not thoughts that are too vague to be contained in words"— or musical or confessional traditions—"but rather too precise,"[32] where his sacred music is not "a mere accompaniment, subordinate to the sacred functions, co-operating with the wax candles and the incense, etc.,"[33] but rather his music expressed a rich experience that incorporated these concepts.

Appendix 2.1
Liturgical Narrative of Opus 39

***Veni Domine*, op. 39, no. 1 (MWV B 24).**
Responsorium of Verspers of third Sunday in Advent.
Mendelssohn's German translation and English text.

Veni Domine et noli tardare! Relaxa facinora plebi tuae, et revocas disperses in terram tuam.
Herr erhöre uns! Und säume nicht länger deinem Volke, und sammle die Zerstreuten in deine Wohnung.
Come Lord and wait no longer! Assuage the suffering of your people. Call the dispersed to return to your dwelling.

Excita Domine potentiam tuam et veni, ut salvos nos facias.
O Herr befreie uns von aller Trübsal und höre die Deinen, die dir vertrauen.
Reveal your power O Lord, and come to save us.

***Laudate pueri*, op. 39, no. 2 (MWV B 30).**
Psalm 113:1–2; Psalm 128:1.
Mendelssohn's German translation and English text (NKJV).

I. Laudate pueri Dominum, laudate nomen Domini.
Ihr Kinder Israel dankt dem Herrn, lobsinget seiner Herrlichkeit.
Praise, O servants of the LORD, Praise the name of the LORD!

Sit nomen Domini benedictum hoc nunc et usque in saecula
Sei hochgelobt des Ewigen Namen von nun an, und immer und ewiglich
Blessed be the name of the LORD from this day forth and forevermore!

II. Beati omnes, qui timent Dominum [qui timent Dominum].
Wohl denen, die ihn von Herzen suchen und seinem Wort gehorsam sind.
Blessed is every one who fears the LORD,

Qui ambulant in viis ejus.
Die im Gesetz des Ew'gen wandeln.
Who walks in His ways.

Surrexit pastor, op. 39, no. 3 (MWV B 23).
Responsorium and Antiphon for Tuesday after Easter.
Easter sequence "Victimae paschali laudes" verse 7.
Mendelssohn's German translation and English text.

I. Surrexit pastor bonus qui animam suam posuit pro ovibus suis.
Er ist ein guter Hirte, der selbst sein Leben lassen wollt' für uns, seine Heerde
The good shepherd, who laid down his life for his sheep, has risen.

Et pro grege suo mori dignatus est. Alleluja!
Er trug für seine Heerde Verfolgung, Schmach und Tod.
And he did not disdain to die for his flock.

II. Tulerunt Dominum meum et nescio ubi posuerunt eum.
Wohin habt ihr ihn getragen, wo habet ihr meines Jesus Leib begraben?
They have taken my Lord, and I do not know where they have put him.

Si tu sustulisti eum, dicito mihi et ego tollam.
Hast du ihn hinweg getragen? Zeig mir die Stätte, hast du ihn hinweg genommen?
If you have borne him hence, tell me where you have laid him and I will take
him away.

III. Surrexit Christus spes mea! Praecedet vos in Galilaeam
Christ ist erstanden vom Tode! Er geht voran nach Galiläa.
Christ, my hope, is risen. He goes before you to Galilee.

Notes

1   Hector Berlioz, letter from Nice, May 6, 1831, quoted in Roger Nichols, *Mendelssohn Remembered* (London: Faber and Faber, 1997), 171.
2   Carl Dahlhaus, "Mendelssohn und die musikalischen Gattungstraditionen," in *Das Problem Mendelssohn* (Regensburg: Gustav Bosse, 1974), 58; Georg Feder, "On Felix

Mendelssohn's Sacred Music," in *The Mendelssohn Companion*, ed. Douglass Seaton (Westport, CT: Greenwood Press, 2001), 272–73; R. Larry Todd, "On Mendelssohn's Sacred Music, Real and Imaginary," in *The Cambridge Companion to Mendelssohn*, ed. Peter Mercer-Taylor (Cambridge: Cambridge University Press, 2004), 167–88.

3   James Garratt, *Palestrina and the German Romantic Imagination: Interpreting Historicism in Nineteenth-Century Music* (Cambridge: Cambridge University Press, 2002), 63.

4   Ibid., 10–12; Mendelssohn had attended Hegel's lectures on aesthetics in 1828, see R. Larry Todd, *Mendelssohn: A Life in Music* (New York: Oxford University Press, 2003), 182–83.

5   See Mendelssohn's letters from Weimar in Peter Sutermeister, ed., *Felix Mendelssohn Bartholdy: Eine Reise durch Deutschland, Italien und Schweiz: Briefe, Tagebuchblätter, Skizzen* (Tübingen: Heliopolis, 1979), 12–22.

6   Todd, *Mendelssohn: A Life in Music*, 166.

7   Garratt, *Palestrina*, 79.

8   Ibid., 62.

9   Todd, *Mendelssohn: A Life in Music*, 177.

10   January 12, 1835, quoted in Garratt, *Palestrina*, 83.

11   Letter from Abraham to Felix, March 10, 1835, in Paul Mendelssohn Bartholdy and Carl Mendelssohn Bartholdy, eds., *Briefe aus den Jahren 1830 bis 1847*, 4th ed. (Leipzig: Hermann Mendelssohn, 1878), 52.

12   Letter to Zelter, October 16, 1830, in ibid., 31: "Vor meiner Abreise aus Wien schenkte mir ein Bekannter Luther's geistliche Lieder, und wie ich sie mir durchlas, sind sie mir mit neuer Kraft entgegengetreten, und ich denk viel davon diesen Winter zu komponieren." Translations are by the author unless otherwise indicated.

13   Reinhold Sietz, ed., *Felix Mendelssohn Bartholdy: Sein Leben in Briefen* (Cologne: Staufen, 1948), 61–62: "Da schicke ich Ihnen denn etwas Musik. . . . Es ist ein Choral, den ich in Venedig komponiert habe. . . . Auch sagten Sie mir einmal, es sei Ihnen sowohl für sich, als für die Akademie unangenehm, daß gar nicht vierstimmiges komponiert würde, sondern alles gleich zweichörig oder achtstimmig, und da ist dies Stück ungefähr die Form hat, die Sie mir damals angaben, und insofern vielleicht mit Ihren Wünschen übereinstimmt, so habe ich es Ihnen denn abgeschrieben. Halten Sie es für wert, auf der Akademie gesungen zu werden, so wäre mir das natürlich die größte Freude."

14   Letter from Abraham to Felix, March 10, 1835, in Mendelssohn Bartholdy and Mendelssohn Bartholdy, *Briefe*, 53: "Eine große Stelle des letztern, in der Mitte, so wie auch das Ende, schienen mir zu künstlich und schwierig für den einfach frommen und allerdings ächt katholischen Styl, welcher übrigens darin vorherrscht."

15   Letter to Zelter, October 16, 1830; in Mendelssohn Bartholdy and Mendelssohn Bartholdy, *Briefe*, 32.

16   November 30, 1830, in Mendelssohn Bartholdy and Mendelssohn Bartholdy, *Briefe*, 51: "Beim Ave, das ein Gruß an die Maria ist, singt nämlich ein Tenor (ich habe mir etwa einen Jünger dabei gedacht) dem Chor immer Alles vor und ganz allein. Da das Stück nun in A dur ist und bei den Worten 'benedicta tu' etwas in die Höhe geht, so mag er sein hohes A nur vorbereiten, —klingen wird es schön."

17   Blanche Gangwere, *Music History During the Renaissance Period, 1520–1550: A Documented Chronology* (Westport, CT: Praeger, 2004), 265.

18   October 23, 1830, in Sutermeister, *Felix Mendelssohn Bartholdy*, 55–56: "Ich habe wieder einen neuen Choral für die Singakademie: 'Mitten wir im Leben sind von dem Tod umfangen, nun suchen wir, der Hülfe thu in der Not uns Armen?' das fragen

die Männerstimmen und nun kommen alle Frauenstimmen piano: 'das thust Du, Herr, alleine.' Dann gibt es bösen Lärm und am Ende 'Kyrie eleison.'"

19   Garratt, *Palestrina*, 82.

20   Ulrich Wüster, "'Aber dann ist es schon durch die innerster Wahrheit und durch den Gegenstand, den es vorstellt, Kirchenmusik . . .': Beobachtungen an Mendelssohns *Kirchen-Musik* op. 23," in *Felix Mendelssohn Bartholdy: Kongreß-Bericht Berlin 1994*, ed. Christian Martin Schmidt (Wiesbaden: Breitkopf und Härtel, 1997), 201.

21   Letter of November 23, 1830, in Sutermeister, *Felix Mendelssohn Bartholdy*, 74: "Der Choral 'Mitten wir im Leben sind' ist seitdem fertig geworden; er ist wohl eins der besten Kirchenstücke die ich gemacht habe, u. brummt bös oder es pfeift dunkelblau."

22   Letter of December 18, 1830; in Mendelssohn Bartholdy and Mendelssohn Bartholdy, *Briefe*, 71: "Ein Lutherischer Choral für acht Stimmen a capella."

23   Letter of November 18, 1830, in Julius Schubring, *Briefwechsel zwischen Felix Mendelssohn und Julius Schubring: Zugleich ein Beitrag zur Geschichte und Theorie des Oratoriums* (Leipzig: Duncker und Humblot, 1892), 15: "Ich schreibe Dir heute so wenig, weil ich eigentlich alle diese Tage sehr wenig Zeit habe, ich arbeite sehr fleißig, und es drängt mich dazu, habe viel Kirchenmusik geschrieben, namentlich einen Choral 'Mitten wir im Leben sind' von Luther, der Dir gefallen würde, denk' ich."

24   Letter of January 2, 1831, in Karl Klingemann, ed., *Felix Mendelssohn-Bartholdys Briefwechsel mit Legationsrat Karl Klingemann in London* (Essen: G. D. Baedecker, 1909), 86: "so rufen deine Gedichte nach dem Klang und da kann der wahre nicht fehlen. Dies habe ich seitdem nur noch einmal in ebenso hohem Grade gefunden und zwar sonderbarerweise, da ich für die Akademie etwas zu komponieren hatte, in den Liedern von Luther, die mir ein Bekannter in Wien schenkte und mit auf die Reise gab; ich bitte Dich, lies sie, oder wenn Du sie nicht gesammelt bekommen kannst so schlag' im Gesangbuch etwa folgende auf: "Mitten wir im Leben sind" oder "Aus tiefer Not" oder "Vom Himmel hoch, da komm ich her," "Ach, Gott vom Himmel sieh darein," "Mit Fried' und Freud," kurz alle. Wie da jedes Wort nach Musik ruft, wie jede Strophe ein andres Stück ist, wie überall ein Fortschritt, eine Bewegung, ein Wachsen sich findet, das ist gar zu herrlich und ich komponiere hier mitten in Rom sehr fleissig daran und betrachte mir das Kloster, wo er gewohnt hat, und sich damals von dem tollen Treiben der Herren überzeugte."

25   See, for example, a letter of December 7, 1830, in Rudolf Elvers, ed., *Felix Mendelssohn: A Life in Letters*, trans. Craig Tomlinson (New York: Fromm International, 1986), 150–51.

26   Letter of December 20, 1830; in Mendelssohn Bartholdy and Mendelssohn Bartholdy, *Briefe*, 73–74: "[ich] bin fleißig bis Elf, und von da an bis zur Dunkelheit thue ich nichts, als Luft athmen. Gestern war seit mehreren Tagen wieder zum ersten Mal ganz heiteres Wetter; nachdem ich also des Morgens ein Stück am "Solomon" gearbeitet habe, ging ich auf den Monte Pincio und spazierte da den ganzen Tag auf und ab . . . kommt dann das Ave Maria, so geht es in die Kirche von Trinità de' Monti; da singen die französischen Nonnen, und es ist wunderlieblich. Ich werde, bei Gott, ganz tolerant und höre schlecht Musik mit Erbauung an, aber was ist zu thun? Die Composition ist lächerlich; das Orgelspiel noch toller; aber nun ist's Dämmerung, und die ganze, kleine, bunte Kirche voll knieender Menschen, die von der untersinkenden Sonne beschienen werden, sobald die

Thüre einmal aufgeht; die beiden singenden Nonnen haben die süßesten Stimmen von der Welt, ordentlich rührend zart; und namentlich wenn die eine mit ihrem sanften Tone das Responsorium singt, was man gewohnt ist von den Priestern so rauh und streng und einförmig zu hören, da wird Einem ganz wunderlich. Nun weiß man noch dazu, daß man die Sängerinnen nicht zu sehen bekommen darf;— da habe ich denn einen sonderlichen Entschluß gefaßt; ich componire ihnen etwas für ihre Stimmen, die ich mir recht genau gemerkt habe, und schicke es ihnen zu, wozu mir mehrere Wege zu Gebote stehen. Singen werden sie es dann, das weiß ich; und das wird nun hübsch sein, wenn ich mein Stück von Leuten, die ich nie gesehen habe, anhören werde, und wenn sie es wieder dem barbaro Tedesco, den sie auch nicht kennen, vorsingen müssen.—Ich freue mich sehr darauf; der Text ist lateinisch, ein Gebet an die Maria. Gefällt Euch nicht die Idee?"

27   Letter of December 20, 1830; in Mendelssohn Bartholdy and Mendelssohn Bartholdy, *Briefe*, 73–74: "die süßesten Stimmen von der Welt, ordentlich rührend zart."

28   Letter of April 4, 1831, in Sutermeister, *Felix Mendelssohn Bartholdy*, 125–32.

29   Siegwart Reichwald, "To Italy and Beyond: Mendelssohn's Concept of Transcendence in Music," *Ars Lyrica* 19 (Fall 2010): 56–92.

30   R. Larry Todd, *Mendelssohn's Musical Education* (Cambridge: Cambridge University Press, 1983).

31   R. Larry Todd, "Of Seagulls and Counterpoint: The Early Versions of Mendelssohn's *Hebrides* Overture," *Nineteenth Century Music* 2 (1979): 197–213.

32   Letter of October 15, 1842, in Mendelssohn Bartholdy and Mendelssohn Bartholdy, *Briefe*, 222.

33   Mendelssohn on January 12, 1835, in Elvers, *Felix Mendelssohn: A Life in Letters*, 235.

Chapter Three

Mendelssohn and the Legacy of Beethoven's Ninth

Vocality in the "Reformation" Symphony

Peter Mercer-Taylor

The unhappy story of the early reception of Mendelssohn's "Reformation" Symphony (MWV N15, op. posth. 107) is a familiar one. While the composer almost certainly embarked on its composition, in 1829, with an eye toward a performance at Berlin's tercentenary celebration of the June 25, 1530, Augsburg Confession, that celebration went forward without the use of Mendelssohn's work. In the course of the two-year *Bildungsreise* upon which he embarked the day after the symphony's completion on May 12, 1830, none of Mendelssohn's several campaigns to secure a premiere for the symphony came to fruition.[1] Perhaps most heartbreaking was the last of these, a projected 1832 performance at the Paris Conservatoire, which Mendelssohn anticipated with unchecked optimism. In a letter of February 13, 1832, detailing the impressive array of Paris performances he was then looking forward to—his A-Minor String Quartet(MWV R22, op. 13), *Midsummer Night's Dream* overture (MWV P3. op. 21), and G-Minor Concerto (MWV O7, op. 25) had all been programmed—he concludes, "But most of all I look forward to the symphony in D minor, which they rehearse next week; I would never have dreamed that I should hear it in Paris for the first time."[2] It is just as well he had not dreamed such dreams, as plans for the Paris performance did not survive that first rehearsal. The piece finally enjoyed a somewhat anticlimactic premiere on November 15, back in Berlin, where the impression it made clearly fell short of Mendelssohn's hopes.[3] He apparently never heard the work again, and it remained unpublished at the time of his death.

The reasons for the failure of the 1830 Berlin performance remain obscure; Judith Silber Ballan has shown that, if a commission for that celebration had ever existed, it had fallen through by mid-April, weeks before Mendelssohn's (long-delayed) mid-May completion of the work.[4] But none of the three possible explanations that Silber Ballan considers most seriously—reluctance to perform the music of a Jewish-born composer at such an event, questions about the appropriateness of a symphony per se, or deference to emerging local composer Eduard Grell's more obvious candidacy—was likely to have stung Mendelssohn as keenly as the grounds for the work's 1832 rejection in Paris, which appear to have been purely artistic. These, too, are obscure (Mendelssohn himself is silent on the topic in his surviving letters), but Ferdinand Hiller's often-cited account—though sketchy, and recorded long after the fact—is compelling: "The end of Mendelssohn's relationship with that splendid orchestra was unpleasant, even hurtful to him. His Reformation Symphony was to be given. A rehearsal took place, which I did not attend; but according to our young friends' account, the work did not appeal to the musicians, and it was not performed. 'It is entirely too learned,' [violinist] Cuvillon told me, 'too many fugatos, too little melody,' etc., etc."[5]

Cuvillon's observation, at least as Hiller recalls it, is more curious than historians have tended to give it credit for. The question of what is "learned" (*scholastisch*) in the work, or melodically lacking, I pass up the opportunity to evaluate (despite a certain severity through stretches of the outer movements, the symphony would appear shot through with ingratiating melody). But it is worth lingering over Cuvillon's somewhat surprising singling out of "fugato," the one musical technique Hiller recalls him actually naming. After all, the "Reformation" Symphony does not include all that much of it. There are only two fugato passages in the whole piece, or, rather, one such passage that appears twice: the transitions of the last movement's exposition and recapitulation, which together account for only some 67 of that movement's 326 measures.[6] These represent a grand total of around 100 seconds of a half-hour work.

As Cuvillon's observation seems to suggest, however, the role of fugato in the climactic final movement of the work—indeed, in the articulation of that movement's own climax—tends to lend it a weight and a memorability out of proportion to its actual duration. The return of the fugato transition in the finale's recapitulation plays host, after all, to the culminating moment in the movement's encounter with the chorale "Ein' feste Burg," whose G-major appearance (attached directly to the movement before) formed the finale's introduction, and whose *Abgesang* had provided subject matter for its development section. It is over the recapitulation of the fugato transition that the chorale's *Stollen* at last appears in the tonic, interwoven for the first time with the formally load-bearing material of the exposition, and in its most celebratory rendering yet. As Benedict Taylor has expressed it, "Finally, the chorale is triumphantly rung out above the striving fugal working of the transition passage, having now attained the D major tonic it had been striving towards. This moment of the double counter-point—the integration of 'external' chorale and finale—is the goal of the movement."[7]

Though the significance of this moment has often been acknowledged, I do not believe it has been fully understood. Taylor and like-minded commentators are certainly not wrong in ascribing such significance as they have to the chorale's appearance in the recapitulation, but I suggest that the picture he paints is an incomplete one. What matters most in this climactic passage may not be what is accomplished for the chorale, but what is accomplished for the fugato itself. For I propose that the fugato is here transformed, undergoing a sea change that forms the crowning event in the symphony-spanning process I seek to tease out in the pages that follow.

The flurry of modern scholarly interest in the "Reformation" Symphony that found a structural downbeat in Judith Silber Ballan's pathbreaking work has focused largely on the issue of the symphony's programmatic content.[8] Surveying the "Palestrina school" counterpoint at the work's outset, the closing movement's entanglements with the Lutheran chorale "Ein' feste Burg ist unser Gott," and those two movements' intimations of agitation, strife, and ultimate triumph, Silber Ballan summarizes the situation thus: "Accepting the broad outline of a narrative suggested by the title, and interpreting the details provided by the music, one may say that the work depicts, in order, the Catholic Church, a struggle, and then the victorious emergence of the Protestants. The inner movements do not unequivocally contribute to the narrative."[9]

This reading has not stood unchallenged. James Garratt has cast into doubt just how Catholic the work's opening invocation of Palestrina-like polyphony would have sounded to Mendelssohn's contemporaries.[10] More recently, Wolfgang Dinglinger has mounted an inventive challenge to the notion that the symphony's middle movements fail to participate in the work's programmatic mission. Drawing a thoughtful distinction between the "picturesque" and the "characteristic" as sources of programmatic content, Dinglinger's is a vision of a work whose deep engagement with the model of Beethoven's Ninth Symphony reaches a climax in which all four movements are manifestly thematically involved (particularly in Mendelssohn's original version, whose final two movements were connected by a twenty-eight-measure transition—later deleted—with manifest debts to Beethoven).[11]

My purpose in the pages that follow is neither to challenge nor to affirm these or other authors in the approaches they have taken to the symphony, much less to resolve such tensions as exist between them. I seek, instead, to suggest that so narrow a focus on the question of programmaticism per se has left unexplored a more obvious interpretive angle, many of whose essential materials (outside of the distinctive approach I will take to the last movement's fugato) are generally acknowledged, but have never been adequately drawn into a synoptic view.

To put the matter in its simplest terms, one of the clearest difficulties with the "Reformation" Symphony is that it is a work committed to serving two masters. On the one hand, the historical topic of the Reformation is clearly in play in the symphony in *some* sense, at least. This much is questioned by no one. On the other, the piece is obviously deeply invested in engagement with the revolution enacted by Beethoven's Ninth Symphony on behalf of the genre through the inclusion of a chorus in that symphony's last movement. (Mendelssohn had taken part in two performances of Beethoven's work by the time he wrote his own D-Minor Symphony.)[12] At the root of this bifocal conception—what made it conceivable in the first place—was the happy fact that Luther's and Beethoven's revolutions both involved, centrally, the triumph of song: both were about the release of the human voice to sing as it had not sung before. For Luther, this meant the creation of chorale, opening for the worshipping public unprecedented vistas of personal musical expressivity and serving as a symbol of the demotic impulse underlying the entire Reformation; for Beethoven, it meant the inclusion of song in a formerly instrumental genre.

I propose that it is upon this highly generalized principle—the triumph of song—that Mendelssohn seized as the central idea of his "Reformation" Symphony. However we might choose to tease out the particularities of the programmatic "Reformation" narrative, and however we might want to detail the particular structural, thematic, or tonal intersections of Mendelssohn's symphony with Beethoven's Ninth, there is a story more essential than either of these to be told. I seek to advance an image of the "Reformation" Symphony as a work that is, at a most fundamental level, about that enigma at the core of Beethoven's legacy in the genre: the principle of symphonic vocality itself.[13]

This argument will unfold in two phases. The first is organized around issues raised in the symphony's first three movements, several of them well-acknowledged in existing literature on the work, though never (to my knowledge) ordered interpretively as I will order them here. In the second phase, I will turn to the last movement, where the curious nature of fugato renders it the ideal vehicle to bring to a dramatic climax the issue of vocality that has, by that point, emerged as the work's central concern.

℞

One of the most striking features of the "Reformation" Symphony—setting it apart from both Mendelssohn's own other work in the genre and the great bulk of his consequential predecessors' work—is just how much of its material not only can be, but seems to demand to be, understood as frankly vocal. More or less explicitly vocal topoi had played a prominent role throughout the symphonic genre's history, of course; it is a rare classical symphony that does *not* contain a certain quotient of material stylistically, or "topically," associated with the singing voice.[14] But it is probably not going too far to suggest that the sheer amount of music in the "Reformation" Symphony that is (to adopt Robert Hatten's interpretive framework) marked for vocality within the instrumental realm that hosts it, and the care with which that marking process takes place, may be the work's single most unusual feature.[15] And the merest glance at the allotment of the vocal material in play in the work's first three movements brings an obvious design into view.

Mendelssohn wastes no time in bringing the issue of vocality to the fore. What strikes us in the first movement's forty-one-measure introduction is not that it contains music of a vocal cast, but that the music's vocal models should be so specific, so abundant, and so diverse. The contrapuntal opening, to begin with (ex. 3.1), is taken by nearly all commentators as a vivid encapsulation of Renaissance vocal polyphony—Palestrina is the usual comparison—freely surrendering the pursuit of melodic originality for absolute conformity to the style's conventions: its melodic kernel, as Thomas Grey points out, "derives from a common intonation formula encountered in Gregorian psalm tones and canticles (such as the Magnificat on the third tone), consisting of a rising major second followed by a minor third."[16]

At measure 23, an altogether different idea is offered by the winds (ex. 3.2), a "portentous recitational . . . figure"[17] (as Grey puts it) that makes a good deal less sense as instrumental melody than as syllabic vocal exhortation. It is on the vocality of this gesture that Hermann Deiters zeroes in imaginatively in his 1868 review of the work, where he describes this as "a new figure, *unisono*, speaking in a firm and powerful voice, as if prophesying something yet to come, in a manner reminiscent of old chorale singing."[18]

Most explicit of all in its referential force is the "Dresden Amen" (ex. 3.3), composed in the 1770s by Johann Gottlieb Naumann for Dresden's Catholic court (and more familiar to most as the "Grail" Leitmotiv in Wagner's *Parsifal*), which appears twice at the introduction's close (mm. 33–35, 38–41).[19]

This introduction's nods to vocal music are thus numerous, variegated, and—particularly in light of the presence of both literal quotation and a suggestive programmatic title—aglow with iconicity. This is not vocal music in the same sense that the first subject of the opening movement of Haydn's Symphony no. 104 sets off from a "singing allegro" topos (nor even, more important, in the sense that the second subject of this movement of the "Reformation" Symphony does the same, at m. 140). This introduction is, instead, shot through with gestures that arrive in the symphonic context without words, but with their vocality flagrantly intact and unreduced. Whatever specific programmatic sense we choose to make of these gestures—and, again, I am setting aside this concern in the pursuit of a more general one—we are obviously missing *something* if we do not hear them as vocal music.

Just as striking is how abruptly and completely that vocality is abandoned as the Allegro con fuoco of the main movement begins. The movement's first subject (ex. 3.4) is obviously related to the introduction's "hortatory" gesture,

Example 3.1. Mendelssohn, "Reformation" Symphony, mvt. 1, mm. 1–5

Example 3.2. Mendelssohn, "Reformation" Symphony, mvt. 1, mm. 23–24 (flutes, oboes, and bassoons)

Example 3.3. Mendelssohn, "Reformation Symphony, mvt. 1, mm. 33–35 (strings)

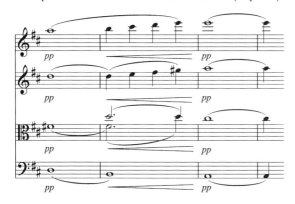

or, rather, to that rhythmically simplified "fanfare" version of the idea that the introduction had already presented (mm. 31–32 and 36–37). Shorn of its syllabic articulation, this version of the melody had already, in the introduction, begun to feel more like trumpet music than vocal music. But the radical expansion of its ambitus at the beginning of the Allegro—the violins leap up a twelfth for the second note, and have covered two octaves by the eighth measure—leaves far behind any hint of vocal performance. The spell of the introduction has been broken, and its melodic denizens will be glimpsed only fleetingly again: the hortatory gesture makes one further appearance (mm.

Example 3.4. Mendelssohn, "Reformation" Symphony, mvt. 1, mm. 42–49 (Violin I)]

247–56) in the middle of the development, and the "Dresden Amen" (mm. 381–84) returns in a reprise of its role at the end of the introduction, to usher in the quieter, gentler recapitulation of the first subject.[20]

But flagrant vocality is not gone for good. Indeed, it is accorded a larger and more central role in the second movement than in the first. The vocality that reaches us from the scherzo's heart may not be as dramatically unreduced as it is in, say, the first movement's "Dresden Amen," but it is scarcely less clear, and the strong possibility of quotation is once more in play.

The scherzo sets off with wind band music, a solidly instrumental idiom that Mendelssohn himself seems to have understood as just that. An often-cited 1830 letter reflecting on Munich's Corpus Christi Pageant finds the composer apparently discerning resonances of his own scherzo in the military wind band he hears there:

> [I] looked around and was very pleased with myself and the initial movements of my *Church* Symphony for I wouldn't have thought that things today would still correspond so well with the contrasts of the first two movements. But if you had heard how the people recited their prayers so monotonously, with one hoarse priest screeching through it all and another reading off the Gospel, and how all of a sudden military music came blasting right into the middle of things . . . I think you would have praised me, as I did myself and was pleased.[21]

The trio, however, is a different matter. Silber Ballan points to the obvious vocality of its lilting oboe duet (the *dolce* marking is an important cue), describing this trio as "a naïve, carol-like song."[22] Song it certainly is, though "carol-like" may not quite get at its character. A most obvious referential grounding point for this melody—indeed, we are verging on a quotation, though one that does not appear to have struck commentators before—is in the duet sung by Ferrando and Guglielmo near the outset of the second act of Mozart's *Così fan Tutte* (see exx. 3.5a and 3.5b). Purposeful allusion seems unlikely, difficult as it is to see what logic could possibly attend an invocation of Mozart's song of seduction. Complicating the matter, however, is the fact that Mendelssohn had a much closer, if much less famous, model readily to hand. In a song dated April 5, 1820, his older sister, Fanny—then fourteen years old—had offered an opening melodic gambit that bears a striking resemblance to the melody Felix would put to work a decade later (ex. 3.6).

Example 3.5a. Mendelssohn, "Reformation" Symphony, mvt. 2, beginning of trio, mm. 65–71

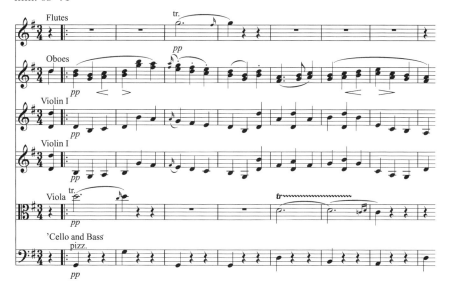

Example 3.5b. Mozart, *Così fan tutte*, no. 21. *Duetto con Coro*, mm. 25–28

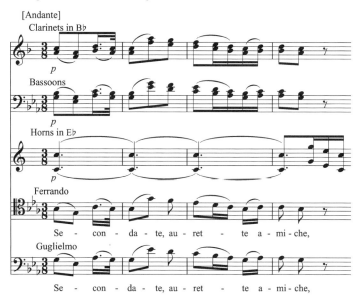

Example 3.6. Fanny Mendelssohn, "Voici venir le doux printem[p]s," vocal incipit. Annette Maurer, *Thematisches Verzeichnis der klavierbegleiteten Sololieder Fanny Hensels* (Kassel: Furore Verlag, 1997), 63.

While the epistolary record appears to have left no remarks on the relationship between this song and the "Reformation" Symphony's trio, it seems unlikely, given their close working relationship, that Felix would have been completely unfamiliar with Fanny's song. The lifting was perhaps unconscious, or perhaps recognized and verbally acknowledged within the family. The issue of literal allusion is ultimately less interesting for my purposes, however, than the testimony such congruities afford to the more basic point at hand: at the very least, it would certainly appear to be song that Mendelssohn has in mind.

And if we compare the two movements considered thus far, the role of vocality is clearly advancing in structural significance and proportional weight. While it is true, on the one hand, that a greater fraction of the second movement is dedicated to patently vocal material than of the first, that material has also moved, in the scherzo, to the movement's structural center. Vocality does not, as in the first movement, play an essentially preludial role, giving way when the principal ideas of the movement arrive. It enjoys a structural room of its own, around which the rest of the movement pivots.

This incremental progress reaches a logical culmination in the third movement, which is generally acknowledged to feel much like a transcription of a vocal number. Silber Ballan calls it "a deeply felt arioso."[23] As Greg Vitercik observes, "The melodic line is clearly vocal throughout."[24] The most striking formal implication of this conception is the movement's sheer brevity, a feature of which commentators rarely fail to take note, but rarely with adequate emphasis. The movement is not just *fairly short, as these things go*. Its performance time of around three and a half minutes—that is taking its fifty-four measures about as slowly as the Andante authorizes, though it is sometimes heard slower—makes for an altogether typical arioso, but probably qualifies it as the shortest movement of concert music Mendelssohn composed for any instrumental ensemble from the 1825 String Octet (MWV R20, op. 20) onward (that is, taking into account chamber music, concertos, overtures, and symphonies).[25] Slow movements of numberless concert works of the Classical and Romantic eras set off from arioso-like material, but extraordinarily rare is the movement that does not build from its vocal point of origin into something else. Indeed, Mendelssohn's conception here is so radical in its start-to-finish dedication to its vocal model as almost to escape the orbit of the symphonic genre altogether.

And it does not really help to suggest that the movement is "clearly treated as a prelude to the finale"[26] (to which it is attached, after all). For that leaves us in the unenviable position of seeking a precedent for a movement that has two fully formed, completely independent slow introductions, as we would thus have to allow Mendelssohn's finale to do.[27] The structural conception is made scarcely less radical.

The foregoing survey of the role of material that is marked for vocality in these three movements is offered as an invitation not to shun the low-hanging fruit. Whatever we make of the "Reformation" program of Mendelssohn's symphony, and however finely we parse structural or thematic similarities between this work and Beethoven's Ninth Symphony, with which it is so clearly in conversation, the issue that may matter most is a more basic one. Beethoven's last completed symphony posed a monolithic challenge to the genre—the symphony must accommodate the singing human voice—and left Mendelssohn's generation with a monumental question: what now? Mendelssohn's response, I propose, was a work *about* the emergence of vocality in symphony, though this principle finds an altogether different formal expression than it did in Beethoven's piece. Where Beethoven turns to vocality only in his last movement, as if in response to a crisis that occurs at that movement's outset, Mendelssohn measures out the incursion of vocality in three distinct, symphony-spanning stages, movement by movement. Where music of a striking vocal cast is put on resplendent display in the introduction of the first movement, that introduction gives way to a movement lodged firmly in the customs of the instrumental genre, within which the vocal ideas of its introduction make only fleeting reappearances. In the trio of the second movement, vocality's role expands to comprise the central event of the movement, securely nested in the wind band music that flanks it, but brought from the periphery to the movement's heart. This incremental process comes to fruition in the slow movement, which trades in its commitment even to the proportional conventions of the symphonic genre in its drive to remain "vocal throughout," an arioso without words.

This brings us to the finale.

The necessity of crafting a climax here is one that Mendelssohn appears to feel no less urgently than Beethoven did in the Ninth Symphony, but it clearly needs to be a different sort of climax, or—to put it more precisely—the same kind of climax played out along a different axis. For Beethoven, the epiphany of the finale lies in the transformation of the latent vocality of its instrumental opening stretch into literal vocality: the recitative-like opening for cellos and basses is reborn as actual recitative for an actual baritone, and the simple, songlike melody to which the orchestra awakens (glimpsed first at mm. 77–80) is reborn as literal song. Mendelssohn's symphony is not about the ascent of the literally vocal from the realm of the instrumental, but about the ascent of instrumental music that is marked for vocality from that which is not. And the epiphany he engineers turns on precisely this axis. What Mendelssohn achieves, I propose, is the revelation of the marking process as a dynamic one, as a process we actually behold taking place. In this finale, for the first time in the symphony, music that is unlikely to strike us as vocal at all the first time we hear it is *turned into* vocal music at its return. Thus, the instrumental is shown not giving way to the vocal, but—the analogy to Beethoven is ultimately quite close—being transformed into it. And fugato is at the heart of the process.

ಚು

The finale sets off with a quotation of vocal music more immediately arresting as such, and more sure to be recognized, than any of those we faced even in the introduction of the first movement: a single flute intoning the chorale "Ein' feste Burg ist unser Gott." The role that this tune—an iconic invocation of Luther's revolution in congregational song, and, by extension, of his whole Reformation—plays in the movement that unfolds from there has often been detailed. The entire melody, save the very last note, is presented in the introduction, as the flute is joined, phrase by phrase, by other members of the orchestra, reaching a full-blooded *ff*, all in the G-major tonality that it shares with the previous movement. Modulating reentries of the opening phrase round out the introduction, culminating in the triumphant arrival of D major, and the first subject of the Allegro maestoso. The chorale tune is absent from the exposition that follows (indeed, just as in the first movement, the vocality of the introduction seems to be cast aside dramatically and purposefully by the very ambitus of the first subject—in this case, two octaves and a third within its first three measures). But successive phrases of the chorale's *Abgesang*, cycling through a range of keys, return to form the bulk of the movement's development section (mm. 166–98). The chorale's *Stollen* makes its thunderous reentry in the fugato transition of the recapitulation (mm. 229–44). This passage represents the first time the tune has appeared in the tonic, and the first time it has intermingled with the principal subjects of this sonata-form movement, prompting Benedict Taylor to label it, as we have seen, "the goal of the movement." The *Stollen* returns one last time, at the coda's close, to comprise the final twenty-one measures of the symphony.

As I have suggested, however, what matters most in the *Stollen*'s reappearance over the fugal transition in the recapitulation may not be the victory that this moment represents for the chorale tune, but the change that this arrival accomplishes for the fugato over which it occurs. It is to that fugato's two appearances—in the exposition (mm. 92–120) and in the recapitulation (mm. 207–45)—that I now turn.

The fact that this exposition contains a passage of fugato is not a surprise. It would have been more surprising if this movement had *not* included a fugal stretch at some point. More to the point, if the onset of the Allegro maestoso exposition seems, in its enormous ambitus, to set its face against the vocality of the introduction's chorale, we have no reason whatever to hear this fugato as a return to the realm of vocality, so tidily does it fit into Mendelssohn's own instrumental practices. Among Mendelssohn's twelve youthful *Sinfoniae* for string orchestra, nos. 1, 5, 6, 7, 8, 9, 11, and 12 (MWV N1, N5–9, and N11–12) all contain fugal material in their finales (*Sinfonia* no. 12 in its first movement, as well). Nor did his taste for fugal work wane as Mendelssohn entered his first compositional maturity: fugato appears in the finales of the Symphony no. 1 in C Minor (MWV N13, op. 11) and the String Octet op. 20, and in the slow movement of the String Quartet in A Minor, op. 13. This list could go on, but the point is simple: there is nothing vocal about this exposition's fugato, no sense whatever that the boundaries of the instrumental genre are being stretched to accommodate music from a different realm. It is even marked *marcato*, after all, a far cry from the *dolce* marking attending the "vocal" music of the second and third movements.

Indeed, setting the "Reformation" Symphony's fugal subject alongside its counterpart in the finale of this work's most direct predecessor, Mendelssohn's Symphony no. 1 in C Minor (1824), we appear to be comparing stylistic siblings. Despite the more conjunct motion of the "Reformation" Symphony's subject, the two are similar in their predominantly quarter-note motion, their onset on the second beat, and the athletic, propulsive performance style prescribed in their expressive markings (*pesante* in the first case, *marcato* in the second; see examples 3.7a and 3.7b). There is even a certain similarity in their melodic contours, with an initial fall from the (local) dominant to the same pitch an octave lower, followed by an upward leap near the close.

When the "Reformation" Symphony's fugato returns in the recapitulation (starting in m. 207), the first clue we get that something new may be afoot is the simple fact that the *marcato* marking has been omitted (this is systemic; every instrument that entered with the subject in the exposition had this marking, and every one lacks it in the recapitulation). Such a detail might seem irrelevant were it not for the fact that a much more profound transformation is in the offing.

What is transformed in the recapitulation, in a most obvious sense, is the countermelody that enters to accompany the fugato as it motors along. The fugato of the exposition had hosted the entry of a new countersubject, introduced by the woodwinds thirteen measures into the fugato's course (ex. 3.8).

In the recapitulation, it is in the twenty-third measure of the fugato that a countersubject appears, and it is no longer the fairly innocuous, melodically static idea presented in example 3.8, but the cantus firmus itself, the mighty return of the chorale's *Stollen* (ex. 3.9).

I want to suggest that the entry of the chorale at this moment sets into motion—or is intended to set into motion—a process of rethinking that is highly subtle, and highly unusual in the kinds of demands it makes upon the

Example 3.7a. Mendelssohn, Symphony no. 1 in C Minor, mvt. 4, mm. 102–4

Example 3.7b. Mendelssohn, "Reformation" Symphony, mvt. 4, mm. 92–95

Example 3.8. Mendelssohn, "Reformation" Symphony, mvt. 4, exposition (flutes, oboes, and clarinets), mm. 104–8

listener, but engineered with extraordinary precision and clarity. I propose that the chorale's entrance abruptly brings into view a feature of the fugal subject itself that Mendelssohn has pointed out before (I will come to this in a moment), but whose salience has not yet been apparent. Like the chorale's opening line, the opening gesture of the fugato subject—the portion leading up to its first disjunct melodic motion—is eight syllables long (four iambs), or would be if it were sung. As the entries of the fugal subject are set alongside the chorale, I propose that Mendelssohn is inviting us to hear these entries as vocal echoes of the chorale, as imaginary bearers of its text in a casual rhythmic diminution of the chorale itself (ex. 3.10). I will turn first to the nature of this invitation as Mendelssohn extends it, then to its implications.

Why should we hear the fugal subject as vocal music in this way (apart from the fact that it readily becomes second nature once we start)? It seems likely that Mendelssohn hoped to prompt just such a hearing in his audience—that is, the Berlin audience he intended the symphony to have in June 1830—by calling on them to undertake two separate acts of musical remembering: to recall music they had heard, in one instance, three minutes before, and, in the other, fifteen months.

If the congruity of syllable count between the opening of the chorale and the opening of the fugato subject is the crucial issue, the countersubject that had joined the fugato earlier, in the exposition (again, ex. 3.8), is the crux of the argument. And it is a crux in a very literal sense, as this countersubject has the unusual property of being manifestly derived from two different subjects. At its first appearance, there is no question—given its offbeat entrance and

Example 3.9. Mendelssohn, "Reformation" Symphony, mvt. 4, mm. 224–41

Example 3.9.—*(concluded)*

Example 3.10. Mendelssohn, "Reformation" Symphony, mvt. 4, fugato subject, mm. 229–31, with imagined text underlay

Ein' fest - e   Burg   ist   un - ser   Gott...

its initial quarter notes on a single pitch—that this countersubject is derived from the fugato subject (comparing ex. 3.7b and ex. 3.8). It is through the gentlest of mental slippages that we immediately accept its rhythmic relationship to that subject's opening gesture despite the fact that it is not precisely the rhythm that has been retained, but what I have termed the "syllable count." Like the opening gesture of the fugato subject, this countersubject is fit for performance with an iambic, eight-syllable text, though we might not put it quite that way just yet.

Yet it is precisely this property that makes the countersubject just as readily recognizable, in retrospect, as a kind of half-formed version of the chorale that supplants it in the recapitulation, once that chorale arrives. As we mentally place the two side by side (which the direct substitution of one for the other obviously encourages us to do, the chorale being offered as the recapitulation of the countersubject), it is nearly impossible *not* to begin mentally attaching the opening words of the chorale cantus firmus to the earlier, simpler countersubject (ex. 3.11). Clearly a transitive property of thematic derivation at once kicks in: if the fugato subject is related to the exposition's countersubject because both are eight syllables long, and that countersubject is related to the first line of the chorale because both are eight syllables long, we have just learned the words to the fugato.[28]

There are thus perfectly sound internal reasons for responding to the arrival of the chorale in the recapitulation (again, ex. 3.9) by immediately mentally testing the idea that what we are hearing is a chorale tune accompanied by a fugato that shares the chorale's text, though delivering that text via a melody that moves along much more quickly than the chorale, and is only tangentially related to it. The challenge to make sense of this mental picture brings with it one obvious question: where have we heard this sort of thing before?

Modern listeners, with access to an abundance of High Renaissance and Baroque choral music, might readily call to mind a host of precedents.[29] But I suggest that the low-hanging fruit once more provides all the sustenance required. The June 1830 premiere Mendelssohn had envisioned for the "Reformation" Symphony was only separated by some fifteen months, after all, from the March 11, 1829, Sing-Akademie revival of J. S. Bach's *St. Matthew Passion* through which Mendelssohn, as conductor, had taken Berlin's musical world by storm and attracted attention across Europe. This was certainly the

Example 3.11. Mendelssohn, "Reformation" Symphony, mvt. 4, fugato's countermelody, mm. 104–8, with imagined text underlay

Ein' fest - e Burg ist   un - ser Gott, Ein' fest - e Burg ist   un - ser Gott...

event, and the piece, with which Felix Mendelssohn's name was most strongly associated for most of the Berlin public (the composer had been out of town for most of the intervening time).

And what is the prevailing texture of the first great finale in *that* work, the closing chorus of its first part? A rendering of "O Mensch, bewein dein Sünde groß," accompanied (where the chorus is concerned) by entries of material that shares the chorale's text, but is generally faster than the chorale, intermittently imitative, and frequently fugal. At points, the resemblance between Mendelssohn's texture and Bach's is startlingly close. Example 3.12a shows the choral lines at the second phrase of Bach's chorale (where the fugato principle kicks in for the first time—the first phrase had been simpler); example 3.12b shows the entrance of the chorale in the "Reformation" Symphony's recapitulation, as it intersects with the fugato material. Up to the beat upon which Mendelssohn's fugato subject, in Violin II, completes the eight (imaginary) syllables of this chorale phrase, that fugato subject is rhythmically identical to the countersubject provided in Bach's tenor line, and stands in an identical relationship to the slower rhythm of the chorale itself, which is also identical (these are boxed in exx. 3.12a and 3.12b).

Another, somewhat more complex, rhythmic issue is brought into view in this comparison. Once this idea is planted in the "Reformation" Symphony—that the fugato has, all along, been an accompaniment-in-waiting to the chorale, and is, in fact, imaginary vocal music that bears the chorale's words—another piece of the puzzle slips into place so conveniently that, though it may not be strictly necessary to the case, it provides a compelling fleshing out of the picture. In order to get the entire fugato we are in the midst of (it has been going for twenty-two measures before the chorale enters) to sound like a setting of the chorale's opening textual phrase, it is presumably necessary to reconcile the entirety of the fugato subject—in the regular form we are by now familiar with (see ex. 3.7b)—with that text. Eight syllables will not get the job done. While the subject opens with a conjunct descending line of eight syllables, four more syllables follow before we reach the fugato subject's second entry. We thus have (retrospectively) to imagine some way to work the text around this, the most obvious being the repetition of the last four imaginary syllables (ex. 3.13). This is precisely how Bach handles exactly the same issue in the tenor of example 3.12a—"darum Christus sein's Vaters Schoß, sein's Vaters Schoß"—as in numerous analogous situations.

Example 3.12a. J. S. Bach, *St. Matthew Passion*, no. 35, voices only, mm. 24–26

Example 3.12b. Mendelssohn, "Reformation" Symphony, mvt. 4, entrance of chorale (chorale and fugato entries only), mm. 229–33

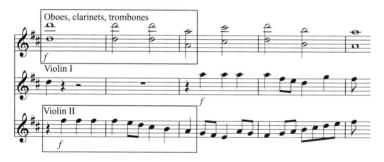

Example 3.13. "Reformation" Symphony, mvt. 4, fugato subject (Oboe II), mm. 207–10, with imagined text underlay

Is Mendelssohn undertaking a quotation of Bach in any meaningful sense? It seems unlikely; even knowing the scores as well as he did himself, it seems altogether possible that the point of specific rhythmic congruity shown in example 3.12 arose unconsciously. And it would be foolhardy in the extreme to imagine that Mendelssohn supposed his audience capable of instantaneously mapping this moment of his own finale onto measures 24–26 of a Bach choral finale they might have heard only once, a year earlier.[30] But it would surely be more foolhardy to assume that these points of congruity mean nothing at all. And if the question is, instead, whether Mendelssohn intended his audience

to hear this stretch of the "Reformation" Symphony as hailing from the contrapuntal world of Bach's *St. Matthew Passion*—that is, whether he intended to
embed "Ein' feste Burg" in a textural housing that would call immediately to
mind the kind of choral counterpoint that Mendelssohn himself had played so
substantive a role in bringing into public view—the answer is surely *yes*. There
seem simply too many points of direct alignment with the world of Bach's choral music to be chalked up to coincidence.

The implications are both obvious and profound. Mendelssohn's exposition
contains a fugato stretch so completely in keeping with his own established
customs for the deployment of instrumental fugato that we have no reason
whatever to move out of that stylistic framework in making sense of it. In the
recapitulation, the arrival of the chorale has the immediate and direct effect
of marking that fugato for vocality: what arises before us is a symphonic finale
transformed—at least for a spell—into a *Schlußchor*. This, I suggest, is the telos
toward which the symphony's entire course has been working. The first three
movements measure out the incremental encroachment of vocal music into
the symphonic realm, culminating in the thoroughgoing vocality of the third
movement. The last movement brings this principle of progressive vocality into
dramatic life, centered on a fugato that is transmuted from instrumental music
to vocal music.

❧

The interpreter's lot is not a happy one where Mendelssohn's "Reformation"
Symphony is concerned, so sparse are those dots we might seek to connect into
a picture of the composer's own understanding of the work and its meanings.
But the picture I have advanced here does stand to bear importantly on how at
least a few of those dots might fit into the whole.

Why, for example, did Mendelssohn—in the course of his revision of this
work before its first performance—do away with the twenty-eight-measure transitional stretch that, in the work's original form, linked the third and fourth
movements? It may well be that the transition, with its recitativo opening
for flute, formed "perhaps too obvious an allusion"[31] to Beethoven's Ninth
Symphony, as Larry Todd has suggested, that so frank an analogy to Beethoven's
work threatened to turn homage into something more like pastiche.

It may also be the case, however, that the problem was not that the resemblance to Beethoven's work was too close, but that it was misleading. The introduction of Beethoven's finale comprises a quest for that which has not yet been
heard, that which is found only in the symphony's radical release into vocality.[32] As I have argued the case of Mendelssohn's "Reformation" Symphony,
just such a release has already occurred by the beginning of the finale, having unfolded through a three-stage process that has already reached a kind
of preliminary culmination in the vocality of the third movement. The fourth

movement becomes climactic, I have argued, not because of what it rejects in the foregoing movements, but because of what it embraces, internalizes, and seeks a new way to dramatize.[33] The trouble is not that Beethoven's and Mendelssohn's symphonies are not engaged in telling the same story—the story of the emergence of symphonic vocality—but that the trajectories of their stories are so different from one another that the conceptual remobilization of the introduction to Beethoven's finale in Mendelssohn's tends only to mislead us into drawing false analogies.

More provocative—if scarcely more conclusive—is the evidence provided by the final known performance of the "Reformation" Symphony in Mendelssohn's own lifetime, which took place in Düsseldorf on December 12, 1837, under the baton of Julius Rietz.[34] In his subsequent report to Mendelssohn, Rietz makes clear (to posterity, that is—Mendelssohn was already aware of it) one curious proviso that Mendelssohn evidently attached to this performance: that the symphony be presented without a programmatic title. "The 'Reformation' Symphony," Rietz writes, "was performed, albeit not with that title, and was enthusiastically received. People were racking their brains trying to figure out what it was supposed to mean, and I quietly enjoyed their various conjectures but was careful not to reveal the correct interpretation."[35]

It was a short time after this performance—in a letter to Rietz of February 11, 1838—that Mendelssohn made his much-discussed denunciation of the piece, foreswearing its publication and declaring it, among his entire output, the piece he "would most like to see burned."[36]

Both Dinglinger and Taylor make reference to this apparent crisis point in Mendelssohn's relationship to the work. The two could scarcely be more different in their assessments of the symphony's ultimate artistic value: for Dinglinger, a fundamental disconnect between form and content is insurmountable; for Taylor, modern listeners may find much to admire here, "used as we are now to the idea of understanding works in relation to their 'extramusical' content."[37] Nonetheless, they are essentially agreed—and evidently in agreement with Rietz himself—about the basic problem this 1837 performance dramatizes. The work only makes sense with the extramusical narrative arc of the Reformation as a guide. Title or no, the Reformation is what the symphony is *about*, and an audience not provided with that information turned out—however much they seem to have enjoyed the work—to be at sea on the topic of "what it was supposed to mean."

The part of this story that does not quite add up is just what Mendelssohn thought he could achieve by insisting that the work be performed without a title. Dinglinger's dismal explanation requires us to envision Mendelssohn in the unlikely position of authorizing the performance of a work he fully acknowledged to have failed in the achievement of its central aim (i.e., "the compositional goal"), evidently hoping that no one would notice, that the resulting lack of clarity might somehow go unremarked: "His refusal to let the symphony be presented with clarification of the compositional goal under which it had been created and first performed is his admission that it failed to achieve this goal. Mendelssohn remained silent regarding his intentions in order not to provide a measuring stick by which the clarity not achieved in the music could be made obvious by other means."[38] Taylor handles Mendelssohn's decision, thoughtfully, as a manifestation of the composer's general disenchantment with the programmatic music of his younger days (the 1834 *Die Schöne Melusine* was the last of his titled overtures, and marked the end of a compositional phase).[39] Taylor does not attempt to probe Mendelssohn's motivations with Dinglinger's explicitness. But if the program of the work really is as central to its sense as he ultimately affirms it to be, it is hard to see how the facile excision of the title could lead to anything other than the strange, almost cruel guessing game Rietz describes. Is this really all Mendelssohn was hoping for?

If my own argument in the foregoing pages is accepted, a much happier possibility comes into view. It may actually be the case that the programmatic backdrop of the Reformation might have served, in Mendelssohn's mind, as just that, but that its removal from the public eye might have been hoped to clear the way for the readier recognition of what was, in fact, the main story of the symphony: the story of symphonic vocality in the wake of Beethoven. From this perspective, the work's undoing in 1837 was not the fact that its various musical allusions—"Ein' feste Burg" chief among them—provided too little information for the audience to go on, but that they provided too much. Had Mendelssohn simply made up a chorale tune, as he so often did in the instrumental works that followed, it seems altogether possible that the course of vocality's advance in the first three movements, and the dramatic transformation of fugato from instrumental music to choral music in the last, might have been much more readily discerned as the central issue of the work. Whether the symphony would have been successful is still very much open to debate (Mendelssohn continued to have strong misgivings about the quality of the material itself). But envisioning the hopes that may have underlaid Mendelssohn's approach to the 1837 performance in this way seems strongly preferable to the attitude of capriciousness or defeatism that seem to undergird our only other available readings.

Finally there is the question of how the reading I have advanced here brings shape to our understanding of Mendelssohn's later approaches to the symphonic genre. If, as I have argued, Mendelssohn reached his early twenties convinced that one of the central challenges in the processing of Beethoven's legacy lay in exploring the issue of vocality in the genre, we can scarcely imagine him to have abandoned that conviction altogether, even if he ultimately rejected a most thoroughgoing early engagement with that principle. And abandon it he clearly did not. For vocality operates in provocative ways, as many have observed, in all three of his remaining contributions to the genre.

The slow movement of the "Italian" Symphony (MWV N16, op. posth. 90) has been understood since the middle of the nineteenth century to be entangled with vocality in some distinctive way.[40] While early commentators tended to draw the analogy to sacred processional song, Eric Werner has also pointed out the resemblance between Mendelssohn's tune and Karl Friedrich Zelter's setting of the Goethe ballad "Es war ein König in Thule," suggesting a biographical motivation.[41] Larry Todd has more recently drawn persuasive links between the movement's opening intonation and Mendelssohn's own Vespers setting, the *Responsorium et Hymnus* (MWV B26, op. posth. 121).[42] Whatever the direct point of origin, there seems little question it is the singing voice we are meant to bear in mind. More compelling in the balance, however, are Mendelssohn's other two symphonic works—the two he actually put into print—both of which approach much more directly that crucial process I have sought to isolate in the finale of the "Reformation" Symphony, whereby the instrumental is made to become vocal before our eyes.

The chief mechanism through which this occurs in the "Lobgesang" (MWV A18, op. 52)—a hybrid of symphony (the first three movements, played without a break) and cantata (the remaining nine)—scarcely takes much explaining. The strapping motto theme presented at the outset of the first symphonic movement (by trombones) returns verbatim early in the fourth movement, but it has now been taken out of the hands of the brass and entrusted to the human voice, bearing the self-descriptive psalm text: "Alles was Odem hat, lobet den Herrn."[43]

More subtle, but clearly relevant to the case at hand, is the coda of the finale of the "Scottish" Symphony (MWV N18, op. 56). Here, the time signature and essential melodic contours of the first movement's opening Allegro subject return to form the foundation of the opening idea of the finale's coda (exx. 3.14a and 3.14b).[44] But this melodic material is now delivered through an orchestral sound that Mendelssohn himself, as many have noted, associated with a *Männerchor*[45] (just what this turn to vocality was intended to mean, I have argued at length elsewhere).[46] The issue of thematic identity is more attenuated here than in either the "Reformation" Symphony or the "Lobgesang"; it is not really the first movement's opening subject greeting us in the finale's coda so much as that subject's more optimistic sibling. But it remains highly provocative, in light of the present discussion, that it is as choral music that Mendelssohn gives us our final glimpse of that melody.

Mendelssohn thus might never again have pursued as subtle and thoroughgoing a confrontation with the issue of vocality in the symphony as I propose he attempted in his "Reformation" Symphony, and, while the principle continued to reverberate through his symphonic work, he does indeed appear to have come to view that early experiment as a failure. But this does not mean we cannot recognize and applaud the unique place the "Reformation" Symphony occupies in his generation's ongoing effort to makes sense of the genre in Beethoven's wake.

Example 3.14a. Mendelssohn, "Scottish" Symphony, mvt. 1, Allegro un poco agitato, mm. 63–67, melody

Example 3.14b. Mendelssohn, "Scottish" Symphony, mvt. 4, Finale maestoso, mm. 396–99, melody

Notes

1   On this dispiriting saga, see Judith Silber, "Mendelssohn and His 'Reformation' Symphony," *Journal of the American Musicological Society* 40, no. 2 (Summer 1987): 324–31. The author will be referred to in the following as Silber Ballan, as she published after her marriage under that double name.

2   "Am meisten freue ich mich aber auf die D moll-Symphonie, die sie nächste Woche vornehmen; das hätte ich mir nicht träumen lassen, daß ich die in Paris zuerst hören sollte." Paul Mendelssohn Bartholdy, ed., *Reisebriefe von Felix Mendelssohn Bartholdy aus den Jahren 1830 bis 1832* (Leipzig: Verlag von Hermann Mendelssohn, 1862), 319. Translations are by the author unless otherwise indicated.

3   Berlin critic Ludwig Rellstab found much to praise, but voiced profound suspicion of the work's programmatic premise, and observed that he "missed . . . melodic invention and a clear presentation and articulation of [formal] sections." In "Überblick der Ereignisse," *Iris im Gebiete der Tonkunst* 3, no. 47 (November 23, 1832): 188; quoted and translated in Silber, "Mendelssohn and His 'Reformation' Symphony," 331).

4   Silber, "Mendelssohn and His 'Reformation' Symphony," 314–16.

5   "Das Ende von Mendelssohn's Verhältnis zu jenem herrlichen Orchester war aber unerfreulich, ja, verletzend für ihn. Seine Reformations-Symphonie sollte gegeben werden. Man spielte sie in einer Probe, der ich nicht beiwohnte; aber nach der Aussage unserer jungen Freunde sprach das Werk die Musiker nicht an und man führte es nicht auf. "Es sei gar zu scholastisch," sagte mir Cuvillon, "zu viele Fugatos, zu wenig Melodie" u. dergl. mehr." Ferdinand Hiller, *Felix Mendelssohn-Bartholdy: Briefe und Erinnerungen* (Cologne: Verlag der M. DuMont-Schauberg'schen Buchhandlung, 1874), 19. Larry Todd has suggested that we may have another brief testimonial on the topic in the form of a remark—recorded in 1858—from Franz Liszt, who observed of Mendelssohn's 1832 Paris sojourn: "'The Overture to *A Midsummer Night's Dream* was a fiasco at the conservatory in Paris some twenty-five years ago (I was there); before the living Mendelssohn not one single note of his composition was played.'" La Mara, ed., *Franz Liszts Briefe*, vol. 3: *An eine Freundin* (Leipzig: Breitkopf und Härtel, 1894), 110; quoted, in translation, in Todd, *Mendelssohn: The Hebrides and Other Overtures* (Cambridge: Cambridge University Press, 1993), 17. In light of the fact that *A Midsummer Night's Dream* overture was

indeed performed by the orchestra on February 19, Todd surmises that Liszt was probably confusing this work with the "Reformation" Symphony.

6   This number goes up by some eleven measures if we include the two brief stretches of Palestrina-like polyphony at the work's opening, though it is difficult to imagine *these* graceful offerings being faulted as unmelodic or overly learned.

7   Benedict Taylor, "Beyond Good and Programmatic: Mendelssohn's 'Reformation' Symphony," *Ad Parnassum* 5, no. 12 (October 2009): 125.

8   This includes both Silber, "Mendelssohn and His 'Reformation' Symphony," and Judith Silber Ballan, "Mendelssohn and the Reformation Symphony: A Critical and Historical Study" (PhD diss., Yale University, 1987).

9   Judith Silber Ballan, "Marxian Programmatic Music: A Stage in Mendelssohn's Musical Development," in *Mendelssohn Studies*, ed. R. Larry Todd (Cambridge: Cambridge University Press, 1992), 155. For earlier approaches to the program of this work—which tend toward a more generalized spirit of religiosity—see, for example, Eric Werner, *Mendelssohn: A New Image of the Composer and His Age*, trans. Dika Newlin (London: 1863), 216–18, and Martin Witte, "Zur Programmgebundenheit der Sinfonien Mendelssohns," in *Das Problem Mendelssohn*, ed. Carl Dahlhaus (Regensburg: Bosse, 1974), 119–27. Hermann Deiters's 1868 review of the symphony (trans. Thomas Grey, in *The Mendelssohn Companion*, ed. Douglass Seaton [Westport, CT: Greenwood Press, 2001], 534–43) already evinces worry over whether the work is better read in terms of a fairly literal programmatic trajectory—via "murky speculations . . . about motives and the interconnection of movements"—or (as Deiters prefers) as a more general "musical glorification of a festal occasion" (534). Deiters's review first appeared in *Allgemeine musikalische Zeitung* 3 (1868): 349–50, 356–57.

10   James Garratt, "Mendelssohn's Babel: Romanticism and the Poetics of Translation," *Music and Letters* 80, no. 1 (February 1999): 25–26. Wulf Konold would offer his own parsing of the musical symbolism of the first movement's introduction, claiming that the contrast between its contrapuntal material and its homophonic, chorale-like material already comprised an embodiment of the Catholic/Protestant struggle at this early stage; see Wulf Konold, *Die Symphonien Felix Mendelssohn Bartholdys* (Laaber: Laaber-Verlag, 1992), 108.

11   Wolfgang Dinglinger, "The Programme of Mendelssohn's 'Reformation' Symphony, op. 107," in *The Mendelssohns: Their Music in History*, ed. John Michael Cooper and Julie D. Prandi (Oxford: Oxford University Press, 2002), 115–33.

12   The first of these took place in Berlin on November 27, 1826, under the direction of Karl Möser; see R. Larry Todd, *Mendelssohn: A Life in Music* (Oxford: Oxford University Press, 2003), 156. A few months later, Mendelssohn took part in another performance of the work in Stettin, where *A Midsummer Night's Dream* overture was premiered on February 20, 1827 (ibid., 167).

13   This argument finds a kindred spirit in Mark Evan Bonds's probing examination of Mendelssohn's later "Lobgesang" (1840) in *After Beethoven: Imperatives of Originality in the Symphony* (Cambridge, MA: Harvard University Press, 1996), 73–108. Toward the end of his thoroughgoing rethinking of the relationship between the "Lobgesang" and Beethoven's Ninth Symphony, Bonds observes that Mendelssohn departs from Beethoven's model in emphasizing continuity and commonality of purpose between his instrumental and vocal sections, where Beethoven's point was discontinuity: "[Mendelssohn] incorporates instrumental manifestations of vocal forms early and often into the instrumental 'Sinfonia.' . . . Unlike Beethoven,

Mendelssohn seeks to demonstrate, in effect, that the gap between the two realms of music—instrumental and vocal—is not in fact as deep as the Ninth might imply" (102). That said, Bonds passes lightly over the "Reformation" Symphony, leaving unexplored the possibility—as I will argue it—that the earlier work embodies an even more sustained, systematic encounter with just such "instrumental manifestations of vocal forms."

14   Victor Kofi Agawu has offered a table of sixty-one of "the more common topics" at work in the "classic repertoire," under the heading "The Universe of Topic for Classical Music," which includes five that are invariably vocal by nature—"aria style," "arioso," "chorale," "singing allegro," and "singing style"—together with a range of others (e.g., "stile legato," "buffa style," "commedia dell'arte," and "pastorale") that have at least the capacity to assume a vocal character, even in instrumental contexts. Victor Kofi Agawu, *Music as Discourse: Semiotic Adventures in Romantic Music* (Oxford: Oxford University Press, 2009), 43–44.

15   On the sense in which I am using the term "markedness," see, for example, Robert Hatten, *Beethoven: Markedness, Correlation, and Interpretation* (Bloomington: Indiana University Press, 1994), esp. 34–38.

16   Thomas Grey, "The Orchestral Music," in Seaton, *The Mendelssohn Companion,* 418. On Mendelssohn's own use of this gesture elsewhere, see Todd, *Mendelssohn: A Life in Music,* 243.

17   Grey, "The Orchestral Music," 421.

18   Deiters, "Review," 535.

19   On the genesis of the "Dresden Amen," see Garratt, "Mendelssohn's Babel," 25. Its further appearances in the symphonic repertoire include its use in the Adagio of Bruckner's Ninth Symphony and the fourth movement of Mahler's First Symphony.

20   The multimovement design I seek to tease out here is simple and straightforward enough that I am reluctant to press into interpretive territory by which many would surely be unconvinced, but the temptation is very strong. As we shall see, I understand vocality itself to take on an ever-increasing role as this work unfolds, and this retransition and recapitulation might well play a role in moving us down that path. The vocality of the "Dresden Amen" was pushed aside abruptly at the outset of the exposition; as we witness the interchange of the "Dresden Amen" upon its return and the chastened, tentative first subject that follows, there is a powerful feeling that the "Dresden Amen" has somehow put the (pointedly instrumental) first subject on notice that changes are afoot, that the status quo cannot hold. Indeed it cannot, as we shall see.

21   Unpublished letter dated June 15, 1830, to his sister Rebecca, cited in Silber, "Mendelssohn and His 'Reformation' Symphony," 327.

22   Ibid., 313.

23   Silber, "Mendelssohn and His 'Reformation' Symphony," 313.

24   Greg Vitercik, *The Early Works of Felix Mendelssohn: A Study in the Romantic Sonata Style* (Philadelphia: Gordon and Breach, 1992), 201.

25   The closest serious contenders are the "Canzonetta" second movement of the String Quartet no. 1 in E-flat Major, op. 12, and the scherzo of the Piano Trio no. 1 in D Minor, which might—if taken extremely quickly—be completed in as little time.

26   Grey, "The Orchestral Music," 420.

27   If we *did* choose to mount such a search, it is clear, at any rate, where we might well begin. The reprise of the scherzo of Beethoven's Fifth Symphony is, after all, so

unlike the scherzo in its original form that we could certainly argue that it represents the first step in the build toward the finale, which is followed by the second step of the transition itself (demarcated by the turn to A-flat). The awkwardness of such an argument is clear, not only in the violence it does to our formal conception of the third movement, but in the fact that the transition feels like just that, nowhere offering new thematic material of anything like the significance of the flute's "Ein' feste Burg" in Mendelssohn's work. Much closer would be an analogy to Mendelssohn's own *Meeresstille und glückliche Fahrt* overture, in which the flute (whose role here has often been compared to its role in the "Reformation" Symphony) does, indeed, seem to breathe a new kind of life into the introduction, to stand apart from it while not yet belonging to the movement that follows. But here, again, the transitional build initiated by the breath of wind the flute introduces into the proceedings does not amount to the exposition of vivid new material that will take on thematic significance later.

28   Among published commentaries on this work, Thomas Grey's has approached this observation as closely as any, as he observes (of the exposition's events) that "the repeated-note fugato subject and its subsequent transformation suggest the opening of the chorale tune, again, without quite citing it" ("The Orchestral Music," 425–26). I clearly agree with Grey that the fugato subject and chorale tune are related (many essentials of the present reading were advanced in my 1995 PhD dissertation, "Felix Mendelssohn and the Musical Discourse of the German Restoration" [University of California, Berkeley], 103–37). And certainly the argument I am in the midst of here—that the relationship between the chorale and fugato subject is recognized only later—*could* be adjusted into a model within which this relationship was, say, recognized as latent in the exposition (a simple matter of thematic derivation, still falling well short of vocal "markedness") and made explicit in the recapitulation (rendered, as we shall see, into a full-blown choral movement). But Grey is not at all interested in the issue of the fugato's "vocality" at its final appearance, approaching the recapitulation in an altogether different, if quite elegant, way ("The Orchestral Music," 426). He therefore has no stake whatever in establishing, as I propose we can, the experiential chronology actually at work, that is, the crucial difference between the presentation of the fugato in the exposition—where its relationship to the chorale is fairly remote, purely speculative, and rather unlikely to be observed—and its presentation in the recapitulation, where a sufficiently attentive listener is provided with musical information that (I argue) practically insists on the recognition of the relationship. Gray himself already has that information as he makes his observations about the exposition, and the question of at what point he obtained it is irrelevant to his own argument.

29   Restricting ourselves to Bach's work alone, a most direct analogy might be to the opening movement of the cantata BWV 3, "Ach Gott, wie manches Herzeleid," in which we find a vocal fugato anticipating (mm. 12–14), then accompanying (mm. 14–18), the chorale cantus firmus whose text it shares.

Given that it is general impressions that matter most, parsing genre reference points too finely may be a fool's errand, but one further point bears teasing out. Fugal *Vorimitation*, in diminution, of a chorale cantus firmus is a frequent occurrence, needless to say, not only in vocal works but in chorale preludes as well (Bach's "Vor deinen Thron," BWV 668, is a locus classicus), thus raising the thorny question of whether the stylistic point of reference in the "Reformation" Symphony's finale might be as much instrumental as vocal. Crucial, however, is the fact that the fugato subject in the "Reformation" Symphony's finale is not really a *Vorimitation* of the kind we generally find in chorale preludes, as it bears only the most remote melodic resemblance to the chorale. The (imaginary) syllable count itself is the fugato subject's real point of commonality with the cantus firmus, thus rooting the movement most clearly, it would seem, in the logic of the explicitly vocal practice at work in, say, the opening movements of the cantatas BWV 3 (as indicated above), BWV 124 ("Meinen Jesum laß ich nicht"), and BWV 125 ("Mit Fried und Freud ich fahr dahin"); each of these develops, as accompaniment to a chorale cantus firmus, a fugato whose subject shares the chorale's text, but little melodic material.

30   The notion that Mendelssohn might have held this specific Bach chorus, "O Mensch, bewein dein Sünde groß," in particularly high esteem is bolstered by Mark Evan Bonds's discernment of "an especially close affinity" (Bonds, *After Beethoven*, 86) between that chorus and the chorale fantasia on "Nun danket alle Gott" that would form the eighth number of Mendelssohn's 1840 "Lobgesang."

31   Todd, *Mendelssohn: A Life in Music*, 226.

32   This interpretation of Beethoven's work—that is, the understanding of the finale as standing in fundamental opposition to the previous movements—appears to have received its first critical articulation in Adolf Bernhard Marx, "On the Form of the Symphony-Cantata. Occasioned by Beethoven's Ninth Symphony" [Über die Form der Symphonie-Cantate. Auf Anlass von Beethoven's neunter Symphonie], *Allgemeine musikalische Zeitung* 49 (1847): 489–98, 505–11.

33   It is worth pointing out that Dinglinger's interpretation places considerable weight on this deleted introductory material and—in part as a consequence—affirms precisely the interpretive stance I have sought to reject. For Dinglinger, the arrival of the chorale is as much "the work's turning point" as Beethoven's baritone recitative had been. Dinglinger, "The Programme of Mendelssohn's 'Reformation' Symphony," 127.

34   On the trail of evidence—long neglected—left behind by this performance, see John Michael Cooper's review of Wulf Konold, *Die Symphonien Felix Mendelssohn Bartholdys* (1992) in *Music Library Association Notes* 50, no. 4 (June 1994): 1375.

35   Quoted in Dinglinger, "The Programme of Mendelssohn's 'Reformation' Symphony," 131.

36   Quoted in, for example, Silber Ballan, "Mendelssohn and the 'Reformation' Symphony," 6.

37   Dinglinger, "The Programme of Mendelssohn's 'Reformation' Symphony," 132–33; Taylor, "Beyond Good and Programmatic," 127.

38   Dinglinger, "The Programme of Mendelssohn's 'Reformation' Symphony," 132. For Dinglinger, the failure of the piece hinges on Mendelssohn's effort "to grapple with the uniqueness and exclusive bond represented by [the] form [of Beethoven's Ninth Symphony], at the same time substituting a historical event for the autobiographical statement articulated by that form" (130).

39   Taylor, "Beyond Good and Programmatic," 117, 121. On Mendelssohn's programmatic "phase" in general, see Silber Ballan, "Marxian Programmatic Music," 149–61.

40   See, on the subject, Grey, "The Orchestral Music," 442–45. As Grey points out, the tradition of linking this movement to processional song of some kind appears to originate in a concert review in the *Rheinische Musikzeitung für Kunstfreunde und Künstler* 2 (1851–52): 566.

41   Werner, *Mendelssohn*, 268.

42   R. Larry Todd, "On Mendelssohn's Sacred Music, Real and Imaginary," in Peter Mercer-Taylor, ed., *Cambridge Companion to Mendelssohn* (Cambridge: Cambridge University Press, 2004), 185.

43   On further, less overt, correspondences between the work's instrumental and vocal sections, see Bonds, *After Beethoven*, 103. See also Benedict Taylor's reading of the "Lobgesang" Symphony in chapter 11 of this volume.

44   The most thoroughgoing exploration of the thematic relationships that bind— or might be seen to, at any rate—this symphony's movements together is Rey M. Longyear, "Cyclic Form and Tonal Relationships in Mendelssohn's 'Scottish' Symphony," *In Theory Only* 4 (1979): 38–48; on this particular association, see Peter Mercer-Taylor, "Mendelssohn's 'Scottish' Symphony and the Music of German Memory," *19th-Century Music* 19, no. 1 (Summer 1995): 76–77.

45   Mendelssohn had written to Ferdinand David that the opening of the finale's maestoso coda should sound "Ordentlich deutlich und stark, wie ein Männerchor" (letter of March 12, 1842, quoted in Witte, "Zur Programmgebundenheit der Sinfonien Mendelssohns," 123).

46   See Mercer-Taylor, "Mendelssohn's 'Scottish' Symphony," 68–82.

Part Two

Mendelssohn and the Organ

Chapter Four

Mendelssohn and the Organ

Wm. A. Little

Felix Mendelssohn's first personal encounter with the organ, for which we have any evidence, occurred in the summer of 1820, when he was eleven years old. While on vacation with his family along the Rhine, Felix played the tiny organ in the St. Rochuskapelle, a pilgrimage church, high on a hill just outside the town of Bingen.[1] Seventeen years later, in 1837, while on his honeymoon, Felix again climbed the same hill, this time with his bride, Cécile. Unfortunately, the chapel was closed. As Cécile noted in their diary, Mendelssohn was deeply disappointed, since he "would have liked to have seen once again the little organ upon which as a child he had played for the first time in his life."[2]

Certainly, Mendelssohn must have heard numerous organs in various Berlin churches during his childhood years, but in the Rochuskapelle he had played the instrument for the first time, and the experience left an indelible impression on him. Only a few months afterward, in the fall of 1820, Mendelssohn began his study of the organ with the Berlin organist, August Wilhelm Bach,[3] and on November 28 of the same year he essayed his first composition for organ, a lengthy Praeludium in D Minor (MWV W2).[4] Although impossible to confirm, it seems reasonable to infer that these events of 1820 were closely interrelated, particularly in view of the fact that two years would elapse before Mendelssohn again composed for the organ. Clearly, by the end of 1820 Mendelssohn's predilection for the organ had been firmly established and would continue to make itself felt throughout his life.

Although Mendelssohn evinced a natural inclination for the organ, he never entertained any thought of becoming a professional organist. In the first place, he was financially independent and did not need the meager salary that most organists were paid. Moreover, he was born into a social class to which few organists had ever belonged, and he moved in social circles from which most organists had always been excluded. Far more important, however, is the fact that from early on Mendelssohn's primary professional locus was not the organ loft but the concert hall; by his early twenties he had already built an enviable international reputation as a composer, conductor, and brilliant keyboard performer. Given the demands of his widespread musical activities, it would have been impossible for him to carry out the normal responsibilities of a church organist or cantor, as he himself recognized, when, in 1842, he declined repeated offers to follow in Bach's footsteps and become cantor of the Thomas-Kirche in Leipzig.

Despite Mendelssohn's deep personal interest in the organ, it could never play more than a subsidiary role in the overall makeup of his professional career. His formal instruction on the instrument had lasted roughly a year to a year and a half, from about the age of eleven to sometime around his thirteenth birthday. His teacher, A. W. Bach, organist of the prestigious Marien-Kirche in Berlin[5] and not much older than his gifted pupil, evidently harbored strong anti-Semitic feelings that may have obliquely or even openly affected the atmosphere in which the lessons were conducted.[6] In any case, Mendelssohn did not benefit significantly from his studies with Bach. Although he may have gained some insight into the fundamentals of registration, his pedal technique failed to advance much beyond an elementary stage.

Once the organ lessons with Bach ceased, Mendelssohn never had any further formal instruction on the instrument, and thus, to all intents and purposes, he was an autodidact. Although he now had to teach himself—and his experience as a pianist enabled him to do just that—the real problem was finding the free time and an instrument on which to practice. Although he later complained how difficult it was in Berlin to find an organ on which to practice,[7] it was far more the problem of finding time to practice, that impeded his progress as an organist. Nonetheless, over the course of the 1820s his pedal technique gradually improved, although not to the extent that he was able to master any of J. S. Bach's most difficult organ works. In a letter from Switzerland, written in 1831, his sense of frustration is almost palpable, when he lamented that "it is a shame that I still cannot perform any of Bach's major works."[8]

In the spring of 1832, at the end of his grand European tour, Mendelssohn traveled to London for the second time. It was an important moment in his life as an organist, because it marked a point of bifurcation. From that time onward Mendelssohn, the organist, lived and moved in two separate and distinct theaters of operation: in Germany the organ remained for him what it had always been, a hobby—indeed, a hobby about which he cared passionately, but nonetheless, a hobby. He explored organ lofts, wherever and whenever the opportunity permitted, and likewise, he played the organ, whenever he could find the occasional spare moment. But his career as a composer, conductor, and pianist preoccupied any momentary indulgences he might have been able to allow himself on the organ. Moreover, until about 1839 he was hampered by an inadequate pedal technique that precluded any thought of more actively entering the fiercely competitive arena of Germany's professional organists. He had only to look about him, at men like Johann Gottlob Schneider in Dresden,[9] or Carl August Haupt in Berlin,[10] or Adolf Hesse in Breslau,[11] simply to name a few of Mendelssohn's most notable contemporaries. In Germany, Mendelssohn realized that, as an organist, he was out of his depth.

In England, on the other hand, Mendelssohn was lionized as an organist and regarded as a beacon of wisdom from the continent: his views on everything from organ construction to organ tempos in Bach were engraved in the minds—and to no small degree in the hearts—of his English hosts. They greeted him with open arms and open organ lofts. At the time of his first visit in 1829 he was taken under wing by Thomas Attwood, for whom he developed a lifelong admiration and affection.[12] Attwood, one of Mozart's last surviving pupils and organist of St. Paul's Cathedral in London, also provided Mendelssohn with an open sesame to London's organ world. Organists from all over London invited Mendelssohn to play or practice on their instruments, and Mendelssohn gratefully accepted.[13] Even today, a century and a half after the fact, London is still awash with churches where lore supports one or more visits by Mendelssohn.[14] And he did, in fact, play here, there, and everywhere; he reciprocated with both public and private, formal and informal, planned and spontaneous recitals. For several Sundays in the summer of 1833, Attwood invited him to play the concluding voluntary at St. Paul's Cathedral.[15] In 1837 Mendelssohn was invited for the first time to perform on the massive new Town Hall organ, as part of the famed Birmingham Music Festival.[16] Three years later, Mendelssohn performed again on the organ during the Birmingham Music Festival, and in 1842 he was invited twice to Buckingham Palace by Queen Victoria, where both he and Prince Albert played the organ and Queen Victoria sang several of the composer's songs.[17] Beyond all question, Mendelssohn felt at ease playing the organ in private and in public in England. Even the traditional English G pedal board seldom elicited the same kind of annoyed impatience that he had voiced so often about the short pedal boards he had encountered in south Germany and Austria.[18]

Altogether, Mendelssohn's English experience as an organist was deeply rewarding, but it was rewarding for England as well. He ardently supported Henry Gauntlett's advocacy of the C pedal board, and Gauntlett, in turn, proclaimed him the greatest organist ever to have visited England from Germany.[19] Although we have no idea who had preceded him from Germany, Gauntlett's opinion was echoed in virtually all quarters. Mendelssohn enjoyed the kind of organist's renown in England that would have been unthinkable in Germany. In Berlin, Leipzig, or Dresden, the C pedal board was the accepted norm, but in the 1830s and early 1840s there were perhaps no more than a half dozen or so C pedal boards in all of England, and probably no more than a dozen organists in the entire country, who had any expertise in playing on them. Small wonder then, that Mendelssohn's performance of Bach's great Prelude and Fugue in A Minor (BWV 543) in St. Paul's Cathedral and Christ Church, Newgate Street, caused such an unprecedented stir—no one had ever heard anything like it.[20] And they clamored for more.

Mendelssohn's appearance on the English organ scene came at a historic turning point: change was in the air, and the moment was propitious for it. The transition from the traditional English G pedal board to the more versatile C or "German" pedal board was but one manifestation of England's transition from parochial to international standards.[21] The rapidly emerging Bach movement in England also brought with it a seismic shift in musical thinking, as the country's musical horizons expanded in unprecedented ways. Although quite inadvertently, Mendelssohn also contributed, at least symbolically, to that transition, when he notified his English publisher, Charles Coventry, that he wanted to change the title of the works he had agreed to compose for him from the insular "Voluntary" to the universally recognized "Sonata."[22]

Mendelssohn's Six Sonatas for the Organ (MWV W56–61, op. 65) represent the culmination of his writings for the instrument and was the second of only two major oeuvres to which he assigned an opus number.[23] They were also the only two of his organ works that were published during his lifetime, despite the fact that he had been composing for organ since the age of eleven. His earliest works have recently become available, and although they show the obvious signs and infelicities of a novice, several of them also reveal conspicuous talent. Among the more attractive of his early works is a short Prelude in D minor, an untitled Passacaglia in C minor (MWV W7, meticulously modeled on J. S. Bach's Passacaglia in C Minor, BWV 582), a partita on the chorale, "Wie gross ist des Allmächt'gen Güte" (MWV W8), and a *Nachspiel und Fuge* (MWV W12) that he composed in Rome in 1831. Five years later he composed a set of Six Preludes and Fugues for Piano (MWV U116/U66, U129/U105, U131/U91, U122/U108, U126/U106, and U135/U128; op. 35), and at about the same time he wrote what he called "Three Grand Fugues" for organ. His original thought was to publish them with that title, but wisely, Breitkopf persuaded him to compose "Three Grand Preludes" to go with them, and thus it is to Breitkopf that we are largely indebted for the existence of the Preludes of opus 37 (MWV W21/W18, W22/W20, and W23/W13).[24]

Preludes and fugues for organ—or for that matter, for piano—were hardly a glut on the early nineteenth-century music market. Although Bach's *Well-Tempered Clavier* was revered in almost all circles, the general attitude toward Baroque forms and styles among organists in the early Romantic period was often tainted by a slightly patronizing air; there was tolerance—at times even reluctant admiration—but seldom enthusiasm. And certainly forms such as prelude and fugue were infrequently attempted, much less cultivated, outside the pedagogical realm.

When Mendelssohn wrote originally to Breitkopf regarding his "Three Grand Fugues," he already had three fugues in hand, one of which (in D minor) he had written two years earlier at Vincent Novello's request, and another of which (in C minor) had evolved from one of the voluntaries he had played at St. Paul's Cathedral in the summer of 1833.[25] The third fugue he had composed in December 1836. As was always the case with Mendelssohn's preludes and fugues, the fugues were composed first, and it was not until afterward, and sometimes long afterward, if ever, that he composed the accompanying prelude.

In March 1837, Mendelssohn married Cécile Jeanrenaud (1817–53) in Frankfurt/Main[26] and was about to leave on his honeymoon, but the need for three organ preludes was not forgotten, and when he packed he included a goodly supply of score paper. With characteristic self-discipline he composed the three preludes on the second, fourth, and sixth of April, and immediately sent them off to both Breitkopf und Härtel in Leipzig and Novello in London.

When composing the three preludes, it seems clear that in at least the first two preludes the composer consciously set out to match the mood of the prelude to its partnered fugue. The driving energy of the Prelude in C Minor anticipates the same vigorous surge of the fugue, just as the pastorale-like G-Major Prelude anticipates with remarkable success the cantilena fugue, with which it is paired. The Prelude in D Minor, however, seems less an attempt to match styles than a conscious juxtapositioning of two opposing styles—the Sturm und Drang improvisatory prelude vis-à-vis the terse and classically severe fugue.

The Three Preludes and Fugues, op. 37, constituted a milestone in Mendelssohn's writings for the organ. From a compositional standpoint he had finally integrated the pedal successfully into the overall structure of a work, but from a broader perspective he had succeeded in restoring the historic balance between prelude and fugue that had been absent since the time of Bach. Moreover, opus 37 provided the impetus for a whole generation of organ composers to reassess their craft and explore the new terrain that Mendelssohn had opened up to them.

Throughout the 1830s Mendelssohn continued to work on his pedal technique, but it was not until the summer of 1839 that he was finally able to find time to achieve mastery of the pedal board. On summer holiday in Frankfurt and briefly unencumbered with official responsibilities, he was able at last to devote the time necessary to bring his pedal and keyboard techniques into rough alignment. In an impressive demonstration of purpose and persistence he practiced daily, either on a pedal piano[27] or on the organ in the Katharinen-Kirche until, by the end of July he at last felt he had achieved his goal. With a newly found sense of self-confidence, he now resolved to give a public organ recital the following year in the Thomas-Kirche in Leipzig. As he wrote to his mother in late August, "I think my pedal technique is now good enough to be heard."[28]

In the summer of 1839 Mendelssohn also turned his attention to organ composition for the first time in three years. Within a span of three days he composed three fugues—in C major, F minor, and E minor, respectively (MWV W25, W26, and W24)—which certainly hint, at least, that he might eventually have planned to pair them with three preludes as a possible sequel to opus 37. In the end, he shelved all three, although five years later he revised the Fugue in C Major and used it as the final movement of his Second Organ Sonata. He also tried his hand at revising the F-Minor Fugue, but the revision failed to satisfy him, and he discarded it.[29] The Fugue in E Minor, however—one of the most brilliant and powerful works that Mendelssohn ever wrote for the organ—was, inexplicably, never revisited, but simply abandoned. It was not published until 1957, but even today it seems still to be relatively unknown and unperformed.

Altogether, the summer of 1839 proved to be productive in a variety of ways, but it was not until a year later that he provided proof of his hard-won mastery of the organ. On August 6, 1840, Mendelssohn gave his one and his only public organ recital in Germany. It was an all-Bach program, and the proceeds from it went toward one of his favorite projects, the erection of a monument to J. S. Bach in the immediate vicinity of the Thomas-Kirche. The recital constituted a critical moment for Mendelssohn, and he practiced relentlessly for it. In a letter to his mother, written several days after the recital, he claimed to have practiced so long that he could walk down the street only in pedal passages.[30] Despite his hard work, however, Mendelssohn evidently harbored fears that his recital would not be well attended, and less than a week beforehand he took the extraordinary step of writing out *by hand* an appeal for subscribers, which he evidently posted either in the Thomas-Kirche itself or in one of Leipzig's music shops. The appeal itself, which consists of five large sheets, has survived and is among the holdings of the Gesellschaft der Musikfreunde in Vienna.[31]

Robert Schumann, who was among the subscribers, subsequently reviewed the recital in extravagant but garbled terms in the *Neue Zeitschrift für Musik*.[32] There is little of substance to be gained from his review, and in spite of his hyperbolic prose, one comes away with the impression that he had written the obligatory review of a friend's performance, but who also felt, as he laconically confided to his wife, Clara, that the program had "lasted rather long."[33]

The program itself deserves a close look, since it is, unintentionally, a highly revealing document (see fig. 4.1). Perhaps most important, it reveals Mendelssohn at his most cautious self. First and foremost, he was determined to leave nothing to chance. The program therefore consisted only of works that had long lain comfortably under his fingers, although it meant that he had to include virtually every organ work of Bach that he had ever learned. With one single impressive sweep he virtually exhausted his entire organ repertoire.

The works that he included on his program also deserve comment, since they illuminate *in nuce* his ambitions and progress as an organist. With obvious intent he sandwiched the Bach works between two improvisations, so that he could ease himself into the program at the beginning, and end it when and

Donnerstag, den 6. August 1840.

ORGEL-CONCERT

in der Thomaskirche

gegeben von

Felix Mendelssohn-Bartholdy.

Erster Theil.

Introduction und Fuge in Es dur.

Phantasie über den Choral „Schmücke dich, o liebe Seele".

Grosses Praeludium und Fuge (A moll).

Zweiter Theil.

Passacaille (21 Variationen und Phantasie für die volle Orgel) (C moll).

Pastorella (F dur).

Toccata (D moll).

Freie Phantasie.

Sämmtliche Compositionen sind von *Sebastian Bach;* die Einnahme ist zur Errichtung eines Denksteins für ihn in der Nähe seiner ehemaligen Wohnung, der Thomasschule, bestimmt.

Billets à **8 Groschen** *sind in den Musikalien-Handlungen der Herren Breitkopf und Härtel, Kistner und Hofmeister und an den Eingängen der Kirche zu haben.*

Anfang 6 Uhr.

Figure 4.1. The program for Mendelssohn's Bach recital.

how he saw fit. He thus reserved for himself both the first and final words. Moreover, the two improvisations served as a kind of nineteenth-century musical framework surrounding the main body of eighteenth-century music.

The Fugue in E-flat Major (BWV 552ii) that followed his short introductory improvisation was a work he had learned on very short notice in the summer of 1837 and performed, together with the Prelude in E-flat Major (BWV 552i), at the Birmingham Music Festival. In July of that year, while still on his honeymoon, Mendelssohn had written to his sister of his decision to play the Prelude and Fugue in E-flat Major, despite the fact that it would not be easy. "It will give me a headache," he confessed.[34] With a lead time of less than two months, Mendelssohn committed himself to learning and bringing to performance level one of Bach's most impressive organ works. When, where, and how he accomplished all this in such a short time is not known, but it was, unquestionably, a remarkable feat.

The second work on the program, "Schmücke dich, o liebe Seele" (BWV 654), was predictably included, not simply as a counterweight to the free works, but because it was Mendelssohn's favorite chorale prelude. It is perhaps important to note, even in passing, that Mendelssohn responded to Bach's chorale preludes quite differently than he did to the free works; they apparently touched an emotional or spiritual nerve and evoked in him a more personal reaction than the free works. On at least two occasions he spoke of "Schmücke dich" to Robert Schumann, saying essentially, that "if life were to deprive me of hope and faith, this single chorale would replenish me with both," or "if everything else in the world were taken from me, this chorale prelude, which alone remained, would comfort me for my loss."[35] What elicited this intensely personal response is impossible to determine, but it is clear that Mendelssohn had internalized the work at an early age and experienced essentially the same emotional response whenever he played it or heard it played later on in life.

The Prelude and Fugue in A Minor (BWV 543) had long been a staple of Mendelssohn's repertoire, and was widely recognized as his signature organ work. He had learned it in the early 1830s, and according to Sir Herbert Oakeley, he was the first to perform the work in England.[36] Alas, he not only introduced it to England, but he played it everywhere and with such frequency that it became popularly known as "Mendelssohn's Bach in A Minor."[37] One aspect of Mendelssohn's performance of this Fugue deserves particular attention, since it sheds light on his whole approach to Bach. Edward J. Hopkins (1818–1901), organist of the Temple Church in London and an acquaintance of Mendelssohn noted that he "threw out points unsuspected before, as in the A Minor Fugue, where he took the episode on the swell, returning to the Great Organ when the pedal re-enters, but transferring the E in the treble to the Great Organ a bar before the other parts"[38] (see ex. 4.1). From Hopkins's report and the memories of others who heard and saw Mendelssohn perform, it is clear that in playing Bach's organ works he changed both registration

Example 4.1. Bach, Fugue in A Minor, BWV 543ii, mm. 93–96

and manuals as he saw fit. It was an iconoclastic approach at the time in many parts of Germany, especially in Berlin. Such treatment of Bach must have been anathema to Carl August Haupt and may be the reason for his complaint that Mendelssohn's organ playing "was that of an amateur."[39]

Perhaps the most demanding work on Mendelssohn's program was the Passacaglia (BWV 582). He had learned it only the year before, in 1839, and it had evidently required an immense investment of time and energy. As he wrote to his sister, "I have practiced mercilessly on the passacaglia for the past two weeks."[40] In practicing for his recital in the summer of 1840, he must have paid particular attention to his registration, since that was the one of the few specific aspects of the recital, singled out for praise by Schumann.[41]

The first movement of the Pastorella (BWV 590i) was one of the first organ works of Bach that Mendelssohn had learned. In 1825 he played it for Sir George Smart, who visited the Mendelssohns during a trip to Berlin.[42] The second and third movements were not published until after Mendelssohn's death, and it is doubtful that he ever played or learned them.

Because there are two Toccatas in D Minor, there has been some question as to whether Mendelssohn played BWV 565 or BWV 538 (the "Dorian") in his Thomas-Kirche recital. Since it is demonstrable that BWV 565 was one of the earliest of Bach's show pieces that Mendelssohn had mastered—probably sometime in the very late 1820s—and had played for Goethe in the Stadt-Kirche in Weimar in June 1830, it may safely be assumed that the Toccata in D Minor that he played in his Thomas-Kirche recital was BWV 565. In his review of Mendelssohn's recital Schumann muddied the waters even further, when he reported that Mendelssohn had played a "Toccata in A Minor, with a Prelude that was typical of Bach's sense of humor."[43] Various critics have attempted to fathom the meaning of Schumann's assertion, but none persuasively.

Although the works Mendelssohn included in his recital constituted almost his entire organ repertoire, he had omitted one or two other works, specifically the triple Fugue in C-sharp Minor (BWV 849) from Book I of Bach's *Well-Tempered Clavier*, which was perhaps the first work by Bach that he had learned to play on the organ. In 1821 he had played it for Johann Gottfried Schicht, who was then cantor of the Thomas-Kirche in Leipzig.[44] He later played it on numerous occasions, the last being in July 1845, when he played it in Kronberg, after having played all six of his Organ Sonatas.[45]

The only other organ work that was part of Mendelssohn's repertoire was the Prelude and Fugue in E Minor (BWV 533).[46] A manuscript copy was owned by his organ teacher, A. W. Bach, but Bach refused him permission to copy it. Undeterred, he persuaded a young friend at the Sing-Akademie, Carl Freudenberg[47] also an organ pupil of Bach, who had been allowed to copy the work, to lend him his copy. Mendelssohn transcribed the prelude and dated it, December 20, 1822. Freudenberg, who later became organist at the Magdalena-Kirche in Breslau, reported that Bach had admonished him not to lend his copy to "the young Jew-boy, who has enough as it is."[48] Certainly, the frosty relationship that existed between the Mendelssohns and Bach is not difficult to understand.

Beyond the Fugue in C-sharp Minor and the Prelude and Fugue in E Minor, only a few chorale preludes of Bach, mostly from the *Orgelbüchlein*, could be considered part of Mendelssohn's organ repertoire.

A number of commentators have suggested that Mendelssohn's organ repertoire was far more extensive than it actually was, but there is nothing to substantiate those assertions. More than a quarter century after Mendelssohn's death, Henry Gauntlett and, later, F. G. Edwards alleged that Mendelssohn had "brought out a number of pedal fugues that were not known here . . . he was the first to play the D Major, the G Minor, the E Major, the C Minor, the short E Minor, etc."[49] Curiously, both Gauntlett and Edwards neglected to mention either the Passacaglia or the omnipresent Prelude and Fugue in A Minor. With or without the Passacaglia or the A Minor, Gauntlett's phrase, "brought out" certainly implies that Mendelssohn had been the first to play these works *in public*. Had Mendelssohn simply played them on a single occasion for one or two friends in an empty church, it would hardly have been worth noting. There is, however, nothing in any contemporary reviews or commentaries to corroborate Gauntlett's claim. If Mendelssohn had indeed played any of these works, whether in public or even in private, surely one of his many friends, colleagues, acquaintances, or fans, who hung on his every word and dogged his every step, would have somewhere noted it. But no one did.

The Prelude and Fugue in D Major (BWV 532) perhaps comes closest to having been part of his repertoire, but even here, the documentation is tenuous at best. Certainly, Mendelssohn had dabbled with the work off and on for many years, but he apparently never honed or polished it to a point where he felt comfortable performing it in public. In the end, Vesque von Püttlingen was probably correct in asserting that Mendelssohn did, in fact, play it privately for him in 1843.[50]

There are also reports that Mendelssohn played the Toccata in F Major (BWV 540) and the Prelude in B Minor (BWV 544i), but they are little more than hearsay.[51] The organist of Leeds Town Hall, William Spark, recalled in his memoirs that he had heard Mendelssohn play Bach's Prelude and Fugue in B Minor at the Birmingham Festival in 1846.[52] Spark did, in fact, hear that work in Birmingham, but it was played by Henry Gauntlett, not Mendelssohn.[53] Mendelssohn, himself, never learned the work.

Looking again at Mendelssohn's recital program in the Thomas-Kirche, he could realistically count it as an unqualified success; his plan to give a second recital the following year, however, was never realized.[54] He doubtless abandoned the idea, when he realized that he had nothing new to offer. Certainly, he could not play the same works again that he had played in 1840, and unfortunately, there was not the time in which to muster either a wholly or even partially new program.

Compared to the extraordinary breadth of Mendelssohn's piano repertoire, his repertoire on the organ was surprisingly narrow. The same, not surprisingly, can be said of his library of organ music.[55] It contained nothing, either by Bach's or by his own contemporaries, with the exception of a few scores of their own works that various composers such as C. F. Becker,[56] J. G. Herzog,[57] and a few others had presented to him. Although Mendelssohn was totally conversant with the broad range of piano literature, he evinced a breathtakingly myopic view of organ literature: there is not the slightest indication that he had any interest whatever in the organ music of any composer, past or present, other than J. S. Bach. At one point in the early 1840s, Henry Gauntlett, presumably in a discussion about notable composers of organ music, made the mistake of asking him, what composer stood next to Bach in greatness, to which Mendelssohn shot back, "No one! There is no composer even remotely close to Bach in greatness."[58]

One of the areas in which Mendelssohn contributed most is also one where his work is least known and recognized. His importance as an editor of Bach's organ music cannot be overstated. In 1833 he coedited anonymously with Adolf Bernhard Marx three volumes of Bach's free organ works—*Noch wenig bekannte Orgelkompositionen von J. S. Bach*—that had not appeared before in print and published them with Breitkopf und Härtel in Leipzig.[59] In an age that demanded all manner of editorial annotations and performance indications, from fingerings to phrasing and tempo markings, Mendelssohn flatly refused to go along. Instead, he insisted on printing only what the composer himself had provided. As a result, these three slim volumes represent what is almost certainly the very first urtext edition of organ music or possibly any music, whether by Bach or anyone else. Although the historic significance of this edition is still not widely recognized, Mendelssohn set the standard for all future urtext editions, including his own. Ten years later, in 1845 and 1846, Mendelssohn single-handedly edited the bulk of Bach's chorale-based organ works for publication by Coventry and Hollier and Breitkopf und Härtel. It was an immense undertaking and included fifteen of the "Great Eighteen" organ chorales, the chorale partitas, and the very first edition of the *Orgelbüchlein*. A recently discovered publication, the *Sechs verschiedene Choräle* (i.e., the Schübler Chorales), although purportedly edited by Mendelssohn, is clearly a rogue volume, in which Mendelssohn had no hand.[60] In all of the bona fide publications edited by Mendelssohn, he maintained the same strict editorial principles he had set for himself, when he and Marx had edited the edition for Breitkopf in 1833. And just as he had when he and Marx had collaborated earlier, he again directed that his name not appear on the title page in the German editions.[61]

While Mendelssohn was actively editing the chorale preludes for Coventry and Hollier, Charles Coventry asked him to compose a set of three organ voluntaries. It had been some five years since Mendelssohn had composed anything substantial for the instrument and he accepted the commission with pleasure. Between late July 1844 and April 1845, he composed, compiled, and culled a total of nineteen movements that were finally shaped into his Six Organ Sonatas. Until about December 1844, however, there was no apparent relationship among any of the movements; they were simply a random collection of pieces in a variety of keys. But then, sometime in December, Mendelssohn realized that all these disparate movements could be sorted into tonal or motivic clusters, and from that point onward the sonatas proceeded rapidly toward completion. Sonatas no. 2 and no. 4 were completed before New Year's Day, which left only the sixth sonata, all four movements of which were composed within a span of three days.

The metamorphosis from voluntary to sonata had occurred fairly early on in the development of opus 65. In August 1844 Mendelssohn had written to Coventry that he would prefer to call these movements "sonatas," because he was not quite certain of what a "voluntary" was. Coventry—who did not care in the least what Mendelssohn wanted to call them—had no objection, and thus the change was effected without incident. Coventry was indifferent and Mendelssohn was relieved. By suggesting the term sonata, Mendelssohn was not proposing a return to traditional sonata form, nor was he proposing a new doctrine of organ sonata. The real reason for Mendelssohn's wish to substitute the term sonata for voluntary was purely practical and came because he intended to publish the works not only with Coventry and Hollier in England, but also with Breitkopf und Härtel in Germany, Schlesinger in France, and Ricordi in Italy, and he needed a practical umbrella-like title that would be recognized in all four countries. Outside England, the term *voluntary* was meaningless, and although it might not have been an insuperable problem to have four different titles in four different languages and in four different countries, all with the same opus number, it would have been awkward at best. All in all, the term *voluntary* was inauspicious.[62]

By mutual agreement, the *Six Grand Sonatas for the Organ* were published and released on the same day, September 15, 1845, and almost immediately they were assimilated into the classic canon of organ literature.[63] In England, Henry Gauntlett reviewed them in ecstatic terms in the *Morning Chronicle*,[64] while they were reviewed more soberly in the *Musical World* and elsewhere. In April 1846, Dr. Edward Chipp, organist at Ely Cathedral, played all six of them in public, probably for the first time, in Walker's organ factory.[65]

Quite without intent Mendelssohn created with his sonatas a wholly new genre for the organ, which in less than a decade became the model for other composers both in Germany and abroad. Neither Whistling's nor Hofmeister's catalogs report the publication of a single sonata for the organ in the years between 1801 and 1845, but from 1845 onward their number becomes legion. In the first decade after the appearance of opus 65, fifteen organ sonatas appeared by ten composers. In the second decade, between 1855 and 1865, another thirteen were published, and Rudolph Kremer has tallied a staggering total of 158 organ sonatas, published between 1865 and 1900.[66]

The structure of the organ sonata became almost formulaic. Typically—and virtually de rigueur—there was a chorale, a movement in $\frac{3}{8}$ or $\frac{6}{8}$ time, and a fugue. Folk-song-like movements and brisk marches were also among the most popular components, and once the formula was digested, the organ sonata could be virtually mass produced. Fink,[67] Kühmstedt,[68] Ritter,[69] van Eyken,[70] and dozens of other composers all wrote at least several organ sonatas, but Dr. Wilhelm Volckmar outdid everyone by manufacturing a total of fifty-eight.[71] Many of the sonata composers were not simply epigones, or as Gotthold Frotscher so tartly put it of Johann Christian Fink, "an epigone of an epigone,"[72] but included some of the most prominent organ composers of the day, such as Gustav Merkel (1827–85), who wrote nine organ sonatas, and Joseph Rheinberger (1839–1901), who produced twenty.

As musical tastes changed in the final years of the nineteenth and early years of the twentieth centuries, Mendelssohn and his works suffered, not from neglect, but from an overload of biased and ill-informed criticism. Led chiefly by English critics such as George Bernard Shaw and Cecil Gray, the consensus developed that Mendelssohn was essentially a composer of very limited talent, whose greatest gift lay in the composition of sentimental miniatures. Such views remained without serious challenge until well into the twentieth century. In 1931, Bruno Weigl, in his *Handbuch der Orgelliteratur*, almost grudgingly conceded that the Preludes and Fugues, op. 37, and the Organ Sonatas, op. 65, were perhaps of some value as pedagogical tools, but added laconically that they were almost never included in the concert repertoire.[73] And then, with the advent of National Socialism in Germany, the prevailing negative view was further reinforced, this time officially, by the government, and unofficially, by the like-minded musicologist, Gotthold Frotscher. His influential *Geschichte des Orgelspiels* (1935) has now gone through at least four postwar unrevised and unrepentant editions, and is still widely quoted. With the disappearance of Mendelssohn's organ works from concert programs and then even from church calendars, absence gradually bred indifference, and in the end simply no one cared any longer.

Until about 1935 or 1936, the entire collection of Mendelssohn's musical manuscripts, including his organ works, lay on the shelves of the Staatsbibliothek in Berlin, available to any scholar who cared to examine them. But no one was interested, and no one bothered to look. Rudolf Werner, who in his book on *Mendelssohn as a Church Musician* devoted a total of twelve pages to Mendelssohn's organ works, was probably one of the last to examine the organ manuscripts.[74] World War II came and went, and with it went all the unknown organ works, leaving only a collection of tantalizing incipits that Werner had dutifully transcribed in about 1930. And it was only from Werner's cursory impressions that the world even knew of the existence of Mendelssohn's youthful works, such as the partita on "Wie groß ist des Allmächt'gen Güte," the "Andante—Sanft" (MWV W6) or the untitled passacaglia (MWV W7) or even the mature works such as the Trio in F (Andante, MWV W46), the Allegro, Chorale, and Fugue (MWV W33), or the three Fugues of 1839.

Clearly, Mendelssohn has about him something of a phoenix-like nature. After the doldrums of the 1900s through the 1930s, it was not until after World War II that Mendelssohn's slow rise from the ashes began in earnest, as musicians, orchestras, and choruses commenced to perform his concertos, symphonies, and oratorios, as organists once again began to play his preludes, fugues, and sonatas, and as scholars decided to take a fresh and serious look at both the man and his work. In terms of the organ, Susanna Vendrey's dissertation—although somewhat unbalanced in its preoccupation with Mendelssohn's "Sonaten-Passion"—deserves credit as the first postwar, full-length, in-depth study of Mendelssohn's organ music.[75] It was the same Susanna Vendrey, now Grossmann-Vendrey, who as late as 1974 opened an article on opus 65 with the comment that "the best-known feature about Mendelssohn's Organ Sonatas is that they are hardly ever played."[76] By 1974, however, Grossmann-Vendrey's observation was more than slightly exaggerated.

As Mendelssohn became rehabilitated and his place in the pantheon firmly reestablished, a stream of dissertations and other serious studies soon followed. In 1974 Douglas Butler's dissertation for the University of Oregon was an important pioneering study that remains a significant source of information and opinion.[77] Over the past several decades there have also been a number of important studies and dissertations, such as those by Paul Jourdan (Cambridge University),[78] François Sabatier (Paris),[79] Friedrich Bötel (Heidelberg),[80] and Pietro Zappalà (Pavia),[81] as well as a master's thesis by Eugene Gates,[82] all of whose works have shed new and significant light on Mendelssohn and the organ. In addition to PhD dissertations, there have also been several DMA dissertations—written from a performer's perspective—by David Lloyd Petrash,[83] Robert Mann,[84] John Stansell,[85] and Caroline Haury.[86] Certainly, some of the most important scholars in recent years who have written on Mendelssohn and the organ are Peter Ward Jones, former music librarian of the Bodleian Library, Oxford,[87] Nicholas Thistlethwaite, author of the magisterial study of the Victorian organ in England,[88] Michael Gailit in Vienna, also author of an important biography of Julius Reubke,[89] and Russell Stinson, in the United States, whose perceptive insights make his books mandatory reading for anyone interested in either Bach or Mendelssohn.[90] In a larger sense, no *Forschungsbericht*, however brief, would be complete without acknowledging the monumental work of R. Larry Todd, whose biography of Mendelssohn is not only a work of immense erudition, but will remain for many years to come the definitive study attesting to Mendelssohn's greatness.[91]

What, finally, is the basis for Mendelssohn's lasting fame and significance in the organ world? Acclaimed by many of his contemporaries as one of the "greatest organists of our time," it is not immediately clear how Mendelssohn acquired such an exalted reputation. He was almost thirty before he finally attained a viable pedal technique. He never held a position as church organist, he never taught organ anywhere, and he left no legacy as an organist. In the course of his entire life he played only one public organ recital in his native Germany, and there is no evidence that he ever played a single organ work by any composer other than himself or J. S. Bach. And even his Bach repertoire consisted of no more than a dozen or so pieces.

Unquestionably, a measure of Mendelssohn's fame as an organist was reflected glory, but in the final analysis, it was not his playing that earned him immortality, but his two groundbreaking publications, opus 37 and opus 65, that assure him a lasting place at the center of organ composition in the nineteenth century.

Notes

This essay written initially for a conference organized by the Eastman Rochester Organ Initiative in the fall of 2009 ("Mendelssohn and the Contrapuntal Tradition") antedates by more than eight months the publication of my book *Mendelssohn and the Organ* (New York: Oxford University Press, 2010) and contains extensive self-quotation and paraphrasing from its pages. I am grateful to Suzanne Ryan, editor in chief at Oxford University Press, for giving me permission to draw on materials from the book.

1   Peter Ward Jones, ed., *The Mendelssohns on Honeymoon: The 1837 Diary of Felix and Cécile Mendelssohn Bartholdy* (Oxford: Oxford University Press, 1997), 62.

2   Ibid. The event was recalled by Cécile Mendelssohn on July 6, 1837. The year in which Felix first visited the Rochus Kapelle is established by the entry of members of the Mendelssohn family in the Guest Book of the Brömserburg in Rüdesheim. I am indebted to Peter Ward Jones for providing me with this information.

3   Bach (1796–1869), unrelated to J. S. Bach, was a pupil of Friedrich Zelter and Ludwig Berger.

4   Felix Mendelssohn Bartholdy, *Complete Works for Organ*, 5 vols., ed. Wm. A. Little (London: Novello, 1987–90), 1:2–7.

5   Bach was appointed to the position in 1816 and remained there until his death.

6   Little, *Mendelssohn and the Organ*, 32–33.

7   Karl Klingemann, ed., *Felix Mendelssohn-Bartholdys Briefwechsel mit Legationsrat Karl Klingemann in London* (Essen: Baedeker, 1909), 222. See also Little, *Mendelssohn and the Organ*, 33.

8   Felix Mendelssohn Bartholdy, *Sämtliche Briefe*, 12 vols., ed. Anja Morgenstern and Uta Wald (Kassel: Bärenreiter, 2009), 2:387. Letter from Lindau, September 3, 1831. "Es [ist] eigentlich eine Schande, daß ich die Hauptsachen von Sebastian Bach nicht spielen kann." Hereafter cited as *Briefe*. Translations are by the author unless otherwise indicated.

9   Schneider (1789–1864), a great virtuoso, was organist at the Evangelische Hof-Kirche in Dresden; Schneider may have coached Mendelssohn informally on the organ from time to time.

10   Haupt (1810–91), organist at the Parochial-Kirche in Berlin. Deeply conservative in his views, he was arguably the leading *Organistenmacher* of his day and prided himself on the large number of American students he had taught.

11   Hesse (1809–63), organist of the Bernadin-Kirche in Breslau, was known primarily as an organ virtuoso and recitalist, whose travels took him throughout Europe. He also composed prolifically for organ.

12   Attwood (1765–1838) was probably Mendelssohn's closest English friend. Mendelssohn dedicated his *Three Preludes and Fugues for Organ* (op. 37) to him in 1837.

13   See the "Organ Atlas" in Appendix A of Little, *Mendelssohn and the Organ*, 372–73: St. John's Waterloo Rd.; St. John's Chapel, Paddington St.; Sepulchre, Holburn, and so on.

14   Little, *Mendelssohn and the Organ*, 375, St. Margaret's, Lothbury.

15   Mendelssohn drafted plans for each of his voluntaries in his diary, which is now in the Bodleian Library—shelf mark: MS. M. Deneke Mendelssohn g.4.

16   The festival took place in September. Mendelssohn played the Prelude and Fugue in E-flat Major (BWV 552), and other works by him were included in the program. For a fuller discussion of Mendelssohn's performances in Birmingham, see Wm. A. Little, "Mendelssohn in Birmingham, 1837 und 1840: Der Komponist als Organist," in *"Dieses herrliche, imponirende Instrument": Die Orgel im Zeitalter Felix Mendelssohn Bartholdys*, ed. Anselm Hartinger, Christoph Wolff, and Peter Wollny (Leipzig: Breitkopf und Härtel, 2011), 187–202 (German) or "Mendelssohn in Birmingham: 1837 and 1840: The Composer as Organist," *American Organist* 43 (March 2009): 72–79.

17   For a more detailed account, see Little, *Mendelssohn and the Organ*, 66–67. Mendelssohn visited Buckingham Palace on June 20, and July 9, 1842.

18   A detailed account of the pedal boards Mendelssohn encountered during his travels, including illustrations of South German/Austrian, English, and North/Central German pedal boards, can be found in Little, *Mendelssohn and the Organ*, 33–35.

19   *Dictionary of Music and Musicians*, 1st ed., ed. George Grove (London: Macmillan, 1880), 2:274. "He was the greatest of the few great German organ players who had visited this country, and the English organists . . . learned more than one lesson from him." Hereafter cited as Grove 1880.

20   For a more detailed account, see Little, *Mendelssohn and the Organ*, 46–49.

21   For a full discussion of this issue, see Nicholas Thistlethwaite, *The Making of the Victorian Organ* (New York: Cambridge University Press, 1990), esp. chapters 6 through 9.

22   Mendelssohn's letter to Coventry of August 29, 1844, is given in Little, *Mendelssohn and the Organ*, 438–39.

23 Mendelssohn designated his Three Preludes and Fugues for Organ (1837) as op. 37.

24 Rudolf Elvers, ed., *Felix Mendelssohn Bartholdy: Briefe an seine Verleger* (Berlin: DeGruyter, 1968), 58–60.

25 Little, "Mendelssohn in Birmingham, 1837 und 1840" (German) or "Mendelssohn in Birmingham: 1837 and 1840: The Composer as Organist" (English).

26 The wedding ceremony, in French, took place on March 28, in the French Reformed Church in Frankfurt/Main, where Cécile's father was minister.

27 Friedrich (Fritz) Schlemmer (1803–90), a lawyer, amateur organist, and cousin of Cécile, had a small English pedal piano in his residence, which he made available to Mendelssohn.

28 Paul Mendelssohn Bartholdy and Carl Mendelssohn Bartholdy, eds., *Mendelssohn Bartholdy, Briefe aus den Jahren 1830–1847*, 2nd ed. (Leipzig: H. Mendelssohn, 2/1870), 393. Letter to his mother of July 3, 1839: "Mein Pedal wird sich jetzt hören lassen können." Hereafter cited as *Briefe* 1870.

29 For a full discussion of Mendelssohn's decision to abandon his revision of this fugue, see Robert Parkins and R. Larry Todd, "Mendelssohn's Fugue in F Minor: A Discarded Movement of the First Organ Sonata," *Organ Yearbook* 14 (1983): 61–77.

30 Letter to his mother, August 10, 1840, in *Briefe* 1870, 416.

31 Mendelssohn's appeal, dated July 29, 1840, plus the list of subscribers is reproduced in Little, *Mendelssohn and the Organ*, Appendix D, 415–28.

32 Schumann's critique, "Mendelssohns Orgelkonzert," appeared originally in the *Neue Zeitschrift für Musik* on August 15 1840, and is reproduced in German and English in Little, *Mendelssohn and the Organ*, Appendix E, 429–32.

33 Eva Weissweiler, ed., *Clara und Robert Schumann: Briefwechsel*, vol. 1 (Basel: Stroemfeld, 1984), 1062.

34 Letter to his mother, July 13, 1837, "sie wird mir brummen," in *Briefe* 1870, 362.

35 *Neue Zeitschrift für Musik*, June 24, 1836, and in *Erinnerungen an Felix Mendelssohn Bartholdy: Nachgelassene Aufzeichnungen von Robert Schumann*, ed. Georg Eismann (Zwickau: Predella, 1947), 39.

36 Edward Murray Oakeley, *Life of Sir Herbert Stanley Oakeley* (London: George Allen, 1904), 77–78.

37 Ibid.

38 Grove 1880, 2:274.

39 More on Mendelssohn's association with Haupt in Little, *Mendelssohn and the Organ*, 169.

40 Postscript to a letter to his sister, July 3, 1839. Not included in the published correspondence. Mendelssohn's manuscript letters in the New York Public Library, no. 408. See also Wm. A. Little, "Mendelssohns Dilemma: Die Sammlung Choralvorspiele oder die Passacaille?" in "*Zu groß, zu unerreichbar*": *Bach-Rezeption im Zeitalter Mendelssohns und Schumanns*, ed. Anselm Hartinger, Christoph Wolff, and Peter Wollny (Leipzig: Breitkopf und Härtel, 2007), 381–93, or "Mendelssohn's Dilemma: The Collection of Chorale Preludes or the Passacaille?" *American Organist* 43, no. 1 (January 2009): 68, 71nn39–40.

41 Schumann, "Mendelssohns Orgelkonzert": "The Passacaille in C Minor, with twenty-one variations, cleverly intertwined with each other and admirably handled in the registers" (see Little, *Mendelssohn and the Organ*, 430).

42 George Smart, *Leaves from the Journals of Sir George Smart*, ed. H. B. Cox and C. I. E. Cox (London: Longmans, Green, 1907), 173.

43 Schumann, "Mendelssohns Orgelkonzert," in Little, *Mendelssohn and the Organ*, 430.

44 Schicht (1753–1823) is chiefly remembered as editor of the monumental *Allgemeines Choral-Buch* (Leipzig: Breitkopf und Härtel, 1819). He also edited a four-volume collection of J. S. Bach's chorale preludes: *J. S. Bachs Choral-Vorspiele für die Orgel mit einem und zwey Klavieren und Pedal* (Leipzig: Breitkopf und Härtel, 1803–5).

45 For a more detailed account, see Little, *Mendelssohn and the Organ*, 330–32.

46 Wm. A. Little, "Felix Mendelssohn and Bach's Prelude and Fugue in E Minor (BWV 533)," in *American Organist* 39, no. 2 (February 2005): 73–83.

47 Carl Freudenberg (1797–1869), a Silesian and quondam student at the Royal Institute of Church Music in Berlin, returned to Breslau, where, as organist of the Magdalena-Kirche, he spent the rest of his life.

48 Carl Freudenberg, *Aus dem Leben eines alten Organisten*, 2nd ed. (Leipzig: Leuckart, 1872), 25.

49 Grove 1880, 2:274 (see Little, *Mendelssohn and the Organ*, 85).

50 Johann Vesque von Püttlingen, *Eine Lebensskizze* (Vienna: Hölder, 1887), 64–66.

51 For a fuller account, see Little, *Mendelssohn and the Organ*, 110–11.

52 William Spark, *Musical Memories* (London: Reeves, 1909), 29–30.

53 For a fuller account, see Little, *Mendelssohn and the Organ*, 72–73.

54 Letter to his mother, August 10, 1840, in *Briefe* 1870, 416.

55 *Catalogue of the Mendelssohn Papers in the Bodleian Library, Oxford*, vol. 3: Printed Music and Books, comp. Peter Ward Jones (Tutzing: Schneider, 1989). Hereafter cited as *Bodleian.*

56 Carl Ferdinand Becker (1804–77), organist at the Nikolai-Kirche in Leipzig and friend of Mendelssohn, inscribed a copy of his *Caecilia: Tonstücke für die Orgel zum Studium, Konzertvortrag und zum Gebrauche beim öffentlichen Gottesdienst*, 1845. *Bodleian*, 22.

57 Johann Georg Herzog (1822–1909), organist and professor at the Munich Conservatory, inscribed a copy of *Der praktische Organist*, vol. 2 (1845), which he had dedicated to Mendelssohn. *Bodleian*, 229.

58 Although the conversation was presumably about organ music, there can be little doubt that Mendelssohn's response referred to Bach's music generally.

59 Little, "Felix Mendelssohn and Bach's Prelude and Fugue in E Minor," 76–77.

60 A copy of the Schübler Chorales, published by Coventry and Hollier, was discovered by the Japanese musicologist, Nobuaki Ebata in late 2012. The account and analysis of his find was published. See Nobuaki Ebata, Yo Tomita, and Ian Mills, "Mendelssohn and the Schübler Chorales (BWV 645–50): A New Source Found in the Riemenschneider Bach Institute Collection," *BACH: Journal of the Riemenschneider Bach Institute* 44, no. 1 (June 2013): 1–45.

61 Letter to Raimund Härtel, February 17, 1845, in Elvers, *Felix Mendelssohn Bartholdy: Briefe an seine Verleger*, 152.

62 For a more detailed discussion of this issue, see Little, *Mendelssohn and the Organ*, 256–59.

63 Coventry wanted to publish them earlier, but Mendelssohn refused (Little, *Mendelssohn and the Organ*, 448–49). There is some evidence, however, that Coventry did publish some copies early, which he may have sent abroad. See Phillip Hale's copy of opus 65 in the New York Public Library, where the first and third sonata are inverted.

64 Henry Gauntlett, "Mendelssohn's Organ Sonatas, an Appreciation," *Morning Chronicle*, March 6, 1846.

65 Chipp (1823–86) evidently played all six sonatas from memory and later received a warm testimonial from Mendelssohn himself after a performance of the Third Sonata. See Little, *Mendelssohn and the Organ*, 333.

66 Rudolph Kremer, "The Organ Sonata since 1845" (PhD diss., Washington University, 1963).

67 Christian Fink (1831–1911), pupil of Schneider in Dresden, organist in Esslingen: five sonatas.

68 Friedrich Karl Kühmstedt (1808–58), organist and Kapellmeister in Eisenach: four sonatas.

69 August Gottfried Ritter (1811–85), organist in Merseburg, later Magdeburg: four sonatas.

70 Jan Albert van Eyken (1823–68), organist in Amsterdam, later Elberfeld: three sonatas.

71 Wilhelm Adam Valentin Volckmar (1812–87), organist and pedagogue in Homberg.

72 Gotthold Frotscher, *Geschichte des Orgelspiels und der Orgelkomposition*, 2 vols. (Berlin: Hesse, 1935), 2:1171.

73 Bruno Weigl, *Handbuch der Orgelliteratur* (Leipzig: Leuckart, 1931), 194.

74 Rudolf Werner, *Felix Mendelssohn Bartholdy als Kirchenmusiker* (Frankfurt/Main: published by the author, 1930).

75 Susanna Vendrey, "Die Orgelwerke von Felix Mendelssohn Bartholdy" (PhD diss., Vienna, 1964).

76 Susanna Grossmann-Vendrey, "Stilprobleme in Mendelssohns Orgelsonaten, op. 65," in *Das Problem Mendelssohn*, ed. Carl Dahlhaus, Studien zur Musikgeschichte des 19. Jahrhunderts 41 (Regensburg: Bosse, 1974), 185–94.

77 Douglas L. Butler, "The Organ Works of Felix Mendelssohn Bartholdy" (PhD diss., University of Oregon, 1973).

78 Paul Jourdan, "Mendelssohn in England: 1829–1837" (PhD diss., Cambridge University, 1998).

79 François Sabatier, "Les grandes oeuvres pour orgue de Mendelssohn," *L'orgue: Cahiers et memoires* 24, no. 2 (1980): 1–29; English translation: "Mendelssohn's Organ Works," trans. J. Christopher O'Malley, *American Organist* 16, no. 1 (1982): 46–56.

80 Friedrich Bötel, *Mendelssohns Bachrezeption und ihre Konsequenzen dargestellt an den Präludien und Fugen für Orgel, op. 37*, Beiträge zur Musikforschung 14 (Munich: Katzbichler, 1984).

81 Pietro Zappalà "Editorial Problems in Mendelssohn's Organ Preludes, op. 37," trans. J. Michael Cooper, in *The Mendelssohns: Their Music in History*, ed. J. Michael Cooper and Julie D. Prandi (New York: Oxford University Press, 2002), 27–42.

82 Eugene Murray Gates, "Towards an Authentic Interpretation of Mendelssohn's Organ Works" (Master's thesis, McMaster University, 1985).

83 David Lloyd Petrash, "Felix Mendelssohn as Organ Composer" (DMA diss., North Texas State University, 1975).

84 Robert Mann, "The Development of Form in the German Organ Sonata from Mendelssohn to Rheinberger" (DMA diss., North Texas State University, 1978).

85 John Stansell, "An Expressive Approach to the Organ Sonatas of Felix Mendelssohn Bartholdy" (DMA diss., Juilliard School of Music, 1983).

86 Carolyn Schott Haury, "Slur Markings in Mendelssohn's Organ Sonatas, op. 65: A Study of the Earliest Prints and Manuscripts" (DMA diss., University of Cincinnati, 1978).

87   Peter Ward Jones has written and edited extensively on Mendelssohn; his most recent book, *The Mendelssohns on Honeymoon*, reveals unique insights into the personal lives of Felix and Cécile Mendelssohn.

88   Nicholas Thistlethwaite, Canon Precentor at Guildford Cathedral, is probably the leading authority on organs and organ building in the United Kingdom; with Geoffrey Weber, he coedited *The Cambridge Companion to the Organ* (Cambridge: Cambridge University Press, 1999).

89   Michael Gailit, organist of the Augustiner-Kirche in Vienna, teaches organ at the Vienna Conservatory and is on the faculty of the Music Department at the University of Vienna. His biography, *Julius Reubke (1834–1858): Leben und Werk* (Langen bei Bregenz: Edition Lade, 1995), remains the standard work on the composer.

90   Russell Stinson, one of the most active American scholars and author of five books, his interests focus on Bach, Bach reception, Mendelssohn, and Schumann.

91   R. Larry Todd of Duke University is the universally recognized dean of Mendelssohn studies. His biographies of Felix Mendelssohn (2003) and of Fanny Mendelssohn Hensel (2009) are regarded as definitive.

Chapter Five

Some Observations on Mendelssohn's Bach Recital

Russell Stinson

There can be little question that Felix Mendelssohn Bartholdy was the most influential champion of J. S. Bach's organ works during the early Romantic era. As a performer, editor, composer, antiquarian, and all-around ambassador, he occupied himself with this music his entire life. In so doing, he helped to bring a historical repertory into the mainstream of musical life in the early nineteenth century.

Of particular importance is the organ recital given by Mendelssohn on August 6, 1840, at the church of St. Thomas in the city of Leipzig, where he had lived since 1835. On that occasion—and for the first and only time in his career as an organist—he offered the public a full-length, all-Bach program, played, no less, in the same organ loft where the great Bach had so often held forth as Thomas-Kantor. And he did so expressly to raise money for a monument to Bach in Leipzig.[1] That monument (see fig. 5.1), which Mendelssohn also helped to design, still stands today just yards from the former site of St. Thomas's School (razed in 1902). Fittingly, the east side of the structure shows an angel playing the organ. All things considered, this performance ranks as the most famous and important organ recital in the history of music.

Mendelssohn's recital is documented primarily by the handbill for the event and by Robert Schumann's review of the performance, published about a week later in the *Neue Zeitschrift für Musik*. Schumann's personal copy of the program (which unfortunately contains no handwritten annotations) is given in chapter 4, as figure 4.1. This document lists, in order, the day of the week, date, location, performer's name, repertoire, and starting time. Also provided are two paragraphs explaining how the proceeds are to be used and where tickets may be purchased.[2] The wording, layout, and typeface match the handbills for

Figure 5.1. Bach monument in Leipzig designed by Eduard Bendemann.
Postcard reprinted with permission from Bild und Heimat Verlag, Reichenbach
(Vogtland), Germany.

concerts at the Leipzig Gewandhaus during Mendelssohn's tenure there as conductor. Between two improvisations (see discussion below) six different Bach works were played, representing six different compositional genres—fugue, chorale, prelude, passacaglia, pastorale, and toccata—but symmetrically arranged into two groups of three works each.

As indicated by the handbill, the recital began not with a prelude but a fugue, which Mendelssohn prefaced with an improvisation. To quote from Schumann's review, "After a short introduction, [Mendelssohn] played a very splendid Fugue in E-flat major, containing three ideas, one built upon the other."[3] Schumann can only be describing the Fugue in E-flat Major (BWV 552/2) that closes part 3 of Bach's *Clavierübung*, the composer's only organ fugue in this key as well as his only double fugue with three subjects, not to mention a rare example by Bach of a double fugue whose second subject is introduced without any counterpoint. This is the same fugue that a few years later would inspire Mendelssohn in the composition of his Six Sonatas for the Organ (MWV W56–61, op. 65), specifically, in the double fugue from the third sonata.[4] In both fugues the second subject is stated first by the left hand, simultaneously with the final cadence of the first main section and with the right hand dropping out until the second statement. Furthermore, both of these second subjects involve perpetual motion in the rhythm equal to one-fourth of the beat of the previous section. Neither is really playable on the pedals.

Mendelssohn appears to have learned Bach's fugue in the summer of 1837, when he and his wife, Cécile, were vacationing in and around Frankfurt. Having agreed to perform on the organ at the Birmingham Music Festival that September, he chose to play this fugue along with the Prelude in E-flat Major that opens part 3 of the *Clavierübung*, reasoning that in both movements he could achieve a variety of organ colors. As he wrote to his mother, Lea, "both in the prelude and in the fugue one can show off the piano, pianissimo, and the whole range of the organ."[5] No doubt he hoped to entertain his Leipzig audience in much the same way, presumably employing registration changes at least between the three main sections of the fugue. Because the St. Thomas organ by this time had expanded to three manuals,[6] these registration changes could have been accomplished simply by switching manuals.

By playing a brief improvisation before the fugue, Mendelssohn was bowing to an old tradition. As early as 1770, for example, German organists are known to have improvised their own preludes to fugues by Bach, regardless of whether Bach had furnished a prelude himself.[7] Two such "Introductions" have survived from the pen of August Wilhelm Bach, a not insignificant fact considering that this Bach (no relation to Johann Sebastian) in the early 1820s had been Mendelssohn's first and only organ teacher.[8] Mendelssohn may also have observed his colleagues in London doing much the same thing, as this had long been a tradition in England too. Indeed, Mendelssohn performed an "introduction and fugue" himself in 1833 at St. Paul's Cathedral, but in that instance he probably improvised both the introduction and the fugue. The larger truth here is the emphasis that musicians have always placed on J. S. Bach as a composer of fugues (and which, if carried to extremes in the context of a prelude-fugue pair, does a great disservice to the preludes). Not by accident does the title of the earliest edition of the so-called Six Great Preludes and Fugues for Organ, BWV 543–48, read *Sechs Praeludien und SECHS FUGEN*.

The second item on the Leipzig recital was a work also in E-flat major, namely, the communion hymn "Schmücke dich, o liebe Seele" from the "Great Eighteen" chorales, BWV 654.[9] Mendelssohn had known this work for at least a decade or so, and by all accounts it was one of his favorite compositions. In 1831, during a visit to Munich, he delighted in playing the piece with two "mellow" reeds and a string stop for the solo melody, and with flutes for the middle voices.[10] Shortly after his move to Leipzig in 1835, he performed the work for Schumann, confessing to his new colleague that, if life were ever to deprive him of hope and faith, this one chorale would restore both. And in 1847, the year of Mendelssohn's death, he recommended the piece to the historian Johann Gustav Droysen as a remedy for Droysen's melancholy over the death of his wife. Schumann revered the composition on his own terms, describing the ornamented chorale tune as "hung with wreaths of gilded leaves,"[11] and writing in his review of Mendelssohn's recital that the work was "as priceless, deep, and full of soul as any piece of music that ever sprang from a true artist's imagination." It might seem odd that the work is listed in the program as a "Phantasie," but compared to the hundreds of organ chorales by Bach (such as those from the *Orgelbüchlein*, a collection published by Mendelssohn in the 1840s) in which the hymn tune appears as an unadorned, continuous melody, this is a decidedly free arrangement.

The first half of the recital concluded with a selection reported on by Schumann to his fiancée, Clara Wieck: "Mendelssohn's concert lasted somewhat long. But you would have taken great joy in it, especially in the Prelude in A Minor (the same one that you play from the 6 Great), which assumed on the organ a very grand, unique, and brilliant character. There might have been a total of 400–500 listeners."[12] Just as Mendelssohn designated this work in his program as "*Grosses* Praeludium und Fuge," Schumann cites it here as one of the "6 *grossen*" preludes and fugues, BWV 543–48, a collection (evidently not compiled by Bach himself) that begins with a piece in A minor. Having gone through five printings by 1840,[13] these very popular works had acquired a nickname befitting their relatively large size. Another point to be made about Schumann's report is that he had apparently never heard the A-Minor played on the organ. Rather, he was used to hearing Clara play her own piano transcription of the piece, which he had introduced to her.[14] It would become a fixture on the countless piano recitals she gave over the next fifty years.

Mendelssohn thus treated his Leipzig audience to the same A-Minor Prelude and Fugue (BWV 543) that he had played to great acclaim in London three years earlier and doubtless at other times too. Indeed, if one can trust the biography of the English organist Herbert Oakeley, Mendelssohn performed this work so frequently in London churches that it became known there not as the "Bach A-Minor" but as the "Mendelssohn A-Minor."[15] In particular, it was the virtuosic pedal part of the fugue that so thrilled the Londoners. According to Oakeley's biography, when Mendelssohn in 1837 essayed the fugue at Christ Church, Newgate Street, he got so excited himself that "when he came to the great pedal solo at the end he just sat on the organ seat and tore his hair." This was the same pedal solo, incidentally, that Mendelssohn had been unable to complete the previous day at St. Paul's, due to the premature departure of the organ-blower.[16] Schumann, for his part, surely had such passages in mind when he wrote in his review of the Leipzig recital that both the prelude and the fugue were "very difficult, even for a master of organ playing." The subject of this fugue also served Mendelssohn as a compositional model, as attested to by the subject of his similarly virtuosic Fugue in C Minor, from the Three Preludes and Fugues for Organ (MWV W21/W18, W22/W20, and W23/W13; op. 37), published in 1837. Not only are both themes conceived along the lines of a gigue in a minor key, but they follow the same melodic contour and phrase syntax as well.[17]

After a brief intermission, the recital resumed with the Passacaglia, or, as Mendelssohn always called it, the "Passacaille" in C Minor, BWV 582. Schumann's remark that the work was "admirably handled in the choice of registers" strongly suggests that Mendelssohn often changed registrations between variations, thereby exploiting the various timbres of that rather substantial organ, which by this date had grown to around forty stops (was he assisted by registrants, who might also have turned pages?). Perhaps, then, he only gradually built up to the "volle Orgel" registration cited in the program. As to the meaning of the word "Phantasie" here, the term must refer to the four-minute-long fugue that concludes the piece.[18] Strictly speaking, this fugue is prefaced not by twenty-one variations, as the program claims, but twenty, implying that the initial, solo statement of the ostinato-bass theme was counted as Variation 1.

Mendelssohn's personal copy of the original print of Bach's passacaglia (F. P. Dunst, ca. 1834) offers further clues about how he might have performed the piece on his recital.[19] This source, housed today at the Bodleian Library, Oxford, contains a multitude of markings in Mendelssohn's hand, most of which are merely corrections of typographical errors. But in several other passages Mendelssohn added his own trills (m. 46, soprano, beat 2, note 2; m. 76, soprano, beat 1; m. 138, alto, beat 3, note 4; m. 194, soprano, beat 2, note 1; m. 196, soprano, beat 1, note 2; m. 259, soprano, beat 2, note 2; and m. 285, soprano, beat 1). Moreover, he prescribed in measure 120 fewer hand changes than the beaming and stemming of the arpeggiated sixteenth notes there would seem to indicate (notes 1–4 are assigned to the left hand, notes 5–6 to the right, notes 7–8 to the left, and notes 9–12 to the right). Since this measure *begins* one of the variations on this eight-measure theme, these markings imply how Mendelssohn might have played the next seven measures as well.

Mendelssohn's recital marks the first time he is ever known to have played Bach's passacaglia, but he obviously knew the work as early as 1823, when he appropriated it as an exemplar for his own Passacaglia in C Minor.[20] In addition to the common key and genre, Mendelssohn, like Bach, based his passacaglia on a theme of eight measures that is first stated as a pedal solo and is then subjected to roughly twenty variations. Further similarities to Bach's passacaglia include the use of the same figuration for two consecutive variations; the transfer of the theme to the right hand midway through, accompanied only by fast scalar figures in the left hand; the arpeggiation of the theme between the hands later on; and the reinstatement of the theme in the pedals to conclude. No other organ work by Mendelssohn so closely follows a Bachian model—even if Mendelssohn's passacaglia is, surprisingly, in duple meter.

The recital continued with the Pastorale in F Major, BWV 590. Only its first movement had been published at the time (under the same title, "Pastorella," found in Mendelssohn's program), which is evidence that it was also the only one performed. To be more exact, this publication was the brainchild of Mendelssohn's erstwhile friend Adolf Bernhard Marx, who in 1825 had issued the first movement as a supplement to his journal, the *Berliner allgemeine musikalische Zeitung*. It was also in this year, when Mendelssohn was still in his midteens, that his family acquired a copy of the work.[21] According to the English conductor and organist George Smart, Mendelssohn rendered the piece that year during a soirée at the family's home in Berlin.

In the commentary provided by Marx to his edition, he was so awed by the music that he could scarcely describe it: "We can hardly venture to say anything about this splendid Pastorale. It is so permeated by the most intimate, truly rustic feeling, and handled so expressively, richly, and charmingly in every voice from the first to the last . . . that one can only sense and marvel and be silent."[22] Marx also considered the movement to be an independent work, and he regarded it merely as a torso due to the way it concludes in A minor, rather like a da capo aria that breaks off right before the repeat of the "A" section: "The composition has been given to us as a fragment. However, it is certainly in and of itself satisfactory, regardless of its beginning in F major and ending in A minor." We can only assume that Mendelssohn, too, thought highly of this movement (highly enough to perform it, anyway). Did he also agree with Marx that it had not survived in its original, complete state? If so, Mendelssohn may have played the first nine measures as a reprise, followed immediately or shortly thereafter by a cadence in F major, which is a practice that has become especially customary when performing just the first movement.[23]

What *is* certain is that the Pastorale impressed Schumann, to quote from his review, as something "mined from the deepest depths in which such a composition may be found." Considering that Schumann mentored his wife, Clara, in

all things Bach, his high opinion of the work might explain why she championed it throughout her long career as a pianist: she played it both in concert
and in her teaching studio, and regarded it as one of Bach's most significant
organ compositions. Clara, in turn, probably introduced the Pastorale to her
dear friend Johannes Brahms, who featured the piece on his piano recitals and
listened to Clara play it on his last visit with her shortly before her death in
1896. In addition, Clara and Brahms sometimes amused themselves by performing the first movement as a piano duet, just as Marx had recommended in
his commentary.

The last Bach work on Mendelssohn's recital was a toccata in D minor,
either the "Dorian" (BWV 538/1) or the infamous Toccata (and Fugue) in D
Minor, BWV 565. Since Mendelssohn knew the "Dorian" not as a toccata but
as a prelude, he must have performed BWV 565, a work he had described as
"learned and at the same time something for the people" when in 1830, at
the beginning of his grand tour, he played it at the town church of Weimar
for the church's organist (the church's superintendent was not amused, for, in
Mendelssohn's words, "he could not study with that much noise going on").[24]
Schumann's response to the opening section of this piece as "typical of Bach's
sense of humor" is seriously at odds with the traditional interpretation of
gloom and doom.

The improvisation that concluded the recital, as described by Schumann,
was a contrapuntal tour de force based on one of Bach's (and Mendelssohn's)
favorite hymns and incorporating Bach's very name, perhaps in the guise of
theme and variations: "Mendelssohn ended with a fantasy of his own in which,
then, he showed himself in the full glory of his artistry; it was based on a chorale (if I am not mistaken, with the text 'O Haupt voll Blut und Wunden') into
which he later wove the name BACH and a fugal passage—the entire fantasy
was rounded out into such a clear and masterly whole that, if printed, it would
appear as a finished work of art."

Schumann was surely correct about this chorale, for the tune known as "O
Haupt voll Blut und Wunden" appears five times in Bach's *St. Matthew Passion*,
a work whose performance under Mendelssohn's own baton in 1829 is credited with launching the so-called Bach revival of the nineteenth century. The
insertion of Bach's name (B♭, A, C, B♮) toward the end suggests the influence
of Bach's Art of Fugue and recalls Mendelssohn's improvisation of an entire
prelude and fugue on B–A–C–H at the organ during his final visit to London
in 1847.[25] The final variation might well have been a fugue on the first phrase
of the chorale, as in the first movement of Mendelssohn's sixth organ sonata. A
little-known, fragmentary organ work by Mendelssohn discovered about twenty
years ago suggests how this improvisation might have begun, for it opens with a
harmonization of this very chorale and, after a two-measure interlude of unac-
companied sixteenth notes in the right hand, continues with a first variation.[26]
Mendelssohn's sixth organ sonata commences in precisely this fashion, and

this fragment may have been intended for the same opus. Another possibility is that it preserves actual material from the Leipzig recital.[27]

Assuming that the opening improvisation, described by Schumann as "short," lasted no more than a couple of minutes,[28] the selections before the concluding improvisation amounted to no more than fifty minutes of music, or only forty minutes, if just the first movement of the Pastorale were played. Therefore, the concluding improvisation must have been one of the longest items on the program, if not the longest. An estimate of fifteen minutes hardly seems excessive, especially considering that Mendelssohn once extemporized at the piano no fewer than twenty variations on "The Bluebells of Scotland."[29] There, too, he demonstrated his keen contrapuntal sense, setting the tune twice as a canon and once as a four-voice fugue with the subject inverted.

Mendelssohn's recital was a great success, both financially and artistically: the proceeds totaled 300 thalers,[30] a sum equal to one-third of the performer's annual salary as conductor of the Gewandhaus orchestra, and the critics raved. An anonymous reviewer for the *Allgemeine musikalische Zeitung* opined that "through the performance of several magnificent compositions by Sebastian Bach, and through the rendition of a free fantasy, Mendelssohn once more proved himself a distinguished organist and great artist; it was a truly splendid artistic treat, for which we are all the more thankful as it is offered to us— alas!—so seldom."[31] Also in attendance was the elderly Friedrich Rochlitz, former editor of that journal, who embraced Mendelssohn afterward and saw fit to paraphrase Simeon's *Nunc dimittis*: "I can now depart in peace, for never shall I hear anything finer or more sublime."[32] Schumann, as usual, said it best:

> How well Mendelssohn understands the treatment of Bach's royal instrument is generally known; and yesterday he laid before us nothing but precious jewels, in the most glorious variety and gradation, which he only prefaced, as it were, at the beginning, and concluded with a fantasy of his own. . . . A fine summer evening shone through the church windows; even outside, in the open air, many may have reflected on the wonderful sounds, thinking that there is nothing greater in music than the enjoyment of the twofold mastery displayed when one master expresses the other.

Appendix 5.1

Mendelssohn's Organ Recital of Bach's Music at the Thomas-Kirche in Leipzig in 1840

Performed on the Craighead-Saunders Organ in Christ Church, Rochester, New York, on October 29, 2009, and September 27, 2012. The 2012 performance can be heard by way of an internet link: www.esm.rochester.edu/organ/mendelssohn.

Program:

Brief Improvised Prelude and Fugue in E-flat Major, BWV 552/2	William Porter
"Schmücke dich, o liebe Seele," BWV 654	Hans Davidsson
Prelude and Fugue in A Minor, BWV 543	David Higgs
Passacaglia in C Minor, BWV 582	William Porter
Pastorale in F Major, BWV 590	Hans Davidsson
Toccata in D Minor, BWV 565	David Higgs
Improvisation (Freie Phantasie)	William Porter

Notes

1   The original manuscript of Mendelssohn's appeal for subscribers to his recital was recently located by Wm. A. Little in the archives of the Gesellschaft der Musikfreunde, Vienna. For a facsimile reproduction with commentary, see Little's monograph, *Mendelssohn and the Organ* (New York: Oxford University Press, 2010), 415–28.

2   For an English translation, see Russell Stinson, *The Reception of Bach's Organ Works from Mendelssohn to Brahms* (New York: Oxford University Press, 2006), 59.

3   Translation from Hans T. David and Arthur Mendel, eds., *The New Bach Reader: A Life of Johann Sebastian Bach in Letters and Documents*, rev. Christoph Wolff (New York: Norton, 1998), 502–3. Schumann was also one of the signatories to Mendelssohn's handwritten appeal for subscribers to his recital, which is hardly surprising given Schumann's own fanaticism for the music of Bach. On his particular affinity for Bach's organ compositions, see Stinson, *Reception of Bach's Organ Works*, 76–101.

4   Stinson, *Reception of Bach's Organ Works*, 64–65.

5   Letter of July 13, 1837. See Paul Mendelssohn Bartholdy and Carl Mendelssohn Bartholdy, eds., *Briefe aus den Jahren 1833 bis 1847 von Felix Mendelssohn Bartholdy* (Leipzig: Hermann Mendelssohn, 1863), 145.

6   Christoph Wolff and Markus Zepf, *The Organs of J. S. Bach: A Handbook*, trans. Lynn Edwards Butler (Urbana: University of Illinois Press, 2012), 52.

7   Peter Williams, "J. S. Bach and English Organ Music," *Music and Letters* 44 (1963): 140–51, esp. 147–48.

8   Andreas Sieling, "'Selbst den alten Vater Sebastian suchte man nicht mehr so lang-stielig abzuhaspeln': Zur Rezeptionsgeschichte der Orgelwerke Bachs," in *Bach und die Nachwelt*, vol. 2 (*1850–1900*), ed. Michael Heinemann and Hans-Joachim Hinrichsen (Laaber: Laaber-Verlag, 1999), 299–339, esp. 307–8.

9   For a discussion of why Mendelssohn must have played this setting and not that cataloged as BWV 759, see Russell Stinson, *J. S. Bach at His Royal Instrument: Essays on His Organ Works* (New York: Oxford University Press, 2012), 43–45.

10 Stinson, *The Reception of Bach's Organ Works*, 23–24, 40–41, and 72.

11 Henry Pleasants, ed., *The Musical World of Robert Schumann: A Selection from His Own Writings* (London: Gollancz, 1965), 93.

12 Eva Weissweiler, ed., *Clara und Robert Schumann: Briefwechsel* (Basel and Frankfurt: Stroemfeld Verlag, 1984–2001), 1062.

13 Stinson, *J. S. Bach at His Royal Instrument*, 120–22.

14   Stinson, *Reception of Bach's Organ Works*, 77, 82–83.

15   Edward Murray Oakeley, *The Life of Sir Herbert Stanley Oakeley* (London: George Allen, 1904), 77–79.

16   See Mendelssohn's own account of this fiasco in Peter Ward Jones, ed., *The Mendelssohns on Honeymoon: The 1837 Diary of Felix and Cécile Mendelssohn Bartholdy Together with Letters to Their Families* (Oxford: Clarendon Press, 1997), 99–100.

17   Stinson, *Reception of Bach's Organ Works*, 36–38.

18   On this matter, see also Matthias Pape, *Mendelssohns Leipziger Orgelkonzert 1840: Ein Beitrag zur Bach-Pflege im 19. Jahrhundert* (Wiesbaden: Breitkopf und Härtel, 1988), 24.

19   On the print itself, see Dietrich Kilian, *Kritischer Bericht* to *Neue Bach-Ausgabe*, series 4, vol. 7 (Kassel: Bärenreiter; Leipzig: VEB Deutscher Verlag für Musik, 1988), 125. On Mendelssohn's personal copy, see Peter Ward Jones, *Catalogue of the Mendelssohn Papers in the Bodleian Library, Oxford* (Tutzing: Hans Schneider, 1989), 3:9. My thanks to Peter Ward Jones and the staff of the Bodleian Library for allowing me to examine this source on my trip to Oxford in 2001.

20   Stinson, *Reception of Bach's Organ Works*, 12–15.

21   Ibid., 16.

22   Stinson, *J. S. Bach at His Royal Instrument*, 47–48.

23   For two different notated examples of this practice, see Hermann Keller, *The Organ Works of Bach: A Contribution to Their History, Form, Interpretation and Performance*, trans. Helen Hewitt (New York: C. F. Peters, 1967), 97; and Anne Marsden Thomas, ed., *Oxford Service Music for Organ: Manuals and Pedals, Book 1* (Oxford: Oxford University Press, 2011), 19.

24   Stinson, *Reception of Bach's Organ Works*, 18–19.

25   Susanna Grossmann-Vendrey, *Felix Mendelssohn Bartholdy und die Musik der Vergangenheit* (Regensburg: Bosse, 1969), 190.

26   R. Larry Todd, "New Light on Mendelssohn's *Freie Phantasie* (1840)," in *Literary and Musical Notes: A Festschrift for Wm. A. Little*, ed. Geoffrey C. Orth (Frankfurt: Peter Lang, 1995), 205–18. For a performing edition, see Christoph Albrecht, ed., *Felix Mendelssohn Bartholdy: Neue Ausgabe sämtlicher Orgelwerke* (Kassel: Bärenreiter, 1993–94).

27   Whatever the case, the opening harmonization of Mendelssohn's fragment is evidently modeled after the last harmonization of this chorale in Bach's *St. Matthew Passion*, as the first phrase of its *Stollen* exhibits the same, striking chromaticism in the tenor voice. See Peter Wollny, "Zur Bach-Rezeption in den Orgelwerken von Felix Mendelssohn Bartholdy," in *"Diess herrliche, imponirende Instrument": Die Orgel im Zeitalter Felix Mendelssohn Bartholdys*, ed. Anselm Hartiger, Christoph Wolff, and Peter Wollny (Wiesbaden: Breitkopf und Härtel, 2011), 133–49, esp. 144–45.

28   Two minutes is also roughly the length of the "Introduction" composed by Mendelssohn's organ teacher A. W. Bach to the Fugue in G Minor, BWV 542/2. For a facsimile reprint, see Sieling, "Zur Rezeptionsgeschichte der Orgelwerke Bachs," 308.

29   R. Larry Todd, *Mendelssohn: A Life in Music* (New York: Oxford University Press, 2003), 546. Fifteen minutes is roughly the length of Rudolf Lutz's reconstruction of Mendelssohn's improvisation. For a description of Lutz's methodology, see his essay, "Eine Orgelsonate über den Choral 'O Haupt voll Blut und Wunden'? Zur Ergänzung von Mendelssohns Fragment GB-Ob, MS. M. Deneke Mendelssohn, b. 5, 28: Ein Arbeitsbericht," in *Die Orgel im Zeitalter Felix Mendelssohn Bartholdys*,

151–71. This publication contains a recording of Lutz's reconstruction, which may also be heard on the CD, featuring Lutz and Martin Schmeding, *Leipziger Orgeln um Felix Mendelssohn Bartholdy* (GEN 89152). The score of Lutz's reconstruction is to be published by Carus-Verlag.

30   According to a letter dated August 10, 1840, from Mendelssohn to his mother. See Mendelssohn Bartholdy, *Briefe aus den Jahren 1833 bis 1847*, 232. This missive also includes the following sentence about Mendelssohn's rigorous preparation for the performance: "I practiced hard for eight days previously, till I could scarcely stand upright, and executed nothing but [pedal] passages along the street in my gait when I walked out."

31   Eric Werner, *Mendelssohn: A New Image of the Composer and His Age*, trans. Dika Newlin (London: Free Press of Glencoe, 1963), 318.

32   Elise Polko, *Reminiscences of Felix Mendelssohn-Bartholdy: A Social and Artistic Biography*, trans. Lady Wallace (New York: Leypoldt and Holt, 1869), 73. Over fifty years earlier, Rochlitz had witnessed another momentous event in the musical history of St. Thomas's Church, for he was a young chorister there when, in 1789, Mozart first encountered Bach's motet, "Singet dem Herrn ein neues Lied." See Friedrich Blume, *Two Centuries of Bach*, trans. Stanley Godman (London: Oxford University Press, 1950), 27.

Chapter Six

"He Ought to Have a Statue"

Mendelssohn, Gauntlett, and the English Organ Reform

Nicholas Thistlethwaite

The reception of the oratorio *Elijah* (MWV A25, op. 70) at the Birmingham Musical Festival in 1846 is a well-rehearsed episode in Mendelssohn biography. Writing to his brother Paul, the composer commented, "No work of mine ever went so admirably at the first time of its execution,"[1] and this impression is largely confirmed by contemporary reviews in the English press. Charles Gruneisen, music critic of the *Morning Chronicle*, a friend of Meyerbeer and (later) one of the first English critics to champion Wagner, penned a lengthy and ecstatic review, which included the following passage:

> The execution of the new oratorio exacts unbounded eulogium [*sic*]. Never was there a greater anxiety to do justice to a composer. Every individual in the orchestra, instrumentalist or vocalist, made the same exertions as if individual fame was at stake. There was not a single hitch; slight blemishes there might have been to the initiated, but the audience could distinguish nothing but the universal desire to accomplish a labour of love. . . . The light and shade were accurately observed, and from the masses in action a real *pianissimo* was actually obtained. The band never was more effective.[2]

Then, to this catalog of superlatives, he adds, "It was also advantageous to have a first-rate organist like Dr. GAUNTLETT on such an occasion."[3] Gauntlett was Mendelssohn's choice as organist. Because the organ keys were placed

eighteen feet in front of the organ case, and immediately below the conductor's rostrum, Gauntlett sat literally (as well as metaphorically) at the composer's feet, with the instrumentalists seated on rising tiers behind the console
and the singers to either side;[4] it was a common arrangement in English musical festivals of the period.[5]

For the organist, it was far from ideal. Unable to see the conductor except
through the agency of a mirror, he was surrounded by instrumentalists and singers, and had to grapple with the heavy key touch (so heavy that Mendelssohn
declined to play at the 1846 festival)[6] and stop actions that, according to the
resident organist, required "the force of a steam engine" to operate.[7] But
this was not the end of Gauntlett's troubles at the first performance of *Elijah*.
Somehow, the organ part had been lost, and hence he was obliged to play from
the full score, "which he did," nineteenth-century writers tell us, "to the composer's entire satisfaction."[8]

But who was Dr. Gauntlett, and how did he come to be entrusted with the
organ part in this first performance of what J. W. Davison, musical critic of the
Times, hailed as the "greatest achievement of Mendelssohn's genius?"[9]

Mendelssohn's good opinion of Gauntlett is sparingly, but unambiguously,
documented. According to an obituary in the *Athenaeum*, Mendelssohn said
of him, "his literary attainments, his knowledge of the history of music, his
acquaintance with acoustical laws, his marvellous memory, his philosophical turn of mind, as well as practical experience, render him one of the most
remarkable professors of this age."[10]

The context is unknown, but Mendelssohn's opinion is partly substantiated by the sale catalog for Gauntlett's library from 1847;[11] the 524 lots
included unique early manuscript collections of English and Italian keyboard
pieces, rare theoretical works such as Gafori's *Practica musicae* of 1512 and
Diruta's *Il Transilvano* of 1625, as well as manuscripts of Handel and Samuel
Wesley (among them, the only surviving full score of Wesley's *Confitebor* of
1799). Alec Hyatt King comments that Gauntlett's collection "typifies the
unsuspected musical catholicity of the lesser Victorians,"[12] and it may have
been an acquaintance with this library that inspired Mendelssohn's tribute to
Gauntlett's learning.

Mendelssohn amplifies his comments in a second document, which survives
in his own hand, and reads as follows:

> I have had the good fortune of becoming thoroughly acquainted with Dr.
> Gauntlett's musical talents and I know but very few of his Countrymen as well
> as of mine whose masterly performance on the Organ, whose skill in writing,
> and whose perfect knowledge of musical litterature [*sic*] of ancient and mod-
> ern times may be compared to his. . . . Accordingly, I most sincerely wish him
> an opportunity of displaying those faculties as much as possible & am certain
> that he will promote the cause of art and prove a high ornament to any scien-
> tific & musical institution.[13]

It is signed by Mendelssohn, and dated "Berlin, January 7, 1844." Reading like a reference, it was indeed a letter of support for Gauntlett's application for the Reid Professorship of Music at Edinburgh University. Five years earlier, Mendelssohn had written in support of the first holder of the chair, the Scottish musician John Thomson (1805–41), who had studied in Leipzig,[14] so Gauntlett's hopes must have been raised by this endorsement. However, he was to be disappointed: in the event, the electors preferred Henry Hugo Pierson (1815–73),[15] a minor composer of songs and theater music.

But it is Mendelssohn's third tribute to Dr. Gauntlett that provides the key to their relationship, and also the title of this chapter. Again, the context is unknown, but an obituary in the *Musical Standard* records what the writer describes as Mendelssohn's "well-known observation," that, "but for him"—meaning Gauntlett—"I should have had no organ to play upon. He ought to have a statue."[16]

Gauntlett himself gives a little more information in a letter written in 1874 to George Grove. Referring to Mendelssohn, he writes:

> I believe when with the Horsleys at this end of the town [i.e., London] he had access to a small organ at St Matthew's[17]—"a crippled" organ as he called the G pedals and key-board—upon which he might certainly gain some sort of facility. Pointing to me one day he said, "But for him there would be no organs to play on." And hard fight it was, for I had Wesley, Turle, Goss, and the whole guild of organists to battle with.[18]

Gauntlett is recalling the campaign he waged between 1837 and 1846 for radical reform in the design of English organs. His campaign was inextricably bound up with the discovery and promotion of Bach's music, and it was inspired (and vitally assisted) by Mendelssohn's practical advocacy of the cause during his visits to England. For Gauntlett, Mendelssohn came to embody the authentic voice and practice of "Sebastian Bach," as the first generation of English Bach enthusiasts liked to call him. Commenting on Mendelssohn's performance of the Prelude and Fugue in E-flat Major (BWV 552) at the Birmingham Festival of 1837, Gauntlett wrote, "He [Mendelssohn] so identified himself with the composer, that one might readily imagine the great Liepsic [*sic*] organist [had] returned to life, and obtained a renewal of his mighty powers."[19]

Gauntlett was romanticizing, of course; he only knew of Bach what Mendelssohn had shown him. But we can sense the genuine excitement at being brought into contact with the great tradition through an individual whose credentials were (it seemed) so impeccable. There was a further attraction. Like Bach, Mendelssohn embodied all that Gauntlett found most admirable in Protestant music. Throughout his life, he had a profound interest in what he called "congregational psalmody"; the organs he planned were designed to support it; the many hymn tunes he composed (reputedly more than one thousand)[20] exemplified it. In his hymn settings, he aspired to capture what he would probably have described as the pure and manly qualities of Lutheran psalmody, and he made no secret of his contempt for the sentimentality and heightened emotionalism of the later Victorian hymn composers. An obituarist made the point succinctly: "He at once parted from the poetical and picturesque aspirations of the newer generation of musicians. The intense Protestant feeling, rather than the realistic poetry, of Sebastian Bach was the attraction which led him early to the study of that master, the fibre of whose choral songs he worked up in his own psalmody."[21]

Gauntlett quoted with approval a comment of Carl Friedrich Zelter, Mendelssohn's teacher, that the chorale constituted "the wall of partition between the Protestant and Catholic Church,"[22] and he observed that Mendelssohn's setting of a chorale tune (in the oratorio, *St. Paul*, MWV A14, op. 36) faithfully reproduced Bach's: "To those who have heard Mendelssohn's oratorio," he wrote, "Bach's mode of treating a chorale in four part harmony, and with a florid accompaniment, will not appear altogether novel."[23] He believed that the broad stream of Protestant psalmody (attaining its highest point in Bach) flowed through Mendelssohn's veins, and it merely confirmed the attraction he felt for him and all that he represented.

Any attempt to describe Gauntlett's role in the reform of the English organ and to examine in detail his relationship with Mendelssohn is hampered by poor documentation. Gauntlett's writings were prodigious, and appeared in various publications over the years, but the author was seldom identified. He was a contributor to the *Musical World* for a short period after its inception in 1836, and briefly its editor; he wrote for the *Morning Post* and *Morning Chronicle* in the 1840s. Sometimes his florid language gives the game away in other publications, but Gauntlett studies await a comprehensive and inevitably time-consuming trawl of Victorian journals and newspapers to lay the foundations of a reliable bibliography.

Henry John Gauntlett was born in 1805, the son of a parson.[24] As a young man he entered the legal profession, but his passion was for music and he took organ lessons from Samuel Wesley (1776–1837), the veteran organist and composer, who, with his companions, the so-called Sebastian Squad, had been promoting a small repertoire of Bach's keyboard and instrumental compositions since the early 1800s.[25]

This repertoire was far from representative, but by the mid-1820s scores of some of the organ works were becoming available, and occasional performances took place. One of the earliest was in 1827, when both Gauntlett and Samuel Sebastian Wesley (son of the elder Samuel) played the "St. Anne" Fugue (BWV 552ii) in the competition for the organistship of St. Stephen's, Coleman Street, in London.[26] Neither was successful, but a significant marker had been put down. In the following year, Wesley played the Preludes in B Minor (BWV 544i) and E Minor (BWV 533i) at Christ Church, Newgate Street, and Gauntlett performed the B-Minor Fugue (BWV 544ii), the final movement of the Trio Sonata in C Minor (BWV 526iii), and (probably) the Prelude in E-flat Major (BWV 552i) at St. James, Bermondsey in 1829.[27]

It is impossible to know what effect these early Bach performances created. They must have been constrained by the limitations of the instruments, in particular, by the pedal boards. Although "German" pedals (i.e., long pedals, spaced sufficiently far apart for the use of toe and heel) were becoming more common by the 1820s, independent pedal pipes remained rare. To complicate matters further, the lowest pedal was nearly always a G and there were seldom more than seventeen or eighteen notes.[28] So the performance of Bach's pedal parts demanded a certain ingenuity.

Tonally, the chief shortcomings, at least for the preludes and fugues, were the lack of 16′ registers on the manuals, with their associated mutations, and the absence of a sprightly secondary chorus as a foil to the Great Organ. (The typical English Choir Organ was a small-scaled division, lacking mixtures, while the Swell was usually physically remote and of short compass.) Later, when English organists began to discover the chorale preludes and trios, the lack of the flute, string, and reed voices commonly found on organs in central and southern Germany was also keenly felt.

Then, there were difficulties of interpretation. Neither Wesley nor any of his collaborators had heard the great Dutch or German organs, with their independent Pedal divisions and well-developed manual choruses. This inevitably hindered their understanding of Bach's intentions. As Gauntlett later wrote, "It was not, that Wesley was unacquainted with [Bach's] Fantasias, Passacaglias, Preludes, and Codas [sic], that he did not introduce them to the English: but never having heard a German organ, with its ponderous pedale, he could not realise the inventions of the author.[29]

Gauntlett probably overstates Wesley's familiarity with the corpus of Bach's organ works, but his general point is valid: Wesley and the "Sebastian Squad" really had very little idea about performance style and registration. There was a further difficulty. Recalling the situation before Mendelssohn's visits in the 1830s, Gauntlett wrote:

> We knew the six Grand Fugues and the Exercises. But what Mendelssohn did was this: He brought out what Marx called the "not well-known" Pedal music. He was the first to play the G minor, the D major, the E major, and the short E minor. . . . And he taught us how to play the *slow* fugue, for [Thomas] Adams [the most celebrated London organist of the period] had played all fugues fast. I recollect Mendelssohn's saying: "Your organists think that Bach did not write a slow fugue for the organ."[30]

Mendelssohn, in other words, showed English organists how to play Bach.

We do not know when Gauntlett first met Mendelssohn. He seems to have been present at St. Paul's Cathedral on September 10, 1837, when the organ blowers were bribed to desert their post, bringing Mendelssohn's account of the Fugue in A Minor to an abrupt end, because he later wrote an indignant account of the episode in the *Musical World*.[31] Possibly it was Gauntlett who then suggested that the disappointed company should reassemble two days later in Christ Church, Newgate Street[32]—where he had been organist since 1836—so that Mendelssohn might resume his performance. We know, too, from Mendelssohn's own account, that Gauntlett was present at Birmingham Town Hall on the morning of September 22, to hear him play the Prelude and Fugue in E-flat Major (BWV 552), shaking the composer's hand as he dashed for the London coach.[33] Critical though these public concerts of 1837 were in ensuring the success of Bach with English organists, and important though they must have been in revealing the shortcomings of English organs, it seems improbable that Gauntlett—scarcely a fading violet—had failed to make Mendelssohn's acquaintance on an earlier occasion.

Certainly, Gauntlett's appreciation of Bach's stature had moved into a different gear from the old "Sebastian Squad" before 1837. Enthusiastic though they were, their knowledge and understanding of Bach's compositions were deficient in many respects. The growing availability of continental editions of the organ music, and the appearance in 1836 of Coventry and Hollier's London edition of *John Sebastian Bach's Grand Studies for the Organ* (accompanied by an arrangement of the pedal part for double bass in deference to the shortcomings of the English pedal organ) ensured that the circulation of Bach's music gathered pace during the 1830s.

Evidence for Gauntlett's campaign to promote Bach is to be found in the *Musical World*. The review of Coventry and Hollier's first volume in April 1836 is almost certainly by Gauntlett. His admiration for the Fantasia in G Minor (BWV 542) was unbounded: "Of all the movements, that of the Fantasia is most wonderful in construction. It is an absolute anticipation of almost every modern invention in harmony. It is as profound as anything that Beethoven ever wrote."[34] (Significantly, Gauntlett had contributed a series of articles on "Characteristics of Beethoven" to the early issues of the journal.)[35] Two months later, the *Musical World* carried an abbreviated version of a lecture by Gauntlett on Bach, delivered "a few weeks ago" at the Islington Literary and Scientific Institution. Having commended Bach to his audience in terms certain to have appealed to a proto-Victorian sensibility ("the works of Bach present ideas of beauty, symmetry, design, expression—the elements of all that is grand and magnificent—and excite emotions of the most lively, varied, and exalted character"),[36] he draws Mendelssohn into his argument: "Among the composers for [the organ] stands first and foremost Sebastian Bach. Mendelssohn was once asked who was the organ composer next in merit to Bach. His reply was 'no one'; meaning that Bach soared so immeasurably above all other writers for the instrument that it would be [an] injustice to rank any other composer with him."[37] In a further article, on Handel and Bach, published in May 1837, Gauntlett again makes the connection between Mendelssohn and Bach, illustrating how closely the reputations of the two composers had become in the minds of the musical cognoscenti: "John Sebastian Bach is the model, and indeed the idol, of Mendelssohn: and this undisguised reverence, emanating from one on whom has fallen the mantle of Beethoven, has had its effect, in turning the attention of his countrymen to the fountain from which he has drunk so deeply."[38] To reapply Gauntlett's metaphor: Mendelssohn is Elisha to Bach's Elijah.

Mendelssohn's organ performances in September 1837 confirmed his prophetic role with the general public; they were received with acclamation. Large crowds lingered in St. Paul's after the service to hear him play; two days later, Christ Church, Newgate Street, was packed with people (appendix 6.1); and, later in the month, Birmingham Town Hall was full to capacity for Mendelssohn's performance on the last morning of the festival (appendix 6.2). Contemporary newspaper reports confirm the extraordinary reception he received on each of these occasions. Gauntlett, writing in the *Musical World*, attempted to explain the phenomenon:

> Although Mendelssohn is admitted to be the greatest extempore performer on the organ in his own country, it may be worthwhile to inquire into the reasons which led to the sensation he produced in our metropolis, and at Birmingham. The instruments he performed on seemed to assume a new character; the *pedale* appeared with a more grand and imposing tone, and the manuals more brilliant and harmonious. This explanation may be offered. Mendelssohn introduced Bach to the English, as an organ composer. Our native artists had known and appreciated him, as a writer for the clavichord, the forty-eight studies had developed his genius, as a profound adept in the strict school of composition; but we had yet to venerate him as the inventor of a set of totally new effects upon the organ.[39]

This is significant for a number of reasons. First, it puts the achievements of Wesley and the "Sebastian Squad" into perspective: clearly, the knowledge of such of the organ works as they possessed had been confined to a small circle of London organists. Second, it confirms that it was Mendelssohn's 1837 performances that finally communicated Bach's genius as an organ composer to English audiences. Third, Mendelssohn's use of the instrument opened Gauntlett's eyes to the deficiencies of the English organ as a vehicle for Bach and (I conjecture) inspired the vigorous campaign for reform that he waged over the ensuing ten years.

It seems that Mendelssohn encouraged Gauntlett to travel to the continent to visit Haarlem and no doubt other organs en route.[40] The timing is uncertain; a late source implies that it was before Mendelssohn's visit and was the direct inspiration for alterations to the Newgate Street organ in preparation for this (see below).[41] This seems unlikely. For one thing, Mendelssohn's performance at Christ Church was probably arranged at short notice after the debacle at the cathedral; for another, major alterations to the organ did not take place until 1838. It is more likely that Gauntlett went abroad with the sound of Mendelssohn's performances ringing in his ears, saw the great Müller organ in Haarlem, and returned to launch his campaign for reform.

Over the next few years, Gauntlett became the driving force behind a radical reform of English organ design. By stipulating C-compasses for manuals and pedals, developing independent pedal organs, extending the manual choruses to include additional mixtures, mutations and subunison registers, expanding the expressive powers of the instrument by creating full-compass Swell divisions, and introducing a wide selection of novel flutes, strings, and reeds (gemshorns, wald flutes, oboe flutes, suabe flutes, viol di gambas, salcionals, cone gambas, the Krumhorn and the Swiss Cromorne-flute among them) he may be said—in collaboration with William Hill, the organ builder—to have invented the Victorian organ. To this new model Gauntlett gave the title "The Anglo-Lutheran or Protestant Organ."[42]

All the evidence points to 1837 being the date of Gauntlett's "Damascus road" experience. The following year, he began to issue his *Choral and Instrumental Fugues of John Sebastian Bach*, derived, it would seem, from the Marx and Clementi editions, though not slavishly following them, and comprising fifty-four pieces of which approximately half are organ compositions and half organ arrangements.[43] In the same year, he began remodeling the Newgate Street organ, with a ten-stop Pedal, C-compasses, and manual subunisons (Appendix 1).[44] By the time Mendelssohn returned to London in 1840, Gauntlett had a completely new organ to show him, which epitomized the new style. This was William Hill's instrument at St. Peter's Cornhill; it had two manuals and pedals, thirty-seven stops, and included all the features of Gauntlett's plan (appendix 6.3).[45]

Mendelssohn visited Cornhill with Gauntlett and Elizabeth Mounsey, the church organist, in September 1840. He played his own Prelude and Fugue in C Minor (MWV W21/W18; op. 37, no. 1) and the Fugue in F Minor, and then Bach's Passacaglia in C Minor (BWV 582), and the Prelude and Fugue in E Minor (possibly BWV 548, the "Wedge").[46] Miss Mounsey recalled how she and Gauntlett stood on either side of Mendelssohn at the console, and that he (Gauntlett) manipulated the stops for him. She continued: "I remember how I imagined that M.[endelssohn] & G.[auntlett] must have consulted together beforehand about the stops, as G. seemed to understand and anticipate what M. would like.[47] In a further letter, she wrote: "Whether playing Bach or his own works, there was always such *a depth of expression*. The organ does not easily lend itself to that, therefore it was the more wonderful to hear him . . . he played Bach *slower* than I expected; but instead of rattling off the semiquavers he made them flow impressively and seriously."[48]

It is clear from this and similar comments that Mendelssohn's performances introduced English organists to a novel style of playing, and it is important to note that it was not only his Bach that was enlightening; his use of the organ, including his taste for "varied shades of tone without any striking change," as Mounsey put it, and the "tenderness and expression," that contemporary writers refer to,[49] reflect Mendelssohn's credentials as a Romantic composer. Gauntlett's vast Swell divisions, and his introduction of colorful new voices, served Mendelssohn's purpose well.

Two years later, in 1842, Mendelssohn returned to Cornhill, where he improvised for half an hour after a service on the theme of "God save the Emperor."[50] He also revisited Christ Church, Newgate Street. Unfortunately, there is no record of what was played, though it seems to have been a public occasion because Mendelssohn commented in a letter to his mother that he feared suffocation, "so great was the crowd and pressure round my seat at the organ."[51] Gauntlett was probably present on both occasions, and certainly at Newgate Street because Mendelssohn (reportedly "much fatigued") lunched at his home in Chatham Place afterward.[52]

During his visits to England in 1837, 1840, and 1842, Mendelssohn clearly spent time in Gauntlett's company. His regard for Gauntlett appears to have been genuine, in contrast to some English musicians who resented Gauntlett out of professional jealousy and (understandably) as a reaction to his abrasive personality. Mendelssohn's friendship is a salutary reminder not to take at face value the attacks made on Gauntlett by a handful of his contemporaries. Had Mendelssohn harbored doubts about his musicianship, he would not have suggested to Coventry the publisher that Gauntlett be asked to check the proofs of the organ sonatas (although, in fact, Vincent Novello undertook the task).[53] When the sonatas appeared in 1846, Gauntlett gave them an ecstatic welcome in a lengthy review in the *Morning Chronicle* in which he described them as the "book of the epoch." Continuing in characteristically extravagant language, he wrote:

> Hitherto religion has had only one organist, Sebastian Bach, the solitary high priest to whom was given that eloquence of song mightier than that of speech. . . . A century has passed, and Mendelssohn—separating himself from his contemporaries, purifying himself by the same loneliness and solitary communion with the parent of all that is good and beautiful—raises the veil. . . . There are now two organ composers—the present epoch has evolved a second in Felix Mendelssohn.[54]

There was much more, in the same vein.

Piecing the evidence together, Gauntlett emerges as one who, more than any of his contemporaries, saw how Mendelssohn's knowledge of Bach and personal celebrity as a performer and pedagogue could be exploited in the cause of reforming English organ design and transforming the culture of the English organist. Crucially, Gauntlett had both the force of personality and the opportunity through his musical journalism to promote the cause during the years between 1837 and 1846. By the time he resigned the organistship at Newgate Street in the latter year, and, at the same time, largely withdrew from designing organs, his work was (astonishingly) complete. So it was particularly apt that Mendelssohn should choose him to play the organ part in the Birmingham premiere of *Elijah*, presiding at an instrument that he (Gauntlett) had redesigned with C-compasses and a "German" pedal organ (appendix 6.2), and accompanying a piece whose conception had been significantly influenced by Bach (the German cantor) and Handel (the naturalized Englishman).

Gauntlett died in 1876. He never got his statue—in Victorian England, it was chiefly generals, admirals, the Queen, and the Prince Consort who got statues—but his legacy, in the form of an organ culture powerfully influenced by his acquaintance with Mendelssohn during those crucial few years, long outlived him and still affects the design of the English organ today.

Appendix 6.1

Christ Church, Newgate Street, City of London

Redesigned by Dr. H. J. Gauntlett
Organ built by Renatus Harris in 1690:

1747, Swell Organ added, probably by John Harris
1827 and 1831, reconstruction and enlargement by Elliott & Hill
1834 and 1837, new stops, pedal board, and coupler added by
William Hill under direction of Henry Gauntlett
1838, reconstructed with C compasses and addition of "German" Pedal
Organ (incomplete) by Hill, advised by Gauntlett

1837		1838	
Great Organ (GG–f³, 58 notes)		Great Organ (C–f³)	
Open Diapason	8	Double Open Diapason	16
Open Diapason	8	Open Diapason	8
Open Diapason (G)	8	Open Diapason	8
Stopped Diapason	8	Stopped Diapason	8
Principal	4	Principal	4
Twelfth	2⅔	Twelfth	2⅔
Fifteenth	2	Fifteenth	2

(continued)

1837		1838	
Great Organ (GG–f^3, 58 notes)		Great Organ (C–f^3)	
Tierce	1^3/$_5$	Sesquialtra	V
Sesquialtra & Cornet	IV	Mixture	V
Posaune	8	Posaune	8
Trumpet	8	Trumpet	8
Clarion	4	Clarion	4
Choir Organ (GG–f^3, 58 notes)		Choir Organ (C–f^3)	
Open Diapason	8	Open Diapason	8
Stopped Diapason	8	Stopped Diapason	8
Principal	4	Principal	4
Flute	4	Stopped Flute	4
Fifteenth	2	Fifteenth	2
Cremona & Bassoon	8		
Swell Organ (G–f^3, with keys to C coupled to Choir)		Swell Organ (C–f^3)	
Double Dulciana	16	Double Diapason	16
Open Diapason	8	Open Diapason	8
Stopped Diapason	8	Stopped Diapason	8
Principal	4	Principal	4
Celestina	4	Flageolet	4
Fifteenth	2	Fifteenth	2
Cornet	V	Sesquialtra	V
French Horn	8	Horn	8
Trumpet	8	Trumpet	8
Oboe	8	Hautboy	8
Clarion	4	Clarion	4

1837	1838	
Pedal Organ (C–g^1)	Pedal Organ (C–g^1)	
Pedal Pipes (32'), G–c^1, 18 notes	Open Diapason (wood)	16
	Open Diapason (wood)	16
	Open Diapason (metal)	16
	Principal	8
	Twelfth	5⅓
	Fifteenth	4
	Sesquialtra	V
	Mixture	V
	Posaune	16
	Clarion	8
Couplers	Couplers	
Great to Pedal	8 couplers (unspecified)	
Choir to Pedal		
"Canto-firmo-copula" [i.e., Swell octave to Pedal]		
Accessories	Accessories	
3 composition pedals to Great	Shifting movement to Swell	
2 composition pedals to Swell		

Sources: Musical World 8 (1838): 279–81; E. J. Hopkins and E. F. Rimbault, *The Organ* (London, 1855), 1:449–50; *Musical Opinion* 20 (1897): 832.

Appendix 6.2

Birmingham Town Hall

Redesigned by Dr. H. J. Gauntlett
Organ built by William Hill in 1834, with 16' manual compasses and three-stop
Pedal Organ:

> 1837, Hill moved the organ into a new recess at the top of the orchestra
> 1840, Grand Ophicleide added (the first high-pressure reed)
> 1842–45, the organ was reconstructed by Hill in accordance with a scheme
> devised by Gauntlett

1834		1845	
Great Organ (CC–f^3)		Great Organ (C–f^3)	
Double Open Diapason (c)	16	Double Open Diapason	16
Open Diapason	8	Open Diapason	8
Open Diapason	8	Open Diapason	8
Open Diapason (wood)	8	Open Diapason	8
Stopped Diapason (wood)	8	Stopped Diapason	8
Dulciana	8	Quint	5⅓
Principal	4	Principal	4
Principal	4	Principal	4
Principal (wood)	4	Twelfth	2⅔
Twelfth	2⅔	Fifteenth	2
Fifteenth	2	Doublette (15.22)	II
Fifteenth (wood)	2	Fourniture	V
Sesquialtra	V	Sesquialtra	V
Mixture	III	Mixture	III
Trumpet	8	Double Trumpet	16
Posaune	8	Posaune	8
Clarion	4	Clarion	4
Octave Clarion	2	Octave Clarion	2
		Grand Ophicleide	8

1834		1845	
Swell Organ (C–f³ + Choir bass)		Swell Organ (C–f³)	
Double Diapason	16	Double Diapason	16
Open Diapason	8	Open Diapason	8
Stopped Diapason	8	Stopped Diapason	8
Principal	4	Principal	4
Harmonica (wood)	4	Fifteenth	2
Fifteenth	2	Sesquialtra	V
Horn	8	Horn	8
Trumpet	8	Trumpet	8
Oboe	8	Hautboy	8
Clarion	4	Clarion	4
Carillon (bells)			
Choir Organ (CC–f³)		Choir Organ (C–f³)	
Open Diapason	8	Open Diapason	8
Open Diapason (c) (wood)	8	Stopped Diapason	8
Stopped Diapason (wood)	8	Dulciana	8
Dulciana (G)	8	Principal	4
Principal	4	Wald Flute	4
Principal (wood)	4	Oboe Flute	4
Stopped Flute	4	Stopped Flute	4
Fifteenth	2	Fifteenth	2
Cremona & Bassoon (GG)	8	Cornopean	8
Combination Organ		Combination Organ	
The fourth keyboard played a selection of registers from the Choir and Swell Organs by means of mechanical duplication		Little changed from 1834	

(continued)

1834		1845	
Pedal Organ (C–c¹)		Pedal Organ (C–f¹)	
Double Open Diapason (m)	32	Double Open Diapason (m)	32
Double Open Diapason (w)	32	Double Open Diapason (w)	32
Trumpet (wood)	16	Open Diapason (m)	16
		Open Diapason (m)	16
		Open Diapason (w)	16
		Bourdon	16
		Principal	8
		Principal	8
		Twelfth	5⅓
		Fifteenth	4
		Sesquialtra	V
		Mixture	V
		Contra Trumpet	32
		Posaune	16
		Clarion	8
		Octave Clarion	4
4 couplers		5 (?) couplers	
Keyboard to play Pedal stops		1 ventil	
9 composition pedals			

Sources: See Nicholas Thistlethwaite, *Birmingham Town Hall Organ* (Birmingham City Council, 1984), 16; Thistlethwaite, *The Making of the Victorian Organ* (Cambridge: Cambridge University Press, 1990), 128–29.

Appendix 6.3

St. Peter-upon-Cornhill, City of London

Designed by Dr. H. J. Gauntlett

New organ in an old case built by William Hill, 1840; tonal scheme by Henry Gauntlett

Grand Organ (C–f³, 54 notes)		Swell Organ (C–f³, 54 notes)	
Bourdon and Tenoroon		Bourdon and Tenoroon	
Diapason	16	Dulciana	16
Principal Diapason	8	Principal Diapason	8
Stopped Diapason	8	Stopped Diapason	8
Claribel-flute	8	Dulciana	8
Dulciana	8	Principal	4
Principal	4	Suabe-flute	4
Oboe-flute	4	Flageolet	4
Wald-flute	4	Twelfth	2⅔
Stopped-flute	4	Fifteenth	2
Twelfth	2⅔	Piccolo	2
Fifteenth	2	Sesquialtera	III
Tierce	1⅗	Mixture	II
Sesquialtera	II	Echo Dulciana Cornet	V
Mixture	II	Cornopean	8
Doublette	II	Tromba	8
Corno-trombone	8	Oboe	8
Cromorne	8	Clarion	4
Corno-clarion	4		

(continued)

		Couplers
Pedal Organ (C–d¹)		Swell to Grand
Grand Diapason	16*	Grand to Pedal
Grand Trombone	16*	Swell to Pedal
* The pedal stops had only 15 notes each (C–d); they repeated in the top octave by means of an octave coupler.		4 composition pedals

Source: William Hill, *Circular* (1841).

Notes

1   Felix Mendelssohn Bartholdy to Paul Mendelssohn Bartholdy, August 26, 1846; quoted in J. Sutcliffe Smith, *The Story of Music in Birmingham* (Birmingham: Cornish Bros., 1945), 33.

2   H. C. G. Matthew and Brian Harrison, eds., *Oxford Dictionary of National Biography* (Oxford: Oxford University Press, 2004), 24:150–51.

3   *Morning Chronicle*, August 27, 1846, 5.

4   Ibid.

5   It may have originated at the Handel Commemoration in Westminster Abbey in 1784, although in that instance the "orchestra" (vocalists and instrumentalists) was directed from the organ keyboard; there was no independent conductor.

6   Elise Polko, *Reminiscences of Felix Mendelssohn Bartholdy: A Social and Artistic Biography*, trans. Lady Wallace (New York: Leypoldt and Holt, 1869), 235.

7   *Musical Opinion* 13 (1890): 470.

8   Leslie Stephen and Sidney Lee, eds., *The Dictionary of National Biography* (London: Smith, Elder, 1890), 21:75.

9   *Times*, August 24, 1846.

10   *Athenaeum*, no. 2522 (February 26, 1876), 306.

11   British Library: Puttick and Simpson sale catalogues (December 17, 1847, to February 25, 1848).

12   A. Hyatt King, *Some British Collectors of Music c1600–1960* (Cambridge: Cambridge University Press, 1963), 46.

13   Facsimile in the collection of the late J. H. Gauntlett, communicated to the author.

14   Matthew and Harrison, *Oxford Dictionary of National Biography*, 54:533.

15   Ibid., 44:275.

16   *Musical Standard* 10 (1876): 134.

17   The Mendelssohns' "honeymoon" diary of 1837 records visiting St. John's, Paddington with the Horsleys and Karl Klingemann on September 8, where "I played fugues by Bach and others on the organ for an hour"; see Peter Ward Jones, ed., *The Mendelssohns on Honeymoon* (Oxford: Clarendon Press, 1997), 97. The organ was built by J. C. Bishop in 1831, and had GG key compasses with an eighteen-note

pedal board commencing at GG. It may be this organ, rather than "St. Matthew's" (not identified) to which Gauntlett referred.

18 "Dr. Gauntlett: His Centenary," in *Musical Times* 46 (1905): 455–56. Samuel Sebastian Wesley (1810–76) was organist successively of a number of English cathedrals and the most significant composer of Anglican church music of his generation. James Turle (1802–82) was Organist of Westminster Abbey, and John Goss (1800–80) of St. Paul's Cathedral.

19 *Musical World* 7 (1837): 42.

20 Stanley Sadie, ed., *New Grove Dictionary of Music and Musicians* (London: Macmillan, 2001), 9:579.

21 *Musical Standard* 10 (1876): 134.

22 *Musical World* 5 (1837): 161.

23 Ibid., 162.

24 Biographical details taken from *Musical Standard* 10 (1876): 134; *Athenaeum*, no. 2522 (February 26, 1876), 305–6; Stephen and Lee, *Dictionary of National Biography*, 21:74–76; "Dr. Gauntlett: His Centenary"; Sadie, *New Grove Dictionary of Music and Musicians*, 9:578–79.

25 See Philip Olleson, "Samuel Wesley and the English Bach Awakening," in *The English Bach Awakening*, ed. Michael Kassler (Aldershot: Ashgate, 2004), 251–313.

26 It had been played previously in a piano arrangement in 1816; see Nicholas Thistlethwaite, *The Making of the Victorian Organ* (Cambridge: Cambridge University Press, 1990), 173.

27 Ibid.

28 Ibid., 98.

29 *Musical World* 8 (1838): 101–2.

30 *Musical Times* 37 (1896): 724.

31 *Musical World* 7 (1837): 8–9.

32 Ibid., 9–10. Gauntlett in his article states that the Newgate Street meeting was on the Tuesday following the debacle at St. Paul's. Mendelssohn in the "honeymoon" diary gives the day as Monday, but Samuel Wesley's most recent biographer supports Gauntlett. See Ward Jones, *Mendelssohns on Honeymoon*, 103; Philip Olleson, *Samuel Wesley, the Man and His Music* (Woodbridge: Boydell Press, 2003), 214.

33 Ward Jones, *Mendelssohns on Honeymoon*, 115.

34 *Musical World* 1 (1836): 46.

35 Ibid., 21–26.

36 Ibid., 181.

37 Ibid., 184.

38 *Musical World* 5 (1837): 146.

39 *Musical World* 8 (1838): 101.

40 Stephen and Lee, *Dictionary of National Biography*, 21:74.

41 Ibid.

42 For a more extended treatment of Gauntlett's contribution to the reform of English organ design, see Thistlethwaite, *Making of the Victorian Organ*, 185–95.

43 Henry John Gauntlett, ed. *Choral and Instrumental Fugues of John Sebastian Bach in continuation of the English edition of his forty-eight preludes and fugues arranged from his masses litanies oratorios and exercises and inscribed to George Gwilt Esq. F.S.A., F.R.A.S.* (London: C. Lonsdale, [1837–38]).

44 For the revised stop list, see Thistlethwaite, *Making of the Victorian Organ*, 463–64.

45 Ibid., 215–22.

46   Russell Stinson, *The Reception of Bach's Organ Works from Mendelssohn to Brahms* (Oxford: Oxford University Press, 2006), 61.

47   Elizabeth Mounsey to F. G. Edwards, February 20–21, 1892; British Library Add Ms 41,572, fols. 10–11v (Edwards Papers, vol. 2).

48   Elizabeth Mounsey to F. G. Edwards, December 3, 1894 (emphasis in the original); ibid., fol. 85.

49   *Musical World* 7 (1837): 10.

50   *Morning Post*, June 20, 1842. Mounsey later recalled that Mendelssohn had also played his Prelude and Fugue in G Major at Cornhill that year, though it is not clear whether it was on the same occasion; see Elizabeth Mounsey to F. G. Edwards, December 3, 1894; British Library Add Ms 41,572, fol. 85 (Edwards Papers, vol. 2).

51   Paul Mendelssohn Bartholdy and Carl Mendelssohn Bartholdy, eds., *Letters of Felix Mendelssohn Bartholdy*, trans. Lady Wallace (London, 1862), 281.

52   Letter of John Boyer to Dr. Gauntlett, November 27, 1874; communicated by the late J. H. Gauntlett.

53   F. G. Edwards, "Mendelssohn's Organ Sonatas," in *Proceedings of the Musical Association*, twenty-first session (1894–95), 3.

54   *Morning Chronicle*, March 12, 1846, 6.

Chapter Seven

Mendelssohn's Sonatas, Op. 65, and the Craighead-Saunders Organ at the Eastman School of Music

Aspects of Performance Practice and Context

Hans Davidsson

Mendelssohn, Bach, and Eighteenth-Century German Organ Culture

Felix Mendelssohn was brought up in a home in which the classical-humanistic education was the ideal and the music of Johann Sebastian Bach (1685–1750) and his circle, the essence. Mendelssohn's mother, Lea Salomon, a student of Johann Philipp Kirnberger (1721–83), took care of the musical education of her children, and made sure that the *Well-Tempered Clavier* (hereafter *WTC*) was studied and played continuously.[1] When Felix, at age eleven, started studying the organ with August Wilhelm Bach (1796–1869), one of the most influential organists in Germany and the leading organ authority in Berlin during the first decades of the nineteenth century, he already knew most of the Preludes and Fugues of the *WTC*. Under the tutelage of A. W. Bach (not related to Johann Sebastian), he tried them out on the organ, and started building his repertoire, primarily focusing on organ works by J. S. Bach. Felix studied the piano with Ludwig Berger (1777–1839), one of the greatest piano virtuosos in Germany of his time, and composition (counterpoint, canon, fugue, etc.) with Carl Friedrich Zelter (1758–1832), the ultimate musical authority of the city.

Zelter was the director of the Berlin Sing-Akademie, and in this capacity initiated and led performances of many of Bach's major choral works. The entire Mendelssohn family, including Felix, his parents, and his sister Fanny, was enrolled in the Sing-Akademie. His great aunt, Sara Levy, had been a student of Wilhelm Friedemann Bach (1710–84), and was now one of Berlin's leading musicians and musical patrons.[2] She possessed many autographs and copies of J. S. Bach's music, and gave Felix a copy of the *St. Matthew Passion* in 1823.

In the late eighteenth and early nineteenth centuries, Berlin was the center for the cultivation of the musical heritage of Johann Sebastian Bach. It was exceptionally well equipped with high-quality eighteenth-century organs. Arp Schnitger and his son, Franz Caspar, were represented with three instruments, and Joachim Wagner, whose instruments Bach had praised, with seven organs, among them three of the largest in the country: the organs in St. Nikolai and St. Marien as well as in the Garnisonskirche in nearby Potsdam. Beginning in 1820, Mendelssohn received his organ lessons at Wagner's most famous instrument, the three-manual organ in the Marien-Kirche. He soon developed his organ technique, performing abilities, and improvisation skills, which led Zelter to take him on a journey in 1821, to present him to cultural icons such as Goethe and the organist Johann Rinck, who later stated: "The boy has gotten a good start in playing the organ; it will be instructive and an honor for him to find the sources from which the good and the proper emanate in our time."[3]

Felix continued to study and play the organ throughout his life; he wanted to further develop his pedal technique, particularly with the aim of mastering the grand masterpieces of J. S. Bach. His knowledge of organ construction enabled him to correct simple problems like ciphers. He engaged in discussions on windchest layouts and pedal-board designs, and his interest in different organ-building styles took him to churches and organs on his grand tour 1830–32, and all of his later journeys. During his honeymoon, for example, he explored organs built by Andreas Silbermann in Alsace, and took his new wife, Cécile, on an organ crawl inside the Silbermann organ in Münster; it was "my first visit inside an organ," she wrote in a letter to a friend.[4] Although mainly active as a composer, conductor, pianist, and director of musical institutions, Mendelssohn was widely considered the greatest organ virtuoso of his time. The organist in the Trinity Church in Berlin, Johann Friedrich Kühnau (1780–1848) held him in special regard: "If I had to compare him with those living among us, I do not know anybody who is his peer."[5] He received similar praise from composer and theorist Johann Christian Lobe (1797–1881): "His organ playing was comparable to his piano performances. One had the feeling that one was hearing a master from previous centuries, who, having occupied himself throughout his life with contrapuntal combinations, effused in improvisations that other and more recent composers were able to calculate on paper only with great effort."[6] In England, where Mendelssohn played all but two of his public organ recitals, Georg Grove stated: "He was the greatest of the few German organ players, who visited the country and the English organists learned more than one lesson from him."[7]

In his repertoire, Mendelssohn had at least twelve of the free organ works by Bach, and probably knew most of the chorale-based works.[8] A collector of Bach autographs and copies, he felt obliged to share Bach's music with the world. The Mendelssohn family's collection of Bach manuscripts contained many organ works. Although a number of them already were available in various editions (chorale-based works published by Breitkopf und Härtel in Leipzig, 1815; free works by Riedl in Vienna, 1817), Mendelssohn saw a need for more correct and expanded editions. In collaboration with his childhood friend Adolph Bernhard Marx, he prepared an edition of eight of the large free works (*Bach's noch wenig bekannte Orgelkompositionen*, Breitkopf und Härtel, 1833). He was the first to edit and publish the *Orgelbüchlein*, the Leipzig Chorales (actually only fourteen of them plus "Wir glauben all an einen Gott," BWV 740), two of the chorale partitas (*44 Short Preludes, 15 Grand Preludes*, and *2 Chorales with Variations*; Coventry and Hollier; Breitkopf und Härtel, 1845/46), and the Schübler Chorales (Coventry and Hollier, 1847).[9] He was a strong proponent of the publication of the source material in unaltered form, and eagerly compared his sources with copies collected by others. By critical editing, he strove to get closer to the authentic version of the compositions, and in this respect he was a pioneer in the development of editions based on musicological and philological research. He wanted editions that *presented* the compositions rather than *interpreted* them. Nevertheless, he always maintained the musician's perspective in the editorial work; in the preface to the *15 Grand Preludes*, he gives rather detailed information regarding registration matters:

The Present 15 Grand Preludes on Corales . . . are published from several old written copies, nearly concordant amongst themselves, and without any modern addition to Time, Selection of Stops, or similar matter.

With regard to the Selection of Stops, it might not be superfluous to remark in general that, for the present compositions, the superscription "Full Organ" does not always mean all the real stops of an Organ: furthermore, that whenever the superscription says "for two rows of Keys and Pedal," only soft Stops ought to be used.

In the Prelude No. 6 on the Coral "O Lamb of God," it appears necessary to change the Stops at the beginning of each new Verse, so that the third Verse is played with the greatest number of Stops (perhaps towards the end with full Organ). In No. 2 also, "Come Holy Ghost," I would recommend here and there to change the Stops after the termination of the different periods of the Cantus firmus, or gradually to increase the power of the Organ to the end. In No. 3 "On the rivers of Babylon," most probably only 8 foot pedal is meant, without any 16 foot Stops. It need hardly be mentioned that for the Prelude No. 8, as well as for the one No. 14, no 16 foot Stop whatever must be used in the Pedal.[10]

The registration recommendations in these "Preliminary Remarks" reflect Mendelssohn's familiarity with German eighteenth-century registration practice, in which "full organ" (*organo pleno*) referred to a variety of registrations, based on full Principal chorus ([16'], 8', 4', 2') with the possible addition of mutations, mixtures, or reeds. He also seems familiar with the general preference for chamber-music-like registrations in chorale works ("auf 2 Clavier") and chorale variations, such as those we find in Georg Friedrich Kauffmann's (1679–1735) "Harmonische Seelenlust" (1733–40).

His remarks concerning "Full organ" may indicate a tendency in his time to nonselectively use loud registrations with insufficient regard to the music, its style and texture. His suggestion of registration changes between the stanzas of "O Lamb of God" is congruent with the general notion that musical texture and sound are interrelated. Similarly, a proposed crescendo toward the end of the Third Stanza points toward the eighteenth-century idea that the *Affekt* of a piece, in this case a text-tone relationship, should influence the choice of registration. His concern for clarity and voice leading is evident in his instructions "to not use a 16 foot" in the bass of "Wir glauben all an einen Gott" (BWV 740), and "Von Gott will ich nicht lassen" (BWV 658, cantus firmus in the pedal; according to instruction in the original print from 1747/48, it should be played with a 4-foot stop) and his preference to use only an 8-foot stop in "An Wasserflüssen Babylon" (BWV 653, double pedal). The idea of making registration changes to the cantus firmus between phrases, or the suggestion to make a crescendo toward the end of the long setting on "Come, Holy Ghost," seem more orchestral and modern.

Johann Schneider (1789–1864), organist in Leipzig, and from 1825 in Dresden, at the Silbermann organ in the Hofkirche, was considered by many, including Mendelssohn, to be the greatest organ virtuoso in Germany. He gave concert tours in many European countries, and as far away as England, mainly presenting organ works by Bach. In his Leipzig years, Mendelssohn recommended that his conservatory students study with Schneider: "Go to Schneider, with him you can learn something first-rate."[11]

On August 6, 1840, Mendelssohn performed his famous Bach concert in Leipzig, as a fundraising event for the Bach Monument, to be placed in the vicinity of the Thomas School. Already a well-known organ virtuoso, particularly in England (Birmingham and London), who had given several recitals performing major Bach works, it was this event that officially established Mendelssohn as one of the foremost proponents of Bach's organ music in his native Germany. Taking into consideration his immersion from early childhood into the musical language and culture of Johann Sebastian; his exposure to many of Bach's keyboard, vocal, and instrumental works, first as a singer and later as a conductor; the direct link to Wilhelm Friedemann (through his great-aunt) and to Kirnberger (through his mother and Zelter); his passion and knowledge of eighteenth-century organ aesthetics and construction;

and his lifelong activity as a Bach organist and editor—an image emerges of Mendelssohn as *the* most significant Bach successor in the first half of the nineteenth century.

Mendelssohn further developed Bach's musical language, adjusting it to the context of his own time. His style of organ playing and improvisation was widely admired; his Preludes and Fugues of 1837 were a success, and it was therefore no surprise that the London publisher Charles Coventry inquired in 1844 whether Mendelssohn would like to compose three voluntaries. His enthusiasm for the commission resulted in a work much larger in scope than had been asked for. Mendelssohn initially described the collection to Mr. Coventry as a School of Organ Playing consisting of Six Sonatas, abandoning the title of Voluntaries altogether.

In the Six Sonatas for Organ (MWV W56–61, op. 65), Mendelssohn combines counterpoint with various compositional techniques in traditional forms (prelude, fugue, trio, toccata), as well as new ones (march, "overture," lyrical movements, "songs without words"), generating comprehensive cyclical forms, filled with emotional potential and content. This new development of musical language and style was immediately recognized by two of Mendelssohn's most distinguished contemporaries. The Magdeburg organ virtuoso August Gottfried Ritter (1811–85) writes in a review: "Some of the sonatas, especially those that are furthest removed from the traditional form, appear as deeply conceived and deeply felt master pieces. . . . Thus we conclude our report on a work that is new and characteristic in many respects: it harbors a great richness of the marvelous and the beautiful and will definitely not be without important consequences for our organ literature, especially that devoted to traditional forms rather than the old spirit."[12] Robert Schumann (1810–56) commends Mendelssohn in a letter dated October 22, 1845: "Finally, I have delved into your organ sonatas. . . . And recognized everywhere the striving forward— that's why you will always be a model for me. These truly poetic forms, as they manifest themselves in every sonata in perfect fashion—especially Nos. 5 and 6 have impressed me as significant."[13]

These observations seem quite far removed from the general perception of Mendelssohn's organ sonatas in our time: namely, that they are quasi-Baroque or Classical in style, inconsistently shaped, with loosely connected movements at best, and with a few pre-Romantic character pieces inserted into them that are stylistically incompatible with the other sections. Accordingly, the six sonatas have mostly been performed on neo-Baroque or eclectic instruments, or in an orchestral style of registration and interpretation on late-Romantic organs. Mendelssohn's sparse instructions about registrations; his seemingly contradictory information regarding slurs, tempo, and metronome markings, have not given much helpful guidance.

It was the premise of the festival organized by the Eastman Rochester Organ Initiative in 2009 that the experience of playing and hearing Mendelssohn's organ works on an instrument built according to late eighteenth-century German aesthetics would bring new perspectives to our understanding of this music. It is the aim of this article to share some observations from this encounter, and to discuss aspects of performance practice in the context of Mendelssohn's Six Sonatas.

A New Research Organ in an Old Tradition: The Craighead-Saunders Organ at Eastman

When the Eastman School of Music at the University of Rochester opened its doors in downtown Rochester, New York, in 1921, its benefactor, George Eastman, made sure that the first class of organ students was met by state-of-the-art facilities and a world-class faculty. In the early twentieth century, Eastman's truly American vision of presenting the pinnacle of the organ art at the institution bearing his name, even allowed that first class to choose whether to study "theater organ" or the "legitimate organ." In order to meet twenty-first-century needs in organ education with an analogous level of energy, vision, and commitment, the school embarked in 2002 on a program called the Eastman Rochester Organ Initiative (EROI). EROI's main goal was to update and expand the school's collection of instruments for the whole range of the organ repertoire, making it a global organ facility. EROI's first major step was to install an antique Italian instrument in the university's Memorial Art Gallery in 2005. It is the largest Italian Baroque organ in North America. The second new instrument, the Craighead-Saunders Organ, was inaugurated in Christ Church Episcopal in October 2008, at EROI's seventh annual organ festival titled "J. S. Bach and the Organ."

The Craighead-Saunders (C-S) Organ is a new two-manual, thirty-three-stop instrument named after David Craighead and Russell Saunders, two venerable organ professors at the Eastman School. It is a scientific reconstruction of an organ from 1776, built by the Königsberg organ builder Adam Gottlob Casparini (1715–88) for the Holy Ghost Church in Vilnius, Lithuania, and represents a Baltic–North European building style from the height of Enlightenment-era Europe. The finished instrument is the result of a six-year interdisciplinary research project between the Eastman School of Music and GOArt (the Göteborg Organ Art Center), a research center at the University of Gothenburg, Sweden, focusing on the organ and its related keyboard instruments. A basic idea shaping GOArt's research environment is to study the organ, not just as a musical instrument but also as a visual object, cultural artifact, and technological construction, and to communicate its research results to students, scholars, and builders. In this very project, GOArt worked in collaboration with a reference group consisting of leading American organ builders as well as key members of Eastman's faculty. The group made decisions by consensus through the entire design and building process.[14]

Thanks to the vigilance of the Lithuanian organ builder and expert Rimantas Guças, over many years, under extremely difficult conditions, no invasive restoration was ever carried out, and the Casparini organ is today one of the best-preserved late Baroque organs in Northern Europe. By studying a signature hidden on the organ case, Guças was able to establish which of the members of the Casparini family built the organ. The Casparini family was active in Europe for most of the seventeenth and eighteenth centuries, with Adam Gottlob as a third-generation organ builder. He apprenticed with his father, and after working under other well-known masters, such as Heinrich Gottfried Trost (1681–1759), he inherited his uncle's organ-building privileges in Königsberg. He built at least forty-four organs, many of them in the churches of Königsberg and its surroundings, but also several in Lithuania. The only intact, full-sized instrument of the Casparini family is Adam Gottlob's organ in the Holy Ghost Church (or Dominican Church) in Vilnius.

The aesthetics of the new instrument in Christ Church gives us the opportunity to interact with an artifact of a kind that has not been experienced anywhere since the end of the eighteenth century. The instrument's soundscape is created by more than 1,800 carefully reconstructed pipes, voiced by Munetaka Yokota, who based his work on strict principles that follow the documentation of the original instrument's design. Its case is like a Baroque theater set; painted in egg tempera and gilded and hand-burnished by German experts led by Monika May. Tuned in an eighteenth-century organ temperament at choir pitch (A = 465), the colorful instrument, on its generously proportioned new timber-frame balcony, provides a unique opportunity to explore eighteenth-century vocal and ensemble music with a large organ as the main continuo instrument, and makes it possible to explore traditional continuo registration practice in this repertoire for the first time in a century. Finally, the new organ brings fresh perspectives on the performance practice of nineteenth-century German organ music, particularly that of Felix Mendelssohn Bartholdy (for specifications, see table 7.1).

Mendelssohn and the Craighead-Saunders Organ

Whereas Königsberg and its surroundings were equipped with Casparini organs, Berlin was supplied primarily with Wagner instruments. In Brandenburg in 1828, Mendelssohn observes: "There are three good organs here built by Wagner, who also constructed our best organs in St. Marien, the Garnisonskirche, and the Parochialkirche (St. Gotthardt)."[15] It is clear that he not only knew but also admired all the Wagner organs in Berlin. He had lessons at the Wagner organ in Marien-Kirche, rebuilt according to Vogler's "Simplification System" by Johann Friedrich Falckenhagen in 1801,[16] and probably referred to this instrument in a letter to Fanny discussing registrations

Table 7.1. The Craighead-Saunders Organ in Christ Church, Rochester New York, 2008. 32/II+P by GOArt, Mats Arvidsson, Munetaka Yokota, reference group: Steve Dieck, Paul Fritts, George Taylor, Martin Pasi, Bruce Fowkes (organ builders), Joel Speerstra, Paul Peeters, Kerala J. Snyder and Eastman organ faculty.

CLAVIATURA PRIMA. (C–d3**)

1. BOURDUN. á 16.	(wood)
2. PRINCIPAL. á 8.	(70% Sn, mostly in front)
3. HOHLFLAUT. á 8.	(C-h wood, c1- metal)
4. QVINTATHON. á 8.	(metal)
5. Octava Principal. á 4.	(metal)
6. Flaut Travers. á 4.	(metal, Koppelflöte form)
7. Super Octava. á 2.	(metal)
8. Flasch Flot. á 2.	(C-h1 stopped, c2-* open cylindrical)
9. Qvinta. á 5.	(metal, Principal scale)
10. Tertia. á 1 3/5	(metal, Principal scale)
11. Mixtura. á 5. Choris.	(incl. Terz)
12. Trompet. á 8.	(block/boot wood, C–c shallot covered, resonator metal)

Claviatura Secunda. (C–d3**)

13. PRINCIPAL. á 4.	(70% Sn, in front)
14. I U L A. á 8.	(wood, open, narrow scale)
15. Principal Amalel. á 8.	(metal, narrow scale, partly in front)
16. Unda Maris. á 8.	(c1- metal, open conical, C-h borrowed from Flaut Major)
17. Flaut Major. á 8.	(wood, stopped)
18. Flaut Minor. á 4.	(wood, stopped)
19. Spiel Flet. á 4.	(metal open conical)
20. Octava. á 2.	(metal)
21. Wald Flot. á 2.	(metal, open conical)
22. Mixtura. á 4. Choris.	(same composition as Man I without Tertia)
23. Vox Humana. á 8.	(70% Sn, same shallot as Man I Trompete, resonator* short cylindrical with flap)
24. Dulcian. á 16.**	(metal, resonator double-cone form with flap)

P E D A L. (C–d1**)

25. Principal Bass. á 16.	(70% Sn, in front)
26. Violon Bass. á 16.	(wood, open, narrow scale)
27. Full Bass. á 12.	(wood, stopped)
28. Octava Bass. á 8.	(partly in front 70% Sn, partly inside wood)
29. Flaut & Quint Bass. á 8.	(wood, stopped, 2 ranks, 8' + 6')
30. Super Octava Bass. á 4.*	(metal)
31. Posaun Bass. á 16.	(resonator wood)
32. Trompet Bass. á 8.	(resonator metal)

Ventil ad Claviaturam Primam.

Ventil ad Claviaturam Secundum.

Ventil Pedall.

Tremulant

Schwebung (Kanal Tremulant)

Bebny (Drum)

Vox Campanorum (Glockenspiel, g-)

Gwiazdy (Cymbelstern)

Dzwonek na kalkujacego (Kalkant bell)

Couplers:	II/I (sliding coupler)
	I/P**
6 bellows (manually operated but also works with an electric blower)	
Pitch: a=465 Hz at 21°C	
Temperament: modified Neidhardt "für das Dorf" ("for a village") 1732	
Pipe materials:	
All front pipes	70% Sn
All inside metal pipes	11% Sn
Wooden pipes	pine for large pipes
	oak for small pipes

Note: Spellings and capitalizations follow the original stop labels from the 1776 Casparini Organ in Vilnius, Lithuania
*Reconstructed
**Added as a whole or partially
Original compass Manuals I and II: C–c3; Pedal: C–c1
Dulcian 16 Man. II did not exist in the original. This position was never occupied on the original windchest. There is no information preserved about the type and pitch of the reed stop once planned for this position.

("You know this already from the Berlin organs").[17] Still, he mostly played eighteenth-century organs in unaltered states. Mendelssohn tried out the registrations of his Six Sonatas at the Stumm Organ (1779) in the Katharinen-Kirche in Frankfurt, together with the dedicatee, Dr. Fritz Schlemmer, the uncle of his wife. In the spring of 1845, he chose to premiere the Sonatas on this instrument in a private performance, although he could have played them on the modern organ next door in the Paulskirche, built by Eberhard Friedrich Walker in 1833. In the summer of 1845, he played the Sonatas again at the Johannes-Kirche in Kronberg on a somewhat smaller organ by Stumm (1802, II/Ped). It is clear that the eighteenth-century German instruments by Wagner, Stumm, and also Silbermann were Mendelssohn's main organ references. When we compare the specifications of the Wagner organ in the Brandenburg Cathedral—the only preserved Wagner organ in this city today—and the Stumm Organ of the Katharinen-Kirche in Frankfurt with the Craighead-Saunders Organ in Rochester, we see a striking resemblance (see appendixes 7.1 and 7.2).

All three instruments are richly equipped with foundation stops (16', 8', 4'), particularly 8-foot stops; they have two rather well-balanced manual divisions (Hauptwerk and Oberwerk/Positiv); full flute choruses (8', 4', 2'); few reeds but mutations that include thirds; and full pedal divisions. It is clear that all three instruments were born out of the same culture; a detailed exploration of the sounds of the Craighead-Saunders Organ may serve as an entrance into this world.

Individual Sounds and Basic Registrations of the C-S Organ: Eight-Foot Foundation Stops of Claviatura Prima and Secunda

In the central and south German traditions, the combination of foundation stops of the same pitch was regarded as an essential part of the concept, as is clear from many sources like Silbermann, Adlung, Agricola, Schröter, Kauffmann, Gronau, and so on.[18] Some organ builders installed dividers in the tone channels of the windchests, to reduce interference between neighboring pipes of the same pitch, and designed the wind supply system to provide sufficient and stable wind.

The ensemble of 8-foot flute stops in the C-S organ includes seven registers with the following character of sounds (for a comprehensive list of specifications, see table 7.1):

CLAVIATURA PRIMA:
PRINCIPAL. á 8.—(façade stop, tin-rich) round, rich, rather vocal toward the treble, and rather stringy toward the bass, natural speech

HOHLFLAUT. á 8.—(metal) main flute of the organ, round, clear speech, distinctive overtone in treble

QVINTATHON. á 8.—(metal) sharp, very colorful, overtone-rich (quint), peculiar, distinct speech

Claviatura Secunda:

I U L A. á 8.—(open wood) full, warm sound, slow/gentle speech, "Traverse flute" in treble

Principal Amalel. á 8.—(metal) stringy, elegant, charming, distinct speech (like the attack of a bow on a string)

Unda Maris. á 8.—(metal, Spitzflöte-construction) tuned sharp, somewhat fluty and stringy at the same time, but less speech

Flaut Major. á 8.—(wooden gedackt)—clear, colorful and elegant, fast speech

All the stops are distinct and diversified in volume, timbre, and speech, but they blend very well together, as they are complementary in volume and timbre. The speech is set so that all stops speak differently, from fast to quite slow speech, causing a minimum of interference. In fact, this is the most important element of the sound concept of this style. This feature developed and expanded in the nineteenth century, particularly in the German style of organ building. It is possible to play the Principal stops alone. They are quite charming and rich in tone. However, combinations with other stops also work very well. The Unda Maris should, of course, not be played on its own. The QVINTATHON is so peculiar that it lends itself best to combinations with either the HOHLFLAUT (colorful, charming, and singing); the PRINCIPAL (full, characteristic, somewhat edgy); together with both of them (full, rich, warm, and colorful); or with one of the two 4-foot stops. Similarly, the IULA, Principal, and Flaut Major of the second manual can be combined two and two, or all three together, creating very different characters. The IULA serves as the warm and quiet string stop of the ensemble; together with Principal Amalel, it produces a rich and rather full string character. The Unda Maris can be used with each one of the three other 8-foot stops to a remarkably diversified effect: with the IULA the sound is round and poetic; with the Principal Amalel it is colorful and stringy, more like an Italian *Voce Umana*. It is possible to use the coupler II/I and combine the "flute and string" chorus (3 + 4 + 14 + 17); a principal 8 chorus (2 + 3 + 14 + 15); and several other combinations, in whatever way these work best with a rather slow and chordal texture.

The number of 8-foot stops in each division grew during the nineteenth century, and the sources give guidelines on how to select combinations. Johann Julius Seidel suggests in 1842:

> In case of soft renditions, when perhaps 2 or 3 registers are combined, one must always avoid mixing voices of the same intonation, because there is no blending of either the overly shrill or the overly mellow organ sound. . . . Thus, it is important to combine voices of opposite character, which help one

another in that the shrill register brings out the mellow one, and, vice versa, the mellow mitigates the shrillness of the other.[19]

Hermann Jimmerthal, organist in the Marien-Kirche in Lübeck wrote in 1854:

> When 3 gamba voices are used at the same time (Viola maj. 16′, Viola di G. 8′, and Violino 4′), then these voices need to be supported through Bordun 16′, Hohlflöte 8′, Gedackt 8′ and perhaps through a Spitzflöte 4′. But the latter voice, if the tuning is not agreeable, can be omitted. . . . When using Salicional 8′, it is advisable to add Gedackt 8′ to achieve a better onset and more rounded appearance of the former. It is also possible, if a richer sound is desired, to add Bordun 16′ and Gemshorn 4′, which blend well with Salicional.[20]

Eight-foot stops of different character but similar volume were usually complementary and worked well in combination, and the soft string stops were usually combined with a Gedackt. If the tuning was negatively influenced by the addition of a stop, particularly of a higher pitch, it was better to exclude it and look for another stop to add color.

Sixteen-Foot and Four-Foot Stops of Claviatura Prima and Secunda

There are five 4-foot stops in the manual division: two principals and three flutes of very different character, and they can be described in the following way:

CLAVIATURA PRIMA:
Octava Principal. á 4.—(metal) rather round, somewhat stringy, natural speech (conceived like an 8-foot Principal beginning on tenor C, not so much speech in the tenor as oftentimes with 4-foot)
Flaut Travers. á 4.—(metal) round, clear, and bold, with prompt flute-like speech in the treble, more stringy and somewhat slower in the bass (construction like Koppelflöte)

Claviatura Secunda:
PRINCIPAL. á 4.—(façade, metal)—full, rather round, and instrumental, more stringy in the tenor and bass, characteristic rich speech, more character in the sustained sound
Flaut Minor. á 4.—(wooden gedackt)—clear, colorful, and elegant, fast speech
Spiel Flet. á 4.—(metal)—full Flute sound with overtones, more stringy in the bass, somewhat slower speech, more consonant, more character in the treble

The Flaut Travers. á 4 is not an overblowing stop and does not have the characteristic traverse speech. It is the main 4-foot flute of the organ and works well together with the Octava Principal. The 4-foot flutes of the Claviatura Secunda also work well together, however, the PRINCIPAL. á 4 sounds best alone or in combination with stops at other pitch levels. There is a rich variety of character available in the combinations of 4-foot and 8-foot stops. In general, however, one should avoid using more than one 4-foot stop in combination with an 8-foot stop. Due to their distinct character, they are less compatible with others. Furthermore, tuning issues occur more easily when stops at this pitch level and higher are doubled.

CLAVIATURA PRIMA:
PRINCIPAL. á 8 + Octava Principal. á 4
HOHLFLAUT. á 8 + Octava Principal. á 4
HOHLFLAUT. á 8 + QVINTATHON. á 8 + Octava Principal. á 4
PRINCIPAL. á 8 + HOHLFLAUT. á 8 + QVINTATHON. á 8 + Octava Principal. á 4
HOHLFLAUT. á 8 + Flaut Travers. á 4
QVINTATHON. á 8 + Flaut Travers. á 4
HOHLFLAUT. á 8 + QVINTATHON. á 8 + Flaut Travers. á 4 (like a soft Nasat-combination)

Claviatura Secunda:
Principal Amalel. á 8 + PRINCIPAL. á 4
Principal Amalel. á 8 + Flaut Major. á 8 + PRINCIPAL. á 4
Principal Amalel. á 8 + I U L A. á 8 + PRINCIPAL. á 4
Flaut Major. á 8 + PRINCIPAL. á 4
Flaut Major. á 8 + Flaut Minor. á 4 (elegant and colorful)
Flaut Major. á 8 + Spiel Flet. á 4 (rich)
I U L A. á 8 + Spiel Flet. á 4 (full and colorful)
I U L A. á 8 + Flaut Major. á 8 + Spiel Flet. á 4 (rich and full)

The BOURDUN. á 16. is a gedackt in the treble with a clear, rather full sound and fast speech. The two lowest octaves are voiced in the direction of a quintadena with an almost stringy bass and distinct speech. This makes it extremely flexible and suitable to all kinds of combinations. It blends very well with all the 8 + 4 registrations mentioned above, and it can also be played with the 8-foot stops, respectively, or in combination.

The Foundation Stops (16', 8', 4') of the Pedal

The five foundation stops in the P E D A L. division offer a variety of volume, timbre, and speech and can be described in the following way:

25. Principal Bass. á 16.—stringy, much overtone, gentle, prompt speech
Violon Bass. á 16.—full and round sound, rather slow speech (like IULA)
Octava Bass. á 8.—(open wood, tin front pipes mixed) full, warm Principal sound, rather stringy and gentle speech
Flaut & Quint Bass. á 8.—very gentle sound, prompt speech
Super Octava Bass. á 4.—(metal) wide sound, and gentle character

Principal Bass. á 16 is softer and more elegant than Violon Bass. á 16, and is, due to its richness of overtones, possible to play alone. The Octava Bass. á 8 is the other choice for a soft bass part. It is almost impossible to tell the difference between its metal and wooden pipes, something that Casparini was proud to have accomplished. The Flaut & Quint Bass. á 8 cannot be used on its own. It functions as an enhancement to the 16-foot bass line in various combinations, the softest together with the Principal Bass. á 16 (like a Quintadena 8). The following registrations are possible examples:

PEDAL.
Principal Bass. á 16 alone
Octava Bass. á 8 alone
Principal Bass. á 16 + Flaut & Quint Bass. á 8
Principal Bass. á 16 + Octava Bass. á 8 [+ Super Octava Bass. á 4]
Violon Bass. á 16 + Octava Bass. á 8 [+ Super Octava Bass. á 4]
Violon Bass. á 16 + Principal Bass. á 16 + Octava Bass. á 8 [+ Super Octava Bass. á 4]
All stops together

The Flutes, Mutations, and Solo Reed of the Manual Divisions

We find 2-foot flutes in both manual divisions. Complete flute choruses (8′–4′–2′) are an important feature of both central and south German eighteenth-century organs.[21] The 2-foot flutes can be described in the following way:

CLAVIATURA PRIMA: Flasch Flot. á 2.—(metal, C–b1 Gedackt, c2–d3 Open) open, round flute in the treble, quite fast speech, more narrow in the tenor and bass
Claviatura Secunda: Wald Flot. á 2.—(metal, Spitzflöte)—elegant Flute, rather round and full in the treble, gentle, fast speech

The names of these stops suggest a different construction and design than we find in the C-S organ. Maybe Casparini preferred to have the 2-foot flute of a Spitzflöte type in the Claviatura Secunda so that it could be combined with the Spiel Flet. á 4. In any case, all combinations of these flutes (8′ + 4′ + 2′; 8′ + 2′; or 4′ + 2′) work well, and provide many possibilities for dialogue or echo performances between the manual divisions.

The only short-length resonator reed is in the second manual, a Vox Humana. á 8. It is overtone-rich and colorful with a rather full bass, and changes character surprisingly much when combined with various flutes or principals (with or without tremulant). Some examples:

Vox Humana. á 8 + Flaut Minor. á 4
Vox Humana. á 8 + Spiel Flet. á 4
Vox Humana. á 8 + PRINCIPAL. á 4

Vox Humana. á 8 + Flaut Major. á 8 + Flaut Minor. á 4

Vox Humana. á 8 + Principal Amalel. á 8 + Flaut Major. á 8 + Flaut Minor. á 4, and so on

A multitude of short-length resonator reeds (such as Dulcian, Regal, Trechterregal, Baarpijp, Vox Humana, Krumhorn) provided overtone-rich ensemble and solo registrations in seventeenth- and early eighteenth-century North German organs. In the eighteenth-century Central and South German organs, the variety of overtone registrations could be accomplished through the combination of overtone-rich flute and well-blending principal, quintadena, string and mutation stops.

The Qvinta. á 5 (original labeling) is in fact a Qvinta. á 3. Whether Casparini originally intended a Quint 5 1/3 is unclear. Although of principal scale, it is somewhat more fluty than the other principal stops, particularly in the treble. It has a rather clean speech in the treble, with somewhat more speech in the tenor and bass. The fluty character makes it possible to combine with HOHLFLAUT. á 8 and Flaut Travers. á 4. The Tertia. á 1 3/5 produces a thin and clear sound, however the treble is also somewhat more fluty. It also blends well with any combination of flutes or principals. Accordingly, it is possible to compose either a rather thin cornet or Sesquialtera solo. August Gottfried Ritter states that quint registers could be either open or stopped and were often wider-scaled, particularly when the wind pressure was moderate.[22]

HOHLFLAUT. á 8 + Flaut Travers. á 4 + Qvinta. á 3 + Flasch Flot. á 2 + Tertia. á 1 3/5

or

PRINCIPAL. á 8 + Octava Principal. á 4 + Qvinta. á 3 + Super Octava. á 2 + Tertia. á 1 3/5

Examples of Chamber Music Registrations: Chorale Works, Trios, and So On

While playing various organs, fascinated by their character and beauty, Mendelssohn constantly searched for registrations that would suit the organ works of Bach, which he also could use and explore in his own improvisations and music. In a letter to his family from September 16, 1831, he writes about his experience in St. Peter's Church in Munich:[23]

In addition, I play the organ every day for an hour, but I was unable to practice as I wanted, because the pedal is too short by five high tones so that no Seb. Bach passage will work on it. However, the instrument has beautiful registers for playing the chorales with figures. I am elated by its heavenly flowing sound: Fanny, I have found here the stops with which one must play Seb. Bach's "Schmücke dich, o liebe Seele." It is as if they were made to order for it and it sounds so moving that it thrills me every day anew, whenever I begin to play it. For the moving voices I have an 8 foot Flute and a very soft 4 foot, which continually hover above the chorale. You know this already from Berlin. For the chorale there is a manual with nothing but reed stops, and there I opt for a soft Oboe, a very gentle Clairon 4 foot, and a Viola; thus the chorale is drawn out so quietly and yet penetratingly, like distant voices, singing from the depth of their hearts.[24]

At the C-S organ, this registration can be carried out in the following way:

CLAVIATURA PRIMA: HOHLFLAUT. á 8, Flaut Travers. á 4
Claviatura Secunda: Vox Humana. á 8, Flaut Major. á 8, Flaut Minor. á 4
  (Tremulant)
P E D A L: Principal Bass. á 16 [Octava Bass. á 8]

There are many alternatives for chorale registrations for 2 Clav. e Ped with solos as follows:

(with or without tremulant)
PRINCIPAL. á 8
PRINCIPAL. á 8, HOHLFLAUT. á 8
PRINCIPAL. á 8, QVINTATHON. á 8
PRINCIPAL. á 8, HOHLFLAUT. á 8, QVINTATHON. á 8

PRINCIPAL. á 4 (octave lower)
Principal Amalel. á 8, I U L A. á 8
Principal Amalel. á 8, Flaut Major. á 8
Principal Amalel. á 8, I U L A. á 8, Flaut Major. á 8
Principal Amalel. á 8, Unda Maris. á 8
I U L A. á 8, Unda Maris. á 8

HOHLFLAUT. á 8 + QVINTATHON. á 8 + Flaut Travers. á 4,
Combinations with Qvinta. á 3 and/or Tertia. á 1 3/5 or
Combinations with Vox Humana. á 8 mentioned above
All accompanied by foundation stops (principals and/or flutes) on the opposite keyboard.

In G. F. Kauffmann's "Harmonische Seelenlust" we find original registrations for chorale settings (2–4 parts) for his organ in Merseburg Dom, built by Thayssner 1698, and rebuilt by Wender 1714–16.[25] There are several registrations for Trio playing, in some cases intended for a four-part setting with the cantus firmus played by a solo oboe together with the organ. In the preface, Kauffmann describes the practice of trio registration, playing the soprano part on a Principal 8, the middle part with the left hand on a separate keyboard on a Principal 4 an octave lower, and the bass in the pedal. There are several registration combinations with the principals on the C-S organ, for example:

Clav. 1: PRINCIPAL. á 8 (RH)
Clav. 2: PRINCIPAL. á 4 (LH)
Pedal: Principal Bass. á 16, Octava Bass. á 8

Clav. 2: Principal Amalel. á 8 (RH)
Clav. 1: Octava Principal. á 4 (LH)
Pedal: Principal Bass. á 16, Octava Bass. á 8

The naming of Octava Principal. á 4 (not merely "Octava") may be explained by this practice of playing an octave lower, like an 8-foot Principal beginning on tenor C. It does not have as much speech in the tenor octave as a 4-foot stop often does.

Trios can also be played with the flutes or with the Vox Humana:

Clav. 1: HOHLFLAUT. á 8, Flaut Travers. á 4
Clav. 2: Flaut Major. á 8, Flaut Minor. á 4
Pedal: Principal Bass. á 16
or
Clav. 2: Vox Humana. á 8, Flaut Major. á 8, Flaut Minor. á 4 (RH)
Clav. 1: PRINCIPAL. á 8, HOHLFLAUT. á 8, QVINTATHON. á 8 (LH)
Pedal: Principal Bass. á 16, Octava Bass. á 8

It is reasonable to assume that Mendelssohn was familiar with all these standard chamber music registrations of the eighteenth-century German organ and explored them even beyond standard use when he searched among the "beautiful registers for playing the chorales with figures."

The Full Organ Registrations (Forte to Fortissimo)

The remaining stops that were part of the *organo pleno* are the principal stops above 4-foot pitch, including the mutations and the mixtures, and the full-length resonator reeds. *Organo pleno* did not necessarily include "all the stops" in the German tradition; the full organ could comprise the full Principal chorus ([16'], 8', 4', 2') alone or with the addition of mutations, mixtures and reeds in different combinations. With the exception of the somewhat fluty mutations (Qvinta. á 3 and Tertia. á 1 3/5) in solo registrations, these stops were not designed to be combined with individual foundation stops (principals, flutes, and strings) in chamber music registrations. They belonged to the *organo pleno* combinations.

The 2-foot Principals are somewhat different from each other and correspond to the general character of the Principals 8 and 4 in their respective divisions. Accordingly, the principal choirs (8' + 4' + 2') are distinctly different in character—"rich and round" (Clav. I) and "sharp and brilliant" (Clav. II). The 2-foot stops can be described as follows:

Clav. I: Super Octava. á 2.—(metal) open, clear and fluty toward the treble, fast and elegant speech (hiss), more speech and principal sound in tenor and bass
Clav. II: Octava. á 2. (metal)—open and clear toward the treble, distinct speech (hiss)

The two mixtures have the same design. They have clearly noticeable octave breaks (between b and c). The mixture in the first manual includes a tierce, whereas the mixture in the second manual is composed exclusively of octave and quint ranks. The following description and schemes of composition show the nature of the mixtures:

CLAVIATURA PRIMA: Mixtura. á 5. Choris. (metal)—rich and colorful with distinct speech ("hiss"), principal character also in the treble, tierce mixture, the low tierce (3 1/5′) from c2 calls for 16-foot bass

C	1′	4/5′	2/3′	1/2′	
c	1′	4/5′	2/3′	1/2′	1/2′
c1	2′	1-3/5′	1-1/3′	1′	1′
c2	4′	3-1/5′	2-2/3′	2′	2′

The tierce (3 1/5′) in the top octave of the Mixture in Clav. I calls for the addition of the BOURDUN. á 16. It is thus not possible to play a plenum with the Mixture of Clav. I without pulling the 16-foot stop. As this was quite common in the Central German tradition, it shows an aesthetical preference for gravity and seriousness, and reflects the main function of the full organ, namely, to accompany congregational song. In 1843, the organist in Münster, Benedikt Jucker, argued for the addition of a 16-foot stop in the Silbermann-Brosy organ: "Any grand composition rendered in a church without a 16-foot foundation stop becomes a caricature; without such a register, the accompaniment of congregational singing sounds dry and empty when performed in the usual manner, but shrill and screaming when performed loudly."[26] The doubling of the higher pitches from c1 (principals 4′, 2 2/3′, 2′) not only enhances the sound but also—because of the rich speech quality similar to the sound when you say "hiss," and clear principal sound—the mixture ranks add an effect that was described by Yokota as "flames in a fire" in seminars on voicing at the Eastman School in November 2007.[27] These ranks blend well with the principal chorus, thanks to the different speech and timbre, and do not cause any tuning issues.

Claviatura Secunda: Mixtura. á 4. Choris. (metal)—same design as for Clav. I, but without tierce—rich and colorful with distinct speech ("hiss"), principal character also in the treble, brings a "flame" effect to the principal chorus, 8-foot based

C	1′	2/3′	1/2′	
c	1′	2/3′	1/2′	1/2′
c1	2′	1-1/3′	1′	1′
c2	4′	2-2/3′	2′	2′

The Mixtures, particularly the tierce mixture of Clav. 1, add a lot of brilliance and force to the sound, and are experienced as the loudest stops of the organ. The effect of the Mixture-plenum with Trompet. á 8 and perhaps manual divisions coupled, is majestic and fiery at the same time. It brings force and brilliance to for instance "Sturm und Drang" fantasies in an electrifying way. The noticeable octave breaks are however creating problems in linear texture, for example, polyphonic music or fugue themes circling around c1 or c2. An addition of the separate tierce stop, Tertia. á 1 3/5, does not eliminate the problem altogether, but lessens the effect of the break.[28] For linear textures, a registration including the Trompet and Tertia but without the mixture is preferable. The Trompet. á 8 is well-balanced between treble and bass, overtone-rich and rather round in the treble, colorful, powerful yet elegant in the bass (C–c shallot covered), and with a prompt speech. It blends very well with all stops, and can be used in many combinations.

The Pedal reeds are more fundamental and can be described in the following way:

Pedal:
Posaun Bass. á 16.—(wooden resonator)—full, fundamental, and clear bass
  with prompt speech
Trompet Bass. á 8.—(metal)—more overtone-rich than Posaune, somewhat
  bright, well balanced, however, more fundamental than Trompet 8 in the
  manual

The pedal reeds can be used alone or in combination with other stops. The Full Bass. á 12 (gedackt 10 2/3′) provides a discrete contour of gravity to the pedal, and is possible to combine with the foundation stops, but works best with a fuller pedal registration. There are many possible combinations for full organ and as a summary of the discussion above, a few are included in the following list:

PRINCIPAL. á 8, HOHLFLAUT. á 8, Octava Principal. á 4, [Qvinta. á 3,]
  Super Octava. á 2
Pedal: Principal Bass. á 16, Octava Bass. á 8, Super Octava Bass. á 4

[BOURDUN. á 16,] PRINCIPAL. á 8, HOHLFLAUT. á 8, [QVINTATHON. á
  8,] Octava Principal. á 4, Qvinta. á 3, Super Octava. á 2, [Tertia. á 1 3/5,]
  [Trompet. á 8]
Pedal: Principal Bass. á 16, Violon Bass. á 16, [Octava Bass. á 8], [Flaut &
  Quint Bass. á 8] Super Octava Bass. á 4, [Trompet Bass. á 8]

BOURDUN. á 16, PRINCIPAL. á 8, HOHLFLAUT. á 8, [QVINTATHON. á
  8,] Octava Principal. á 4, Qvinta. á 3, Super Octava. á 2, [Tertia. á 1 3/5,]
  Mixtura. á 5, [Trompet. á 8]

Possibly coupled to Clav II:
[Principal Am. á 8, (Flaut Major. á 8), PRINCIPAL. á 4, (Octava. á 2), Mixtura. á 4 (Dulc. 16)]
Pedal: Principal Bass. á 16, Octava Bass. á 8, Flaut & Quint Bass. á 8, [Full Bass. á 12] Super Octava Bass. á 4, Posaun Bass. á 16, Trompet Bass. á 8

The flutes of 4-foot and 2-foot pitch should not be included, since they do not blend well with the principal stops and cause tuning issues. The general character of the divisions corresponds well to Boxberg's description of the Hauptwerk and Oberwerk of Central German instruments: "The principal ranks differ from manual to manual. The one is of wider, the other of narrower scale, so that each manual might have a particular and distinct sound. The Hauptwerk sounds grand (*prächtig*); the Oberwerk, very piercing and keen; the Brustpositiv, keen and delicate."[29] The opposite character of the two main divisions was useful in the concerto style of the eighteenth century with its dialogue between solo instruments (or groups of instruments) and the ensemble (ripieno/tutti) that could be realized by the organist through manual changes in dialogue: "But there are also compositions with two, three, and four choirs that alternate in dialogue fashion. The organists can imitate such changes on their instruments, when they have more than one manual."[30] The powerful, penetrating and brilliant full plenum, with reeds and mixtures, and with manuals coupled, is ideal for the accompaniment of congregational singing in a full church.

> The organ is the instrument to lead and elevate congregational singing. To achieve the first goal, it needs, depending on the size of the church and the congregation, a strong sound; to realize the second requires a beautiful tone of the individual stops as well as of the full work. The 8-foot registers of the manual constitute the core of the sound; they need to assert themselves above the others through number and strength. The 16-foot stops of the manual imbue the organ sound with seriousness and dignity; 4- and 2-foot voices add life and freshness; the mutation stops serve to amplify the sound.[31]

It is also better suited to the texture of free fantasias than to complex contrapuntal works.

In 1773, Johann Friedrich Agricola (1720–84) wrote a set of instructions for conducting an organ audition in the Nikolaikirche in Berlin, where he asked each candidate: "Finally, to perform either an organ work of his own choice composed by a great master, if he wishes, to improvise a fantasy of his own devising. In the latter case, however, he must skillfully shift among three contrasting manuals."[32] Manual changes for variation and dynamic contrast were part of the performance practice at least into the second half of the nineteenth century.[33] Friedrich Konrad Griepenkerl (1782–1849) gives instructions for registration (foundation stops without mixtures) and manual changes in the Prelude and Fugue in E-flat Major, BWV 552, in the preface to volume 3 of the

1844 Bach edition by C. F. Peters.[34] An article published by Griepenkerl in the *Allgemeine musikalische Zeitung* in 1846 reveals that Wilhelm Friedemann Bach also seems to have preferred an *organo pleno* without mixtures and couplers:

> If, however, we are made to believe that dignity and grandeur in performance depend on mixtures, on coupled manuals, and on strong dynamics in general, I cannot help but recall an anecdote that Forkel long ago related to me with amiable modesty. In 1773, Friedemann Bach spent some time with Forkel in Göttingen, when the latter was still a buoyant young man. After Friedemann had repeatedly played the *clavier*, he was asked to be heard also on the organ, and Forkel took him to a church. Friedemann improvised on the organ for more than an hour, but without any mixtures and without using the full strength of the instrument. The young Forkel did not like this, and he dared to remark on it critically. In response, Friedemann patted him on the shoulder and said: "Oh, just let it be, it's all right!"[35]

Also in the nineteenth century, organists were careful and somewhat selective in their choice of stops for full organ. Strings with slow speech should, for example, not be included in "Volles Werk." We should once again remind ourselves of Mendelssohn's words in the preface to the Grand Chorales: "The superscription 'Full Organ' does not always mean all the real stops of an organ."[36] Organists aimed at clarity in polyphonic music, and paid attention to the musical texture, searching for the appropriate sound for different musical ideas, rhetorical figures, gestures, and, as times evolved, emotional characters, or "Stimmungen."

The Eighteenth-Century Central German Organ: Particular Features That Set It Apart From the Neo-Baroque Organ

The fascinating and rich sonorities of the C-S organ are very different from the idea of a Baroque sound that many of us have received through our experience with neo-Baroque organs or new instruments inspired by the Baroque style. A careful listening to the sound characteristics of individual stops leads to some observations. The speech of the principals is rich, particularly in the Principal 4 of the Clav. II, but in a very different way than the spitting sounds of neo-Baroque principals. The proportion between speech and character ("noise") in the sustained sound varies with the type of speech. The richer the speech, the more character we perceive in the sustained sound; the more gentle and focused the speech, the cleaner the sustained sound. This contributes to the wide-ranging variety of color and character in the different categories of stops. Moreover, most stops display some variety in timbre (vowel) and speech (consonant) over the register (bass, tenor, alto, soprano). The PRINCIPAL. á 8 (Clav. I) for example, has a round, rich, and rather vocal treble register, with natural speech, but becomes rather stringy toward the bass with richer speech in the tenor range. The I U L A. á 8 has a full and warm sound with rather slow and gentle speech; in the bass it is also rather stringy; in the treble it widens, however, and the speech is enriched so that the stop takes on the character of a "Traverse flute." The subtle character differentiation over the register results in a transparency in polyphonic texture, and makes it easy to distinguish the individual parts in a four-part setting when played on a single principal stop. Almost all flute stops have a noticeable treble ascendancy: an increase of volume and sound toward the treble, and a different character in the bass, which is softer, somewhat restricted, often narrow. This quality helps bring out treble and bass in homophonic textures and gives a sense of dynamic gesture to solos on individual stops, for example, the I U L A. á 8 mentioned above. Furthermore, in one and the same range of a single stop (for example, the tenor [c–c1] or the alto [c1–c2] octave registers), one might notice slight variations in vowel and speech characteristics, a feature Harald Vogel has described as one of the main factors that gives the Principal sound a vocal character. When a four-part setting is played on such a stop, our perception is similar to that of a vocal ensemble singing a text with different consonants and vowels in the various parts on each note. The sustained sound of individual notes of a single stop, might vary in the vowel sound from AHH to EHH or from AHH to OHH. These unpredictable shifts of timbre and speech are very subtle, otherwise they would disturb the general character and stick out from their neighbor notes, but they are noticeable enough to bring a sense of life to a polyphonic texture.

A summary of the most significant features in eighteenth-century organ building will tell us the following:

- All stops have a distinct character.
- All stops have a particular speech.
- All stops have a clear and colorful sustained sound.
- they easily blend with other stops, including foundation stops of similar pitch.
- Combinations of stops generate new characters of almost indefinite numbers.

The variation of character in the different registers within a single stop contributes to the transparency of texture, and the treble ascendancy brings out melodies in the top range of the compass. Each individual stop and all combinations of stops present a character with emotional quality and expression.

The aesthetics only gradually changed with time, as the following comparison will show. In nineteenth-century organs

- many stops maintain the same character as their eighteenth-century counterparts; however, the speech is generally reduced;

- variation of timbre and speech in individual stops is abandoned for consistency and linear development;
- the treble ascendancy of the flute stops, particularly the foundation stops, is often enhanced; and
- most stops blend well with each other.

In neo-Baroque organs

- the timbre and speech are consistent throughout the registers within a stop;
- the speech of principals and flutes is distinct, although the sustained sound is clean, producing the well-known "spitting" effect, which reduces the aptness for blending, particularly of foundation stops of the same pitch;
- individual sounds are clean and emotionally neutral (abstract), whereas the full organ registrations produce an effect of brilliance, sharpness, and power, but with a lack of balance between treble and bass;
- the blending is reduced or eliminated; and
- the tenor range often stands out as the loudest register.

Registering Mendelssohn's Opus 65: The Instructions in the Preface and the Edition

On September 15, 1845, Mendelssohn's Six Sonatas for the Organ appeared in print in four countries simultaneously: Germany (Breitkopf und Härtel), England (Coventry and Hollier), Italy (Giovanni Ricordi), and France (M. Schlesinger). The German, English, and Italian editions contained a short preface by Mendelssohn that provides us with important information, particularly regarding registration:

> Much depends in these Sonatas on the right choice of the Stops; however, as every Organ with which I am acquainted has its own peculiar mode of treatment in this respect, and as the same nominal combination does not produce exactly the same effect in different Instruments, I have given only a general indication of the kind of effect intended to be produced, without giving a precise List of the particular Stops to be used. By "Fortissimo," I intend to designate the Full Organ; by "Pianissimo," I generally mean a soft 8 feet Stop alone; by "Forte," the Great Organ, but without some of the most powerful Stops; by "Piano" some of the soft 8 feet Stops combined; and so forth. In the Pedal part, I should prefer throughout, even in the Pianissimo passages, the 8 feet & the 16 feet Stops united; except when the contrary is expressly specified; (see the 6th Sonata). It is therefore left to the judgment

of the Performer, to mix the different Stops appropriately to the style of the
various Pieces; advising him, however, to be careful that in combining the
Stops belonging to the different sets of keys, the kind of tone in the one,
should be distinguished from that in the other; but without forming too vio-
lent a contrast between the two distinct qualities of tone.[37]

Mendelssohn underlines the significance of the choice of registration for a
successful performance of the Sonatas. But due to the individuality of each
organ, he kept his guidelines short and general. We recognize the two main
categories of registrations from the preface of his Bach edition (see above):
soft registrations (2 Clav. and Pedal) and "Full Organ" (and the differentiation
of the latter in "Forte" and "Fortissimo"). The description of the soft registrations, particularly the definition of "Piano," reflects the practice of combining
soft 8-foot foundation stops for contrast in tone and character, both for one-
manual and two-manual performances (in solo and accompaniment textures
or alternating passages).

At the beginning of 1846, Mendelssohn's Sonatas were reviewed by Eduard
Krüger (1807–85) in *Neue Zeitschrift für Musik* (*NZfM*) (January 1, 4, and 8,
1846), and by August Gottfried Ritter (1811–85) in *Allgemeine musikalische
Zeitung* (*AMZ*) (February 11, 1846). Krüger, a teacher at the Gymnasium in
Emden, Ostfriesland and frequent contributor to the *NZfM*, wrote a partly
critical review (divided into three installments) discussing general matters such as form (terminology and structure), style (sacred and secular),
fugal style, organ-idiomatic writing, the aspect of virtuosity, and so on, with
examples taken from the Sonatas.[38] Although Krüger was mainly a regional
authority, he was active as a writer on the national stage, and he performed
recitals including music by Sebastian Bach.[39] Concerning the preface to the
Sonatas he wrote:

> This preface is anxiously concerned about proper performance; even in its
> brevity it makes explicit the striving for expression (affect) by giving pointers
> for *forte, piano*, registration, etc., which are a hindrance for good organists.
> The sonatas are not written for the bad ones, and the expert will remember
> that he never will fail with S. Bach who provided only the most general and
> vaguest information such as 2 Clav. Ped., 8- or 4-Foot, *organo pleno*, rarely *forte*
> and *piano*. Nothing else.[40]

Krüger does not find the preface useful or even desirable. He argues that the
Sonatas are written for professional organists who know how to handle registration, manual changes, and dynamics. He is particularly opposed to *piano*
and *forte* annotations. His arguments mainly reflect the guild mentality: that
knowledge should not be shared outside the circle of qualified practitioners, in
this case professional organists. Krüger may also represent a somewhat conservative attitude against the new trends of dynamic expression in performance,
or at least against the compositional trend proscribing dynamics by means of

detailed instructions: organists should be free to make their own decisions about the interpretation.

In his review in the *AMZ* (see above), August Gottfried Ritter,[41] criticizes the preface from a different point of view:

> The remarks about registration, provided in the score, are mostly limited to general aspects, *forte* and *piano*, etc. The composer has avoided giving special indications for individual registers, since each organ demands a different treatment in this respect, "in that even registers of the same name do not always produce the same sound on different instruments." The latter statement may be alright, but the difference in sound is never so significant that, say, a register whose timbre is penetrating or string-like would sound similar to another one requiring, by its nature, a full and rounded tone. It matters for the sound of a composition whether a movement is performed with a voice of this or that timbre. Indicating the registers would therefore have been desirable. If the required register was not available on the organ, it could easily be replaced by a similarly sounding one.[42]

Ritter does not question that organs are individual, however, he argues that the musical texture and the character of the main categories of softer stops (strings and flutes) are so closely interrelated that they should be included in the annotations of the edition. If not literally applicable, the performer can adopt the detailed instructions with similar effects at various instruments. Ritter further develops his argument in the context of a detailed discussion of the Sonata II:

> I have already mentioned earlier in my general remarks that the composer has neglected to indicate the individual registers and that therefore the score does not include a direct elaboration of the art of registration. But the thoughtful player, by cleverly exploring different manuals, has been indirectly given the opportunity to juxtapose and compare the different voices of his organ, search for the most appropriate colors in the movements designed to be performed on several manuals and, possibly, switch them in the course of the movement. The Adagio of the second sonata, because of the peculiar and distinctive treatment of the individual manuals (and the Pedal should be included here as well), represents an orchestra-like texture. The melody performed by the right hand on the second manual is given to wind instruments, while the violins, performed in the left hand on the first manual, accompany it in song-like flowing passages; and the basses—in the pedal—indicate the harmonic foundation in the form of pizzicato tones. If this interpretation is correct, the organist would have to select full and somewhat sonorous stops for the second manual (voices that also have resonance in the lower tones), transparent and flexible stops for the first manual, and, finally, for the pedal: rounded stops that respond well and quickly. However, considering that the first manual usually includes voices with wide scalings and the second manual voices with narrow scalings appropriate for accompaniment, we would have

to reverse the nomenclature for the manuals as used in the score. The use of the manuals and the voice-leading are, as stated earlier, very clever, and will be a great pleasure and advantageous for the player.[43]

Ritter gives a rather detailed example from the Adagio of the Second Sonata of how "the art of registration" can be applied based on the "clever" notation of "the use of the manuals and the voice-leading." He describes the musical texture and associates its different voices with instruments of a chamber orchestra: solo for wind instruments, string-bass pizzicato, and the flowing accompaniment parts with violins. The organist should thoughtfully explore different sonorities in different manuals and, in doing so, ensure that clarity for all voices would be attained: the choice of stops for the solo voice should be such that it could also be heard when it is hidden in the tenor range. Ritter argues that the fuller sound of the wider-scaled stops of Manual I would therefore be more suited for the solo, and that the narrow-scaled stops of Manual II would be more suited for the accompaniment parts, bringing more clarity to them. Based on this observation, he states that the order of manuals suggested by Mendelssohn should be reversed. Not only the sound characteristics but also the key-touch characteristics of the manuals would be more suitable to the texture in Ritter's suggested distribution. The key action of the second manual is lighter and more elegant than the action of the first manual, and the flowing parallel sixths in sixteenth notes are easier to play on this division. The fact that he does not comment on the consequences for the change of registration in the transition from Grave to Adagio indicates that he assumes either that this can be arranged in some other way or a performance on a three-manual organ would be required. Ritter suggests the reversed order of manuals also for the third movement of Sonata IV, and it is indeed more convenient to play the sixteenth notes as suggested in *pianissimo*, for example on the Gedackt 8′, on Manual II, in which one can more easily control the touch and reduce the action noise by staying in contact with the keys.

Ritter's commentary gives us valuable insight into the philosophy of the nineteenth-century art of registration and particularly that of soft registrations. It shows that the concept of orchestration was the point of departure, and a "thoughtful" player should carefully explore contrasting tonal qualities that could clarify the voice leading and that would be idiomatic to the texture by using appropriate categories and combinations of stops and distribution of the parts on different manuals.

The editions of Ritter's own Sonatas provide registrations with a level of detail that he would have liked to have seen in Mendelssohn's edition. In Ritter's Sonata III in A Minor, the recitative is annotated with dynamics (*f, fp, mf, mp, p, pp*) and pitch levels for the pedal (8′ and 16′, respectively), and in the character movement (*Nicht schleppend—piano*) we find a carefully orchestrated interpretation with solo registrations (for example, Gedackt 8′; Gedackt and Principal 8′; Gedackt 8′ and Flöte 4′; Viola da Gamba 8′), wind ensemble registrations (I: Tromp. and V d Gambe; Ped: Violon, Posaune, Tromp), and Pedal with alternating 16-foot or 8-foot pitch, partly pizzicato, and occasionally solo (Violoncello 8′), and the distribution of the parts on the main and secondary manuals (*Haupt- und Neben-Manualen*) takes into consideration both character of tone and touch, for example, assigning a fast arpeggio figuration that should be played with a Gedackt 8′ to the lighter action of the second manual. The outer movements are mainly composed for forte registration with some dynamic differentiation (*mf, f, ff*) and twice a diminuendo down to the extreme (*pp*). The registration annotations can be successfully realized almost literally on the C-S organ (Iula 8′ instead of Viola da Gamba 8′, and, in the pedal, Octava 8′ instead of Violoncello 8′).[44]

Mendelssohn included more detailed registration indications for the Sonatas III and VI. In Sonata VI, the three first variations have indications similar to those found in Ritter's Sonata, however, no stop names are mentioned. The fugue in the first movement of Sonata III is the first example of a nineteenth-century German fugue, in which a gradual crescendo and accelerando toward the end is integrated as part of the form. Neither Krüger nor Ritter comments on the difference in detail of registration annotations between the Sonatas. However, Ritter reports on the unusual annotation in Sonata III and describes the development of this double fugue to its culmination and conclusion as follows:

> With the instruction "Da questa parte fino al Maggiore poco a poco animato e più forte," the chorale is accompanied in sixteenth notes instead of the eighth notes that prevailed earlier. After it has sounded the final tone of the cantus firmus for a long time, even the pedal finally joins the ever increasing motion. While the manuals repeat the main segment of the theme in full chords and in high registers, the pedal burrows down into the depth in wild and thunderous passages to ascend subsequently from the low E via F, G-sharp, B, d, f, g-sharp, b to the high d. From there, it slowly and gradually descends leading to a return of the first movement in A major, which, except for a very few but effective and characteristic changes (for instance, in the fifth and sixth measures), is repeated almost literally.[45]

Overview of Registration Information for the Sonatas: Its Application to the Craighead-Saunders Organ

In the following list, the different dynamic levels described in the preface are combined with the more detailed indications from the individual movements[46] In addition, examples of relevant combinations of stops from the C-S organ are included, with a few observations regarding their qualities and character, reflecting general knowledge of the registration practice on eighteenth- and early nineteenth-century German organs.

Pianissimo (A Single Soft 8′ Stop Alone)

[In Sonatas I: 2, 3; II: 1b; IV: 3; VI: 2]

Cl. II: The softest stop of the organ is the Flaut Major. á 8. The I U L A. á 8 (warm and somewhat stringy) would be the other alternative. Mendelssohn's preference for soft Flute stops, and the fact that FM8 is the quietest stop speaks in favor of this choice. Unda Maris. á 8 combined with either the FM8 (gentle and colorful) or I8 (full and warm) could be considered (for example in the recitative of I: 3).

Cl. I: HOHLFLAUT. á 8 is the softest stop. H8 combined with FM8 (Cl. II— round and clear). Flaut Travers. á 4 (played an octave lower).

Pedal: Principal Bass. á 16 or Octava Bass. á 8

Piano (Several of the Soft 8′ Stops Together)

[In Sonatas III: 2 (*piano e dolce*); IV: 2; V: 2; VI: I, 4; 7 (*piano e dolce*)]

Cl. II: Flaut Major. á 8 combined with I U L A. á 8. Unda Maris. á 8 combined with I8. Flaut Minor. á 4 and Spiel Flet. á 4 combined (played an octave lower).

Cl. I: HOHLFLAUT. á 8 coupled to I8 (warm and round) or FM8 (Cl. II—round and clear) or combined with both (warm, rich and round). QVINTATHON. á 8 combined with H8 (round, rich, and colorful). Flaut Travers. á 4 combined with FM4 (round and clear) or SF4 (colorful and warm) or both.

Pedal: Principal Bass. á 16 or Octava Bass. á 8

Mezzo Piano (A Combination of Several Softer 8′ Stops, or 8′ and 4′ Stops)

[In Sonatas IV: 2; VI: 1, 2]

Cl. II: [I U L A. á 8], Flaut Major. á 8, Flaut Minor. á 4 or Spiel Flet. á 4 (colorful and warm); or I U L A. á 8, FM8, Principal Amalel. á 8 (full, warm and rich); or Unda Maris. á 8 combined with PA8 (full and rich).

Cl. I: HOHLFLAUT. á 8, Flaut Travers. á 4 [QVINTATHON. á 8]; H8, [Q8] combined with I8, FM8, [and PA8] (Cl. II)

Pedal: Principal Bass. á 16 and Octava Bass. á 8

Mezzo forte (A Combination of 8′ and 4′ Stops, Most Likely Principals)

[In Sonata VI: 2, and in V, first movement Mendelssohn asks for the addition of a 16′ stop]

Cl. II: I U L A. á 8, Flaut Major. á 8, Principal Amalel. á 8, and Spiel Flet. á 4 or PRINCIPAL. á 4

Cl. I: [BOURDUN. á 16], PRINCIPAL. á 8, HOHLFLAUT. á 8, QVINTATHON. á 8 (and Octava Principal. á 4)

Pedal: Principal Bass. á 16, [Violon Bass. á 16], [Flaut & Quint Bass. á 8] and Octava Bass. á 8

Forte (Full Organ, but without Some of the Most Powerful Stops: Mixtures and Full-Resonator Reeds)

[In Sonatas II: 1a, 4; III: 1; IV: 1; V: 3; VI: 6]
PRINCIPAL. á 8, HOHLFLAUT. á 8, Octava Principal. á 4, [Qvinta. á 3,]
   Super Octava. á 2
Pedal: Principal Bass. á 16, Octava Bass. á 8, Super Octava Bass. á 4
or
BOURDUN. á 16, PRINCIPAL. á 8, HOHLFLAUT. á 8, [QVINTATHON. á
   8,] Octava Principal. á 4, Qvinta. á 3, Super Octava. á 2, [Tertia. á 1 3/5,]
Pedal: Principal Bass. á 16, Violon Bass. á 16, Octava Bass. á 8, [Flaut & Quint
   Bass. á 8] Super Octava Bass. á 4, [Trompet Bass. á 8]

Fortissimo (Full Organ, Including the More Powerful Stops)

[In Sonatas I: 1, 3, 4; II: 3; III: 1; IV: 4; VI: 5]
BOURDUN. á 16, PRINCIPAL. á 8, HOHLFLAUT. á 8, [QVINTATHON. á
   8,] Octava Principal. á 4, Qvinta. á 3, Super Octava. á 2, Tertia. á 1 3/5,
   [Mixtura. á 5], Trompet. á 8
Possibly coupled to Clav II:
Principal Am. á 8, [Flaut Major. á 8,] PRINCIPAL. á 4, [Octava. á 2], Mixtura.
   á 4 [Dulc. 16]
Pedal: Principal Bass. á 16, Violon Bass. á 16, Octava Bass. á 8, Flaut & Quint
   Bass. á 8, [Full Bass. á 12,] Super Octava Bass. á 4, Posaun Bass. á 16,
   Trompet Bass. á 8

Pedal (8′ and 16′ Stops Combined unless Otherwise Indicated)

Principal Bass. á 16 can be used alone (overtone rich). Octava Bass. á 8
should be used alone in VI: 2 and V: 2, and possibly in II: 1b; VI: 4. The
combination of PB16 and OB8 is too loud for the *pianissimo* and often
also for the *piano* registrations.

Performance on Two Manuals
and with Manual Changes

Manual indications are quite frequent in the edition. We find them in thirteen
of the twenty-three movements, namely, in I: 1, 2, 3; II: 1b; III: 1, 2; IV: 2, 3, V: 2
(3); and VI: 2, 3, 4. The abbreviations Cl. I and Cl. II are used to indicate either
solo and accompaniment or dialogue (alternation) between manuals.

Ritter was particularly fond of the resulting differentiation of color and
character. In general, he was less in favor of Sonata IV, primarily because he
found the outer movements less idiomatic to the organ. However, he appreciated the inner movements and commented as follows: "The Adagio religioso
that follows, however, makes up for it completely (it again uses alternating

manuals appropriately), and so does the ensuing Allegretto in $\frac{6}{8}$ meter—it is as exquisite and gentle, as only Seb. Bach's Pastorella can be."[47]

Mid- and late nineteenth-century sources reflect this practice taken a step further; for example, Lichtwark (around 1900)[48] and Pearce (1902) recommend and encourage the performer to alternate between three or four manuals of similar yet contrasting color in orchestral fashion in the lyrical movements of Mendelssohn's Sonatas. Pearce suggests an unusual two-manual performance for the last movement of Sonata VI, Finale, with two parts in the right hand and two parts in the left hand (mm. 1–4; 9–12; 17–26; 29–34).

In the manuscript for the edition Mendelssohn included thirty-eight manual indications for the final movement of Sonata V, Allegro maestoso—most likely a documentation of how he often played this movement.[49] A dialogue performance of this kind makes a great deal of sense on an eighteenth-century-style German organ with two well-balanced manual divisions of different characters. A two-manual *forte* registration on the C-S organ results in a transparent and colorful version of the piece:

Registration for Sonata V, Allegro maestoso

CLAVIATURA PRIMA:
PRINCIPAL. á 8, HOHLFLAUT. á 8, QVINTATHON. á 8, Octava Principal. á
   4, Qvinta. á 3, Super Octava. á 2
Claviatura Secunda: Principal Amalel. á 8, I U L A. á 8, Flaut Major. á 8,
   PRINCIPAL. á 4, Octava. á 2
Pedal: Principal Bass. á 16, Violon Bass. á 16, Octava Bass. á 8, Trompet Bass. á 8

It is clear that performance on two manuals (solo/accompaniment) or alternation between manuals was an essential part of Mendelssohn's performance style, and it is carefully indicated primarily for the movements with softer registrations in the edition. The main musical purpose was to create differentiation and transparency of sound and to provide for subtle alternation of character and contrast. It is possible that he also used the dialogue practice (see above) more extensively in other movements, for example, in the final movement of Sonata V, at least, when he played German-style organs. Mendelssohn was familiar with this practice from Sebastian Bach's organ music and the "Dorian" Toccata and Fugue in D Minor (BWV 538), in which the manual parts are supposed to alternate between the manual divisions (*Werk* and *Oberwerk*) in accordance with the concerto grosso style. As reported by the organist of the Temple Church in London, Edward J. Hopkins (1818–1901), Mendelssohn "threw out points unsuspected before, as in the A Minor Fugue, where he took the episode on the swell, returning to the Great Organ when the pedal re-enters, but transferring the E in the treble to the Great Organ a bar before the other parts."[50] Thus, he used manual changes for the enhancement of the musical form. Gauntlett's English edition of Bach's Passacaglia from 1838 includes rather detailed performance instructions with regard to registration, manual changes, and tempo, and Little has suggested that it may reflect Mendelssohn's interpretation of this piece.[51]

Crescendo and Diminuendo
and the Role of the Registrants

Several sources describe Mendelssohn's organ playing and frequently mention that he changed registrations with regard to texture and character (between variations or movements) and often employed crescendo and diminuendo. In a letter to his mother in the summer of 1842, Mendelssohn reports on his visit with Queen Victoria and Prince Albert, who wanted to show him their chamber organ before he left England. Prince Albert played Mendelssohn "a chorale by heart, with pedals, so charmingly and clearly and correctly that many an organist could have learned something from it." Mendelssohn continues:

> Then I had to play, and I began my chorus from "St. Paul," "How lovely are the Messengers!" Before I got to the end of the first verse, they both began to sing the chorus very well, and all the time Prince Albert managed the stops for me expertly—first a flute, then more at the forte, the full organ at the D Major part, then he made an excellent diminuendo with the stops, and so on to the end of the piece—and all by heart—and I was greatly pleased.[52]

Crescendo and diminuendo accomplished by change of stops was already known at the end of the eighteenth century. The first description of a register crescendo appears in Justin Heinrich Knecht's Organ School (1796):

> When one wants to imitate the crescendo of orchestral music on the organ, one should start on the manual with stopped 8- and 16-foot stops, pulling them one after the other to render the transition from *pianissimo* to *piano*; then one takes the open 8-foot stops to increase the crescendo somewhat, after that come the 4-, 2-, and 1-foot stops to move to *forte*, and, finally, reeds and mixture-like stops are added to achieve *forte* and *fortissimo*. In the pedal, one starts the *pianissimo* with the subbass alone, adds a 32-foot stop if available, and then successively pulls 16-, 8-, and 4-foot, partly principal and partly flute stops, but the reeds and mixtures are reserved for *forte* and *fortissimo*.[53]

The design and arrangement of the stop knobs at the key desk of eighteenth-century German-style organs, was such that it was rather difficult for the performer to reach and change stops while playing. The stop actions consisted of substantial parts of solid wood and iron, and the resulting mass required some force to be moved. Accordingly, for the execution of gradual crescendos and diminuendos on an eighteenth-century-style organ, registrants were needed. Adolph Friedrich Hesse (1809–63) requested to be assisted by two registrants on his concert tours, and Mendelssohn asked for assistance from registrants when he performed publicly in England. Several reports from his informal performances show that he often had one assistant or more.

At Christ Church in London, Miss Mounsey and Dr. Gauntlett assisted Mendelssohn twice. Miss Mounsey recalled that in playing his Fugue from the Sonata in F Minor "he wished to have the swell stops varied, as he proceeded, giving varied shades of tone without any striking changes."[54] In 1828, however, Mendelssohn reported from Brandenburg, playing the Wagner organ in the Gotthards-Kirche, that he had set his registrations himself since he did not have a registrant available. He played a free fantasy "on the chorale 'Christe, du Lamm Gottes,' which I first played with flutes, then gradually stronger and stronger (I had to register myself in the absence of the organist) and finally I concluded with the chorale, again quietly."[55]

Whether he had assistance or not, Mendelssohn seems to have played using an orchestral approach, at some point including register crescendos and diminuendos. Performing repertoire without assistance required a clever distribution of the voices, so that one hand would be free to pull or push stop knobs when a gradual dynamic change was desired. In improvisation, and the composition of new works, this was, of course, easier to integrate. In Johann Gottlob Schneider's 1831 *Fantasie und Fuge* in C Minor the following footnote gives detailed instruction about how the performer himself can manage a decrescendo: "During these two measures, the player, having one hand free for registration, can remove the loud stops leaving only two soft 8-foot stops." And Schneider continues: "This chord is played by one hand alone, so that the other hand is free to remove one 8-foot stop, thereby producing the pianissimo."[56]

This registration practice can also be traced in Mendelssohn's Sonatas, for example, in Sonata II, between the Grave and Adagio (rests in all parts but the soprano) and the third and fourth movements (attacca la fuga—from *ff* to *f*), and in Sonata VI, there is just enough time between all variations, primarily thanks to the short interludes, and before the Fugue (reduction of stops from *ff* to *f*) and the Finale (from *f* to *piano e dolce*) to change the necessary stops.

An important feature of Mendelssohn's organ compositional style, including counterpoint, is the frequent subtle increase and decrease of the number of parts.[57] On paper, this may appear as an inconsistency and deficit, however, when experienced in sound on an eighteenth-century German organ, the variation of density of texture results in a gentle, dynamic expression of shading. In his essay on Mendelssohn's Organ Sonatas, Charles William Pearce (1856–1928) argues that "Mendelssohn wrote as he played,"[58] and that the variation in texture may reflect spontaneous, expressive gestures, as well as practical concerns. It is also possible that Mendelssohn arranged the texture so that it could be performed by English organists who did not have access to an organ with the requested pedal compass, or who simply preferred playing them "with a little extra manual dexterity" without using the pedal at all.[59] Indeed, when the pedal part moves in faster note values, we can observe the tendency that the manual parts can almost always be played by one hand. From the German perspective, we may argue that this feature probably also reflects how Mendelssohn played and occasionally changed stops while he was playing.

In the final movement of Sonata II, the Fugue, there are several places where one of the hands is free to add stops, for example, in measures 63, 67, 76, 77, 85, 92, 96, and 102. The dynamic indication is *forte* and no registration changes are indicated. A performance on one registration (*forte*), as indicated in the edition, can be convincing if the principal chorus is full, rich, colorful, and transparent so that all parts can be heard clearly. However, we can also easily imagine Mendelssohn playing the fugue in his typical orchestral crescendo fashion, adding some of the remaining loud stops along the way and reaching *fortissimo* in measure 96.

As mentioned above, the double fugue of the first movement of Sonata III is a crescendo fugue. The crescendo starts in measure 58, where the second theme is presented in sixteenth notes. However, the texture of the manual parts of the double fugue is consistently dense and it is harder to find places where one hand would be free to add stops. Moving from *poco meno forte* (for example, on the C-S organ: [B16], P8, HF8, O4) to *fortissimo* (m. 113) would only require the addition of four to five manual stops (for example, Super Octava. á 2, Qvinta. á 3, [BOURDUN. á 16], Trompet. á 8, Tertia. á 1 3/5, and Mixtura. á 5). From a structural point of view, the first two most logical places (mm. 80 and 97) would require assistance, whereas some additions on the last page (for example, mm. 103, 106, and 111–12) would possibly allow one hand to be free for the addition of stops.

In the summer of 1845, when Mendelssohn played the Sonatas in Kronberg, the composer and writer Emil Naumann (1827–95) was in the audience. He gives a rather detailed description of the performance, including orchestral crescendos of the kind requested in the fugue of Sonata III:

> So many times we encountered the organ being played with tiresome monotony in its sound effects or, vice versa, with cheap showmanship in juxtaposing contrasting timbres, but in Mendelssohn's hands it seemed to be transformed into an entirely new instrument, not heard so far. Never again did we hear the organ sing in this manner, never again did we encounter such crescendos, carefully prepared and soothing in the addition of the reed stops. The instrument became a full-sounding orchestra, and one believed to hear hovering above the voices of a singer or of entire choirs.[60]

Naumann is lyrical about Mendelssohn's art of registration, and sets it apart from what he recognized as typical extremes of contemporary organ performance, monotonous and nondynamical playing versus frequent and dramatic tonal change, simply with the purpose to create effects. Mendelssohn's performance was transparent since he knew how to combine the appropriate stops for a certain musical texture, and expressive since he explored combinations of stops that evoked the character of instrumental and vocal music. Mendelssohn expanded the eighteenth-century art of registration, particularly with more frequent changes of color and orchestral crescendo and diminuendo, something that Naumann especially appreciated and perceived as a rendering of the "deeply conceived and deeply felt" meaning of the music. The continuous change of colors through registration and manual changes was perceived as an integral part of the interpretation, as necessary means to render the emotional character of the music. The color and emotional character of the individual stops and ensembles of the C-S organ, and historical instruments like it, is well suited to bring this dimension to the performance.

Depending on the size and type of organ, whether he had assistants or not, and the nature of the event, Mendelssohn adjusted his registration to the context of the performance. Although he does not seem to have changed his style of playing as radically as one might expect, the rendering of an interpretation was not set in stone. The limited information about registrations in the edition of the Six Sonatas mirrors his performance style only to a certain degree. Ritter's critique against the lack of detail is understandable; however, the complexity of Mendelssohn's performance style, the fact that the edition was published in four countries simultaneously, and that the initiative originated in Coventry, England, made it too complicated to include detailed instructions pertaining to different styles of organ. Primarily, the edition presents the *compositions* and not their detailed performance. This is most likely also the explanation for the varying degrees of information for different Sonatas. A careful study of the information provides the basis for historically informed interpretations, but performance-practice decisions should not be restricted to the limited level of detail of the edition. A study of the Six Sonatas on the C-S organ brings fascinating new perspectives to the understanding of the music and its sound. Naturally, the art of registration is the basis for the tonal rendering of the performance, but the organ's sensitive key action also influences the resulting sound much more than one may imagine. From this perspective, Naumann's statement: "Never again did we hear the organ sing in this manner" gains an additional meaning: Mendelssohn handled the organ with such skill and care that it sounded like an entirely new instrument. Indeed, eighteenth-century historical organs (including the C-S organ) sound completely different when played by organists who are sensitive to the behavior of the wind and pipe speech. Mendelssohn not only mastered the art of expressive and colorful registration but also played with such fine touch and articulation that the organ sound was transformed to that of a singer, a choir, and a complete orchestra.

Mendelssohn's Articulation and the C-S Organ

The varied key-touch characteristics of the C-S organ generated a new awareness of how the performer can influence the speech ("Ansprache," attack or
onset) and the ending of a tone ("Absprache," release). There were excited
daily discussions between Eastman students and teachers on the organ balcony
at Christ Church: "Listen to the sound, play with the wind, play 'in the keys,'
stay in contact with them, use the weight of the arm, focus on the attack and
particularly on the release, connect the notes with a slow release, listen to the
shape of the sound, let the organ breathe."

The proportion of the key-fall and pallet opening is approximately 1:2
(whereas 1:1 or a little bit less is common in modern organs), a proportion
that will distribute the opening of the pallet (pluck point) over a longer distance of the key-fall. The speech of the pipes is set so that the influence on the
buildup of the tone is maximized, which gives the player direct contact with
the wind and better control of the attack and the release. A slow release has
the effect of a decrescendo. When playing two successive notes, one can let
the hand movement during the gradual release of the weight on the first note
(the decrescendo) transfer sideways to the next note, in order to make a gentle
buildup (slow onset) of the second note to avoid an accent. When playing *forte*,
the touch should be firm with the attention turned to the onset, applying various degrees of fast attacks, yet keeping the fingers in contact with the keys for
a controlled release. Eighteenth-century stringed keyboard instruments and
organs had sensitive actions that offered the player a maximum range of articulation possibilities. The main difference between the systems was the amount
of weight that needed to be applied for the onset.

Otto Goldschmidt (1829–1907), noted pianist and husband of Jenny Lind,
described Mendelssohn's touch: "Though lightness of touch and a delicious
pearliness of tone were prominent characteristics, yet his power in *forte* was
immense." Joseph Joachim (1831–1907) described his "staccato as the most
extraordinary thing possible," and Henry Gauntlett (1805–76), amazed by
Mendelssohn's technique and touch, stated: "One thing which particularly
struck our organists was the contrast between his massive effects and the lightness of his touch in rapid passages. The touch of the Christ Church organ was
both deep and heavy, yet he threw off arpeggios as if he were at a piano."[61]
Mendelssohn obviously mastered both force and brilliance.

Playing the *fortissimo* arpeggio figures in Sonata VI: 1, var. 4 on the C-S
organ, Gauntlett's observation came to mind. At first it seemed very difficult
due to the heavy action. Our students soon could manage however, thanks to
several years of clavichord playing with a weight technique as described by the
Bach scholar and organist, Johann Nikolaus Forkel (1749–1818). The arpeggio figuration requires a weight application from the arm on the first note
(left hand) and on the chord on the fourth beat (left hand, right hand), both

reaching the keybed. The first impulse is transferred through all fingers playing the fast sixteenth notes of the arpeggio, with intense key contact, but without reaching the keybed. The result is a seemingly effortless cascade of notes and a striking contrast between the accent and following gesture, between force and brilliance.

Mendelssohn was critical and specific about the organs he played in England. He considered it necessary to have the wide Central German scaling of the pedal board, that "contrived that the keys have the breadth which feet and boots usually require,"[62] and he considered the key actions of some organs too heavy. To open the pallet of a key at the St. Peter's organ in London, half a pound of weight (227 g) had to be applied.[63] This might appear as an unusual amount, but Mendelssohn was used to actions that required similar amounts of weight. A *forte* registration at the C-S organ, according to key measurements undertaken by GOArt experts, requires the following weight:[64]

Man I (B16, Pr8, O4, Q3, SO2—key-fall: bass: 10 mm, treble: 9 mm)
F: 286 g
f: 224 g
f1: 172 g
f2: 164 g

Man II (I8, Pr8, Pr4, O2—key-fall: bass: 9, treble: 8 mm)
F: 136 g
f: 168 g
f1: 140 g
e2: 147 g

It is possible that Mendelssohn's complaints concerned some property of the action other than the weight. The proportion between key-fall and pallet opening may have been different, the key-fall deeper than he was used to (9–11 mm), or the required weight to keep the pallet open at the keybed more than he was used to. At the C-S organ, the weight needed to move the key after the pluck point is less than 60 percent on Clav I and 50 percent on Clav II of the initially applied weight. The player can thus reduce the applied weight (force) immediately after the first impulse, and balance the arm against the remaining counterforce, and transfer the energy to the following figure or group of notes. When this balance is achieved, the action feels "lighter" and one feels a sense of relative relaxation.

Perhaps John C. Horsley's description of Mendelssohn's behavior at the organ reflects how he intelligently adjusted his posture at the organ to engage maximum natural weight in his performance, also supporting the pedal playing in the high and low compass by "swaying": "At times, especially at the organ, he leant very much over the keys, as if watching for the strains [i.e., melodic lines] which came out of his fingertips. He sometimes swayed from side to side, but usually, his whole performance was quite quiet and absorbed."[65]

Pedal Playing

Since his youth, Mendelssohn complained about how difficult it was to get access to organs for practice. There were several obstacles: the church had to be free, he had to pay rent, he needed bellows treaders, and it was too cold in the winter. He continued to seek opportunities to play the organ, whenever possible "an hour every day."[66] In the summer of 1839, Fritz Schlemmer provided Mendelssohn with a pedal piano. It is possible that he had access to such pedal instruments at other times too.[67] Several sources witness that he had developed an excellent pedal technique. Among them the organist in the Mendelssohn family parish in Berlin, Johann Friedrich Kühnau: "Several times I had the occasion to admire his manual and pedal skills on my organ in the Dreifaltigkeitskirche [Trinity Church]. As far as the pedal is concerned, he knew how to use the heel and toe of the foot so skillfully at the right time and with appropriate flexibility that it was a real pleasure to listen to him."[68]

In organ methods of the first half of the nineteenth century, three categories of pedal applications were mentioned: (1) alternating toes, (2) consecutive toe-heel with the right foot in the top octave and the left foot in the bass octave, and (3) a combination of (1) and (2).[69] In accordance with category (3), the "mixed applications," Mendelssohn used the heels when needed ("at the right time") for pedal passagework and small-interval motives outside the center of the pedal keyboard. Ten out of twenty-three Sonata movements contain pedal scales or virtuoso figurations in fast note values. Most of them are easily playable with alternating toes and occasional use of heels, for example, at turning points of scales or arpeggio figures (Sonatas I: 1, 4; II: 3, 4; III: 1; IV: 1, 4; V: 2, 3; V: 3). The bass lines in Allegro movements are fully integrated in the musical texture, and require the same approach to articulation as the manuals. In some of the lyrical and character movements, he gave the bass line a "lightness of touch" by composing a pizzicato-style bass. In 1845, the young English organist William Rockstro (1823–95) witnessed the first performance of the Six Sonatas in Frankfurt: "He played [the Sonatas] exquisitely—the whole six, straight through, from the neatly written MS. We remember noticing the wonderfully delicate staccato of the pedal quavers in the second movement of the Fifth Sonata, which he played upon a single 8-ft. stop, with all the crispness of [the great double-bass virtuoso] Dragonetti's most highly-finished *pizzicato*."[70] As in the C-S organ, the Pedal Octave 8′ in Central German organs was usually an open wood stop, rather round and fundamental with a stringy speech. The sensitive pedal action of the C-S organ makes it easy to control the speech of Octave 8′, or Principal 16′. To play a "pizzicato," one must keep the key down just long enough for the tone to bloom, and then gently release, thus making a short note with a slow release. A consistent toe application makes for the easiest control. In addition to the Andante con moto of Sonata V and the second variation of Sonata VI, three more movements contain bass parts with short note values separated by rests. Ritter describes the first and third as examples of pizzicato:[71]

- Sonata II: 1b Adagio—with the exception of the consecutive small seconds (sighs) in mm. 46:3–49:3—C/B; B-flat/A; A-flat/G;
- Sonata IV: 3 Allegretto—the tenor solo from m. 24 requires a 16′ stop to avoid voice crossings;
- Sonata VI: Variation 3—no change of registration indicated—possible to play with 8′ alone.

The Sacred and Solemn Organ Style

Around 1800, the appreciation of varied articulation gradually shifted into an aesthetic where the sustained sounds on the organ were particularly appreciated, and became its main style. The organ was associated with music of a solemn and sacred character. In organ methods, slow musical texture (e.g., in chorales), was described as particularly idiomatic to the organ and was to be played with long, singing notes: "The organ is particularly suited for solemn performance, or for pieces with serious and gentle characters, because the tones can be rendered in an appropriately sustained and singing manner."[72] Gradually, the legato touch became the point of departure for slow and soft organ pieces: "Legato . . . always means only that the tones are not to be separated, but that they are to be performed as linked as closely as possible, as if they were flowing into each other, so that no temporal space can be perceived between them."[73]

Legato playing on the C-S organ requires careful control. Consecutive notes must be played with equally slow attack and release, with consistent weight transfer and avoidance of over-legato. The second note should not be heard before the first ends, but one should also not notice a distance between the notes. Legato is easiest to accomplish on soft stops with slow speech. When stops with faster speech and more volume are used, inevitably more contour of the notes will be noticeable.

Examples of the slow and solemn style among the Sonata movements can be found in Sonata V: 2, mm. 16–18, 20–29 as well as the three chorales (Sonatas I: 1; V: 1; VI: 1). These sections can be played with or without finger substitution.[74] All other movements with soft registrations are composed in lyrical style (I: 2; II: 1b; III: 2; IV: 3; V: 2; VI: 2, 7) and have a distinct rhythmical character and melodic gesture (Adagio, Andante movements) with a frequent use of slurs. They can be associated with the *galant* style, often characterized by a solo voice accompanied by short chords or figurations. All fast and loud movements (Allegro and *forte*) belong to the brilliant style and should be performed with articulation, often referred to as staccato ("detached" or "abgestossen"). This is the style most frequently associated with Mendelssohn and his admired "lightness of touch."

Slurs

In performance practice literature for early nineteenth-century repertoire, there are four categories of slurs:[75]

1. accentuation slurs: group of notes corresponding to one or more units of a measure;
2. articulation slurs: group of a few notes, motives;
3. legato slurs: one measure long; and
4. phrasing slurs: longer than one measure.

The meaning and execution of the rich and inconsistent slurs in Mendelssohn's Sonatas have been given substantial attention without reaching consensus.[76] The experience of playing melodic lines on the C-S organ sheds new light on the seemingly unresolvable conflict between accentuation slurs and the natural shape of a melody. David Higgs reports:

> In the Allegretto movement of Sonata IV, with the running sixteenth-notes and the melody of eighth-notes, the slurs seem at first to be opposed to the phrase and the breathing. If the slurs are observed as very discreet "enunciations," as well as indications of timing before a new slur, one sees how Mendelssohn was a master of organ expression. I think this is his most brilliant example (also possibly the final movement of the Sonata VI). The slurs not only enunciate and give specific shape to the melodic line, as if there were a text (Song without Words), which can be effectively realized on an organ with mechanical key action by altering the speed of attack and release, . . . but they also elucidate the larger phrase shapes that correspond with the printed meter (i.e. the second half of a measure is not as strong as the first half in $\frac{6}{8}$), and they indicate the goal of each phrase (the melody begins with four upbeat eighth-notes, rather than just one: A–B-flat–C–D / C–A–G–B-flat / A, then a slur which could indicate no "breath") since Mendelssohn wants us to move to the next down beat, which is also the next harmonic arrival point). Thus these slurs seem to show small enunciation, medium size phrase shape, *and* large harmonic direction in a hierarchical manner, and they can be observed using both articulation (various ways of connecting the notes), touch (various speeds of attack and release), and timing, all indicated by those same slurs.[77]

Based on his experience of the C-S organ, David Higgs presents a new perspective on how to understand the slurs: articulation is a way to *connect* rather than to separate notes. This is self-evident for singers and most instrumentalists; organists, however, talk about articulation as pauses, breaks, or distances between notes, assuming a constant legato is the only option to play a melodic line. The possibility to connect notes with varied attacks and releases opens up new possibilities for expressive playing. Subtle releases between groups of notes in a melodic line create a dynamic shape similar to a vocal line with text. A slow release of the last note under a slur, and a gentle weight-transfer (guided by the arm) to the first note of the next slur, results in a natural and dynamic connection between groups of notes, the effect of a subtle "enuncia-tion." The perceived danger of shortening the last note under a slur can turn into an opportunity to shape the melody dynamically, given there is a sensitive key action, and the organist develops a differentiated touch of Mendelssohn's caliber. The intention should be to shape a line with diversified subtle articula-tion but without accentuating individual notes.

In eighteenth-century performance practice, accentuation was the most important parameter of musical expression, and theorists distinguished between three categories of accents:[78]

  a.   grammatical accents: the strong beats, good notes, of a metrical hierar-chy indicated by time signature;
  b.   oratorical accents: first note of a motive not coinciding with the gram-matical accents; and
  c.   emotional accents—"pathetisch": single note or chord of extreme nature relative to its context.

In the eighteenth-century literature, the close relation between dance rhythms and musical meter was often underlined and explored. The movements of a dance generated a rhythmical pattern that was associated with a certain charac-ter (*Affekt*). It could be understood as the result of a combination of the basic categories of accents. The meter of poetry ("Klangfüße" as Mattheson calls them in *Der vollkommene Kapellmeister* of 1739) was also associated with instru-mental music. In vocal music, the text generated complex patterns of accen-tuation that should be convincingly rendered in performance, something that was also integrated in instrumental music, for example, by Mendelssohn in his *Songs Without Words.*[79]

In his violin treatise, Leopold Mozart stated that the first note of a group of "two, three, four and even more [slurred notes] must be somewhat more strongly stressed, but the remainder slurred on to it quite smoothly and more and more quietly."[80] Mozart's definition is valid for accentuation and articula-tion slurs (categories [1] and [2]). At the clavichord and the organ, this accent and gradual diminuendo is accomplished through a weight application impulse on the first note, and a transfer of the weight onto the fingers that play the fol-lowing notes, successively reducing the weight.[81] The notes within such a gesture can have a wide range of articulation, primarily shaped by movements initiated at the first finger joints. Grammatical accents and accentuation slurs are related ([a] and [1]), and oratorical accents are indicated with articulation slurs ([b] and [2]), and they can be interpreted in the same way, namely, showing which notes should be played within one gestural impulse. Slurs of category (3) are not very frequent in the Sonatas. Since the phrasing slurs of category (4) only occasionally are longer than two measures (for example, in the chorale in Sonata I: 1), a similar interpretation can be applied: the performer must move the music from the beginning of one slur to the beginning of the next slur, without losing direction toward the goal by emphasizing the grammatical accents of the hierarchy of the meter. Nineteenth-century organ methods consistently state that the last note under a slur should be shortened ("abschleifen").[82] Put in context, it could mean everything from a subtle "enunciation" to a very short note with fast release that produces a strong accent on the next note.

The upbeat motive, a common feature of eighteenth-century *galant* style, is often indicated with a slur. The first note of the slurred motive must be accentuated, despite the fact that the beginning of the slur does not coincide with the hierarchy of the meter. Mendelssohn uses such motives with pairs of notes rather frequently, for example in Sonata II: 1 Grave and in the fugue in Sonata III: 1. In the pair-note motive of Sonata II: 1 Grave, the upbeat is an eighth note followed on the downbeat by a quarter note (and an eighth-note rest). On the clavichord, one can make a subtle decrescendo from the first to the second note. On the organ, such an effect can be achieved only if the second note is shorter than the first. Thus, the sounding value of the quarter note should not exceed the length of an eighth note, unless you would like to emphasize the downbeat. The articulation of both notes must be clear, so that the onset of the second note can be heard and the meter perceived. In the Grave (common time and *forte*), the motive should be played with the sounding length of two eighth notes, with a rather fast release of the first note, and a slow release of the second and no noticeable "distance" between the two. The Grave is succeeded by the *Adagio*, in which a slurred downbeat motive of two paired eighth notes forms a *suspiratio* or "sigh" motive. In this case, a decrescendo (dissonance and resolution) can only be accomplished if the sounding length of the second eighth note is noticeably shorter than that of the first. This motive may be played with the sounding length of an eighth note followed by a sixteenth note with slow releases of both.[83]

The articulation is determined by more parameters than just the slurs: the style of the piece, the time signature, the tempo, harmonic pulse, smallest note value, dynamics, and character annotation (Adagio, Allegro, etc.). Accordingly, slurs in different contexts would require different articulation. For example, the *fortissimo* bass lines in the following movements require a slightly different approach: in Sonata I: 1, measures 97–106 (C: Allegro moderato e serioso, the smallest note value is an eighth note), the bass should be played with firm legato; in Sonata I: 4, measures 108–12 (Alla breve: Allegro assai vivace, the smallest note value is an eighth note), the articulation of the bass should be more focused and clear; in Sonata IV: 4, measures 22–24 (C: Allegro maestoso e vivace, the smallest note value is a sixteenth note), the articulation should be light and brilliant ("staccato").

The different readings of the slurs in the English, German, Italian, and French editions of the Sonatas, included in the Novello edition (edited by Wm. A. Little), have caused confusion, primarily because they were interpreted merely as indications of modern legato.

If the slurs are interpreted as suggested above, in dynamic interaction with meter, harmonic direction, and character of the music, the inconsistencies are less conflicting. Georg Stauffer discusses the different versions of slurring of the solo motive in Sonata IV: 2, measures 10–14 and 20–24): "The point is not that he was inconsistent, but rather . . . that he used each form at least twice. To me, that would say, that the two-slur and one-slur versions are equally valid."[84] Also in the Andante religioso, the varying lengths and placement of the slurs in dynamic interaction with meter and pulse indicate small enunciations, phrase shape, and large harmonic direction. In his *Historical Performance Practice in Organ Playing, Part 2,* Jon Laukvik presents a detailed analysis of the Finale in VI: 3 and demonstrates how one can observe the slurs through articulation, touch, and timing. The full meaning of the slurs only emerges when they are seen in the context of meter and tempo.[85]

Tempo

Mendelssohn's "lightness of touch" had its correspondence in a brilliant performance style, and his tempos were considered fast by many. "Das Brilliante Spiel," an extroverted performance style described in organ and piano methods as the fast Allegro,[86] suited Mendelssohn's temperament well, and many praised the energy, fire, and drive of his performance. Clara Schumann (1819–96) recalled that he "would sometimes take the tempi very quick, but never to the music's disadvantage."[87] A statement from the famous conductor Hans von Bülow (1830–94) confirms Clara Schumann's view that the character of the music was integral to Mendelssohn's choice of tempos: "His style of playing had definitely a modern character, it was interesting and poetical, whereas the style of those organists who could not play the piano was hard without energy—in short, dry and leathery."[88] Bülow, known for taking great freedom with the tempo in his Wagner interpretations, recognized an unusual expressivity in Mendelssohn's organ playing.

In the third part of his Pianoforte-School, "Von dem Vortrage" (1839), Carl Czerny (1791–1857) states: "Now we have reached the third and almost most important means of performance, the various modifications of the prescribed tempo by way of rallentando and accelerando."[89] The flexible meter should be applied in general: "Regardless, there very often are, almost in every line, single notes or passages where a subtle retardation or acceleration, often hardly noticeable, is necessary to render the performance more beautiful and to increase interest."[90] Czerny considered this style "die grosse Kunst des guten Spielers"—the great art of the performer.

Tempo modification "durch der Affekt gegründet" can be traced back to the keyboard style of Carl Philipp Emanuel Bach (1714–88) and Daniel Gottlob Türk (1750–1813), who both generally favored sudden contrast and change of character.[91] Czerny in contrast recommends flexible meter, but without sudden fluctuations: "Not only an entire composition but also each individual passage expresses a certain sentiment or at least allows one to render such sentiment in performance."[92] Czerny presents a four-measure lyrical piano phrase with four alternative versions of interpretation. He prefers the (third) version with accelerando followed by rallentando, but states that all four versions are possible. He encourages the performer to explore various patterns of expressive playing, and requests variation whenever a section is repeated. "When such a passage occurs several times within a composition, the performer has not only the option but even has the obligation to vary its rendition each time in order to avoid monotony."[93] The necessity of variation in repetition is constant throughout music history. In the Baroque era, a repeated section would entail elaborate ornamentation on individual notes; in the *galant* style, recurring motives would call for a variation in the small-scale rhetorical shaping; and in the nineteenth century, longer phrases were expected to be shaped differently each time.

The English edition of Mendelssohn's Sonatas is the first collection of organ pieces published with metronome markings, added on request of the publisher rather than based on any desire of Mendelssohn's. In his memoirs, Hector Berlioz (1803–69) recalls:

> One day when I spoke of the metronome and its usefulness, Mendelssohn said sharply, "What on earth is the point of a metronome? It is a futile device. Any musician who cannot guess the tempo of a piece just by looking at it is a duffer." A few days later [he visited me again and] asked to see the score of the King Lear overture, which I had just composed in Nice. He read it through slowly and carefully and was about to begin playing it on the piano (which he did with incomparable skill), when he stopped and said, "Give me the right tempo."[94]

Mendelssohn's critical attitude is easy to understand: a skilled musician would immediately recognize the style, and if not, should be able to judge the tempo by identifying the character, time signature, smallest note values, and so on.[95] The use of the metronome as a device for student's practice, advocated by many teachers of the day, including Czerny,[96] was of no interest to Mendelssohn either, although he might have agreed that it could be useful for musicians unfamiliar with a particular style. The main use of the metronome was to document the composer's preference for pulse for future reference.[97]

The metronome numbers for some of the slow and lyrical movements of the Sonatas might seem fast at first—for example, II: 1; II: 2; IV: 2; IV: 3; and VI: Finale—but, if taken as a reference tempo for an expressive performance with constantly flexible meter, the result is convincing. A piece played with exact pulse is perceived as faster than when played with flexible meter. In fact, the combination of a rather fast reference pulse and flexible meter renders a compelling balance between energy and expressivity, and evokes an attractive and poetic effect.[98] A study of the relation between character designation, meter, smallest note value, harmonic pulse, and metronome indication shows that Mendelssohn, with almost no exception, followed the notational practice of his time, and was very careful in his choice of character designations as well as metronome indications. Table 7.2 presents an overview of all movements with information about character designation, meter, smallest note value, harmonic pulse, and Mendelssohn's metronome indications.

Table 7.2. Overview of Mendelssohn's organ sonatas

	Character designation	Meter	Smallest note value	Harmonic pulse	Mend. M.M.
I.1	Allegro moderato e serioso	C	eighth note	4 harm/m. 2/m. in 'chorale'	♩=92
I.2	Adagio	$\frac{3}{8}$	sixteenth note	2 harm/m.	♪=100
I.3	Andante Recitativo	C	eighth note	1 or 2 harm/m.	♩=80
I.4	Allegro assai vivace	Alla breve	mainly eighth notes, sixteenth notes at the end	mostly 1 harm/m.	𝅗𝅥=88
II.1	Grave	C	eighth note	2 harm/m.	♩=69
II.2	Adagio	$\frac{2}{4}$	sixteenth note	2 harm/m.	♪=72
II.3	Allegro maestoso e vivace	$\frac{3}{4}$	eighth note	1 or 3 harm/m.	♩=92
II.4	Fuga. Allegro moderato	Alla breve	eighth note	2 harm/m.	♩=132
III.1	Con moto maestoso	C	eighth note	2,(4) harm/m.	♩=72
	piu animato e piu forte	C	sixteenth note	1,2,4 harm/m.	♩=72–100
	tempo primo	C	eighth note	2,(4) harm/m.	♩=72

	Character designation	Meter	Smallest note value	Harmonic pulse	Mend. M.M.
III.2	Andante tranquillo	3/4	eighth note	3 or 1 harm/m.	♩=76
IV.1	Allegro con brio	C	sixteenth note	2 harm/m.	♩=100
IV.2	Andante religioso	C	eighth note	4 harm/m.	♩=84
IV.3	Allegretto	6/8	sixteenth note	2 harm/m.	♪=138
IV.4	Allegro maestoso e vivace	C	sixteenth note	4 harm/m. when eighth note is smallest; 2 harm/m. when sixteenth note is smallest	♩=100
V.1	Andante	Alla breve	half note	2 harm/m.	♩=100
V.2	Andante con moto	6/8	eighth note	2 harm/m.	♪=126
V.3	Allegro maestoso	C	eighth-note triplets	1 harm/m.	♩=126
VI.1	Choral	Alla breve	half notes	2 harm/m.	♩=100
	Andante sostenuto	Alla breve	sixteenth notes	2 harm/m.	♩=63
	12/8	12/8	eighth notes	4 harm/m.	♩.=63
	C	C	sixteenth notes	4 harm/m.	♩=63
	Allegro molto	Alla breve	sixteenth notes	2 harm/m.	𝅗𝅥=69
VI.2	Fuga–sostenuto e legato	3/4	quarter note	1 harm/m.	♩=96
VI.3	Finale–Andante	6/8	eighth note	6 (2) harm/m.	♪=100

Mendelssohn's attention to detail can be demonstrated by a comparison of a few pieces with the same character designations but different metronome indications. The numbers for I: 1 (Allegro moderato e serioso) and II: 4 (Fuga Allegro moderato) are quite far apart ($\quarternote$=92 and $\quarternote$=132). The latter is in alla breve, with a harmonic pulse of two per measure throughout; thus, it moves faster than a piece in common time, with four harmonies per measure. The II: 3, IV: 4, and V: 3 have the character designation Allegro maestoso [e vivace] but the metronome indications differ ($\quarternote$=92, $\quarternote$=100, $\quarternote$=126). The II: 3 is rather slow at 92 since it only has eighth notes, and often moves at one harmony per measure, resulting in a character of a maestoso march in triple meter. The V: 3 is set at 126. Its smallest note value, eighth-note triplets, is not as small as the sixteenths in IV: 4, and the harmony shifts only once per measure, resulting in a faster pulse.

The two Andante movements in $\frac{6}{8}$, V: 2, Andante con moto [$\eighthnote$=126], and VI: 3, Finale. Andante [$\eighthnote$=100], have different harmonic pulses, that is, two versus six harmonies per measure—ample reason to play V: 2 faster, even if con moto had not been added. It is interesting to note how the changes of harmonic pulse and smallest note value contribute to the distinct and contrasting characters within both of the movements III: 1, Con moto maestoso and IV: 4, Allegro maestoso e vivace.

The metronome number for II: 2, Adagio is set on the eighth note, which may indicate that it should be played as a $\frac{4}{8}$ rather than a $\frac{2}{4}$, as was sometimes the case with early eighteenth-century pieces in $\frac{2}{4}$. An early version of the piece was notated in $\frac{4}{4}$ with the character designation Andante con moto. The final choice of notation indicates a more singing and expressive character.

An overview of the Sonata movements ordered after meter is shown in table 7.3.

The chart enables us to see the variation of pulse with regard to time signatures. For common time, we notice an orientation of the metronome indications around three numbers:

1. $\quarternote$=60 (no character designation)
2. $\quarternote$=80 (Andante)
3. $\quarternote$=100 (Allegro)

The interval between the quarter notes of (1) and (2)—$\quarternote$=60 and $\quarternote$=80, respectively—corresponds to the range of *tempo ordinario* in the eighteenth century. Hymns seem to have an orientation around 50 beats per minute (I: 1, V: 1, and VI: 1). The figure for pieces in $\frac{6}{8}$ with (two harmonies per measure) $\eighthnote$≈120 (100–138) [Andante] is also in line with eighteenth-century practice.

The six Allegro movements all have quite different characters as captured in the qualifiers con brio, maestoso e vivace, maestoso, moderato e serioso, assai vivace, and the variation of the pulse from 88 to 126. Czerny, giving ten

Table 7.3. Overview of Mendelssohn's organ sonatas (ordered according to meter)

	Character designation	Meter	Smallest note value	Harmonic pulse	Mend. MM
IV.1	Allegro con brio	C	sixteenth note	2 harm/m.	♩=100
IV.4	Allegro maestoso e vivace	C	sixteenth note	4 harm/m. when eighth note is smallest; 2 harm/m. when sixteenth note is smallest	♩=100
V.3	Allegro maestoso	C	eighth-note triplets	1 harm/m.	♩=126
I.1	Allegro moderato e serioso	C	eighth note	4 harm/m. 2/m. in 'choral'	♩=92
III.1	Con moto maestoso	C	eighth note	2,(4) harm/m.	♩=72
	piu animato	C	sixteenth note	1,2,4 harm/m.	♩=72–100
	e piu forte	C			
	tempo primo		eighth note	2,(4) harm/m.	♩=72
I.3	Andante Recitativo	C	eighth note	1 or 2 harm/m.	♩=80
IV.2	Andante religioso	C	eighth note	4 harm/m.	♩=84
II.1	Grave	C	eighth note	2 harm/m.	♩=69
I.4	Allegro assai vivace	Alla breve	mainly eighth notes, sixteenth notes at the end	mostly 1 harm/m.	𝅗𝅥=88
II.4	Fuga. Allegro moderato	Alla breve	eighth note	2 harm/m.	𝅗𝅥=132
V.1	Andante	Alla breve	half note	2 harm/m.	𝅗𝅥=100

(continued)

Table 7.3.—*(concluded)*

	Character designation	Meter	Smallest note value	Harmonic pulse	Mend. MM
VI.1	Choral	Alla breve	half notes	2 harm/m.	♩=100
	Andante sostenuto	Alla breve	sixteenth note	2 harm/m.	♩=63
	12/8	12/8	eighth note	4 harm/m.	♩.=63
	C	C	sixteenth note	4 harm/m.	♩=63
	Allegro molto	Alla breve	sixteenth note	2 harm/m.	𝅗𝅥=69
II.2	Adagio	2/4	sixteenth note	2 harm/m.	♪=72
II.3	Allegro maestoso e vivace	3/4	eighth note	1 or 3 harm/m.	♩=92
III.2	Andante tranquillo	3/4	eighth note	3 or 1 harm/m.	♩=76
VI.2	Fuga– sostenuto e legato	3/4	quarter note	1 harm/m.	♩=96
I.2	Adagio	3/6	sixteenth note	2 harm/m.	♪=100
IV.3	Allegretto	6/8	sixteenth note	2 harm/m.	♪=138
V.2	Andante con moto	6/8	eighth note	2 harm/m.	♪=126
VI.3	Finale– Andante	6/8	eighth note	6 (2) harm/m.	♪=100

examples, underlines that Allegro can have many different characters and meanings, from "calm, gentle, and ingratiating" (ruhig, sanft und einschmeichelnd), "profound or enthusiastic" (tiefsinnig oder schwärmerisch) to "stormily fast, very wild, excited, and exuberant" (stürmisch schnell; sehr wild, aufgeregt und ausgelassen), and "furious" (furios).[99] The metronome numbers for II: 3, Allegro maestoso e vivace, ♩=92, and I: 4, Allegro assai vivace, 𝅗𝅥=88, seem on the slow side, considering the *vivace* designation. They certainly fit, however, within the wide range of characters given by Czerny. The tendency for an Allegro in common time seems to be an orientation around ♩=100. This is the "new tempo," the faster pulse for an Allegro mentioned in many sources in the first half of the nineteenth century.[100]

In the seventeenth century, the smallest note value of organ pieces (in our modern editions notated as sixteenth or even thirty-second notes) were at least as fast as the same note values in the nineteenth-century Allegro. The pulse was, however, generally slower. Several seventeenth-century sources refer to the difference between the pulse (which is slow) and the movement (the actual notes, which can be fast), of which the seventeenth-century chorale fantasia is a good example.[101] In the Allegro movements of the eighteenth-century concerto style, there is still a difference, now between the slow harmonic pulse and the fast note values. In the nineteenth-century Allegro, this difference is reduced; there is a higher frequency of accents, which makes the music sound "faster." This important character was a feature of Mendelssohn's style, and is well represented in the Sonatas.[102]

Romantic Musical Speeches: Form and Meaning in the Sonatas

With the opus 65 Sonatas, Mendelssohn attempted to "develop thoughts suitable for the organ,"[103] partly with a pedagogical purpose, but also (and primarily) with the intention of creating an artful and comprehensive collection. Most likely, he had in mind examples like the Six Trio Sonatas and other collections, or selections thereof, by Johann Sebastian Bach, such as the *WTC* or the Six Partitas, Wilhelm Friedemann Bach's Twelve Polonaises and Carl Philipp Emanuel Bach's Eighteen *Probestücke*, Six Prussian Sonatas, and Six Württemberg Sonatas. In his *Sieben Charakterstücke* (MWV U56, U44, U59, U55, U60, U61, and U62; op. 7 [1827]) and Six Preludes and Fugues (MWV U116/U66, U129/U105, U131/U91, U122/U108, U126/U106, and U135/U128; op. 35 [1832–37]) for piano, Mendelssohn had already presented similarly ambitious collections that exploited Baroque idioms and counterpoint, contrasting and combining them with a contemporary style. With opus 65 he took a step further in terms of bringing these worlds together while creating cyclical and comprehensive forms. This would not just be randomly gathered movements of genre pieces like the *Lieder ohne Worte*, but rather complex, intertwined, even experimental Sonatas, corresponding to the eighteenth-century "Klang-Reden," musical speeches, a term coined by Johann Mattheson in 1739, when he described the nature and form of the multisectional organ works of the German master organists.[104] Schumann, as we have seen, considered the Sonatas "truly new poetical forms" (ächt poetischen neuen Formen), and Ritter, in his 1846 review of opus 65, takes a similar stand:[105] "The term 'sonata' here is completely justified by the necessary context of the individual movements. By this we do not mean merely external connections provided by key or melody, but those invisible relations that, being rooted in the spiritual structure of the piece, are prepared here and find a resolution there. Viewed from this angle, some of the sonatas, especially those that are furthest removed from the traditional form, appear as deeply conceived and deeply felt masterpieces."[106] Ritter does not question Mendelssohn's use of the term Sonata, although it is hard to find examples of traditional sonata form in the music. He recognizes how tightly knit the Sonatas are through the "external connections" of thematic and harmonic relationships, but also through a "spiritual structure," evident mostly in the Sonatas that show divergences from traditional form.

The Interpretation of Mendelssohn's First Sonata: A Case Study

Mendelssohn's creative use of form and contrasting ideas generates dramatic tension and associations that attract Ritter. In fact, it motivates him to give a rather detailed analysis of his favorite Sonatas, the first and the third, in the review:

> Sonata 1 . . . begins with full-voiced, powerful chords that, initially, are rather general and preparatory, but already in measure 11 lead to a principal idea of a speaking nature. As [do] all the themes presented in the entire work, this one has such an expressive character that it is completely justified to use the term "speaking." It is the despondent lament of a depressed heart, which utters itself here in tones, ever louder and more frightful the closer the feared fate approaches. Then, after a cadence in C minor [m. 40], a chorale-like section sounds; it seems to be carried by angelic voices and brings consolation from the heaven above. True, it alternates with interjections—sometimes shorter, sometimes longer—of the principal idea, which is now treated with increased liveliness, and at times its texture is even invaded by the lament. But soon the song of consolation sounds in victorious elevations, high above earthly suffering. The movement concludes in gentle chords reinforced by the powerful stream of the full organ sound. And yet, it is not a jubilant triumphal song; the minor third reminds us of the earlier laborious struggle. The heart comes to rest not until the following Adagio (A-flat major, $\frac{3}{8}$ meter) and the Recitatives [Andante], the latter functioning as a transition to the final movement. The lament has been silenced. Being saved, our hero erupts in joyful sounds, as they can be felt only by a human heart: Allegro assai vivace. Shimmering, fiery chords, supported by the powerful tones of the basses, resound in animated arpeggios. And as the rejoicing heart in its initial ecstasy searches in vain for a definitive expression and only finds the right words after it has calmed down somewhat, so do the chords initially move back and forth seemingly without direction and only gradually gain coherence and structure. Finally, the chords swarm around the jubilant melody, which now resounds below and above, and ultimately ends in a full and bright F-major chord with the third in the top voice. This is the real conclusion of the sonata. The arpeggios, in the following four measures, perhaps not entirely appropriate for the organ, are to be considered an appendix.[107]

Indeed, Ritter associates the composition with a musical speech. After an exordium of eleven measures, the main idea (*propositio*) is presented. He underlines the "speaking" nature of the theme in view of its particularly expressive nature. It contains a descending diminished fourth (c^2–g^1–ab^1–e^1) that generates an atmosphere of "despondent lament of a depressed heart." Ritter describes the chorale as "carried by angelic voices" that "bring consolation from the heaven above." It is played with soft sounds (*mp*) on a separate manual, and is notated on two separate staves above the three staves of the dramatic fugue (*ff*), which visually enhances the contrast between the two themes.[108] The last two phrases of the chorale are treated in sequences on different pitches, with full organ over a fast figuration in the pedal ("high above earthly suffering"), a dramatic juxtaposition of fugue and chorale. In the last nine measures of the movement, the conflict between heaven and earth has dissolved; what remains is the slow chorale in simple harmony, played softly at first, but ending with full organ in *fortissimo* and in F minor with the minor third suggesting that the "struggle" on Earth has not yet been resolved.

In the recitative we are dramatically reminded of the conflicting elements of the first movement. However, Ritter states that the resolution arrived already with the *Adagio* ("the heart comes to rest"). The final movement paints the emotion of a rejoicing heart "in ecstasy," from measure 68 rendered by a jubilant melody. Ritter draws our attention to the (spiritual) contrast between the minor third of the first movement, emphasized by expressive harmony and *fortissimo* in the last five measures, and its resolution in the major third of the top voice of the final movement in measure 134. The "jubilant melody" of the last movement starts with a five-note motive that responds as a mirror-gesture to the theme of the fugue; Ritter stresses the importance of the four-measure long F-major chord with the third (a'') in the top voice as the ultimate resolution of the struggle on Earth, and he considers the following arpeggios unnecessary and unsuitable to the organ. Perhaps he noticed that at the end of the movement, the fugue theme appears in the top voice in augmented form in major (c^3–g^2 in m. 133; a^2 in mm. 134–37; e^2–f^2 in mm. 143–44), however interrupted by the fast arpeggios (mm. 138–41), which he considers a rhetorical "appendix."

Earth and Heaven are symbolically represented by the fugue and the chorale, respectively, in the first movement. The contrast between these two worlds is expressed in the overall form by the juxtaposition of old and new, by Baroque (fugue, chorale, and recitative) and Romantic forms (character pieces based on melody and harmony), by Bach's and Mendelssohn's tonal worlds, and the shift between minor and major tonality.[109] In the spiritual dimension of the Sonata, Ritter sees a poetic form that takes the lonely soul from lament and depression to resolution and jubilation. Larry Todd has shown the resemblance between the principal theme of the fugue with that of the recitative (no. 25) from Bach's *St. Matthew Passion,* Jesus's prayer at Gethsemane. Bach presents the theme with its descending forbidden diminished fourth (*saltus duriusculus*) over a pedal point, juxtaposed with the choral: "Herzliebster Jesu, was hast du verbrochen?" (Ah, holy Jesus, how hast thou offended) in the key of F minor. A few moments later (no. 31), he brings in the chorale "Was mein Gott will, das g'scheh allzeit," which is the chorale that Mendelssohn chose for his Sonata—as a response to Jesus's prayer "My father, if this cannot pass unless I drink it, your will be done." According to Todd, "the first movement of the sonata impresses as a musical reading, or improvisation, on Bach's music and uses Bach's preferred instrument to penetrate the spirit of the Passion. . . . Ultimately, the sonata, and Op. 65 as a whole, remains paradoxically Janus-faced, eyeing the baroque splendors of Bach through the lens of Felix's own stylistic identity."[110]

In the spiritual dimension of the Sonata, Ritter sees a poetic form that takes the lonely soul from lament and depression to resolution and jubilation. Particularly, his detailed description of how the music reflects the initial phase of spiritual ecstasy ("as the rejoicing heart in its initial ecstasy searches in vain for a definitive expression and only finds the right words after it has calmed down somewhat") shows his recognition of the Sonata as a composition not only of spiritual structure but of spiritual nature. It is more than a musical speech. It is a musical rendering of religious sentiment and spiritual transformation. Through the association with Bach's *St. Matthew Passion*, Mendelssohn takes us from the despair and solitude of Christ in Gethsemane to his Resurrection, which brings salvation and eternal communion with God. (This is a recurring theme in Mendelssohn's music in the 1840s, also recognizable in other Sonatas, and it is at the core of the Symphony Cantata "Lobgesang" [MWV A18, op. 52] in which the composer presents a magnificent example of such a transformation *per musica*, the ultimate triumph of light over darkness.[111])

A Lost Program for the Sonatas?

The case study of the First Sonata shows that Mendelssohn's contemporaries interpreted it as a musical speech with poetic meaning and imbued with a spiritual nature. Ritter gives a detailed analysis also of the Third Sonata, in which he recognizes the dramatic contrast between the outer movements ("calm and joyful confidence") and the tritone theme of the double fugue ("frightening") composed over the choral "Aus tiefer Not schrei ich zu dir" (From deepest woe I cry to thee) in the bass, which is resolved by the Andante tranquillo, perceived "as a quiet and deeply felt prayer of Thanksgiving."[112]

The Sonatas continued to be interpreted as poetic forms and toward the end of the century in England, literary references were common practice. In 1902, Charles William Pearce reports:

It has also been stated that the composer issued to the subscribers to the first edition of his work, a sort of prospectus or circular, giving a kind of explanatory programme for each Sonata. This circular—evidently because of its detached or "inset" character—has unhappily become so rare as to be practically extinct; but in the absence of Mendelssohn's own ideas I have tried to show that it is by no means difficult for any appreciative player or listener to form his own ideal conception of the composers meaning, or at any rate to attach a poetical signification of a definite and intelligible kind, which when considered in connection with the music may be said in some degree to express very much the same ideas in ordinary verbal language. This definiteness of purpose and aim may not be altogether an unimportant factor in the success which has attended these Sonatas for the last half century or more.[113]

Whether Mendelssohn wrote literary commentaries to the Sonatas or not, we do not know. I have not been able to find any reference to such elsewhere in the literature. Nevertheless, it is clear that Pearce considers it important for performers and listeners alike, to develop an interpretation of the meaning of the Sonatas, or at least to attach a poetical significance. He gives examples of suitable poems for several of the Sonatas and some individual movements, for example the Allegretto (IV: 3), which he considers "a veritable Frühlingslied" (Spring Song).[114] And he equates the various sections of Sonata VI with the verses of the Lord's Prayer,[115] an interpretation that has been picked up by critics later in the twentieth century.[116] In this context it is perhaps worth recalling that Robert Schumann was particularly impressed by the unusual poetic form of Sonata VI.

Following a similar mode of hermeneutic interpretation, Christopher Petit has recently observed that the number of movements of Sonata I corresponds to the number of verses of the hymn "Was mein Gott will, das g'scheh allzeit." Although it is only the first movement of Sonata I that quotes this hymn, it is still possible that Mendelssohn used the hymn text as inspiration for the form. Petit finds the similarities between musical *Affekt* in the four movements and the character of the text striking and suggests the following interpretation:

The first verse depicts a fair, just God who both assists and punishes, a typical Old Testament presentation of omnipotence. It seems appropriate, then, that Mendelssohn's first movement would be serioso and contrapuntal. The second stanza paints the picture of the New Testament Christ as shepherd. He "counts our individual hairs," comforts us, and watches over us. Mendelssohn's setting is, likewise, a pastoral aria. The opening, descending-fifth motive of the recitative is an extreme change of character, but the hymn's third verse does open with "Now must I, a sinner from this world!" It seems highly appropriate that such an awareness of the human, flawed self would be set as a plaintive and stormy recitative. The last seven measures of the recitative consist of rising, four-voice chords that lead to the dominant of the toccata's F major. Their character departs from the previous drama of the recitative, but so does the last sentence of the third stanza: "You, holy God, have overcome for me sin, hell, and death." Perhaps the chromatically rising bass line depicts our hope in salvation. If so, then the final, exuberant toccata represents the final words of the entire hymn: "I say joyfully: Amen!"[117]

Petit's interpretation of the four hymn verses indeed supports Ritter's analysis of the Sonata and the interpretation discussed above in the case study. The hymn text is a paraphrase of Christ's prayer in Gethsemane and simultaneously a prayer for every Christian who identifies himself with Jesus and is prepared to follow his example. The pastoral *Affekt* ($\frac{3}{8}$, Adagio, *pianissimo*) convincingly renders the general character of the text of verse two; verse three provides a libretto that Mendelssohn almost literally rendered in the recitative, particularly in the second half (mm. 29–52) with its slow diminished arpeggio chord, repeated a half step higher each time ("Mein' arme Seel'/ Ich Gott befehl' / In meiner letzten Stunden" [I relinquish my poor soul to God in my last hour]); and the modulation in the last seven measures provides the perfect bridge to the jubilant ecstasy of the Allegro assai vivace.

Mendelssohn deliberately chose to integrate chorales in a genre of instrumental music, Sonatas, in which they normally would not be found. We have seen that, most likely, he also used hymn texts as form-creating parameters. However, integrating chorales into opus 65 was an essential part of his experimental way of developing musical thoughts for the organ.

The Chorale: Its Symbolism and Role in the Sonatas

In the nineteenth century, music was generally considered the supreme medium to evoke and transfer emotion to the listener, as the language of the senses (*Sprache des Gefühls*).[118] Also in theology, music was considered to be a language without words. The theologian Friedrich Schleiermacher (1768–1834), founder of liberal theology and very influential to the evangelical theology of the nineteenth century, argued that religion is essentially an intuition and feeling, and he considered music a speech that without words brings the feeling of the eternal to the individual souls. In fact, one would not need to understand the words of a text since the music itself communicated their emotional meaning.[119]

Mendelssohn's *Songs Without Words* embody this concept, and we recognize examples of this genre among the soft character pieces of the Sonatas. Nevertheless, it is the chorale that stands out as the most significant thematic material in his opus 65; he chose to use chorale melodies with well-known texts in three of his Sonatas (I, III, and VI) and a chorale without words in another one (V).

In the nineteenth century, the chorale was associated with the sublime and "became a symbol of religious exaltation." Its slowly moving parts and homophonic texture were perceived "as musical symbols of a universal and enduring validity."[120] Mendelssohn begins the last two Sonatas with such chorales and in the character of the sublime. At the organ, it was natural for him to improvise on chorale melodies, and to play the chorales by Bach. He was convinced that Bach's chorale "Schmücke dich o liebe Seele" in itself bore the potential to evoke a true sense of comfort and hope, beyond and above what words can communicate, and that anyone who listened to it would experience its spiritual dimension and healing effect.[121] Another Bach chorale that attracted him immensely was "Wir glauben all an einen Gott" (BWV 740). Meischein has shown the connection between this chorale and the Adagio of Sonata II, which is particularly obvious in the notation and the shape of the final melodic cadence in the first version of this movement.[122] The composer created a work with close affinity to its source of inspiration, in character as well as in texture (flowing eighth notes, a flourish of sixteenth notes at the end). Instead of a pure chorale, Mendelssohn created what we may call an aria-chorale, rendering the sense of belief and hope he found in Bach's setting. The atmosphere of the Adagio sets the stage for the jubilant character of the following movement, Allegro maestoso e vivace.

The Cycle of Romantic Musical Speeches: An Overview and Some Observations

Mendelssohn's collection of Sonatas continues the eighteenth-century German tradition of comprehensive keyboard and organ collections that served as educational resources in the broadest sense. They were not merely methods conveying technical and musical material, but were created and compiled according to the principles and ideals of art and science.

Based on Pearce's report, it is reasonable to assume that Mendelssohn created all of his Sonatas with programs according to Romantic musical speeches, as we saw in the case study of Sonata I, and that he organized the collection according to a particular concept.

The following chart presents the fundamental tonalities of all the movements and the chorales included.

Sonata I	("Was mein Gott will, das g'scheh allzeit")	f–Ab–[f]–F
Sonata II	(Aria-Chorale Paraphrase "Wir glauben all an einen Gott")	c–C
Sonata III	("Aus tiefer Noth")	A–a–A–A
Sonata IV		Bb–Bb–F–Bb
Sonata V	(Chorale)	D–b–D
Sonata VI	("Vater unser im Himmelreich")	d–D

In three of the Sonatas (II, III, and VI) all movements have the same tonic, but they shift mode between minor and major. Two Sonatas (I and V) shift to the relative key in the second movement. Two Sonatas (I and IV) have more complex schemes including tonic, its relative major or dominant. In general, the tonal schemes of the individual Sonatas are surprisingly simple: no unexpected change of pitch between movements as means of character change (as in the *Eighteen Probestücke in Sechs Sonaten* by C. P. E. Bach) and no chromatic order (as in the *WTC*). The tonal schemes are similar to those of the Baroque suite. The only third relations noticeable are between Sonatas II and III (C–A) and between Sonatas IV and V (B♭–D). It is interesting to note that the last two Sonatas have their fundamental pitch in common, D, the key in which Mendelssohn liked to begin his improvisations.

Sonata IV does not have a chorale as thematic material and no reference to a chorale like Sonata II.[123] It has the most traditional four-movement form of all Sonatas with two Allegro movements surrounding an Andante and an Allegretto. Ritter identifies the first movement as a transcription of an orchestral piece,[124] and this Sonata follows the form-pattern of the classical symphony more than any other. Sonata I also has four movements. It is logical to see the collection organized as two sets of three sonatas each. Each of the sets begins with a four-movements Sonata with a somewhat more complex tonal scheme.

The fundamental pitches of the first three Sonatas (F–C–A) played together form an F-major chord. The pitches of the last three Sonatas (B♭–D–D) form a major third. The first set is dominated by descending motives, often a minor sixth, and in a few movements, as a relief, this is inverted to an ascending major sixth. The second set is dominated by ascending motives, often octaves, or major thirds, or tenths. The two groups of three Sonatas are organized in a V to I (dominant-tonic) relation with the pitches F (Sonata I) and B♭ (B in German) (Sonata IV). It is possible that Mendelssohn organized the sets according to the letters F and B of his name: Felix Mendelssohn Bartholdy.

Mendelssohn ended his Bach recital in Leipzig in 1840 with a *Freie Phantasie*, based on the passion chorale "O Haupt voll Blut und Wunden," and a fugue with Bach's musical signature: B–A–C–H. This improvisation impressed Schumann very much, and he wrote in a review that it sounded like a "finished composition." Felix's homage to Bach inspired Schumann to use the same theme in his Six Fugues on B–A–C–H, op. 60, "trying to perpetuate something of Felix's twofold mastery," that of "one master emulating another."[125]

The pitches of A and B (B♭), the two first letters of Bach's name, are the fundamental pitches of Sonata III, ending the first set of three, and Sonata IV, beginning the last set of three. The pitch of Sonata II is C and the pitch of Sonata V: 3 is H (B). Sonatas II, III, IV (1, 2, 4) and V (2) contain the pitches that correspond to Bach's musical signature B–A–C–H. We can see that Mendelssohn has ordered the Six Sonatas with regard to pitch so that the combination of Bach's name and his own (F–B) form the basis for the collection. Bach's name can also be found within some of the movements of the Sonatas, for example, in I: 1, measures 126–28 (treble); in II: 1, measures 46–48 (bass); in III: 1 (second part of theme, mm. 26–28); in IV: 3, measures 66–68 (bass); in V: 2, measures 20–22; and in VI: 1, measures 110–11 and measures 174–78.

Conclusion

Most likely, Mendelssohn created the Six Sonatas as a homage to the Thomas-Kantor in Leipzig. He juxtaposes the *old* (counterpoint, hymns, traditional techniques, and genres) with the *new* (vocal, instrumental, and orchestral styles, and character pieces). The connections in key relationships and thematic material between the Sonatas and between individual movements are carefully crafted and deliberately designed. The chorales were the center of the vocal and instrumental works by Bach, and they are also key for the understanding of Mendelssohn's Sonatas. In fact, even though he does not engage in text painting (one of the principal compositional means of relating text and music in the Baroque era), Mendelssohn uses the chorale texts as form-generating factors. The first three Sonatas are characterized by the main theme of Sonata I: the Gethsemane drama as Mendelssohn experienced it in Bach's *St. Matthew Passion.* All three Sonatas move from darkness, suffering, and struggle to resolution and jubilation, or, at least, as in the case of Sonata III, relief. The fourth and the fifth Sonatas are characterized by jubilation, life and energy, however the sixth has a more serious character; it explores the central prayer of Christianity, the Our Father. Instead of an expected jubilant ending corresponding to the doxology of the prayer, Mendelssohn's Sonata culminates in the middle with a dramatic outburst, like a "Sturm und Drang" fantasia by W. F. Bach, that never completely resolves. The majestic and jubilant beginning and ending of Sonata III: 1 stands in stark contrast to the ever-increasing struggle and despair rendered by the crescendo chorale fugue, which also never completely resolves. In these six Romantic musical speeches, we may find yet another dimension: the enlightened Romantic artist's perception of the human dilemma, societal conflict and injustice in the time of democracy's birth in Europe.[126] The fact that they were perceived as expressive and dramatic musical speeches among his contemporaries challenges our perception and interpretation of the Sonatas. Performing them on an organ of eighteenth-century style, character, sensitivity, and expressive color, like the C-S organ in Christ Church in Rochester, New York, brings truly new dimensions of experience to performers and listeners alike.

Appendix 7.1

Brandenburg Dom, Joachim Wagner, Berlin 1725

Hauptwerk I C, D–c3	
Bordun	16′
Principal	8′
Rohrflöte	8′
Quintadena	8′
Viola da Gamba	8′
Octave	4′
Spitzflöte	4′
Quinte	2 2/3′
Octave	2′
Cornett 5f.	8′
Scharff 5f.	1 1/3′
Cimbel 3f.	1′
Trompete	8′

Oberwerk II C, D–c3	
Quintadena	16′
Principal	8′
Gedackt	8′
Octave	4′
Rohrflöte	4′
Nasat	2 2/3′
Octave	2′
Terz	1 3/5′
Sifflöte	1′
Mixtur 4f.	1 1/3′
Vox Humana	8′

Pedal C, D–c1		
Principal	16'	
Violon	16'	
Gemshorn	8'	
Quinte	6'	
Octave	4'	
Mixtur 6f.		
Posaune		16'
Trompete		8'

Source: Hermann Busch, "Es kommt . . . auf richtige Wahl der Register sehr viel an: Zur Orgelpraxis Felix Mendelssohn Bartholdys," in *Zur Deutschen Orgelmusik des 19. Jahrhunderts,* eds. Hermann J. Busch and Michael Heinemann, 3rd ed. (St. Augustin: Dr. J. Butz Musikverlag, 2006), 147–53, esp. 147.

Appendix 7.2

Frankfurt am Main, Katharinenkirche

Franz und Johann Michael II. Stumm, Rhaunen-Sulzbach, 1779

Specifications from a source dated 1845.

Hauptwerk I C–d3	
Groß Bordun	16'
Principal	8'
Viola da Gamba	8'
Gedackt	8'
Quintadena	8'
Octave	4'
Flöte	4'
Salicional	4'
Quinte	2 2/3'
Superoctave	2'
Waldflöte	2'

Hauptwerk I C–d3 *(continued)*	
Cornett 5f.	8'
Mixtur 4f.	2'
Cimbel 2f.	1'
Trompete Bass/Disk.	8'

Positiv II C–d3	
Hohlpfeife (Gedackt)	8'
Flauttravers (Diskant) 8'	
Salicional	8'
Principal	4'
Rohrflöte	4'
Quinte	2 2/3'
Octave	2'
Mixtur 4f.	
Krummhorn	8'
Vox Humana	8'

Echowerk III C–d3	
Hohlpfeife (Gedackt)	8'
Flöte	4'
Spitzflöte	4'
Octave	2'
Quinte	1 1/3'
Krummhorn	8'
Vox Humana	8'

Pedal C–c1	
Principal	16'
Subaß	16'
Violon	16'
Octave	8'
Superoctave	4'
Mixturbaß 5f.	2'
Posaune	16'
[Trompete	8'?]
Clarine	4'
Kornett	2'

Source: Hermann Busch, "Es kommt . . . auf richtige Wahl der Register sehr viel an: Zur Orgelpraxis Felix Mendelssohn Bartholdys," in *Zur Deutschen Orgelmusik des 19. Jahrhunderts,* eds. Hermann J. Busch and Michael Heinemann, 3rd ed. (St. Augustin: Dr. J. Butz Musikverlag, 2006), 147–53, esp. 149.

Notes

The author gratefully acknowledges the help he received from Ulrika Davidsson, Paul Peeters, Joel Speerstra, and Munetaka Yokota in finalizing this essay. His thanks extend also to Jacques van Oortmerssen, who gave inspiring masterclasses on Mendelssohn's organ music at the Craighead-Saunders Organ during the EROI Festival 2009 and who generously shared his thoughts on the issues addressed in this chapter.

1   Friedhold Bötel, *Mendelssohns Bachrezeption und ihre Konsequenzen dargestellt an den Präludien und Fugen für Orgel op. 37* (Munich and Salzburg: Emil Katzbichler, 1984), 21.

2   Wm. A. Little, *Mendelssohn and the Organ* (New York: Oxford University Press, 2010), 6.

3   Cited in Bötel, *Mendelssohns Bachrezeption*, 34. "Der Knabe hat einen guten Anfang gemacht im Orgelspielen und es wird ihm zur Lehre und Ehre werden, die Quellen zu finden, aus welchen in unserer Zeit Gutes und Rechtes kommt." Unless a published English translation is cited, the tranlations of German quotations in this article are provided by the editor.

4   Markus Zepf, "Felix Mendelssohn Bartholdy in Süddeutschland: Ein Beitrag zur oberrheinischen Musikkultur im 19. Jahrhundert," in *"Diess herrliche, imponierende Instrument": Die Orgel im Zeitalter Felix Mendelssohn-Bartholdys*, ed. Anselm Hartinger, Christoph Wolff, and Peter Wollny (Wiesbaden, Leipzig, Paris: Breitkopf und Härtel, 2011), 203–26, esp. 220.

5   Cited in Bötel, *Mendelssohns Bachrezeption*, 32. "Soll ich ihn mit einem unter uns Lebenden vergleichen, so weiß ich keinen anderen neben ihn zu stellen."

6   Cited in ibid. "Wie sein Pianofortespiel, war auch sein Orgelspiel, man glaubte einen Meister aus vergangenen Jahrhunderten zu vernehmen, der lebenslänglich sich mit kontrapunktischen Combinationen beschäftigt hat, und in Improvisationen ausströmen ließ, was andere und Neuere nur mühsam auf dem Papiere auszurechnen vermögen."

7   Cited in ibid.

8   Little, *Mendelssohn and the Organ*, 132–38.

9   See Bötel, *Mendelssohns Bachrezeption*, 36; Little, *Mendelssohn and the Organ*, 104–18; and Nobuaki Ebata, Yo Tamita, and Ian Mills, "Mendelssohn and the Schübler Chorales (BWV 645–50): A New Source Found in the Riemenschneider Bach Institute Collection," *BACH: Journal of the Riemenschneider Bach Institute* 44, no. 1 (June 2013), 1–45.

10   Little, *Mendelssohn and the Organ*, 136.

11   Cited in Andreas Glöckner, "Bach-Organisten des frühen 19. Jahrhunderts und ihre Repertoire," in Hartinger, Wolff, and Wollny, *"Diess herrliche, imponierende Instrument,"* 333–42, esp. 341. "Gehen Sie noch zu Schneider, da können Sie was Tüchtiges lernen." Today, we probably would consider Adolph Friedrich Hesse (1809–63), *Oberorganist* in St. Bernhard in Breslau and student of Johann Christian Heinrich Rinck (1770–1846) in Dresden from 1828 to 1829, as the most well-known "Bach organist" among Mendelssohn's contemporaries. In 1831–32, he toured the main cities of Germany, including Leipzig, Kassel, Hamburg, and Berlin, performing mainly works by Bach. In 1844, he was invited to play in Paris at St. Eustache where he presented five large Bach works before an audience of 10,000 listeners (pp. 339–40). It was this event that sparked interest in Bach's organ music in France. Today, the idea that Hesse was a "direct link" from Johann Sebastian Bach

to the French organ tradition down to the twentieth century (Kittel–Rinck–Hesse–Lemmens–Widor–Dupré) is regarded as a legend.

12 August Gottfried Ritter in *Allgemeine musikalische Zeitung* 46 (February 11, 1846), 97–102, esp. 97 and 102. "erscheinen einige der Sonaten, und gerade jene von der herkömmlichen Form am Meisten sich entfernenden, als tiefgedachte, tiefempfundene Meisterstücke. . . . Somit schliessen wir unser Referat über ein Werk, das, in vielfacher Hinsicht so neu und eigenthümlich, einen grossen Reichthum des Vortrefflichen und Schönen birgt und gewiss nicht ohne wichtige Folgen für unsere, den hergebrachten Formen mehr, als dem alten Geiste huldigende Orgelliteratur bleiben wird."

13 Cited in Gerd Zacher, "Die riskanten Beziehungen zwischen Sonate und Kirchenlied," in *Felix Mendelssohn-Bartholdy* (*Musik-Konzepte* 14/15), ed. Heinz-Klaus Metzger and Rainer Riehn (Munich: Johannesdruck Hans Pribil, 1980), 34–45. "Noch zuletzt haben wir uns in Ihre Orgelsonaten versenkt. . . . Und dabei doch Überall das Vorwärtsstreben, weshalb Sie mir immer als Vorbild dastehen. Diese ächt poetischen neuen Formen, wie sie sich in jeder Sonate zum vollkommenen Bild runden—vor allem haben mir Nr. 5 und 6 bedeutend geschienen."

14 For a thorough presentation of the methodology of the project, see Joel Speerstra, "Opening a Window on the Enlightenment: A Research Organ for the Eastman School of Music," in *Keyboard Perspectives: Yearbook of the Westfield Center for Historical Keyboard Studies*, vol. 1, ed. Annette Richards (Ithaca, NY: Westfield Center, 2008), 113–35.

15 Cited in Bötel, *Mendelssohns Bachrezeption*, 29: "Drei sehr gute Orgeln sind hier von Wagner gebaut, demselben, der unsere besten in der Marien-, Garnison- und Parochialkirche [St. Gotthardt] aufgesetzt hat."

16 Little, *Mendelssohn and the Organ*, 8.

17 Burkhard Meischein, "Stimmung, Choral und Text: Mendelssohn und die Geburt der religiösen Empfindung aus dem Geiste der Hermeneutik," in Hartinger, Wolff, and Wollny, *"Diess herrliche, imponierende Instrument,"* 37–56, esp. 46. "Du kennst das schon von Berlin her."

18 For more details see, for example, Quentin Faulkner, *The Registration of J. S. Bach's Organ Works* (Colfax: Wayne Leupold Editions, 2008).

19 "Bei sanften Vorträgen, wo man vielleicht 2 oder 3 Register mit einander verbindet, muß man stets darauf sehen, daß man nie Stimmen von gleicher Intonation zusammenstellt, weil sonst keine Vermittelung des entweder zu schneidend oder zu dumpf klingenden Orgeltons eintritt. . . . Es müssen also Stimmen von entgegengesetztem Character mit einander verbunden werden, diese treten dann einander helfend entgegen, indem die schneidende Stimme die dumpf klingende hebt und die dumpf klingende das Schneidende der andern mildert." See Hermann J. Busch, "Zur Registrierungskunst der deutschen romantischen Orgel," in *Zur Deutschen Orgelmusik des 19. Jahrhunderts*, ed. Hermann J. Busch and Michael Heinemann, 3rd ed. (St. Augustin: Dr. J. Butz Musikverlag, 3/2006), 63–74, esp. 67.

20 "Bei gleichzeitiger Anwendung der 3 Gamben (Viola maj. 16′, Viola di G. 8′ und Violino 4′) müßen diese Stimmen noch durch Bordun 16′, Hohlflöte 8′, Gedact 8′, und allenfalls noch durch Spitzflöte 4′ unterstützt werden. Doch kann letztere Stimme, sollte sie nicht recht rein stimmen, auch fehlen. . . . Beim Gebrauch des Salicional 8′ ziehe man stets Gedact 8′ hinzu. Man erzielt dadurch eine bessere Ansprache und vollständigere Tonentwicklung der ersteren Stimme. Auch kann man, beabsichtigt man mehr Fülle, noch Bordun 16′ auch Gemshorn 4′ hinzu

nehmen, mit welchen Stimmen sich Salicional sehr wohl verträgt." See Joachim Walter, *"This Heaving Ocean of Tones": Nineteenth-Century Organ Registration Practice at St. Marien, Lübeck* (Göteborg: Göteborg University Press, 2000), 191, 197.

21   See Markus Zepf (note 4), 205, on South German instruments.

22   August Gottfried Ritter, *Kunst des Orgelspiels*, vol. 1, op. 15, facsimile (Niedernhausen: Edition Kemel, 2010), 9.

23   Markus Zepf argues that Mendelssohn may have found this registration at the Stein organ in Lindau: Evangelische Kirche St. Stephan, Georg Marcus Stein 1783, 29/II/Ped—however, this instrument had full pedal compass. Zepf, "Felix Mendelssohn Bartholdy in Süddeutschland," 204.

24   Cited in Meischein, "Stimmung, Choral und Text," 46: "Auch spiele ich täglich eine Stunde Orgel; kann aber leider nicht üben wie ich wollte, weil das Pedal um fünf hohe Töne zu kurz ist, so daß man keine Seb. Bach'sche Passage darauf machen kann. Aber es sind wunderschöne Register darin, mit denen man Choräle figuriren kann; da erbaue ich mich denn am himmlischen strömenden Ton des Instruments, namentlich, Fanny, habe ich hier die Register gefunden, mit denen man Seb. Bach's "Schmücke dich, o liebe Seele" spielen muß. Es ist, als wären sie dazu gemacht, und klingt so rührend, daß es mich allemal wieder duchschauert, wenn ich es anfange. Zu den gehenden Stimmen habe ich eine Flöte, 8 Fuß, und eine ganz sanfte, 4 Fuß, die nun immer über dem Choral schwebt—Du kennst das schon von Berlin her. Aber zum Choral ist ein Clavier da, das lauter Zungenregister hat, und da nehme ich denn eine sanfte Hoboe, ein Clairon, sehr leise, 4 Fuß, und eine Viola. Das zieht den Choral so still und durchdringend, als wären es ferne Menschenstimmen, die ihn aus Herzensgrund singen." English translation partly by Wm. A. Little (*Mendelssohn and the Organ*, 89), and partly by the editor.

25   Georg Friedrich Kauffmann, *Harmonische Seelenlust 1733–1740*, facsimile ed. (Corlay: Editions J. M. Fuzeau S.A., 2002), xiii.

26   Zepf, "Felix Mendelssohn Bartholdy in Süddeutschland," 213: "Jede großartige Composition, in einer Kirche ohne 16füßige Grundstimme vorgetragen, wird zu einer Carricatur, und ebenso klingt die Begleitung des Gemeinde Gesangs ohne ein solches Register bei gewöhnlichem Spiele trocken und leer, bei starkem Spiele aber schrillend und schreiend."

27   In the fall of 2007 a lecture series was held at the Eastman School of Music called "Culture vs. Technology" within the humanities project "The Organ in Society: Culture and Technology," sponsored by the College Music Department and the Department of History at the University of Rochester, New York.

28   Joachim Wagner's organs did not have mixtures with tierce ranks, however the Scharfs often had a high tierce rank $(4/5')$ in the tenor and bass octaves. Communication from Paul Peeters on January 25, 2014.

29   Faulkner, *The Registration of J. S. Bach's Organ Works*, 9.

30   Johann Gottfried Walther, *Musikalisches Lexikon; oder Musikalische Bibliothek* (1732), facsimile repr. ed. Richard Schaal (Kassel: Bärenreiter, 1953), 204: "Es giebt aber auch Compositiones auf 2, 3 und 4 Chöre, so Gesprächs-weise alterniren. Die Organisten imitiren dergleichen Umwechselungen auch auf den Orgeln, wenn sie mehr als ein Clavier haben."

31   Ritter, *Kunst des Orgelspiels*, 23: "Die Orgel soll das Mittel sein, den Kirchengesang zu leiten und zu erheben. Für den ersten Zweck bedarf sie des nach der Grösse der Kirche und der Gemeinde abgemessenen starken, für den andern Zweck des schönen Tones der einzelnen Stimmen wie des vollen Werkes. Die achtfüssigen

Stimmen des Manuals bilden den Tonkern; sie müßen sich also durch ihre Zahl und Stärke vor den andern geltend machen. Die sechzehnfüßigen Manual–Stimmen verleihen dem Orgeltone Ernst und Würde; Vier und Zweifusston giebt ihm Leben und Frische; die Füllstimmen dienen zur Verstärkung."

32 Faulkner, *The Registration of J. S. Bach's Organ Works*, 89.

33 Peter Williams, "Further on changing manuals in works of J. S. Bach," *The Organ Yearbook* 29, 59–74.

34 Faulkner, *The Registration of J. S. Bach's Organ Works*, 92–93.

35 Friedrich Konrad Griepenkerl, "Die neue Ausgabe der Compositionen für die Orgel von J. S. Bach, im Bureau de Musique von C. F. Peters, betreffend," *Allgemeine musikalische Zeitung*, no. 8 (February 1846), 146–48, esp. 147: "Gibt man aber zu verstehen, dass Würde und Erhabenheit im Vortrage von Mixturen, von gekoppelten Clavieren, überhaupt von der Stärke abhängig sei, so muss ich mich an eine Anekdote erinnern, die mir Forkel einst selbst mit liebenswürdiger Bescheidenheit erzählte. Friedemann Bach hielt sich nämlich 1773 einige Zeit bei Forkel in Göttingen auf, als dieser noch ein junger, lebhafter Mann war. Als Friedemann nun sehr häufig auf dem Claviere gespielt hatte, sollte er sich auch auf der Orgel hören lassen, und Forkel führte ihn in die Kirche. Hier phantasirte nun Friedemann über eine Stunde auf der Orgel, doch ohne Mixturen und ohne die ganze Kraft der Orgel zu gebrauchen. Dies gefiel aber dem jungen und lebhaften Forkel nicht, und er wagte es, darüber eine Bemerkung zu machen. Da klopfte ihn Friedemann freundlich auf die Achsel und sagte: 'Na, lassen Sie's nur gut sein!'"

36 For nineteenth-century registrations of Mendelssohn in St. Marien, Lübeck, see Joachim Walter, *"This Heaving Ocean of Tones,"* 121–23, 132–34, and 141–44.

37 Little, *Mendelssohn and the Organ*, 281.

38 For a more detailed discussion, see ibid., 333–36.

39 Andreas Glöckner, "Bach-Organisten des frühen 19. Jahrhunderts und ihre Repertoire," in Hartinger, Wolff, and Wollny, *"Diess herrliche, imponierende Instrument,"* 333–42, esp. 335.

40 Eduard Krüger, "Felix Mendelssohn-Bartholdy, 'Sechs Sonaten für die Orgel Opus 65.'" *Neue Zeitschrift für Musik* 21 (January 4, 1846), 5: "Dies ist die für guten Vortrag ängstlich besorgte Vorrede, die selbst in ihrer Kürze die Bemühung um Ausdruck (Effect) ausspricht, indem sie Fingerzeige für Forte, Piano, Registrierung etc giebt, dergleichen einem guten Organisten ein Hinderniß sind. Für schlechte Organisten sind die Sonaten nicht geschrieben, und der kundige wird sich erinnern, wie er bei S. Bach nie fehlgreifen kann, der nichts als die allgemeinsten, unbestimmtesten Bezeichnungen angiebt: 2 Clav. Ped., 8 oder 4 F, org. pleno,—selten f. p.—weiter nichts."

41 August Gottfried Ritter was born in Thuringia but educated in Berlin; like Mendelssohn, he studied the organ with A. W. Bach and piano with Ludwig Berger. He was organist in Erfurt (1831–44), and at the cathedrals of Merseburg (1844–47) and Magdeburg (1847–85).

42 Ritter, *Allgemeine musikalische Zeitung* 48 (February 11, 1846), 97: "Die im Laufe der Stücke angegebenen Bemerkungen über das Registriren beschränken sich zumeist auf die allgemeineren Zeichen des Piano und Forte u. s. w. Eine spezielle Angabe der einzelnen Register hat der Componist vermieden, weil jede Orgel in dieser Hinsicht eine andere Behandlungsart erfordert, 'indem selbst die gleichnamigen Register nicht immer bei verschiedenen Instrumenten die gleiche Wirkung hervorbringen.' Diese letztere Behauptung hat zwar ihre Richtigkeit; allein der Unterschied des Klanges ist niemals so bedeutend, dass z. B. ein Register, zu dessen

eigenthümlicher Klangfarbe das Schneidende oder Streichende gehört, einem anderen ähnlich klänge, welches seiner Construction nach einen vollen, runden Ton haben muss. Aber gleichgiltig für die Wirkung einer Composition kann es keineswegs sein, ob ein Satz mit einer Stimme dieses oder jenes Toncharacters ausgeführt wird. Deshalb wäre die Angabe der Register wünschenswerth gewesen; und hätte sich eines der vorgeschriebenen nicht in der Orgel gefunden, so war es leicht durch ein ähnlich klingendes zu ersetzen."

43 Ritter, *Allgemeine musikalische Zeitung* (February 11, 1846), 99: "In den dieser Anzeige vorausgeschickten allgemeineren Bemerkungen ist es bereits erwähnt worden, dass der Componist die Angabe der einzelnen Register unterlassen hat und somit eine unmittelbare Erweiterung der Regisrirkunst hier nicht gegeben wird. Indessen erhält der denkende Spieler durch die vortreffliche Anwendung der verschiedenen Manuale auf mittelbare Weise Gelegenheit, die verschiedenen Stimmen seiner Orgel gegen und miteinander zu vergleichen, und die zu dem Vortrage der für mehrere Manuale berechneten Sätze passendsten auszusuchen, und nach Umständen im Verlaufe eines Satzes mit einander zu vertauschen. Das Adagio der zweiten Sonate bildet bei der eigenthümlichen und unterscheidenden Behandlung der einzelnen Claviere (wozu das Pedal mitgezählt wird) einen orchestermässigen Satz. Die Melodie, von der rechten Hand auf dem zweiten Manuale gespielt, wird von den Blasinstrumenten vorgetragen; die Violinen begleiten in gesangvollen, fliessenden Gängen, und werden auf dem ersten Manuale mit der linken vertreten; die Bässe endlich—das Pedal—deuten die harmonischen Grundtöne pizzicato an. Ist diese Darstellung eine richtige, so würden für das zweite Manual volle, etwas streichende, und darum auch der Tiefe hervortretende, für das erste durchsichtige und bewegliche, für das Pedal endlich gut und schnell ansprechende runde Stimmen gewählt werden müssen. Nach dem gewöhnlichen Gebrauche indessen, welcher das weit mensurirte Hauptmanual das erste nennt, würde die in der Sonate gebrauchte Bezeichnung der Claviere umzukehren und die linke Hand auf das, gewöhnlich mit solchen Stimmen, welche wir oben als zur Begleitung brauchbar bezeichneten, versehene eng mensurirte Nebenmanual zu verweisen sein. Die Benutzung der Manuale, die Führung der Stimmen ist, wie schon ausgesprochen, höchst geistreich und vortrefflich, und wird dem Spieler grossen Genuss und vielen Vortheil gewähren."

44 August Gottfried Ritter, *IIIte Sonate A-moll für die Orgel*, op. 23 (Magdeburg: R. Sulzer, no year; repr. Winterthur: Orgelreihe der Stadtkirche Winterthur, 1986).

45 Ritter, *Allgemeine musikalische Zeitung* (February 11, 1846), 100: "Mit der Bezeichnung 'Da questa parte fino al Maggiore poco a poco più animato e più forte' tritt statt der bisherigen Begleitung des Chorals in Achteln eine in Sechszehnteltheilen auf. Der immer mehr sich steigernden Bewegung schliesst sich endlich auch das Pedal an, nachdem es den Schlusston des Cantus firmus im Orgelpuncte längere Zeit ausgehalten. Während die Manuale den Hauptschritt des Thema's in vollen Accorden und in den höchsten Lagen wiederholen, wühlt es in wilden, donnernden Passagen hinunter in die Tiefe, um vom Grundton *E* durch die Töne *F*, *Gis*, *H*, *d*, *f*, *gis*, *h* nach dem hohen *d'* hinaufzusteigen. Ruhiger und ruhiger senkt es sich von da allmälig hinab und leitet nach dem ersten Satze—A-dur—wieder ein, welcher bis auf einige weniger, aber sehr wirksame und bezeichnenden Veränderungen (z. B. im fünften und sechsten Tacte) fast wörtlich wiederkehrt."

46 See Hermann J. Busch, "Es kommt . . . auf richtige Wahl der Register sehr viel an: Zur Orgelpraxis Felix Mendelssohn Bartholdys," in Busch and Heinemann, *Zur*

Deutschen Orgelmusik des 19. Jahrhunderts, 147–53, esp. 150; and Little, *Mendelssohn and the Organ,* 281–82.

47   Ritter, *Allgemeine musikalische Zeitung* (February 11, 1846), 100–101: "Dafür entschädigt aber vollkommen das Adagio religioso, welches die abwechselnden Manuale wieder trefflich benutzt, und das sich anschliessende Allegretto, 6/8-Tact, letzteres so reizend und zart, wie nur Seb Bach's Pastorella sein kann."

48   Walter, *"This Heaving Ocean of Tones,"* 132–40.

49   Little, *Mendelssohn and the Organ,* 101–8.

50   Ibid., 85.

51   Ibid., 87.

52   Ibid., 67.

53   Cited in Busch, "Zur Registrierungskunst der Deutschen romantischen Orgel," 69: "Wenn man das Crescendo (Anwachsende) einer Orchestermusik auf der Orgel nachahmen will, so ziehe man anfangs, was das Manual betrifft, eine gedeckte 16 u. 8füßige Stimme nach der andern, um den Uebergang des Pianissimo zum Piano auszudrücken, allmählig heraus; alsdann nimmt man nach und nach die offenen 8füßigen Register, wenn das Crescendo a poco angehen soll; hernach kömmt die Reihe bei dem Crescendo il forte an die 4, 2, u. 1füßigen, und endlich auch bei dem Forte und Fortissimo selbst and die Schnarrwerke und mixturartigen Stimmen. Im Pedal fängt man das Pianissimo mit dem Subbaß allein an, gesellet dann ein 32füßiges Register, wenn eines vorhanden ist, und nach und nach mehrere 16, 8 u. 4füßige theils Principal- theils Flötenstimmen dazu; erst aber bei dem Forte und Fortissimo warden die Pedalschnarr- und Mixturwerke gezogen."

54   Little, *Mendelssohn and the Organ,* 88.

55   Ibid., 38.

56   Cited in Busch, "Es kommt . . . auf richtige Wahl der Register sehr viel an," 151: "Während dieser zwei Takte kann der Spieler, da ihm eine Hand zum Registrieren frei bleibt, die starken Stimmen bis zu 2 schwachen 8 füßigen Registern abstoßen. . . . Eine Hand allein übernimmt diesen Akkord, damit die dadurch freigewordene eine 8füßige Stimme abstoßen, und damit das pp hervorgebracht werden kann."

57   Rudolf Lutz, "Eine Orgelsonate über den Choral 'O Haupt voll Blut und Wunden'? Zur Ergänzung von Mendelssohns Fragment GB-Ob, MS.M.Deneke Mendelssohn, b. 5, 28. Ein Arbeitsbericht," in Hartinger, Wolff, and Wollny, *"Diess herrliche, imponierende Instrument,"* 151–74, esp. 153.

58   Charles W. Pearce, *Mendelssohn's Organ Sonatas* (London: Vincent Music, 1902), 4.

59   Ibid., 75.

60   Cited in Bötel, *Mendelssohns Bachrezeption,* 30: "Die Orgel, bei deren Behandlung wir so häufig entweder einer ermüdenden Monotonie der Tonwirkungen oder umgekehrt einer derben Effekthascherei durch den Wechsel scharfer Kontraste in den Klangfarben begegnen, schien hier unter Mendelssohns Händen zu einem ganz neuen, bisher unbekannten Instrumente zu werden. Nie haben wir wieder in solcher Weise auf der Orgel singen gehört, nie wieder so harmonisch vermittelte und wohltuende Steigerungen in der Anwendung der Zungen gehört. Das Instrument verwandelte sich in ein volltönendes Orchester, über welchem man die Stimmen eines Sängers, bald die Stimmen ganzer Chöre zu hören glaubte."

61   All three citations in Little, *Mendelssohn and the Organ,* 79.

62   Cited in ibid., 72.

63   Ibid., 82.

64 Mats Arvidsson and Carl Johan Bergsten, "Key Action Measurements in the Craighead-Saunders Organ," unpublished documentation, GOArt 2009.

65 Little, *Mendelssohn and the Organ*, 80.

66 See Meischein, "Stimmung, Choral und Text," 46.

67 R. Larry Todd, *Mendelssohn: A Life in Music* (New York: Oxford University Press, 2003), 377.

68 Cited in Bötel, *Mendelssohns Bachrezeption*, 32: "Mehrmals hatte ich Gelegenheit, auf meiner Orgel in der Dreifaltigkeitskirche seine Fertigkeit in Manual und Pedal zu bewundern. Was letzteren besonders anbelangt, so wußte er Absatz und Zehenspitze des Fußes so geschickt zur rechten Zeit mit gehöriger Abrundung zu benützen, daß es eine wahre Lust war ihm zuzuhören."

69 See Christoph Kaufmann, "Es ist also sicherer, auf alle Fälle gefasst zu seyn: Aussagen zu Artikulation und Pedalapplikatur in Orgelschulen des späten 18. und frühen 19. Jahrhunderts," in Hartinger, Wolff, and Wollny, *"Diess herrliche, imponierende Instrument,"* 303–32, esp. 328; also Jacques van Oortmerssen, "Johannes Brahms and the 19th-Century Performance Practice in a Historical Perspective, in *Proceedings of the Göteborg International Organ Academy 1994*, ed. Hans Davidsson and Sverker Jullander (Göteborg: University of Göteborg Press, 1994), 353–82, esp. 368.

70 William S. Rockstro, *Mendelssohn* (The Great Musicians) (New York: Scribner and Welford, 1884), 99–100.

71 Ritter, *Allgemeine musikalische Zeitung* (February 11, 1846), 99 and 101.

72 Cited in Vidar Vikøren, "Studier omkring artikulasjon i tysk romantisk orgelmusikk, 1800–1850 med ett tillegg om registreringspraxis" (PhD diss, Göteborg University, 2007), 12: "Für die Orgel paßt vorzüglich der schwere Vortrag, oder Stücke von ernsthaftem, sanften Charakter, weil man da die Töne gehörig lang und singend vortragen kann."

73 Cited in ibid., 8; "Legato [. . .] zeigt immer nur an, daß die Töne nicht abstoßen, sondern so gebunden als möglich, in einander fließend gleichsam, daß kein Zwischenraum der Zeit zwischen ihnen wahrgenommen wird, vorgetragen werden sollen."

74 For a more detailed discussion of legato playing and articulation, see Oortmerssen, "Johannes Brahms and the 19th-Century Performance Practice," 369–70; Vikøren, "Studier omkring artikulasjon," 11–13; and Hans Fagius, "The Organ Works of Mendelssohn and Schumann and Their Links to the Classical Traditions," in Davidsson and Jullander, *Proceedings of the Göteborg International Organ Academy 1994*, 325–52, esp. 330–33.

75 Ludger Lohmann, "Notated Slurs in Organ Music: Approaches to Interpretation," in *GOArt Research Reports*, vol. 1 (Göteborg: University of Göteborg Press, 1999), 193–200.

76 See Little, *Mendelssohn and the Organ*, 283–88.

77 Cited in ibid., 286–87.

78 See also Ludger Lohmann, *Studien zu Artikulationsproblemen bei den Tasteninstrumenten des 16.–18. Jahrhunderts* (Kölner Beiträge zur Musikforschung, vol. 125) (Regensburg: Gustav Bosse Verlag, 1982), 50–53.

79 Jean-Claude Zehnder, "Tanzen oder Schwimmen: Rhythmische Konzepte in der Orgelmusik zwischen 1700 und 1900," in Hartinger, Wolff, and Wollny, *"Diess herrliche, imponierende Instrument,"* 91–110, esp. 96–98.

80 Leopold Mozart, *A Treatise on the Fundamental Principles of Violin Playing*, trans. Edith Knocker (London: Oxford University Press, 1951), 123–24, quoted from Sandra

P. Rosenblum, *Performance Practices in Classic Piano Music* (Bloomington: Indiana University Press, 1988), 159.

81   Joel Speerstra, *Bach and the Pedal Clavichord: An Organist's Guide* (Rochester, NY: University of Rochester Press, 2004), 114–17.

82   Jacques van Oortmerssen, "Johannes Brahms and the 19th-Century Performance Practice," 370.

83   Zehnder, "Tanzen oder Schwimmen," 92–95.

84   Cited in Little, *Mendelssohn and the Organ*, 285.

85   Jon Laukvik, *Orgelschule zur historischen Aufführungspraxis, Teil 2, Romantik* (Stuttgart: Carus-Verlag, 2000), 254–57.

86   Carl Czerny, "Von dem Vortrage (1839) Dritter Theil," in *Vollständige theoretische-practische Pianoforte-Schule*, op. 500, facsimile ed., ed. Ulrich Mahlert (Wiesbaden: Breitkopf und Härtel, 1991), 58–64.

87   Little, *Mendelssohn and the Organ*, 81.

88   Ibid., 78.

89   Czerny, "Von dem Vortrage (1839) Dritter Theil," 24: "Wir kommen nun auf das Dritte, und beinahe wichtigste Mittel, des Vortrags, nähmlich auf die mannigfachen Veränderungen des vorgeschriebenen *Tempo's* durch das *rallentando* und *accelerando* (Zurückhalten und Beschleunigen)."

90   Ibid.: "Aber diesem unbeschadet, kommen sehr oft, fast in jeder Zeile, einzelne Noten oder Stellen vor, wo ein kleines, oft kaum bemerkbares Zurückhalten oder Beschleunigen nothwendig ist, um den Vortrag zu verschönern und das Interesse zu vermehren."

91   Zehnder, "Tanzen oder Schwimmen," 99–102.

92   Czerny, "Von dem Vortrage (1839) Dritter Theil," 24: "Nicht nur jedes ganze Tonstück, sondern jede einzelne Stelle drückt entweder wirklich irgendeine bestimmte Empfindung aus, oder erlaubt wenigstens, eine solche durch den Vortrag hineinzulegen."

93   Ibid., 25: "Wenn übrigens eine solche Stelle sich an mehreren Orten eines Tonstücks wiederhohlen sollte, dann steht es dem Spieler nicht nur frei, jedesmal eine andere Vortragsweise anzuwenden, sondern es ist sogar eine Pflicht, um die Einförmigkeit zu vermeiden."

94   Little, *Mendelssohn and the Organ*, 81.

95   Czerny, "Von dem Vortrage (1839) Dritter Theil," 50: "Die zuverlässigste Idee zur sicheren Auffindung des wahren Tempo kann gefunden werden, 1stens aus dem Charakter des Tonstücks; 2tens aus der Zahl und dem Notenwerthe der geschwindesten Noten, welche in einem Takte vorkommen." (The most reliable clue for finding the right tempo can be found, first, in the character of the piece; second, in the number and the durational value of the fastest notes occurring in a bar.)

96   Ibid., 49–50.

97   Ibid., 48: "Das Metronom hat einen mehrfachen Zweck: 1stens kann man das von Tonsetzer gewünschte Tempo auf das Genaueste erfahren, und für alle Zukunft aufbewahren." (The metronome has a multiple purpose: to ascertain most precisely the tempo desired by the composer and to preserve it for the future.)

98   See Oortmerssen, "Johannes Brahms and the 19th-Century Performance Practice," 372–75; and Zehnder, "Tanzen oder Schwimmen," 108–9.

99   Czerny, "Von dem Vortrage (1839) Dritter Theil," 50.

100   Zehnder, "Tanzen oder Schwimmen," 106.

101 See Hans Davidsson, *Matthias Weckmann: The Interpretation of His Organ Music*, vol. 1 (Stockholm: Gehrmans Musikförlag, 1991), 70.

102 Harald Vogel, "Das Wohltemperierte Clavier I," Unpublished handout, Norddeutsche Orgelakademie (Bremen: Organeum, 2010).

103 Burkhard Meischein, "Stimmung, Choral und Text," 52: "die Orgel zu behandeln und für dieselbe zu denken."

104 Johann Mattheson, *Der vollkommene Capellmeister* [Hamburg: Christian Herold: 1739], facsimile repr. (Kassel: Bärenreiter, 1987), 160–70, 180–85.

105 See also Zacher, "Die riskanten Beziehungen zwischen Sonate und Kirchenlied," 35.

106 Ritter, *Allgemeine musikalische Zeitung* (February 11, 1846), 98: "Die Benennung Sonate ist hier vollkommen gerechtfertigt durch den nothwendigen Zusammenhang, in welchem die einzelnen Sätze stehen. Wir meinen nicht jenen blos äusseren Zusammenhang, welchen etwa die Tonart und die Melodie vermittelt, sondern jene unsichtbaren Beziehungen, welche, in dem geistigen Baue des Tonstückes wurzelnd, hier eine Vorbereitung, dort eine Auflösung finden. Von dieser Seite betrachtet, erscheinen einige der Sonaten, und gerade jene von der herkömmlichen Form sich entfernenden, als tiefgedachte, tiefempfundene Meisterstücke."

107 Ibid., 98–99: "Sonate 1 . . . beginnt mit vollgriffigen kräftigen Accorden, welche, anfangs mehr allgemein und vorbereitend gehalten, bereits schon im eilften Tacte zu einem sprechenden Hauptgedanken hinführen. Wie überhaupt alle in dem ganzen Werke vorkommenden, zeigt auch dieser ein so ausdrucksvolles Charactergepräge, dass er die Bezeichnung 'sprechend' vollkommen rechtfertigt. Es ist die unmuthsvolle Klage eines bedrückten Gemüths. Welche hier in Tönen immer lauter und ängstlicher erklingt, je näher das gefürchtete Schicksal herantritt. Da, nach einem Schluss in C moll, erklingt, von Engelstimmen getragen, ein choralmässiger Satz. Er bringt Trost aus Himmelshöhen. Zwar wird er, bald kürzer, bald länger, von dem mit gesteigerter Lebendigkeit behandelten Hauptsatz unterbrochen, zwar tönt die Klage in ihn selbst hinein; bald aber erschallt er in siegreicher Höhe, weil erhaben über das irdische Leid, das Lied des Trostes. In sanften Accorden, dann von dem mächtigem Strome des vollen Orgeltones getragen, schliesst er den ersten Abschnitt. Noch ist es kein jauchzender Triumphgesang. Die kleine Terz erinnert an den bestandenen mühevollen Kampf. —Erst in dem nun folgenden Adagio (Asdur, $\frac{3}{4}$-Tact) und in dem die Ueberleitung zum letzten Satz bildenden Recitative gelangt das Herz zur Ruhe. Die Klage schweigt. In Freudentönen, wie sie nur die menschliche Brust zu fühlen vermag, jauchzt der Gerettete (Allegro assai vivace). Glänzende, feurige Accorde erschallen in lebendiger Bewegung, von den brausenden Tönen der Bässe getragen. Und wie das von hoher Freude erfüllte Herz in seiner ersten Wallung vergebens nach bestimmtem Ausdrucke ringt und nur beruhigter die rechten Worte findet: so schweifen die Accorde anfänglich in unbestimmterer Richtung hin und her, gewinnen aber allmälig an Zusammenhang und Gruppirung, und umschweifen endlich . . . die jubelvolle Melodie, welche nun fort und fort, in der Tiefe und in der He, erklingt und endlich in den vollen, lichten Fdur-Accord mit obenliegender Terz führt. Hier ist der eigentliche Schluss des Ganzen. Die nun folgenden, vier Tacte ausfüllenden Arpeggiaturen, zugleich der Orgel nicht ganz angemessen, sind als ein Anhang zu betrachten."

108 Zacher, "Die riskanten Beziehungen zwischen Sonate und Kirchenlied," 38.

109 See Martin Weyer, *Die deutsche Orgelsonate von Mendelssohn bis Reger* (Kölner Beiträge zur Musikforschung 55) (Regensburg: Gustav Bosse Verlag, 1969), 51.

110 Todd, *Mendelssohn: A Life in Music*, 490.

111 See chapter 11 for a detailed discussion of the work by Benedict Taylor.

112 Ritter, *Allgemeine musikalische Zeitung* (February 11, 1846), 99–100, esp. 100: "als ein stilles, tiefempfundenes Dankgebet."

113 Pearce, *Mendelssohn's Organ Sonatas*, 75.

114 Ibid., 39.

115 Ibid., 65–67.

116 For instance by Rudolf Werner, *Felix Mendelssohn Bartholdy als Kirchenmusiker* (Frankfurt/Main, 1930), 123–25; Susanna Grossmann-Vendrey, "Stilprobleme in Mendelssohns Orgelsonaten, op. 65," in *Das Problem* Mendelssohn, ed. Carl Dahlhaus (Regensburg: Bosse, 1974), 185–94, esp. 193–94; and Zacher,"Die riskanten Beziehungen zwischen Sonate und Kirchenlied," 42–45.

117 Christopher Petit, Notes to Mendelssohn's Sonata I in booklet accompanying Loft Recordings CD 1115 (2011): The Craighead-Saunders Organ: Hans Davidsson, David Higgs, William Porter.

118 Meischein, "Stimmung, Choral und Text," 39.

119 Ibid., 44.

120 John Michael Cooper and Julie D. Prandi, eds., *The Mendelssohns: Their Music in History* (Oxford: Oxford University Press, 2003), 126.

121 Meischein, "Stimmung, Choral und Text," 46–47.

122 Ibid., 41–43, 48–49.

123 Charles William Pearce believes, however, that Sonata IV is reminiscent of the Prelude in E-flat Major (*WTC* I, no. 7) both in terms of thematic material and the ternary form (Pearce, *Mendelssohn's Organ Sonatas*, 35–37).

124 Ritter, *Allgemeine musikalische Zeitung* (February 11, 1846), 100–101: "Der erste Satz der vierten Sonate . . . besteht grösstenteils in der Bearbeitung eines mehr orchester-, als orgelmässig gedachten Hauptsatzes."

125 Todd, *Mendelssohn: A Life in Music*, 401–2.

126 Zacher, "Die riskanten Beziehungen zwischen Sonate und Kirchenlied," 44.

Part Three

Mendelssohn's Inherited Legacies in Context

Chapter Eight

The Bach Tradition among the Mendelssohn Ancestry

Christoph Wolff

The rediscovery of Johann Sebastian Bach and his music long after the composer's death in the Romantic period belongs among the most widespread misconceptions and misconstructions in the historiography of music. A statement like the following is symptomatic in this regard: "Bach and his works have met a strange fate at the hands of posterity. They were fairly well recognized in their day; practically forgotten by the generations following his; rediscovered and revived; and finally accorded an eminence far beyond the recognition they had originally achieved."[1]

Scholarship of recent decades has found it necessary to turn away from a Bach image that resembles the metaphorical paradigm of "Death and Resurrection," the characteristic heading of the pertinent chapter in Albert Schweitzer's *J. S. Bach: le musicien-poète* of 1905 and its expanded German edition of 1908—arguably the most influential Bach book of all times.[2] Informed by scholarship that was greatly inspired by the influential first edition of *The Bach Reader* and significantly substantiated by the groundbreaking source studies conducted in conjunction with the *Neue Bach-Ausgabe* (1954–2007), today's view differentiates between two complementary aspects of the Bach reception in the eighteenth and early nineteenth centuries. There is first the uninterrupted and rather broad, deep, and educationally focused Bach tradition as it spread throughout the decades after 1750 in professional musical circles where Bach's compositions were regarded as a continuing challenge, a source of inspiration, and a yardstick for measuring quality.[3] Then there followed, largely after 1800 and as the result of a continuously growing interest in the music of the past among musical amateurs, a more widely based public reception of Bach's music in the early nineteenth century, for which the 1829

Berlin performance of the *St. Matthew Passion* conducted by the young Felix Mendelssohn Bartholdy represented the most decisive landmark.[4] This essay focuses on a third and much less explored aspect as it surfaced in a small circle of early bourgeois Bach devotees in late eighteenth-century Berlin and in an atmosphere of emerging musical historicism.

The phenomenon of musical historicism had various origins, manifested itself in different ways, and eventually led to an ostensibly irreversible paradigm shift. Whereas contemporary music unquestionably dominated musical life until the early nineteenth century, by the end of that century the music of the past had clearly taken over the lead function, canonic repertoires were established, and new composition—according to today's classical performance statistics—definitively put into a marginalized position. In Germany, it was the Berlin Sing-Akademie, a bourgeois choral society founded in 1791 by C. P. E. Bach's former assistant and successor Carl Friedrich Fasch on the model of the London Academy of Ancient Music, which explored, in private reading sessions rather than public performances, the music from earlier times with a preference for the vocal repertoire from seventeenth-century Italy. From 1800, under its second director Carl Friedrich Zelter, the Sing-Akademie more regularly cultivated also the music of Bach and Handel in both private study and public presentation.

This background is directly and concretely connected with the Mendelssohn family. For, shortly after Abraham Mendelssohn donated in 1811 the Bach manuscript scores of unpublished works to the Sing-Akademie, Zelter began to perform excerpts from the Passions, Masses, and cantatas of J. S. Bach based on the donated materials. Meanwhile, the Mendelssohn family relocated to Berlin. At age ten, Felix joined the Sing-Akademie and, more important, was put under Zelter's private tutelage. He could have had no better teacher who, among other things, exposed him to Bach's vocal works, including the *St. Matthew Passion*, but almost exclusively in the form of excerpts. Zelter did not consider the large-scale work performable, for musical-technical reasons as much as for its "wretched texts" (ganz verruchte deutsche Kirchentexte),[5] referring to the Baroque-style sacred poetry. However, young Felix eagerly wanted to see and study the whole piece and, finally, grandmother Bella Salomon fulfilled his wish, had a professional copy made from the manuscript score of the unpublished work in the collection of the Sing-Akademie, and gave it to him as a present. Felix was fourteen years old then and it took him another five years to persuade his teacher Zelter to agree to a complete performance.

The effect of the 1829 performance of the *St. Matthew Passion* was beyond question, but in the context of the advancement of musical historicism during the early decades of the nineteenth century, another major programmatic milestone was set by Felix Mendelssohn Bartholdy. In 1835, his first season as music director of the Leipzig Gewandhaus, he established "Historische Concerte," which specifically featured works of the past. Music by Johann Sebastian Bach played an essential role in this respect and in one such program Mendelssohn presented the Keyboard Concerto in D Minor (BWV 1052), himself performing its solo part. The work, unknown at the time, received great praise from the general public and notably from the music critic Robert Schumann, who called it a "sublime work" (ein erhabenes Werk).[6] Nobody, however, including Mendelssohn himself, knew that this same concerto had actually been presented in public almost thirty years earlier, before Mendelssohn was even born, by a certain Sara Levy at a public concert of the Berlin Sing-Akademie.

Family Connections: Itzig–Mendelssohn–Bach

Madame Levy, who stands at the center of this discussion, was none other than Mendelssohn's great-aunt, the younger sister of his maternal grandmother Bella Salomon. The young Mendelssohn is generally credited with bringing about one of the most seminal events in musical historicism, the aforementioned 1829 performance of Bach's *St. Matthew Passion* at the Sing-Akademie in Berlin. He certainly deserves credit as the inspired and energetic youthful musical leader of this most influential performance, which was attended by King Friedrich Wilhelm III, the royal family, the Prussian nobility, and the intellectual elite of the capital, headed by the theologian Friedrich Schleiermacher, the philosopher Georg Wilhelm Friedrich Hegel,[7] the historian Gustav Droysen, the poet Heinrich Heine, and the writer Rahel Varnhagen. However, the true origins of that particular event must be sought in the remarkable musical traditions of Mendelssohn's extended family—a tradition underemphasized, underresearched, or neglected if not suppressed by earlier historical German scholarship for reasons of an apparent anti-Semitic bias.

Johann Friedrich Reichardt, the last Kapellmeister in the service of King Friedrich II ("the Great") of Prussia, refers in his autobiography of 1813 to "a veritable Sebastian and Emanuel Bach cult"[8] as it transpired in the early 1770s at the house of Daniel Itzig, the father of Sara Levy and Bella Salomon, banker of the king and the most privileged Jew in all of Prussia, in fact, the first Jew to acquire citizenship. In professional circles of the later eighteenth century, familiarity with Bach's name, even a certain Bach enthusiasm would not have been anything special—one need only consider Beethoven's growing up with Bach's *Well-Tempered Clavier* or Haydn's 1799 reference to Bach as "the man from whom all true musical wisdom proceeded."[9] Yet, neither Haydn, nor Mozart, nor Beethoven pursued anything like a Bach cult. Hence, this particular characterization of reverence and cultivation in the Itzig family is a most unusual phenomenon. Moreover, it indicates a surprising continuity of interest in the music of Johann Sebastian Bach almost thirty years after his death, an interest not traceable elsewhere in bourgeois families.

Daniel Itzig, born 1723 in Berlin, began his banking career as principal supplier of the Prussian mint to the court and the army and was instrumental in assisting the king in funding the Seven Years' War (1756–63) against Maria Theresa's Austria. While it is conceivable that Itzig heard first about Bach on the occasion of the latter's widely publicized visit to the Prussian court in 1747, he certainly would have known Bach's second son, Carl Philipp Emanuel, who served as a prominent member of the Prussian Hofkapelle until 1768. Be that as it may, Itzig had great interest in music, found the best possible music instructors for his children, and paid them well. For his two oldest daughters, Hanna and Bella, he hired Johann Philipp Kirnberger, one of Bach's most prominent students and Kapellmeister for Princess Anna Amalia, the king's sister.

Bella Itzig, who was to become Felix Mendelssohn's maternal grandmother, coincidentally shared her music instructor with Felix's future paternal grandfather, Moses Mendelssohn, who took lessons in both keyboard performance and music theory from Kirnberger. Moses Mendelssohn, a faithfully practicing Jew, successful businessman, eminent philosopher of the German Enlightenment, along with Daniel Itzig and David Friedländer (the latter's son-in-law), "devoted himself to the emancipation, both civil and intellectual, of Europe's ghettoized Jewish community."[10] Abraham Mendelssohn, his second son, received no particular musical training, but in 1793 became a member of the newly established Sing-Akademie, where he met his future wife, Lea Salomon, who in 1796 joined the same organization. He probably knew her through earlier family connections, for she was the daughter of Bella Itzig, now married to the Berlin banker Levin Jacob Salomon. An accomplished pianist, Lea Mendelssohn is known to have played the *Well-Tempered Clavier* regularly. (Table 8.1 may clarify the family connections.)

The newly wed Mendelssohns moved to Hamburg in 1804, the year in which Carl Philipp Emanuel Bach's daughter Anna Carolina, last custodian of the Bach family estate, died there. When the estate came up for auction in 1805 the Mendelssohns decided to buy the bulk of the music in order to donate it eventually to their former common musical home, the Sing-Akademie in Berlin, now under the direction of Carl Friedrich Zelter, with whom they developed a warm relationship. Mendelssohn's acquisition of the Bach estate, which included a significant portion of the works of C. P. E. Bach but also a major segment of the surviving works of J. S. Bach, represented a genuine rescue operation with respect to the latter's music. Its importance for the survival of J. S. Bach's music, contained in more than 100 unique autograph scores, must not be underestimated. It is safe to say that, without Abraham Mendelssohn's efforts, the losses of Bach's music would be substantially greater than those already suffered. Hence, the acquisition of the Bach estate for the Berlin Sing-Akademie formed an essential background for the later performance of the *St. Matthew Passion* under the baton of his son—a fact usually not taken into consideration.

Table 8.1. Family Tree.

ITZIG		MENDELSSOHN
Daniel Itzig, 1722–99		Moses Mendelssohn, 1729–86
∞ Miriam Wulff, 1727–88		∞ Fromet Guggenheim, 1737–1812
15 children, among them:		6 children, among them:
Sara, 1761–1854	Bella, 1749–1824	
∞ Samuel S. Levy	∞ Levin Jacob Salomon	
no children	4 children, among them:	
	Lea, 1777–1842	∞ Abraham M. (Bartholdy), 1776–1835
		4 children, among them:
		Felix Mendelssohn Bartholdy, 1809–47

After her marriage in 1783 to the banker Samuel Salomon Levy, an accomplished amateur flutist, Sara Levy established a salon at her stately home in old Berlin's poshest neighborhood with a strong focus on music. For about ten years, from 1774 to 1784 she took keyboard lessons from Wilhelm Friedemann Bach, J. S. Bach's oldest, and became a keyboard virtuoso in her own right. The silverpoint portrait by Anton Graff of 1786 shows a very attractive young woman age twenty-five (fig. 8.1). As keyboard soloist she regularly performed at the weekly afternoon gatherings in her home but also elsewhere in Berlin, during the 1790s notably in the public concerts at the mansion of Joseph Fliess (at the so-called Fliessische Concerte).[11] Her repertoire extended from keyboard and chamber music to concertos, for the music room in her mansion could easily accommodate an orchestra of standard eighteenth-century size.[12] She owned a number of keyboard instruments of various kinds and was particularly fond of the fortepianos by Friedrich Silbermann of Strasbourg.

After the death of her husband in 1806 she became more engaged in the concerts of the newly established "Ripienschule" founded in 1807 by the entrepreneurial C. F. Zelter as an amateur orchestral society running parallel to, and complementing, the activities of his Sing-Akademie. There she appeared regularly from 1807 to 1810 as soloist with orchestra, performing concertos by Bach and his sons and also by other composers. Sometime after 1815, however, in her mid-fifties, she stopped performing in public so that her grand nephew Felix most likely never heard her play.

Figure 8.1. Sara Levy, Silverpoint Drawing by Anton Graff, 1786. Traditionally identified with Sara Levy, nee Itzig, the original portrait refers only to a younger sister of Isaac Daniel Itzig (1750–1806) of whom there are eight. However the date of the drawing in combination with the presumable age of the sitter makes her a plausible candidate. Bach-Archiv Leipzig.

Figure 8.2. Sara Levy in old age, photograph, c. 1850. Bach-Archiv Leipzig.

An undated early photograph from around 1850 (fig. 8.2) depicts Sara Levy in her old age; she survived her grand nephew by almost seven years. The silverpoint and the photograph in juxtaposition show very dramatically the contrast of two different centuries, not just as reflected in the different age, changed face, body, clothing, and habit of one and the same woman, but also reflected in the technique of portraiture: drawing versus photography. More than that, the new industrial age left no room for the salon culture of the late eighteenth and early nineteenth centuries. Sara Levy observed and experienced this firsthand.

Sara Levy not only arranged for musical performances, she and her flut-ist husband also commissioned new works occasionally and became major patrons, in particular for the two elder Bach brothers. Wilhelm Friedemann Bach probably wrote the *Cantilena nuptiarum* "Herz, mein Herz, sei ruhig" (Fk 97) for the Itzig-Levy wedding in 1783. He lived in Berlin from 1774 for the last ten years of his life as a freelance musician. The Levys apparently sup-ported him financially and he, in turn, provided them with music. It remains unknown when they established direct contact with Friedemann's younger brother Carl Philipp Emanuel, who had left Berlin for Hamburg in 1768 when Sara was just seven years old. It may well have been only around or after the time of Friedemann's death on July 1, 1784. However, their music collection already contained already sixteen keyboard concertos by the Hamburg Bach when they commissioned him in 1788 to write the three piano quartets Wq 93–95 as well as a concerto for harpsichord, fortepiano and orchestra. The lat-ter Concerto in E-flat Major (Wq 43) turned out to be C. P. E. Bach's last com-position. After his death, the widow Johanna Maria Bach kept in touch with Madame Levy.[13]

When Sara Levy died at age ninety-four, childless, she left her considerable fortune to charity by establishing a foundation for a Jewish orphanage in Berlin. Otherwise, like the rest of the Itzigs, Mendelssohns, Salomons, Ephraims, Friedländers, and others in her extended family, she fit perfectly into the envi-ronment of intellectual, cultural, and to some extent political liberalism in a period quite unique in German history, the quarter century from 1780 to 1806, when Napoleon conquered Prussia. This was also a period in which a group of wealthy Jewish women in Berlin "achieved social glory by entertaining the cream of gentile society."[14] The literary and philosophical salons of Rahel Varnhagen, Henriette Herz, Rebecca Friedländer, and Dorothea Schlegel were among the most prominent and best known, and the success of these Jewish salonières "was based on defiance of the traditional boundaries separating noble from commoner, gentile from Jew, man from woman. The public happi-ness achieved in these salons was a real-life enactment of the ideal of *Bildung*, encompassing education, refinement, and the development of character."[15]

Continuing Fascination with Counterpoint

After giving up public concertizing and perhaps performance altogether, the widowed Sara Levy donated the bulk of her very large music collection to the library of the Berlin Sing-Akademie. There it seems to have been of some use during the Zelter era, but after his death in 1832 it went into oblivion. The music archive of the Sing-Akademie, never a research library and never inven-toried or properly evaluated, was virtually unavailable for study through gen-erations. Only a few unique items, among them the above-mentioned concerto

(Wq 43) and the piano quartets (Wq 93–95), were eventually published. During the turmoil of World War II and its aftermath the Sing-Akademie materials were completely inaccessible for more than half a century.[16]

Fortunately, since the music archive of the Sing-Akademie was repatriated from Kiev to Berlin in 2001 and placed on permanent deposit in the Staatsbibliothek Berlin, the now fully cataloged materials can be examined.[17] Recent research by the Leipzig Bach Archive included a systematic examination of the Berlin Bach tradition as it specifically relates to the Mendelssohn ancestry.[18] The documentation now available of Sara Levy's Bach holdings and that of her extended family permits a long overdue reevaluation of the significant contribution to the early Bach reception history made by the Itzig and Mendelssohn families well before Felix Mendelssohn Bartholdy was born.

Sara Levy's large music library, the bulk of which is in the Sing-Akademie archive, reflects the repertoire of instrumental music that dominated in Berlin between 1760 and 1800, with keyboard, chamber, and orchestral works by the brothers Johann Heinrich and Johann Gottlieb Graun, Johann Gottlieb Janitsch, and other Berlin musicians, as well as by Handel, Pergolesi, and King Friedrich II. However, within this rich material the works of Johann Sebastian Bach and his four composer sons represent a significant portion without parallel elsewhere. Within the Bach holdings of the Itzig family, Sara (and Solomon) Levy's collection was by far the most extensive one, also containing sources of some unique works by W. F. and C. P. E. Bach. However, the complementary materials—manuscripts and printed editions—that belonged to her father, brothers, and sisters are by no means negligible.

Of J. S. Bach's music, the holdings comprise virtually all of the major keyboard works including both parts of the *Well-Tempered Clavier*, some chamber music, including the violin and flute sonatas as well as the sonata from the *Musical Offering*, most of the concertos for one to three harpsichords, the Brandenburg Concerto no. 5 and the Triple Concerto (BWV 1044). The W. F. repertoire comprises much of his keyboard solo music, his chamber trios, a flute concerto (probably commissioned by Salomon Levy), and three concertos for one to two harpsichords. C. P. E. Bach's output is particularly well represented with most major works for solo keyboard, many of the chamber duos, trios, and quartets, two flute concertos, a large number of keyboard concertos, and five orchestral symphonies. The works of the two younger Bach brothers are less extensive, but altogether still impressive. Most important, however, is the fact that the entire holdings represent an active collection for performance, indicating that this repertoire was primarily in use throughout the last three decades of the eighteenth century if not beyond. Sara Levy herself retired from public performances around 1810, turning over much of her collection to the Sing-Akademie. Her collection and similar ones amassed by Carl Friedrich Zelter over the years for the music archive of the Sing-Akademie became primarily teaching materials but continued to be used for performance as well.

During his lifetime and increasingly after 1750, J. S. Bach was considered the unmatched master of the fugue. Not only did his posthumously published *Art of Fugue* confirm his reputation, it was bolstered further by the first theoretical treatise on the fugue, published by Friedrich Wilhelm Marpurg under the title *Abhandlung von der Fuge* (Berlin, 1753) and dedicated to W. F. and C. P. E. Bach as heirs apparent of their father's musical achievements. A relevant later publication promoting the art of strict composition and codifying the teachings of J. S. Bach was Johann Philipp Kirnberger's two-volume *Die Kunst des reinen Satzes in der Musik* (Berlin, 1772 and 1774), a book that also benefited from the philosophy of Kirnberger's student Moses Mendelssohn.[19]

Bach's strict polyphonic style is particularly well represented in Sara Levy's collection. Of particular interest are copies of the *Well-Tempered Clavier* that lacked preludes and contained fugues only or copies of the contrapuntally sophisticated organ trio sonatas (BWV 525–30) apparently for performance on two harpsichords. For Madam Levy, her circle, and indeed music lovers in Berlin and elsewhere in general, the "Bach tradition" did not by any means imply primarily, let alone solely Johann Sebastian Bach, but included the sons, notably the two older ones. Both of them had for a long time been active in Berlin. Therefore, it is worth noting that Sara Levy and her sister Fanny Arnstein of Vienna owned the two major sets of fugues composed by W. F. and C. P. E. Bach: Eight Fugues (Fk 31) and Six Fugues (Wq 119). An early copy of the latter fugues had even been in the possession of their father, Daniel Itzig. This all suggests a particular fascination with fugal and strict counterpoint that most likely was shared by others in her circle. Moreover, the fugues of the two Bach sons demonstrated—in further pursuit of the innovative fugal examples of the second part of the *Well-Tempered Clavier* and the *Art of Fugue*—that fugue as a genre could well be adapted and integrated into modern styles.

Notes

1   Hans T. David and Arthur Mendel, eds., *The Bach Reader: A Life of Johann Sebastian Bach in Letters and Documents* (New York: Norton, 1945), 358.

2   The chapter title was clearly influenced by Schweitzer's previous book, *Geschichte der Leben-Jesu-Forschung* (Tübingen: I. C. Mohr, 1906), his revised theological dissertation of 1901.

3   Christoph Wolff, "On the Recognition of Bach and 'the Bach Chorale': Eighteenth-Century Perspectives," in *Bach: Essays on His Life and Music* (Cambridge, MA: Harvard University Press, 1991), 383–90.

4   Martin Geck, *Die Wiederentdeckung der Matthäuspassion im 19. Jahrhundert* (Regensburg: Bosse, 1967); Celia Applegate, *Bach in Berlin: Nation and Culture in Mendelssohn's Revival of the "St. Matthew Passion"* (Ithaca, NY: Cornell University Press, 2005).

5   Zelter in a letter to Goethe of April 5, 1827, cited after Werner Neumann, ed., *Sämtliche von Johann Sebastian Bach vertonte Texte* (Leipzig: VEB Deutscher Verlag für Musik, 1974), 14. Translations are by the author unless otherwise indicated.

6   Robert Schumann, *Gesammelte Schriften über Musik und Musiker*, ed. Martin Kreisig, vol. 1 (Leipzig: Breitkopf und Härtel, 1914), 314.

7   Schleiermacher himself and Hegel's wife, Marie Hegel, actually sang in the choir as members of the Sing-Akademie; see Ingrid Schobert, ed., *Wahrnehmung der christlichen Religion* (Berlin: LIT-Verlag, 2006), 135.

8   Christoph Wolff, "A Bach Cult in Late-Eighteenth-Century Berlin: Sara Levy's Musical Salon," *Bulletin of the American Academy of Arts and Sciences* 58, no. 3 (2005): 25–31; Peter Wollny, *"Ein förmlicher Sebastian und Philipp Emanuel Bach-Kultus": Sara Levy und ihr musikalisches Wirken* (Leipzig: Breitkopf und Härtel, 2010).

9   Hans T. David and Arthur Mendel, eds., *The New Bach Reader. A Life of Johann Sebastian Bach in Letters and Documents*, rev. and enlarged by Christoph Wolff (New York: Norton, 1998), 374.

10   Steven P. Meyer, "Moses Mendelssohn and the Bach Tradition." *Fidelio Magazine* 8, no. 2 (1999): 27.

11   About her performances and repertoire, see Wollny, *Sara Levy*, 38–40.

12   For a historical picture of her very large house located on what today is the Museumsinsel, see Wollny, *Sara Levy*, 47.

13   Letter of September 5, 1789, in Wollny, *Sara Levy*, 49–51.

14   Deborah Hertz, *Jewish High Society in Old Regime Berlin* (New Haven: Yale University Press, 1988), 3.

15   Ibid., 3–4.

16   Christoph Wolff, "Recovered in Kiev: Bach *et al.* A Preliminary Report on the Musical Archive of the Berlin Sing-Akademie," *Notes* 58 (2001): 259–71.

17   Axel Fischer, ed., *Das Archiv der Sing-Akademie zu Berlin: Katalog* (Berlin: de Gruyter, 2010).

18   Wolfram Ensslin, ed., *Die Bach-Quellen der Sing-Akademie zu Berlin. Katalog*, 2 vols., Leipziger Beiträge zur Bach-Forschung, 10.1–2 (Hildesheim: Olms, 2006); Wollny, *Sara Levy*.

19   Laurenz Lütteken, "Zwischen Ohr und Verstand: Moses Mendelssohns Bedeutung für Johann Philipp Kirnberger und die zeitgenössische Musikästhetik," *Musik und Ästhetik im Berlin Moses Mendelssohns*, ed. Anselm Gerhard (Tübingen: Niemeyer, 1999), 135–63.

Chapter Nine

Music History as Sermon

Style, Form, and Narrative in Mendelssohn's "Dürer" Cantata (1828)

John Michael Cooper

In the spring of 1828 the Royal Academy of the Arts in Berlin commissioned the nineteen-year-old Felix Mendelssohn Bartholdy to compose a grand cantata for the official ceremonies commemorating the tercentenary of the death of Albrecht Dürer (1471–1528). The existence of this cantata is hardly a secret; it is mentioned in every major Mendelssohn biography and many minor ones. Yet most biographers, undaunted by the fact that they have neither seen nor heard the music, have dismissed it as an occasional piece based on an inferior text by a mediocre court poet. Indeed, the cantata remained unpublished until 2012, and apart from a 1995 DMA dissertation on it and the 1822 *Gloria* (MWV A1), the only source to have consulted the score and discussed it with any thoroughness is Larry Todd's authoritative Mendelssohn biography.[1] Since neither of those contexts permitted the sort of detailed examination that a seventy-minute cantata for soloists, chorus, and full orchestra contemporaneous with masterpieces such as the *Midsummer Night's Dream* overture (MWV P3, op. 21), the *Hebrides* overture (MWV P7, op. 26), and the Symphonies in D minor and A major (MWV N15 and N16, opp. posth. 107 and 90, respectively, also known as "Reformation" and "Italian") warrants, the secular cantata that resulted from Mendelssohn's first commission remains obscure.

No amount of explanation and apology is likely to change the fact that to assign the text of this cantata to the annals of literary mediocrity would be an insult to the annals of literary mediocrity. Nevertheless, musical settings of texts can be better than the texts themselves. Mendelssohn's *Große Festmusik zum Dürer-Fest* (MWV D1) thus warrants closer examination than it has heretofore been accorded—if only because of its significance in his career and the importance of the event for which it was written.[2] The method and the premise for approaching the work are simple: since Mendelssohn's music naturally reflects the text and the text was in turn directly tailored to the occasion of the festivities, that text and its relationship to the contemporary context offer a glimpse into Mendelssohn's compositional goals and strategies in setting it and addressing himself to the tercentenary of Dürer's death as that momentous occasion was understood in Prussia in the 1820s.

Such an examination shows that the "Dürer" Cantata is not just a hastily tossed-off occasional work—an unlikely proposition to begin with, given the importance of a first commission to any young composer. Rather, it is a cyclically organized essay in large-scale unity that attempts to deliver the message of its text in a fashion consistent with the contemporary view of Dürer as the Renaissance messiah of German art. In the process, it also guides listeners through a series of movements whose stylistic eclecticism is comparable to that of Bach's B-Minor Mass or Mozart's C-Minor Mass, into an inner sanctum where Dürer's own identity is fused with that of Christ, and then out again into their own present reality. Mendelssohn's music thus ultimately amounts to a sort of guided tour through the masterworks of music history as he understood them, and suggests a decidedly didactic approach geared to using music's historical legacies to overcome the problems of the obviously prosaic text and edify listeners. In other words, Mendelssohn accords to contrapuntal tradition as represented in the styles of Bach, Handel, Mozart, and Beethoven the same messianic import that the cantata's text accords to Dürer. We thus encounter in this 1828 cantata an extremely public pronouncement of a vision of music history in which historical and contemporary styles and forms coexist as equals—the first example of one of the most important hallmarks of Mendelssohn's distinctive musical style.

Dürer as Christ: Creating a Historical Messiah for Germans

The most important factor shaping the occasion for which Mendelssohn wrote this public pronouncement was the sweeping cultural-historical project that had begun to take shape in the German lands at the turn of the nineteenth century. Deeply aware of the revolutionary break with tradition and eager to develop a coherent national consciousness despite the fragmented political condition of their lands, Germans fervently sought historical figures who could serve as examples of a German cultural greatness rivaling or surpassing that of France and (especially) Italy. This collective process of creating and developing a distinctively German cultural memory extended beyond cultivated enterprises such as architecture, literature, law, music, and the visual arts, into the realms of folktales and myth.[3] In the latter capacity, the Romantic obsession with universal, timeless concepts that explain and encompass all history and culture led figures such as Friedrich Creuzer, Joseph Görres, and Jacob Grimm, as well as Herder, Schelling, Friedrich and August Wilhelm Schlegel, and Schopenhauer, to reexamine the relationships between history and myth, myth and religion, religion and philosophy, and philosophy and art—and, in widely varying ways, to dispense with received notions that (in the eyes of these commentators) reinforced arbitrary and artificial divisions among those disciplines and obscured the organic truths that underlay them. Removing these artificial distinctions would make it possible for art and culture to assume their rightful roles in human experience. This project was fueled in part by the well-documented but inadequately explained phenomenon of profoundly moving religious experiences that were triggered by artworks—a phenomenon central to the poem and music that are the subject of this chapter.

Two examples will suffice to illustrate the ramifications of these ideas for the case at hand. First, if, as Creuzer and his many followers asserted, the biblical narrative was a parable-like myth that ancient priests developed in order to make abstract sacred principles comprehensible to an uneducated populace, then the key to understanding the actual events and personages known from the historical accounts of the Abrahamic religions was to intermingle them with those of other faiths and theological systems and to retroactively construct the metanarratives of which they were a part, in the process disregarding contradictions as conveniences that had been contrived for the sake of the individual narratives.[4] Second, if myth itself was a poetic distillation of divine revelation, incapable of reduction to literal history, then Christ himself was not a sacrosanct historical individual, but a symbol whose identity resided in what Christ represented.[5]

The first of these meant that any infiltration of heathen subject matter into portrayals of Christian history was inherently more factual, not less, than a literal portrayal of Christian accounts. The second meant that individual figures who participated in one or more of the individual narratives out of which the great myth was constructed were only partial manifestations of the actual identity represented by them and others who shared their significance and at least some of their beliefs. In this view, Christ was not *the* Messiah, as the Christian church conventionally suggested, but part of a greater messianic identity that could be recognized as such only when Christ and other great individuals were recombined into an aggregate persona that may never have existed as such, but that became perceivable when those individuals' identity was understood to exist in their deeds and the principles that these represented. To fuse the identities of two great individuals—in this case, Dürer and Christ—was not to create a fiction, but to recognize a fact.

The general themes and issues entailed in this process of "becoming histori-cal" (to borrow Toews's formulation) are well known. Less well known are the extraordinary symbolic potency Dürer possessed for this project and the ways in which the various factions who were striving to propagate their own vision of a German nation appropriated the life and work of Dürer to advance their own cause. Most generally, because Dürer became the first German artist to win widespread acclaim from his contemporaries in Italy and the Low Countries— nations celebrated for their long and distinguished artistic heritages—and eventually had artists from those countries flocking to his humble *Werkstatt* in order to study with him, he became a historical exemplar of the potential of humble German patriotism to win international acclaim—that is, of German genius's potential for greatness in leadership. Moreover, since one of the great-est obstacles to any envisioning of a unified German nation in the early nine-teenth century was the deep theological division between Protestantism and Catholicism and the historical legacy of German-on-German violence born of that rift, Dürer's success at attaining artistic and cultural eminence—working with thematic material that was profoundly spiritual in nature—during pre-cisely the era in which those conflicts erupted made him an instance of a pro-foundly spiritual German greatness that transcended the Protestant/Catholic schism. Third, by using his own likeness to portray Christ—most famously in his 1500 self-portrait (see fig. 9.1), the 1513 *Veil of St. Veronica*, and the 1520 images of *Christ as Man of Sorrows*—Dürer made significantly easier the work of nineteenth-century voices who proclaimed him a figure of messianic import in the German cultural-historical project. Such a view began to emerge already in the decades after his death, as the gravesite visitations and other regular practices of Dürer's posthumous admirers assumed religious, almost cultlike features—and during the tercentennial year its religious potency was further enhanced by the fact that his death date (April 6, in the Julian calendar) fell on Easter Sunday.[6]

The importance of Dürer's posthumous role in this project of reenvisioning Germany as a political unity rather than (to borrow Metternich's notoriously apt description of early nineteenth-century Italy) a "geographical expression" was hinted at by the fact that the plans for an opulent 1828 Prussian celebra-tion of the tercentenary of Dürer's death were hatched in April 1820—in the wake of a festival hosted by Berlin's Royal Academy of the Arts commemorating his illustrious Italian contemporary Raffaello Sanzio da Urbino (1483–1520).[7] The leaders of the Berlin celebration—the sculptor Gottfried Schadow (1764– 1850), the architect Karl Friedrich Schinkel (1781–1841), and the composer and conductor Karl Friedrich Zelter (1758–1832)—began actively planning the event in the spring of 1828.[8] They initially envisioned a public spectacle that would be free of charge, but eventually opted instead for a highly struc-tured and exclusive state festivity, by invitation only, to be attended by the crown prince and his family themselves. Apparently in an effort to maximize

Figure 9.1. Albrecht Dürer, *Self-Portrait at Twenty-Eight Years Old Wearing a Coat with Fur Collar*, 1500. Reproduced with permission from Alte Pinakothek, Munich.

the public response despite this less-than-egalitarian approach, the directors mounted something close to a full-scale propaganda campaign during the weeks leading up to it. On April 8, the first day of public activities after Easter, the Berlin Wissenschaftlicher Kunstverein (scholarly art club) held a solemn public lecture and banquet commemorating Dürer's death, including a display of Dürer's woodcuts and etchings and a life-size statue of him, and lectures by Christian Friedrich Tieck (1776–1851; sculptor and younger brother of Ludwig Tieck), Schadow, Heinrich Gustav Hotho (1802–73; art historian, Right Hegelian, and docent at the university), and Christoph Friedrich Förster (1791–1868).[9] Hotho's lengthy speech was printed in installments over the next several issues of the *Berliner Conversations-Blatt für Poesie, Literatur und Kritik*,[10] and reflections on Dürer and his significance for art history and Germans especially became ubiquitous in the popular press.[11] The renowned medalist Johann Ludwig Jachtmann (1776–1842) produced a commemorative bronze medal that was sold to the public and eventually became a collector's item, and on the eve of the festival proper there was a public dress rehearsal of the complete program. This rehearsal reportedly filled the hall to capacity (approximately eight hundred), with many more turned away because of lack of seating.[12]

Held inside the main auditorium of the Sing-Akademie, the ceremony proper began at 11:30 on April 18.[13] Approximately 180–200 students of the Royal Academy of the Arts were seated in the balcony of the auditorium and nearly six hundred other invited guests were in their places on the main floor when the assembled senior faculty of the academy began their procession from the courtyard of the university out onto Unter den Linden, and then past the Neue Wache, entering the Sing-Akademie through its courtyard, where throngs of the uninvited public were gathered. The interior of the building, sumptuously appointed in greens and golds, was adorned with images and figures that alternately allegorized Dürer's artistry and were based on his works (see fig. 9.2). At the front of the hall, mounted on a stylobate, was an array of five plaster statues, the central figure being a six-foot statue of Dürer by the sculptor Ludwig Wichmann (1788–1859), depicting the cloaked artist holding a pen to slate, in the process of creating a new work. This was flanked on each side by gold-inlaid plaster statues by Friedrich Tieck representing architecture, perspective, painting, and the graphic arts of printmaking, drawing, and sculpture. Spanning the entire width of the space above the row of statues, in the form of an arch, was a gigantic oil painting by Heinrich Anton Dähling (1773–1850) based on Dürer's 1511 woodcut *Die heilige Dreifaltigkeit* (commonly known in English as *The Adoration of the Trinity* or *The Peace of the World Redeemer in the Lap of the Holy Father*). The side walls and the space above Dähling's painting were draped in a rich green, with a crown of stars at the ceiling—and in the center of the orchestra level, placed atop a richly ornamented pedestal approximately four feet high, was Christian Daniel Rauch's model for the ten-foot

Figure 9.2. Schinkel, Sketch for the auditorium decorations for the Berlin Dürer celebrations, 1828. Georg Galland, *Eine Dürer-Erinnerung aus dem romantischen Berlin* (Straßburg: J. H. Ed. Heitz, 1912).

Dürer monument that had been commissioned by King Ludwig I of Bavaria, for which the foundation stone had been unveiled in Nuremberg a few weeks earlier, on April 6.

All totaled, the ceremony lasted three hours.[14] This festival clarified that the day's pomp and splendor were committed in service of a cause that was a matter of church and state as well as art history. After the court entourage had been seated, the festivities began with Mendelssohn's C-Major ("Trumpet") overture (MWV P2, op. posth. 101),[15] followed by a lengthy address by the archaeologist, art historian, and theologian Ernst Heinrich Toelken (1786–1869), the secretary of the Akademie der Künste and professor of art history at the university in Berlin. Toelken's address did precisely what one might expect of any early nineteenth-century German:[16] it celebrated aspects of Dürer's life that would resonate with the cause of the German cultural project, situating him in the glorious age ("glorreiche Zeit") of Michelangelo, Correggio, Raphael, Titian, and Leonardo da Vinci, espousing him as the founding father of German art, and portraying him as a proud German whose works, despite his humble beginnings and a life and career centered on his native Nuremberg, became at least internationally sought after as those illustrious contemporaries from the more artistically and politically established countries of France, Italy, and the Low Countries.[17] Moreover, for Toelken and his (Protestant) Prussian contemporaries, Dürer was a Roman Catholic who also had grave reservations about Catholicism, "[taking] up the renewed doctrine of the Gospel with all his heart and soul"[18] and "recogniz[ing] in advance" that "from that point on the highest calling of art [would] lie in public life, that of individuals as well as governments and states."[19] In this sense, Dürer's supposedly enthusiastic embrace of Protestantism was a stand against Catholic (i.e., non-German) religious and territorial hegemony—at best an exaggeration, at worst a distortion, even though Dürer did harbor some sympathy for Luther and Protestantism. His use of religious artworks even for civic purposes thus symbolically encouraged later Germans to envision a politically unified Germany that formed a superstructure for individual confessional beliefs as well as for religion generally. Dürer thus anticipated the vision of the sacred political and cultural cause of German national unity that was specifically endorsed by Prussia, and that would eventually become known as the *Kleindeutsche Lösung*.[20]

The Poetic Text

If the propaganda-like pomp and splendor of the setting and the sacred-nationalistic fervor of Toelken's speech left any doubt that the goal of the day's festivities was to use Dürer's life and works to arouse mass enthusiasm for the explicitly Protestant version of the quest to create a unified German nation, the second half of the program did not. It comprised a seventy-minute

Große Festmusik zum Dürer-Fest by Mendelssohn, based on a 276-line "lyric poem" (lyrische Dichtung) titled *Albrecht Dürer* by Konrad Levezow (1770–1835).[21] An archaeologist by profession, Levezow was originally a student of theology, but became deeply involved in the philological study of ancient texts under the tutelage of Friedrich August Wolf (1759–1824) and Christian Gottlob Heyne (1729–1812). Both were influential figures in the Romantic reenvisioning of the pan-cultural relationships among myth, religion, and history, and Heyne specifically mentored the diplomat Christian Bunsen (1791–1860) in the development of his ideas on the Prussian mission in creating a German nation based on language and belief.

Levezow's text reflects the specifically Prussian bent of the ceremony's commemoration of Dürer in that it elevates sculpture and architecture (the principal fields of the Berlin ceremony's animating spirits, Schadow and Schinkel) to the same exalted level of aesthetic experience as those that were actually represented in Dürer's work. Moreover, as it progresses, Levezow's poem adopts themes that emphasize subjective and sometimes mystical experiences as essential elements of the collective universal feeling and faith—themes that reflect his years of study with Heyne, and that are decidedly closer to those of pietism and the theology of the Prussian theologian Friedrich Schleiermacher (1768–1834) than they are to those of Dürer or his native Nuremberg.

More importantly, Levezow's poem, like Toelken's speech that preceded it, adopted the already well-defined enthusiasm for portraying this "Holy Spirit of German Art" (heiliger Geist der deutschen Kunst)[22] as a Christlike cultural hero for German art and for Germanness generally by creating a textual narrative that depicts a sacred temple of the arts (no. 1), establishing Dürer as the key for the opening of the temple's gates (nos. 2–3), and identifying the characteristics of Dürer's art as a "testimony to German power" (ein Zeugniß deutscher Kraft) that have occasioned their plea for entry into that shrine of German greatness (nos. 4–7). Once inside, individual soloists, groups of soloists, and the full chorus reverently pray that "what [their] eyes have seen in these images" will be revealed to their hearts (no. 8).[23] They then (no. 9) reach the goal of their spiritual and national journey: Dürer's deep and abiding Christian faith, with a direct reference by a quartet of solo voices to the massive adaptation of Dürer's *Adoration of the Trinity* that loomed above the five statues by Wichmann and Tieck that adorned the stylobate at the front of the hall (see fig. 9.2):[24]

Ruhend nun im Vaterschoße,	Resting now in His father's lap,
Er, der Ewige, der Große,	he, the Eternal, the Great,
Einer Hölle Überwinder,	Conqueror of Hell,
Heiland aller Menschenkinder.	Savior of all children of humanity.

The crux of the narrative in Levezow's poem occurs in no. 10. Based on the Parable of the Unjust Steward (Luke 16:1–12) with a direct quotation from Psalm

143:2, this movement is a contemplation of the plight of those who have been entrusted with a sacred legacy, their acknowledgment of their obligations, and the mystery of redemption through grace. Levezow likens the delinquent steward of the Biblical parable to the heirs of Dürer's sacred legacy who have admitted their delinquency and renewed their vows to make good on that legacy's promise. In the sort of mystical wedding of art and religion typical of the German cultural project during the first quarter of the nineteenth century, the poem's final strophe actually fuses the personae of Dürer and Christ. The culmination occurs as Dürer/Christ directly addresses the poem's pilgrims (i.e., the German Christian faithful who have inherited Dürer's great legacy), acknowledging their plea for mercy and giving them another chance to make good on the sacred promise of that with which they have been entrusted:

Solo:
Manche Tränen sah' ich fallen
von des Menschen Angesicht,
doch die heißeste von allen
fließt, wenn Reu die Herzen bricht;

Wenn das Aug' auf *ihn* sich wendet,
der zum Sünder "Gnade" spricht,

wenn der Flehende geendet:

"Geh mit mir nicht ins Gericht!"
Blick auf Dürers *heil'ge* Werke,
schau des Heilands Angesicht—
und du *fühlst* des Trostes Stärke,

siehst der Hoffnung strahlend Licht,
hörst die Stimme von dem Munde

Lieb und Frieden wie sie tönt
zu dem neuen ew'gen Bunde
Gott und Menschen fest versöhnt.

*Mit dem Chor (pianissimo ohne
    Instrumente)*
Deine Zähren sah ich heiße fallen

und das Herz dir mächtig überwallen

von der Wehmut-Freude heiligstem
    Gefühl!

Solo:
Many a tear I saw falling
from the face of man,
but the most fervent tears of all
flow when our heart breaks in
    repentance.
When we turn our eyes to *Him*
who imparts [His] grace to the
    sinner
when the supplicant has finished,
    [saying:]

"Do not be judged with me!"
Look upon Dürer's sacred works,
behold the savior's face,
and you will *feel* the strength of
    comfort,
see the streaming light of hope;
you will *hear* the voice of that
    mouth,
uttering love and peace,
for the new eternal covenant,
God and Men firmly reconciled

*With chorus (pianissimo, a
    cappella)*
I have seen your tears falling
    fervently,
and your heart overtaking you
    mightily
with that holiest of all
    feelings, anguished joy!

234 JOHN MICHAEL COOPER

Thus blessed, the chorus (now speaking in the first-person singular and addressing Dürer/Christ in the second-person familiar) proclaims its praise for the "great, divinely gifted man" whose "miracles" it "can see and feel," and who "elevates [them] to divinity" (no. 11).[25] In no. 12 one voice hears the "joyous call" (Jubelruf) of the fatherland, where "a thousand voices . . . united in spirit" (tausend Stimmen . . . im Geist vereint) resound into the starry heavens, then beseeches the ancient Greek sculptors Lysippos (ca. 395–305 BCE) and Praxiteles (ca. 370–330 BCE) to lend "the great soul [and] pious German spirit" (die große Seele, den frommen deutschen Sinn) to the great bronze statue of Dürer that dominates the platform at the front of the hall so that they can know him as his own world did. A final recitative and aria proudly tell exalted Rome that it may honor Raphael, but that Germany will praise "her Dürer," closing by portraying those two great artists as brothers who shine in the furthest reaches of the richly colored ether like the Dioscuri (Castor and Pollux) in the firmament (no. 14).[26] The poem closes as the collective voices ask the favor of the "goddess of the rainbow" (Göttin mit dem Farbenbogen) and exhort their comrades to strive bravely toward that lofty goal alluded to in no. 11, whence they are beckoned by victory's garlands, also bestowed by genius at the summit of fame (no. 15).

Mendelssohn's Music

The unenviable challenge of setting Levezow's dramatically imaginative but poetically turgid text to music fell first to Zelter, who, as director of the Sing-Akademie and a close friend of Schadow, was an obvious choice. At a meeting of the festival's directors on January 25, however, Zelter informed the other directors that due to his advancing age he would be unable to complete the music in time for the festival, recommending that his star student Mendelssohn be offered the opportunity instead.[27] Mendelssohn thanked the directors for the commission and tentatively accepted it on January 12, but shied away from definitive acceptance until he had seen the text because "it could easily happen that [the demands of] Professor Levezow's poem exceed my [compositional] abilities, which have only recently reached their maturity," adding (diplomatically but astutely): "all the more so because, as you yourself state in your letter, my honorable teacher, Zelter, must have feared that he would not be able to finish the work in the available time."[28]

Precisely when Mendelssohn approached Levezow and received a copy of the poem is unknown,[29] but he must have been repelled by the text's virtuosic blend of turgidity and insipidness. That notwithstanding, he ultimately decided to take on the challenge. He reported on his reaction in a letter to Karl Klingemann dated February 5, 1828:

Now the Royal Academy of the Arts has commissioned me to write a grand cantata for chorus and orchestra and a festive symphony for a ceremony in honor of Dürer that they will be giving in April. Between those two works there will be a speech by Toelken; Schadow and Wichmann are decorating the hall of the Sing-Akademie with statues [and] Wach is contributing a painting, and since five other cities are giving [Dürer] festivals on that same day the occasion is too full of honor for me not to turn a blind eye to the text, wretched though it is, and set it unencumbered by that.[30]

The last sentence of that passage is telling, for there is little to corroborate the notion—first submitted by Eduard Devrient in 1869 and implicit throughout the cantata's subsequent reception history—that Mendelssohn set Levezow's text dispassionately or merely tossed the work off as an "occasional piece."[31] On the contrary, there is considerable evidence that he read Levezow's poem and endeavored not only to make his music respond appropriately to its gamely expressed ideas, but also to improve its effectiveness.

The most obvious indication of this effort at musical compensation for textual deficiency is that whereas Levezow's poem offers a straightforward linear sequence of events whose thickly layered references to Classical mythology, art history, and German folk themes threaten to obscure its narrative progress, Mendelssohn's cantata is constructed as an obvious cycle. The most straightforward device employed to this end is the theme of the instrumental introduction to no. 1 (see ex. 9.1), which recurs numerous times, complete or in part, over the course of the cantata. After no. 1, its most complete statement is in the slow introduction to no. 15, where it constitutes both the slow introduction (now provided with text and entrusted first to the vocal quartet and then to the entire chorus) and the majestic conclusion. Its first and last phrases also recur at the very end of no. 13. The opening phrase also recurs at the beginning of nos. 2, 6, and 14, and the signature thematic incipit of a 3–2–1 descent in the uppermost voice, usually followed by a gap and then a further descent, is present in the first phrase of most of the cantata's main themes.

Subtler but equally important are a number of fragmentary statements of this theme, with its character transformed according to the mood or idea of the movement at hand, at various points in the course of the cantata. The most important of these thematic cross-references comes when the expansive plagal cadence that opens the first movement returns, embellished, after the choral jubilation at having received grace from the fused personae of Christ and Dürer; this tranquil statement in A major (see ex. 9.2; c.f. ex. 9.1) depicts the "joyous call from the distant homeland" (Jubelruf aus heimatlichen Fernen) called for in the text. Indeed, the cadence is restated in this form at the end of this movement before returning in its original majestic form at the outset of no. 15, as the pilgrimage is completed.

Example 9.1. Mendelssohn, "Dürer" Cantata, no. 1, mm. 1–23, Cyclical theme in slow introduction

Example 9.2. Mendelssohn, "Dürer" Cantata, no. 12, mm. 1–6

More remarkable is that Mendelssohn constructs a musical analogue to the text's central idea of a pilgrimage across space and time—that is, from the festival's home in Prussia to the artist's home in Nuremberg, and from the nineteenth century to the sixteenth. One important musical acknowledgment of this textually symbolic departure and return is the cantata's tonal structure: the opening and closing movements are both firmly rooted in D major, opening and closing in that key, but D major and D minor are conspicuously absent from all the intervening movements (see table 9.1). Mendelssohn's cantata thus sets out on a tonal pilgrimage beginning with no. 2 and returns home only when the text does—at the beginning of no. 15, the moment of cyclical conclusion.

Similarly, Mendelssohn's slow introduction to no. 1 presages the subsequent movements' historical retrogression by giving increasingly prominent voice to archaisms that are somewhere between what Jonathan Bellman has termed the early nineteenth century's "chivalric style"—the use of non-functional, modal, or modally tinged harmonic progressions, often in tandem with martial or other "exotic" stylistic signifiers, to evoke the musical language of a pretonal past (and with it that brave and noble distant past itself)—and the *stile antico* polyphony that came to epitomize Renaissance Catholicism in the Romantic imagination.[32] The subject of this introduction, as noted above, is the theme that also serves as the main agent of the cantata's cyclic structure, recurring numerous times over the course of the work. Although this theme's quadratic phrase structure and overall harmonic language situate it firmly in the musical present of the early nineteenth century, its central section (phrases 2 and 3) also evokes an archaic style—indeed, in increasing measure and with increasing insistence at each of its three presentations. As shown in example 9.3a, the first statement turns toward the dominant (A major) in measure 9 and reaches a half cadence in that key (i.e., V of V in D) in measure 11, but then resolves this half cadence by turning to ii of D major in measure 12. Preceded as it is by the dominant of A major, the change of the chords' third from G♯ to G♮ at this point gently suggests the minor dominant (v) of that key, a useful component in the arsenal of musical devices used to evoke the modal musical past.

The second and third statements of the theme deploy this device more assertively. The second statement (mm. 24–43) is preceded by a short martial figure, *pianissimo*, in the trumpets and timpani, and remains essentially the same through the half cadence at the end of phrase 2, except for the addition of the martial rhythm in an arpeggiated ascent in the basses in measure 31. Then, however, the original mildly evocative deceptive cadence at the turn to phrase 3 is replaced by a full-fledged harmonic regression (V–IV) as a G-major triad replaces the E-minor triad of measure 12 (ex. 9.3b). Finally, in the third statement, now *forte*, the half cadence in D major at the end of phrase 2 is followed by C major—that is, flat-VII, a sonority whose modal implications

Table 9.1. Mendelssohn, Dürer Cantata, overview of organization, keys, genres, and stylistic references

No.		Keys	Notes	Stylistic referent
1	Chorus	D		"Chivalric style" in O, otherwise current
2		G–V/B♭	(recit)	
3		B♭		Beethoven
4		F		Current
		B♭ (Da Capo)	[3]	Beethoven
	Recit.	B♭–V/A		(recit.)
5		A		Mozart
6	Accomp.	F–V/E		Current
7		E		Handel
8		F		Current
		F–B♭	recitative	(recit.)
9		E♭		Current
10		g–G		Bach / [late Beethoven]
11		C		Current
12		A		Mozart
[13] ("12")		A – F	(recit)	
[14] ("13")		B♭		Beethoven
15 ("13")		D		Current

made it one of the most potent conveyers of archaic connotations in the early nineteenth century (ex. 9.3c).

The slow introduction's suggestion of progressively more remote moments in musical history is also acted out in what may be the cantata's most provocative and problematic feature: its frank appropriation of easily recognizable stylistic features of other composers from the German lands' recent and distant musical past—specifically, Bach, Handel, Mozart, and Beethoven—and its intermingling of those styles with others that are squarely rooted in Mendelssohn's and his contemporaries' own present.

As shown in table 9.1 above, this obvious stylistic eclecticism is also systematic, beginning with the recent past and moving back to Sebastian Bach, the composer whom Mendelssohn had by 1828 already come to revere as the *fons et origo* of great music. The cantata's music-historical pilgrimage begins in no. 3, in which the chorus for the first time names Dürer as the cause for their

Example 9.3. Mendelssohn, "Dürer" Cantata, introduction to no. 1; Harmonic archaism at junctions of phrases 2 and 3: (a) mm. 9–15; (b) mm. 29–35; and (c) mm. 49–59

pilgrimage (evidently in response to the question posed by the vocal quartet in the B section of no. 1). The first indication of the musical importance of this moment in the cantata's text is that Mendelssohn calls for this chorus to be repeated da capo after no. 4—a decision that would be understandable if the poet had requested it or the repetition somehow furthered the plot of the narrative, but that is decidedly odd when the work is already perilously long and based on a text as weak as this one. As shown in example 9.4, however, the forceful, irregular rhythms and asymmetrical phrasing of no. 3 are redolent of Beethoven's works, especially the "Eroica" Symphony (first movement) and the secular cantata *Der glorreiche Augenblick*, op. 136 (1814). Although in 1828 that cantata dated from the relatively recent musical past, Berlin's growing community of performers and audiences who were familiar

Example 9.4. Mendelssohn, "Dürer" Cantata, no. 3, Main theme, mm. 1–23

with Mendelssohn's usual idiom probably would have noticed that this chorus was unusually brusque and asymmetrical for him. In the context of the plot and purpose of the cantata's text, that stylistic departure acquires a greater significance. By invoking Beethoven (specifically the works of the "heroic" period, which until the 1840s were most widely accepted as Beethoven's greatest), Mendelssohn was invoking the most recently deceased representative of greatness in German music; and by calling for a repeat of no. 3 after no. 4 he underscored the stylistic juxtaposition.

The next station in this retrogressive exploration of German musical greatness is Mozart, who is not far from view in no. 5: the soprano aria "O wie lieblich" (O how lovely). The orchestration of this aria is lighter than that of the preceding numbers (indeed, than that of most of Mendelssohn's music prior to this date): it is scored for doubled woodwinds (sans oboes) and strings only, suggesting a scoring more typical of orchestral music before ca. 1800 than after that point. Adding to this, the movement employs the sort of inflective chromaticism, transparent textures, and elegant writing for the vocal soloist that were well known to the growing Mozart cult of the early nineteenth century (see ex. 9.5).

The next step in the journey is Handel, whose style was well known to Sing-Akademie audiences by the 1820s. This is the chorus "Hoffnung läßt nicht zu schanden werden, was Glaub' und Liebe auferbaut" (Hope does not allow the destruction of what is built on faith and love; no. 7), arguably one of the more successful movements of the entire cantata.[33] That this movement represents an earlier music-historical era is most obvious from the fact that of all the movements so far, it is the one most thoroughly suffused with imitative counterpoint. Beyond this, its orchestration is consistent with that of late eighteenth- and early nineteenth-century reorchestrations of music from the earlier eighteenth century: there are no flutes, but two oboes and two clarinets that generally double the upper vocal lines, and two bassoons that double the cellos and basses; trumpets and timpani enter at the exclamation "Heil ihm! Heil dem Sohn der Erden" (Hail to him! Hail to the son of the world). Finally, the walking-bass accompaniment to the main theme is reminiscent of Handel's celebrated continuo lines (ex. 9.6a), and the final cadence of the movement is thoroughly Handelian in its rhetorical construction—first establishing the tonic with an authentic cadence that fails to disrupt the contrapuntal texture, then offering another authentic cadence with a more homophonic texture, then suspending the cadential resolution before closing with a homorhythmic plagal progression that includes the leading tone and supertonic as passing tones moving to the final chord (ex. 9.6b).

The communal acclamation of no. 7 gives way to prayerful supplication in no. 8 ("Nehmt uns auf im Geist" / Take us up in this spirit) and then, in no. 9, to a contemplation of Christ in the lap of God by the quartet of vocal soloists (see ex. 9.7)—both movements whose scoring and musical language is more germane to Mendelssohn's own idiom than to that of any previous composers. With no. 10, however, the text brings the cantata's pilgrims into the inner sanctum of German art's sacred history—and here, as in the da capo statement of no. 3 after no. 4, Mendelssohn deliberately lengthens the cantata without any obvious textual or narrative reason for doing so. As shown above (p. 233), Levezow's text consists of three sections: a rumination on tears of penitence before the thought (and implicit image) of Christ on the cross (lines 1–8); an admonishment to take spiritual solace in Dürer's works (lines 9–16); and the voice

Example 9.5. Mendelssohn, "Dürer" Cantata, no. 5, Main theme, mm. 21–45

of Christ/Dürer himself, addressing the pilgrim's tears and imparting grace (lines 17–19). Mendelssohn introduces the first of these sections with a lengthy violin solo; states both of the first two sections twice; and inserts a third statement of the first section before moving to the third (see table 9.2). Although Levezow's libretto called for this third section to be stated a cappella and *pianissimo*, Mendelssohn sets it as an exclamation by the full choir and orchestra, *forte*. Once again, Mendelssohn's obvious contravention of the poet's directives suggests that his own reading of that text called for different musical means

Example 9.6a. Mendelssohn, "Dürer" Cantata, no. 7, main theme (text in S and T only), mm. 7–28

Example 9.6a.—*(concluded)*

Table 9.2. Synopsis of no. 10 of the "Dürer" Cantata

1–16	Introduction (A)	g	Vn solo
17–52	A	g–D	T, Vn solo
53–71	B	B♭	T, ww, str
71–99	A′	B♭ - g: V	T, Vn solo
100–110	B	G	T, ww, str
110–34	A″	g–V	T, vn solo
135–59	C	g : VI–G	ch, orch

in order to realize its ideas effectively—and the fact that his chosen means for accomplishing this improvement necessarily lengthened a work that by this point had already lasted at least forty-five minutes requires explanation.

Some insights are offered by the fact that this movement reflects the presence of not one, but two voices from German speakers' illustrious musical past. The first of these voices is that of J. S. Bach, whose searching, affective chromaticism

Example 9.6b. Mendelssohn, "Dürer" Cantata, no. 7, conclusion (text in S only), mm. 112–21

and angular melodic lines are vividly evoked in the A section ("Manche Träne sah' ich fallen"; see ex. 9.8). By this point, of course, Mendelssohn and a circle of friends had already begun rehearsing the *St. Matthew Passion,* and it is safe to assume that that work's musical language made itself felt in this movement of the cantata.[34] Less obvious but perhaps equally important is the church cantata *Herr, gehe nicht ins Gericht,* BWV 105 (1723). Like no. 10 of Mendelssohn's "Dürer" Cantata, BWV 105 is in G minor and employs a prominent violin obbligato—perhaps a reflection of the circumstance that the manuscript copy that Mendelssohn kept in his library from 1827 until at least 1844 was prepared by his closest boyhood friend, Eduard Rietz (1802–32)—a violinist.[35] Moreover, Mendelssohn, prompted by Levezow's text, also seems to allude to the rhetorical structure of the last movement of BWV 105: just as Levezow's text assures its pilgrims that faith in Dürer's works will bring solace to their troubled nation and offer the key to salvation, the text of the closing chorale of BWV 105 promises salvation through faith and belief. Bach graphically depicts the stilling of the sinner's troubled soul called for by the text,[36] beginning in G minor with *concitato* repeated sixteenth notes in the accompaniment for the first two lines and then slowing this to triplets, dactyls, and trochees, before closing in

Example 9.7. Mendelssohn, "Dürer" Cantata, no. 9, Quartetto, mm. 48–66

G major with even quarter notes (ex. 9.9). No. 10 of the "Dürer" Cantata parallels this rhetorical structure by beginning in a ruminative G minor, becoming increasingly anguished at each of the tenor solo's and solo violin's repetitions of the A section, adopting a rhetorically concentrated affect of profound sorrow as the voice of Dürer/Christ acknowledges the troubled souls of the penitent pilgrims as they are overtaken by anguished joy at the C section, and closing in a relieved G major as Dürer/Christ imparts the "love and peace" promised in the B section (ex. 9.10).

But Bach is not the only voice of musical salvation explicitly alluded to in no. 10 in Mendelssohn's "Dürer" Cantata. The other is Beethoven, whose voice is present in the B section ("Blick auf Dürers heil'ge Werke") via two works: the "Joy" theme of the Finale to the Ninth Symphony and the Finale of the Fantasia in C Minor for Chorus and Orchestra, op. 80 (1808), on a text by

Example 9.8. Mendelssohn, "Dürer" Cantata, no. 10: A theme, mm. 24–47

Example 9.8.—*(concluded)*

Christoph Kuffner (1777–1846).[37] In the late 1820s, the Choral Fantasy was the better known and more widely accepted of the two, but at least some members of the Dürer Festival's audience had been introduced to the Ninth Symphony already in November 1826, when Karl Möser had conducted it with Mendelssohn playing in the orchestra.[38] In both cases, Beethoven's theme performs the same function as the B section of no. 10 in Mendelssohn's cantata: the resolution of conflicted, anguished, soul-searching trouble (musically expressed by intense chromaticism, abrupt dynamic changes, and unpredictable changes in texture and tonal motion) into a lyrical calm, the reassurance of peace and joy (see ex. 9.11).

As noted above, no. 10 represents the dramatic turning point of the narrative in Levezow's text: the German *Volk* who petitioned for entry into the temple of the arts in no. 1 have been granted access and have gradually made their way into the inner sanctum, where the truth and beauty of Dürer's rendering of the crucifixion move their troubled spirits to an artistic and spiritual *Durchbruch* that grants them overwhelming peace, love, and joy. Thus inspired, they first sing praises to the source of their renewal (the exultant chorus "O du Herrlicher," no. 11) and then begin their egress toward the outer world/fatherland whence they have come.[39]

Example 9.9. Bach, *Herr, gehe nicht ins Gericht*, BWV 105, last mvt. (chorale tune and accompaniment only): (a) mm. 1–3; (b) mm. 6–8; (c) mm. 9–10; (d) mm. 14–20

Logically enough, this artistic and spiritual retracing of steps back to the journey's starting point is paralleled by a music-historical retracing—that is, by now moving forward through music history. The first step in this return pilgrimage is Mozart, who is obviously present in the virtuosic sonata-form coloratura aria "O Kunst Lysipps" (O art of Lyssipos; see ex. 9.12a–b); the second, Beethoven. No. 13 (the bass aria in contemporary style, "Hohe Roma, reich die Sternenkrone" / Exalted Rome, hand the starry crown) likens Dürer and Raphael to the Dioscuri shimmering as brothers in the ether, and in no. 14

Example 9.10. Mendelssohn, "Dürer" Cantata, no. 10: C theme, mm. 130–47

the bass solo promises honor to Dürer, who, "shining brightly high in the starry wreath," will "have [his] praises spread from mouth to mouth," "bringing the fatherland its laurels."[40] And here, as the mystically inspired populace returns to the present in order to strive with renewed fervor to realize the promise that Dürer had bequeathed them at his death three centuries earlier, Mendelssohn obviously refers to the mysterious passage at "über Sternen muss er wohnen" (beyond the stars he must abide) in the recapitulation, just before the double fugue on "Seid umschlungen ihr Millionen" and "Freude, schöner Götterfunken" (ex. 9.13a–b). Although it would be at best difficult to argue that the dominant-seventh sonority in the closing measures of no. 14 rivals the mystery of the fully diminished seventh in its counterpart passage in the Ninth Symphony, the dynamics, instrumentation, registration, and rhythmic language of this passage clearly hearken back to the Ninth's musical depiction of the starry heavens that are home to Schiller's and Beethoven's supreme deity. Mendelssohn's decision to draw on the Ninth as

Example 9.11. (a) Beethoven, *Choral Fantasy*, op. 80, finale theme; (b) Beethoven, Symphony no. 9, finale, "Joy" theme; (c) Mendelssohn, "Dürer" Cantata, no. 10, theme of B section

the cantata's narrative returned to the here and now was entirely logical, since in 1828 the Ninth still represented a little-understood milestone at the threshold of progress in musical history.

This guided tour through music history has thus reached its goal. The Finale articulates the cyclical completion of the cantata's journey by returning to the introduction to no. 1—but now entrusted first to the vocal quartet and then to the entire chorus (ex. 9.14a–b). As one would expect from a pilgrimage in which the present's inspiration was achieved by its recognition and assimilation of the magnificent legacies of the past, this closing movement of Mendelssohn's cantata adsorbs many of the music-historical voices that were heard in the preceding movements. Most generally, the rhetorical strategy of the finale of the Ninth Symphony is present, in that the originally purely instrumental introduction from no. 1 here attains fulfillment through the addition of words. This slow introduction's shimmering textures and hymnic ethos are also redolent of Mozart, via works such as the *Ave verum corpus* (K. 618; likewise in D major), which was well known in the growing Mozart cult by the early 1820s. Bach is most obviously present in the lengthy fugue that makes up the movement's B section (mm. 85–156). And Handel, too, makes a final appearance in the work's closing measures, via a suspended cadence that also offers Mendelssohn's predilection for a 3–2–1 descent to closely massed choral sound in *fortissimo* conclusions of choral/orchestral works (ex. 9.15). Significant here, however, is that, while this Finale contains obvious references to the musical past, it never surrenders itself to those bygone musical moments entirely, as those earlier movements had. Instead, the musical present achieved here is richly informed and inspired by musical history, but autonomous and self-fulfilling—an apt musical counterpart to the lesson of Levezow's poem, Toelken's speech, and the motivation of the Berlin tercentenary celebrations generally.

Example 9.12. Mendelssohn, "Dürer" Cantata, no. 12: (a) first subject, mm. 8–15; (b) second subject, mm. 30–38

Example 9.13a. Beethoven, Symphony no. 9, finale "Über Sternen muss er wohnen" in recapitulation

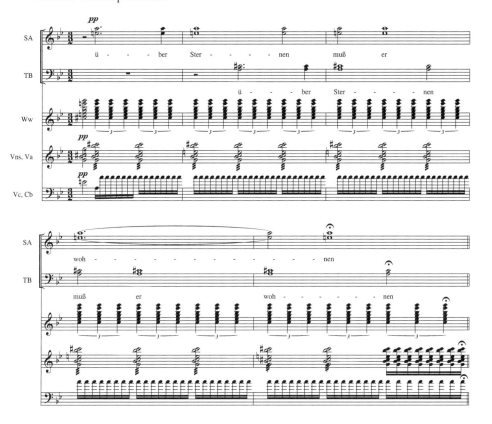

Example 9.13b. Mendelssohn, "Dürer" Cantata, no. 14, conclusion, mm. 17–21

Example 9.14. Mendelssohn, "Dürer" Cantata, no. 15: (a) cyclical theme from introduction to no. 1 entrusted to vocal quartet, mm. 1–7; (b) cyclical theme from introduction to no. 1 entrusted to full chorus and orchestra, mm. 20–23

Example 9.15. Mendelssohn, "Dürer" Cantata, no. 15, conclusion, mm. 164–79

Conclusions: "Denn in Sebastian, da sey alles zusammen"

The above remarks have left two important questions unanswered. First, why does the cantata's pilgrimage into the music-historical past proceed only in alternating movements, rather in a steady progression? And second, why is Beethoven's voice so obviously present in the movement of this cantata otherwise devoted to Bach, whose position at the early end of a journey into the musical past (as it was known in Prussia in the 1820s) is understandable?

The answer to the first of these questions may well be simply that of context. Few if any of the audience members or performers involved in the Berlin Dürer Festival would have had the grasp of music history that Mendelssohn did, and on first hearing most would have needed some sort of aid in order to appreciate the stylistic devices by which Mendelssohn, following the text's concept of a journey from the present to the past and back again, musically articulated the increasing distance from the language of the musical present. The alternate movements provided that aid. By dispensing with the stylistic continuity that would have faithfully reproduced gradual changes in musical style and instead moving back and forth between contemporary idioms and progressively more remote stations on that journey, Mendelssohn emphasized the distance between the present and the historical legacies that he and Levezow asserted as the sources of inspiration for spiritual, artistic, and national renewal.

The answer to the second question, I believe, is that Mendelssohn viewed Bach and Beethoven as historical figures who were both frequently misunderstood and underestimated, but of comparable historical importance, for German music and music generally. In April 1828, the epoch-making performances of the *St. Matthew Passion* by which the Sing-Akademie would make the nascent Bach revival a full-blown public affair were still a thing of the future. Bach had, however, become a potent symbol in print culture's project of articulating a national community of German-speakers, even though few of his works were widely known, public performances of his music were few, and even fewer composers had attempted compositional engagement with his legacy. The same was true of Beethoven, especially with regard to the works of the 1820s: until the 1840s the body of believers in the works of the late Vienna period was passionate but small, performances were few and controversial, and composers' comprehension of this legacy rarely if ever adequate to permit them to address themselves to it compositionally. In other words, one answer to the question of why Beethoven shared with Bach the musical counterpart to Levezow's inner sanctum of holy German art as unrealized promise for creating national community is that for Mendelssohn, both were historically different manifestations of a single German genius that happened to have been realized at different historical moments. Collectively, their legacies offered a single, as-yet-unrecognized but potent promise for bringing untold glory to the fatherland and to art generally. (Obviously, the subsequent reception history of both composers suggests that he was correct on this count.)

Moreover, Mendelssohn seems to have believed that the German genius realized in Bach and Beethoven was historically transcendent. In this sense, the theme of the Finale in Beethoven's Choral Fantasy was as timeless as the idea that inspired it, and thus not in historical contradiction to no. 10's position, within the narrative of this cantata's plot, in the age of Sebastian Bach. Likewise, Bach's genius, which in the eyes of the growing cult of his admirers in the 1820s was a gift to their generation, was not strictly a thing of the past, as its position in contemporary musical life would seem to suggest. Rather, it was a specific historical moment's expression of an idea that was timeless, one whose promise for bringing together Germans through art was both untold and almost unimaginable—a position entirely congruent with the contemporary ideas of Creuzer, Grimm, and others named above, even if Mendelssohn did not explicitly subscribe to their ideas. The composer's account of Thibaut's analogy for the roles that Bach and Tomás Luis de Victoria could play in contemporary life might well be transferred to his "Dürer" Cantata to explain the presence of Beethoven's voice in a movement centrally based on Bach's: "Since I had said some things about Sebastian Bach to [Thibaut] and had told him that he did not yet know the fountainhead and most important thing, because all that was encompassed in Sebastian, he said as I was leaving: 'Farewell, and we will build our friendship on Luis de Victoria and Sebastian Bach, like two lovers who promise each other to look at the full moon and then no longer feel far from one another.'"[41]

I would suggest, then, that Mendelssohn's little-known but oft-dismissed "Dürer" Cantata is not the halfhearted assemblage of motley movements that scholars and other musicians have generally assumed—usually, it must be noted, without providing any evidence of having examined the music they so readily dismissed. But does that mean that the work succeeds in delivering its music-historical sermon, or that its aesthetic merits make it a worthy peer of the Octet for Strings, the *Midsummer Night's Dream* overture, or his other acknowledged masterpieces of the late 1820s? Of course not—or, at least, not necessarily.

At the most specific level, the significance of recognizing that Mendelssohn made his first public contribution to the cultural project of creating German cultural unity through the celebration of a shared historical past is that his intellectually elegant method for realizing the modern implications of historicism has eluded previous commentators on the work not because of its sophistication, but because scholars have repeated previous scholars' verdicts on the work without ever troubling to examine the score or read Levezow's text closely. Although the message of Mendelssohn's "sermon" did not get through to at least some of his contemporaries,[42] Eduard Devrient's simple dismissal of the work as an "occasional piece" (Gelegenheitsmusik) that "made no impression" (machte keinen Eindruck)[43] is not consistent with the reports of other contemporary sources—all of which were contemporaneous with the event itself rather than recollected more than forty years after the fact. The same reviewer who chided Mendelssohn for the work's lack of stylistic unity also applauded the work for its "ingenious drive" (genialen Schwung) and noted the "undeniably . . . genuine, important talent" (das ächte, bedeutende Talent) of the composer.[44] An anonymous reviewer in the *Berliner Kunst-Blatt* described the cantata as "flowing, pleasing, melodious, in some places tending toward languorousness," and noted that it "captured every heart."[45] The Berlin Künstlerverein inducted Mendelssohn as an honorary member.[46] Another Berlin periodical noted "with gratification" that Mendelssohn had "adopted Beethoven as the model for his instrumentation," that "several choruses were reminiscent of Handel," and that "the solos were rich in beautiful melody."[47] Perhaps most tellingly, Zelter (who conducted the performance) reported to Goethe that the cantata's "[compositional] craft was masterly throughout," and "in response to many requests" a second performance of the work was scheduled for May 8.[48] For reasons that Zelter does not provide, this planned repeat performance was canceled—but in any case Devrient's dismissal of this reception is unjustified, and the failure of subsequent commentators to look further is even more problematic.

What is at issue here, then, is not what Mendelssohn's "Dürer" Cantata is *not* (a masterpiece), but what it *is*: a large-scale exploration of the creative potential of music-historical legacies not simply as items in an imaginary museum of musical works, but as poetic sparks in the living, breathing, ongoing tradition collectively represented by the works of Bach, Handel, Mozart, Beethoven, and of course Mendelssohn himself. That the cantata has for so long been ignored and dismissed altogether is regrettable—for in overlooking it, we have overlooked an early and impassioned argument for the integration of the great contrapuntal tradition into the discourse of musical modernity.

Notes

1   Kent Eugene Hatteberg, "*Gloria* (1822) and *Große Festmusik zum Dürerfest* (1828): Urtext Editions of Two Unpublished Choral-Orchestral Works by Felix Mendelssohn, with Background and Commentary" (DMA diss., University of Iowa, 1995); R. Larry Todd, *Mendelssohn: A Life in Music* (Oxford: Oxford University Press, 2003), 185–87.

2   The autograph for the cantata is held in volume 17 of the original *Mendelssohn Nachlaß* in the Staatsbibliothek zu Berlin–Preußischer Kulturbesitz. An (inadequate) edition was included in volume 2 of Hatteberg, "*Gloria* (1822) and *Große Festmusik zum Dürerfest* (1828)." The work was published in series VII of the *Leipziger Ausgabe der Werke von Felix Mendelssohn Bartholdy*: Felix Mendelssohn Bartholdy, *Festmusik* ("Dürer Festival Music"), MWV D1, ed. Annette Thein and Birgit Müller (Wiesbaden, Leipzig, Paris: Breitkopf und Härtel, 2012).

3   See John Edward Toews, *Becoming Historical: Cultural Reformation and Public Memory in Early Nineteenth-Century Berlin* (Cambridge: Cambridge University Press, 2004); further, George S. Williamson, *The Longing for Myth in Germany: Religion and Aesthetic Culture from Romanticism to Nietzsche* (Chicago: University of Chicago Press, 2004).

4   The most influential text to have developed this viewpoint was Friedrich Creuzer's four-volume *Symbolik und Mythologie der alten Völker, besonders der Griechen* (Leipzig: Heyer und Leske), which ran to four editions between 1810 and 1843. For a summary of the text and its influence, see Williamson, *The Longing for Myth*, 127–50.

5   See Friedrich August Wolf, *Prolegomena ad Homerum, sive de operum Homericorum prisca et genuina forma variisque mutationibus et probabili ratione emendandi* (Halle: Libraria Orphanotrophei, 1795; trans. Anthony Grafton, Glenn W. Most, and James E. G. Zetzel as *Prolegomena to Homer, 1795* [Princeton, NJ: Princeton University Press, 1985]); Joseph Görres, *Die teutschen Volksbücher* (Heidelberg: Mohr und Zimmer, 1807); Jacob Grimm, "Gedanken über Mythos, Epos und Geschichte," *Deutsches Museum* 1 (1812): 53–75; Wilhelm Martin Leberecht De Wette, *Beiträge zur Einleitung in das Alte Testament* (Halle: Schimmelpfennig, 1806–7); De Wette, *Über Religion und Theologie: Erläuterungen zu seinem Lehrbuch der Dogmatik* (Berlin: Realschulbuchhandlung, 1815). These lengthy and often difficult texts are summarized in Williamson, *The Longing for Myth*, 72–120.

6   The best documentary exploration of this phenomenon is Heinz Lüdecke and Susanne Heiland, *Dürer und die Nachwelt: Urkunden, Briefe, Dichtungen und*

wissenschaftliche Betrachtungen aus vier Jahrhunderten (Berlin: Rütten und Loening, 1955). See also the Introduction in Jane Campbell Hutchison, *Albrecht Dürer: A Guide to Research* (New York: Garland, 2000), 1–24, and her "Der vielgefeierte Dürer," in *Deutsche Feiern*, ed. Reinhold Grimm and Jost Hermand (Wiesbaden: Akademische Verlagsgesellschaft Athenaion, 1977), 25–45.

7   See Georg Galland, *Eine Dürer-Erinnerung aus dem romantischen Berlin* (Strassburg: J. H. Ed. Heitz, 1912), 5.

8   For a documentary history of the preparations, see the Anhang (appendix) to Galland, *Eine Dürer-Erinnerung*, 25–34. The earliest document of these preparations cited in the published literature is a lengthy letter from Schinkel dated January 8, 1828, but a letter from the author of the cantata's text, Konrad Levezow, to Carl Friedrich Zelter now held in the Library of Congress in Washington, DC, reveals that the cantata's text was already written by that point, and further reflects earlier conversations on the matter (Gertrude Clarke Whittall collection, box 9, no. 8). I wish to thank James Wintle of the Performing Arts Division for assistance in locating and accessing this little-known letter.

9   "Albrecht Dürers Gedächtnißfeier in Berlin," *Berliner Conversations-Blatt für Poesie, Literatur und Kritik* 2, no. 73 (April 14, 1828): 290.

10   [Heinrich Gustav Hotho], "Zur Charakteristik des Geistes und der Werke Albrecht Dürers," *Berliner Conversations-Blatt für Poesie, Literatur und Kritik* 1 (1828): 290–92, 295–96, 297–98, 300–302.

11   For an overview of these activities and a summary of the festivities in other German cities, see especially Lüdecke and Heiland, *Dürer und die Nachwelt*, 382–95. See also Paul Münch, "Changing Historical Perceptions of the Historical Role of Albrecht Dürer," in *Dürer and His Culture*, ed. Dagmar Eichberger and Charles Zika (Cambridge: Cambridge University Press, 1998), 198–210.

12   "Albrecht Dürers Säcular-Feier zu Nürnberg am 7ten April und zu Berlin am 18ten April 1828," *Berliner Kunst-Blatt* 1 (1828): 114–15.

13   Conveniently, Dürer's death date of April 6, 1528 (Julian calendar) converts to April 18 in the Gregorian calendar. Because of this coincidence, the Berlin festivities were able to claim that in some sense they fell on Dürer's death date.

14   "Albrecht Dürers Gedächtnißfeier," 310.

15   See Todd, *Mendelssohn: A Life in Music*, 185.

16   For the complete text of Toelken's address, see "Albrecht Dürers Säcular-Feier," 116–29. A small excerpt of the address is also given in Lüdecke and Heiland, *Dürer und die Nachwelt*, 209–10.

17   "Albrecht Dürers Säcular-Feier," 116: "Die vaterländische Kunst, als deren begründender Meister Albrecht Dürer heute gefeiert werden soll." All translations are by the author.

18   "Albrecht Dürers Gedächtnißfeier," 126: "Albrecht Dürer . . . wandte sich mit ganzer Seele zu der erneuerten Lehre des Evangeliums."

19   "Albrecht Dürers Säcular-Feier," 126–27: "Er (ahnte) voraus, die höchste Beziehung der Kunst werde von nun an das öffentliche Leben, des einzelnen, wie der Regiergungen und Staaten, seyn."

20   There were two principal visions for politically unifying the German lands in the early and mid-nineteenth century. The *Großdeutsche Lösung* (Greater German Solution) was espoused by the Kingdom of Bavaria and other southern lands, and envisioned an officially Catholic German state that would include Austria as well as the German states to the north. The *Kleindeutsche Lösung* (Lesser German Solution), espoused by the northern, predominantly Protestant lands, with Prussia

---

in the lead, envisioned an officially Protestant German state that did not include Austria.

21 Levezow's poem was published by A. W. Hayn in 1828 and sold at the entrance to the festivities; the proceeds were to go to the fund for the Dürer monument in Nuremberg. Two exemplars of this publication survive in the Library of Congress (Washington, DC).

22 The phrase is Hutchison's; see "Der vielgefeierte Dürer," 29.

23 "Mag die Andacht uns erfüllen, / laßt im Glauben uns voll Ehrfurcht nah'n. / Dann wird sich dem inner'n Sinn enthüllen, / was in Bildern uns're Augen sah'n" (May we be filled with devotion, / may we approach faithfully and reverently. Then will be revealed to our inner thoughts that which our eyes saw in [those] images).

24 See also example 9.7.

25 "O du herrlicher, du großer, / gottbegabter Mann! / Selig, daß ich deine Wunder sehn und fühlen kann! . . . Nein, die Seele mir entrückest / zu der Künste höchstem Ziel, / mich zu dem Göttlichen erhebst" (O you glorious, great, divinely gifted man! Blessed, that I can see and feel your miracles. . . . No, you carry my soul away to the loftiest goal of the arts, and elevate me to the divine!)

26 Levezow and Mendelssohn apparently wrote and composed no. 12 late in the cantata's genesis. Its text is not included in the libretto that Levezow sent to Zelter on January 1, 1828, although it is included in the printed libretto that was sold at the ceremony itself. The script of Mendelssohn's score for this movement bears signs of obvious haste, and in the recapitulation the soprano line is not notated (though the absence of rests in that staff indicates that the soprano was obviously intended to sing—a task that could be realized easily enough because the movement is in sonata form; Mendelssohn may well have written out the soprano part himself and supplied the notes there). The score also includes, in Zelter's hand, the annotation "Statt No. 12 u. 13" (instead of nos. 12 and 13) at the heading of the soprano recitative and aria, and the scores of nos. 13 and 14 are headed "No. 12" and "No. 13," respectively. Additionally, the header for the original no. 12 bears the original autograph heading "Recit. und Aria," but the latter two words are crossed out (it is unclear whether this deletion is in Mendelssohn's handwriting or Zelter's). Since the printed libretto includes all three of these texts in that sequence, however, it is also possible that Zelter's indication that the soprano recitative and aria were to replace the original two movements was a suggestion. For the latter to have been removed at the performance but included in the printed libretto that was distributed there would have been an obvious flaw in the otherwise consummate professionalism that the festivities presented to the public and the royal court.

27 There were also other complications, of course. Most obviously, Zelter (then seventy-three) was still actively directing the Sing-Akademie, which had an active schedule of rehearsals and performances in preparation for Holy Week and Easter.

28 Galland, *Eine Dürer-Erinnerung*, 25–26: "Da es nun aber leicht möglich seyn könnte, daß das Gedicht des Herrn Prof. Levezow meine noch lange nicht zur Reife ausgebildeten Fähigkeiten überstiege . . . um so eher, da, wie Sie selbst in Ihrem geehrten Schreiben sagen, mein geehrter Lehrer Zelter gefürchtet haben muß, das Werk nicht in der bestimmten Zeit beendigen zu können."

29 A manuscript copy in the poet's hand survives in the Bodleian Library, Oxford MS M. Deneke Mendelssohn c.27, fols. 52–57. This copy concurs with the final version in most essentials, but contains obvious signs of revision by the poet. It does *not* contain texts for one movement set by Mendelssohn (no. 12, which was, however,

included in the printed libretto sold at the Berlin celebration), and does contain some texts that Mendelssohn did not set.

30 "Jetzt hat mir die königliche [*sic*] Akademie der Künste zu einem Feste, das sie im April in Gemeinschaft mit dem Künstlerverein und der Singakademie Dürern zu Ehren geben wird, den Auftrag gegeben, eine grosse Kantate für Chor und Orchester und eine Feiersymphonie zu komponieren; dazwischen hält Tölken eine Rede, Schadow und Wichmann dekorieren den Saal der Singakademie mit Statuen, Wach malt ein Bild dazu, und da noch fünf andere Städte an demselben Tage ein Fest geben, so ist mir die Gelegenheit zu ehrenvoll, als dass ich nicht ein Auge zudrücken und den Text, wie schlecht er auch sei, frischweg komponieren sollte." Quoted from Karl Klingemann [Jr.], ed., *Felix Mendelssohn-Bartholdys Briefwechsel mit Legationsrat Karl Klingemann in London* (Essen: G. D. Baedecker, 1909), 48.

31 Eduard Devrient, *Meine Erinnerungen an Felix Mendelssohn-Bartholdy und seine Briefe an mich* (Leipzig: J. J. Weber, 1869), 44.

32 See Jonathan Bellman, "*Aus alten Märchen*: The Chivalric Style in the Music of Schumann and Brahms," *Journal of Musicology* 13 (1995): 117–35; further, James Garratt, *Palestrina and the German Romantic Imagination* (Cambridge: Cambridge University Press, 2002).

33 When this text entered Levezow's libretto is unclear. It is not in the manuscript libretto that the poet delivered to Zelter on January 1, 1828, but it is in the printed libretto sold at the premiere, and the script, writing implement, and placement of autograph folio numbers in the score are in the same as those of the preceding movements but different from those of the following portion of the manuscript, suggesting that nos. 1–7 belong to one phrase of composition and nos. 8–15 to another.

34 See especially Martin Geck, *Die Wiederentdeckung der Matthäuspassion im 19. Jahrhundert: Die zeitgenössischen Dokumente und ihre ideengeschichtliche Deutung* (Regensburg: Gustav Bosse Verlag, 1967); Celia Applegate, *Bach in Berlin: Nation and Culture in Mendelssohn's Revival of the "St. Matthew Passion"* (Ithaca, NY: Cornell University Press, 2005).

35 See Rudolf Elvers and Peter Ward Jones, "Das Musikalienverzeichnis von Fanny und Felix Mendelssohn Bartholdy," *Mendelssohn-Studien* 8 (1993): 90. This manuscript survives in the Bodleian Library as MS M. Deneke Mendelssohn c.64.

36 "Nun ich weiß, du wirst mir stillen, mein Gewissen, das mich plagt; es wird deine Treu' erfüllen, was du selber hast gesagt: daß auf dieser weiten Erde Keiner soll verloren werden, sondern ewig leben soll, wenn er nur ist glaubensvoll" (Now I know that you will quiet the conscience that troubles me; your steadfastness will fulfill what you yourself promised: that no one in this whole world who believes in you shall be lost, but shall live forever.)

37 It is worth noting that the theme of the Finale of the Choral Fantasy is in turn based on Beethoven's song *Gegenliebe* ("Wüsst' ich, daß du mich lieb'"), WoO 118/2. This song was first published in 1836, however, and there is no evidence that Mendelssohn knew it.

38 See Todd, *Mendelssohn: A Life in Music*, 156.

39 In this sense, the dramatic function of this turning point in Mendelssohn's musical narration of Levezow's text clearly points to the Choral Fantasy as the immediate point of inspiration, since the closing quatrain of that work's text admonishes listeners to go forth with renewed inspiration, as Levezow's text does in its final lines: "Nehmt denn hin, ihr schönen Seelen, / froh die Gaben schöner Kunst: / Wenn sich Lieb und Kraft vermählen, lohnt den Menschen Göttergunst" (So go forth,

you beautiful spirits, taking with you the gifts of beautiful art: when love and power are united, humans are blessed with the favor of the gods).

40 "Strahle hoch im Sternenkranze; / großer Dürer, sei verehrt! / Mit des Ruhmes ew'gem Glänze / hast du Deutschlands Ruhm gemehrt! / Spät noch wird im Lauf der Zeiten / sich der Jubeldank erneu'n, / Mund zu Mund dein Lob verbreiten / und des Vaterland die Lorbeer streu'n" (Radiate high in the starry wreath; O great Dürer, honor to you! With the luster of your eternal renown you have magnified the fame of Germany. Still later in the course of ages the joyous thanks will be renewed from mouth to mouth your praises will be spread, bringing the fatherland its laurels).

41 Sebastian Hensel, *Die Familie Mendelssohn, 1729 bis 1847: nach Briefen und Tagebüchern*, 16th ed. (Berlin: Georg Reimer, 1918), 1:190–91: "da ich ihm manches von Seb. Bach erzählte und ihm gesagt hatte, das Haupt und das Wichtigste sei ihm noch unbekannt, denn in Sebastian da sei alles zusammen, so sprach er zum Abschiede: 'Leben Sie wohl und unsere Freundschaft wollen wir an den Luis de Vittoria und den Sebastian Bach anknüpfen, gleichwie sich zwei Liebende das Wort geben, in den Vollmond zu sehen und sich dann nicht mehr fern voneinander glauben.'"

42 For example, an anonymous reviewer from the Leipzig *Allgemeine musikalische Zeitung* specifically chided the young composer for its lack of stylistic unity and the too-obvious influences of Bach, Handel, Mozart, and Beethoven (*Allgemeine musikalische Zeitung* 30, no. 22 [May 28, 1828]: 362).

43 Devrient, *Erinnerungen an Felix Mendelssohn-Bartholdy*, 44. Although J. Rigbie Turner has established and corrected the problems of textual fidelity that pervade Devrient's presentation of Mendelssohn's letters to him (see "Mendelssohn's Letters to Eduard Devrient: Filling In Some Gaps," in *Mendelssohn Studies*, ed. R. Larry Todd [Cambridge: Cambridge University Press, 1992], 200–239), a thorough reexamination of Devrient's relationship with Mendelssohn is long overdue. Aside from the liabilities to which memoirs as a genre are prone, Devrient's case is complicated by the fact of his close collaboration with Richard Wagner in the Dresden Court Theater in 1842–44, their shared views on the nature and means for developing a German national theater, his passive participation in the development of the concept for the *Ring*, and their close collaboration in the Court Theater at Karlsruhe from 1852 to 1859. The two had a falling-out at that point, and Devrient's memoirs of Mendelssohn were written another decade later—but during nearly fifteen years of collegial work with Wagner many of his assessments of Mendelssohn's work were certainly influenced by the power and elegance of Wagner's own. Given this context, the fact that Devrient always regards Mendelssohn with affection but often concurs with Wagner in his assessment of Mendelssohn's works is surely no coincidence.

44 *Allgemeine musikalische Zeitung* 30, no. 22 (May 28, 1828): 362.

45 "Albrecht Dürers Säcular-Feier," 129: "fliessend, gefällig, melodisch, an einigen Stellen selbst zum Schmelzenden sich hinneigend, bemeisterte dieselbe sich aller Herzen."

46 Ibid., 129–30.

47 "Albrecht Dürers Gedächtnißfeier," 310: "Wir bemerken jedoch mit Vergnügen, daß Hr. Mendelssohn was die Instrumentierung betrifft, sich Beethoven zum Muster genommen hat, mehrere Chöre erinnerten an Händel, die Solos waren reich an schönen Melodien."

48 Letters of April 26 and May 8, 1828, from Zelter to Goethe, quoted in Lüdecke and Heiland, *Dürer und die Nachwelt*, 210–11.

Chapter Ten

Mendelssohn's "Authentic" Handel in Context

German Approaches to Translation and Art and Architectural Restoration in the Early Nineteenth Century

Glenn Stanley

> Either the translator leaves the author at peace as much as possible and moves the reader toward the author, or he leaves the reader at peace as much as possible and moves the author toward the reader.
>
> —Friedrich Schleiermacher, "Über die verschiedenen Methoden des Übersetzens" (On the different methods of translating) 1813/1838

Felix Mendelssohn's efforts to reform the performance style of early music (notably Handel oratorios) have received only some of the attention they rightfully claim: in 1969 Susanna Grossmann-Vendrey touched on the subject in her book on Mendelssohn and historical music; in the 1990s I published a short essay on his Handel performances at the Lower Rhine music festivals against the backdrop of eighteenth-century performance traditions (Mozart's arrangements of Handel) and their discussion in the musical press; and in 2008 Ralf Wehner presented the most detailed discussion of Mendelssohn's Handel performances to date.[1] In this study I will broaden the focus by placing Mendelssohn's work as well as the contemporary debate on arrangements of historical music—Handel was the focus—in their cultural-historical context and by examining comparable developments in architecture, the visual arts, and literature.

Our appreciation of the singularity, in his time and for many decades thereafter, of Mendelssohn's vision of a historically correct performance style should not obscure the fact that his reforms, and the aesthetic and cultural-historical perspective that informed them, comprised just one current in a broad stream of cultural historicism that stimulated efforts in Germany and in other, primarily northern European, countries to preserve art and literature of the past and to make it available and understandable to a modern public. The alternatives for translators that Friedrich Schleiermacher proposed in the passage cited above establish, perhaps over-reductively, the antipodes framing the field of divergent perspectives and practices about unfamiliar music, literature, and the visual arts. Because they can be applied, in their general form, not only to literature, but rather to all these areas, they also provide something of a unifying conceptual field for my topic, which lends some measure of methodological integrity to the difficult task of discussing very different artistic media. However different their materials and forms were, artists and theorists in all these areas were faced with the same problem: how to preserve and present old and unfamiliar, even foreign artifacts to the contemporary recipient. As Carl Dahlhaus has remarked, the spirit behind Mendelssohn's epochal performance of the *St. Matthew Passion* in 1829 "invites us to compare the Bach renaissance to the completion of the Cologne Cathedral."[2] That great undertaking in Cologne is a chapter in my story, and the idea that the Bach and Handel revivals actually constitute one revival, and one in which Mendelssohn played a crucial and major role, hardly needs stating.

ဢ

The direct stimulus for Mendelssohn's engagement with Handel performance practice arose in 1833, when he was asked to conduct *Israel in Egypt* at the Lower Rhine Music Festival in Düsseldorf. It came, ironically, in a negative form: the festival committee had originally wanted to use the English edition by Arnold, but later decided in favor of the arrangement by Ignaz von Mosel that included additional wind parts. The committee also voted for the addition of several settings for solo voice from a collection of Handel psalm settings, because it felt that the oratorio lacked a sufficient number of arias. (The judgment about the arias departed decisively from the perspective that guided the elimination of arias from the *St. Matthew Passion* in the Berlin performance of 1829.) The measures concerning instrumentation were common at the time; indeed, in the late 1820s, Mendelssohn had prepared arrangements of the *Dettingen Te Deum* and *Acis und Galatea* for the Berlin Sing-Akademie that included additional wind parts; a year later the performance score of the *St. Matthew Passion* included minor changes to the instrumentation and the deletion of numerous numbers. But now Mendelssohn had changed his position. In a letter to his English friend William Horsley in January 1833, he expressed strong displeasure about Handel arrangements—with the exception of Mozart's, which were done with "the utmost delicacy and carefulness after much study." But for the most part, "Handel is improved by tedious imitations & sentimental dissonances, there are flute and clarionets [*sic*] which make me shudder."[3] Shortly thereafter Mendelssohn traveled to England, where he studied Handel manuscripts and discovered movements in the libretto and score of *Israel in Egypt* that had not been included in any printed edition. Mendelssohn informed the committee of his discoveries and his wish to perform them using a score based on original sources. After much negotiation, a compromise was reached: Mosel's score was retained, but Mendelssohn was permitted to incorporate in his performance some of the movements he discovered in England into the performance in Düsseldorf. This partial success was the first step toward his goal of performing Handel in a way that approached the composer's own practice, in modern musicological parlance, with all its problems, "authentically."

The next and decisive step followed in 1835, when he was engaged to conduct *Solomon* at the Lower Rhine Music Festival in Cologne. Now Mendelssohn informed the committee that he would perform the work with an organ part and no additional winds. He convinced the committee to purchase an organ for the venerable Gürzenich Hall, the performance venue, and wrote the organ part himself, based on his research.[4] He continued this practice in performances of *Israel in Egypt* and *Messiah* in Leipzig in 1836 and 1837 and *Joshua* in Cologne in 1838 and, whenever possible, he performed Handel in this way. But, as Wehner has shown, he was flexible enough to accept additional wind parts when there was no opportunity to perform with an organ, and in his performance of historical music, including that of J. S. Bach, he also constructed "continuo" parts for cellos and doubles basses and sometimes for the entire string ensemble.[5] Mendelssohn also was interested in the problems of the translation of the texts into German, the correct sequence of numbers, the inclusion of movements that had not been included in printed editions, and the placement of the choir and orchestra in the concert hall. It appears that Mendelssohn did not think about the size of the orchestra and the chorus, which, of course, for our modern historical performance practice is a fundamental concern. That this was not an issue for him is understandable for several historically legitimate reasons. The wish to bring together amateur singers and players en masse was a fundamental principle of the music-festival movement, especially in its early stages. This social character of the festival complemented the general preference for large ensembles that characterizes nineteenth-century performance practice of symphonic and choral music. Moreover, performing Handel with many singers and players possessed a degree of authenticity in the early nineteenth century. It represented a tradition of monumental Handel performances in England that were epitomized by the Handel "Commemoration" concerts in Westminster Abbey in 1784, about which Germans could read in Charles Burney's writings.[6] Mendelssohn's concern for authenticity (a term he never used) also surfaced in the full-score and piano-vocal editions of *Israel in Egypt* that he prepared for the British Handel Society (published in 1846), about which Wehner has written in detail. After some contentious wrangling, Mendelssohn prevailed in his determination to print a score with an organ part and no additional wind parts. Having agreed to provide nonautograph tempo and dynamic markings, he insisted that they be identified as such in a foreword to the edition.[7] (Mendelssohn's preface to the edition is presented in excerpts as appendix 10.1 at the end of the chapter.) In the end, the score edition (see ex. 10.1) included two organ parts, one labeled "Organo" that consisted of a bass line with some figures, one labeled "Organo (by the editor) Col Pedale" that was fully realized, as well as a "Pianoforte Adaptation" with dynamic indications and metronome markings ("Maelzel's Metronome"), which were placed between the organ realization and the piano arrangement.

The practice of enriching Handel's orchestration is typically associated with Mozart's arrangements for Gottfried van Swieten circa 1790, but its origins extend much further back into the eighteenth century: to 1766 in conjunction with a performance of Handel's *Alexander's Feast* (*Alexanderfest*) in Berlin that was conducted by Christian Gottfried Krause.[8] Another pre-Mozartian arrangement was prepared by Johann Adam Hiller in 1786 for performances of *Messiah* in Berlin and Leipzig. Nevertheless, Mozart's arrangements were the most prominent and influential, certainly because of his renown, and also because they were published and hence accessible to choral societies whose concerts often featured Handel oratorios. The increasing frequency of Handel performances and the success of Mozart's arrangements spurred composers like Mosel to make new arrangements in the 1820s and thereafter. Despite their popularity, these arrangements were subject to criticism and earlier ones had also faced opposition. In 1770 Christoph Daniel Ebelin found Krause's scoring of *Alexanderfest* to be "beautiful and modern, but not in Handel's style and therefore not appropriate."[9] In these remarks, Ebelin seems to have been more concerned about the stylistic unity of the piece than a sense of obligation to the composer. The work and its style, not the composer, is his focus. Later arguments for authentic performance and publication, especially in conjunction with the authentic-performance movement of the late twentieth century, often stressed the necessity to respect the compositional intentions of the genius composer. One perspective does not categorically exclude the other, and they coincide in their efforts on behalf of authenticity. In my view, the work orientation enjoys aesthetic priority, and the style orientation expresses true music-historical reflection, while the composer orientation is, strictly speaking, both ahistorical and nonmusical. Mendelssohn subscribed to both perspectives: he certainly thought in terms of masterworks by master composers, and he certainly was committed to the idea of presenting a historical work in its original style and form for its own sake.

Example 10.1. Handel, *Israel in Egypt*, first chorus, Mendelssohn's edition for the Handel Society, London

The announcement of the publication of Mozart's *Messiah* arrangement—it was most likely written by Gottfried van Swieten himself—reveals
that even Mozart's work required explanation and defense. It is legitimate
for aesthetic and practical reasons, argued the author: the "more liberal use
of wind instruments" enriches Handel with the "charms of newer music" and
the larger orchestra helps to realize the "colossal effects" that are only latent
in the score. The arias were reduced in length in order to alleviate their ste-
rility and monotony. (These are curious admissions in an announcement of
a publication. And the point about the arias anticipates the performance of
the *St. Matthew Passion* in Berlin.) Mozart's version also helps performers who
are not accustomed to such thinly orchestrated music. The announcement
appeared as an "Intelligenzblatt" (no. 14) in the Leipzig *Allgemeine musikalische Zeitung* [AMZ] of 1802, which was edited by Friedrich Rochlitz. Rochlitz
played an active role in the publication of the arrangement by Breitkopf und
Härtel (the publisher of the *Allgemeine musikalische Zeitung*). But Rochlitz
harbored (or soon came to harbor) reservations about the arrangement,
which he expressed in an essay that he published in a literary journal in 1804.
Rochlitz wrote primarily about the arias, viewing them in their relationship to
the choruses. As individual movements they profit from the additional wind
parts, but they have become, as a result of their enrichment, overly prominent and hence weaken the effect of the choruses, the only movements that
were richly orchestrated by Handel himself. In describing the arrangements,
Rochlitz drew on analogies to painting: the arias resemble the too "charming
secondary figures and illuminations at the perimeters of a painting and thus
divert attention from the choruses, "the primary group." And almost all the
arias, in and of themselves, "have lost something" through their reorchestra-
tion, in the same way that "an old gray knights' assembly hall [Rittersaal] suf-
fers from [even] the most charming repainting."[10]
 In Rochlitz's analogy between Handel's music and an old fortress, we
sense the spirit of Romantic cultural historicism. In his description of the
richly orchestrated choruses, we hear the words of the professional critic
and connoisseur of Baroque music, who reminds us of Ebelin in the latter's
critique of "vacillations between old and new," and who also calls for a new
edition, with a better translation into German, that is based on the most reliable English sources from Handel's own time. A work-and-style orientation
is evident, which also informs his essay on Handel that appeared in the first
volume of his collection of essays, *Für Freunde der Tonkunst*, of 1824. In this
later essay, a new thought is striking: Mozart's *Messiah* arrangement should be
made superfluous through performances with an organ! A year later Anton
Friedrich Justus Thibaut, in *Über Reinheit der Tonkunst*, a polemic against modern church music, rejected arrangements as "an immodest presumption that
one could forgive a Mozart, but no one else."[11] The remark embodies the
composer orientation in two ways: the charge of presumption is raised in the

shadow of the genius Handel; and only the genius Mozart is to be forgiven for this transgression. It is highly likely that Adolf Bernhard Marx knew of the essays by Rochlitz and Thibaut, or at least was aware of the discourse on arrangements. Marx, who at this time was, or wished to be, a mentor for Mendelssohn, argued in an essay of 1824 for Mozart's arrangement in part as a compensation for the absence of the organ in modern performance venues. Without one or the other of these, the work was "less" in its effect than in its conception (a typically idealistic point of view on Marx's part) and "less" than the modern public expects.[12]

Mendelssohn, the avid reader, most probably knew of these recent writings, as well as an anonymous defense of Mosel's arrangements that appeared in 1827 in the *Allgemeine musikalische Zeitung* (cols. 689–96). He met von Mosel, and also Franz Hauser, an important collector of Bach manuscripts, and Raphael Georg Kiesewetter in Vienna in 1830. We can well imagine discussions about performance practice with them, and with Marx, Rochlitz, and Zelter. Mendelssohn also knew leading figures in literature and in the visual arts interested in the question of older and foreign art and its place in contemporary culture. Schleiermacher was a member of the Berlin Sing-Akademie and a regular visitor to the Mendelssohn's home. Mendelssohn attended lectures by Hegel, who attended the revival of the *St. Matthew Passion* in Berlin, at the Berlin University. Hegel's lectures on aesthetics, which discuss art, literature, and music in the entire Western tradition, have been cited in literature on Mendelssohn's interest in historic music.[13] Yet Hegel says nothing about the problems of literary translation, musical arrangements, or restorations of art and architecture. Goethe, however, as we will see, took an active interest in the problems of restoring paintings and publishing old German stories. In Berlin Mendelssohn also knew Wilhelm von Schadow, a painter and one of the leading figures of the so-called German Nazarene School, whose members cultivated a Romantic-historicist style based on Italian and German Renaissance painting. It was Schadow, in the 1830s the director of the Academy of the Arts in Düsseldorf, who was primarily responsible for bringing Mendelssohn to Düsseldorf. It is highly likely that Mendelssohn, who painted and drew, translated Terence's comedy *Andria* into German, and had nearly universal intellectual interests, discussed these issues with his friends: the historian should acknowledge the likelihood and significance of irrecoverable conversation in the dissemination of information and the development of opinion.

Rochlitz did not pluck his metaphor of the "Rittersaal" from thin air. On the contrary, it suggests a consciousness of correspondences between the Handel arrangements he discussed and similar efforts and problems in the visual arts. The restoration of historical art and architecture developed quickly after the end of the Napoleonic period: in part as a by-product of burgeoning historicism and Romantic nostalgia for a so-called golden age before the Enlightenment epitomized by Novalis's essay "Die Christenheit oder Europa" of 1799; in part through the necessity of preserving and restoring historical art and architecture that had suffered often substantial damage during the French invasion and occupation of much of Germany. Of course, this necessity was only felt because the objects themselves were considered to possess value in the contemporary culture and society. German cultural historicism originated in the eighteenth century; "Von deutscher Baukunst," Goethe's nationalistic essay in praise of the Strasbourg Cathedral (1773) is considered to be a landmark in its early stages. Forty years later, the ravages left by the French occupiers and the shock of the German capitulation epitomized by the collapse of the Holy Roman Empire in 1806 promoted an increased sensitivity and concern for national culture and tradition.

℘

As one of the oldest regions of German culture, the Rhineland, notably the Mittelrhein with Cologne as its heart, was an important center of cultural historicism, whereby the Cologne Cathedral, still very unfinished in the early nineteenth century, claimed particular significance as an artistic, religious, and national cultural icon. The first attempts to promote interest in the cathedral and argue for its completion were made in the period of the French occupation of the city, which began in 1794 and continued until the defeat of France in 1813.[14] The Cologne native, Ferdinand Franz Wallraf (1748–1824), a professor of medicine, and a Catholic preacher and theologian, was one of the earlier proponents; his efforts on behalf of the visual arts were, however, more significant and will be discussed later. Friedrich Schlegel visited the city circa 1802 and wrote at length about the cathedral in his collection of travel letters from his two-year tour of Western Germany, Switzerland, and France.[15] After the withdrawal of French forces, decisive impulses came from the art collector and historian Sulpiz Boisserée (1783–1854, also a native of Cologne), the Hessian architect Georg Moller (1784–1852), and Karl Friedrich Schinkel (1781–1841), who designed many buildings for the Prussian monarchy and served in the Prussian administration as director of all public building (Oberbaudirektor). In 1814 Moller discovered one half of a large medieval blueprint containing plans for parts of the facade of the cathedral. He published a facsimile of it in 1816.[16] Boisserée, the leading figure in the early campaign for the cathedral, found the other half in Paris in 1816. Boisserée published extensive original plans and contemporary drawings of the cathedral in 1821 and a history of the cathedral (first published in 1823) that contained historical images, such as the drawing of the south facade from the early sixteenth century (fig. 10.1).[17] Their work became the most significant basis for the monumental tasks of restoring the finished part of the building and completing it. Also in 1816, Schinkel wrote a memorandum to Friedrich Wilhelm III, king of Prussia, in which he reported on the cathedral's grave state of disrepair and pleaded for

Figure 10.1. Cologne Cathedral at the beginning of the sixteenth century.
Sulpiz Boisserée, *Geschichte und Beschreibung des Doms von Köln*, 2nd ed. (Munich, Literarisch-artistische Anstalt, 1842), [123].

its preservation. He did this in his official capacity as a Prussian civil servant, because the Rhineland had been ceded to Prussia as a consequence of the negotiations at the Congress of Vienna in 1814.

Restoration work began in the 1820s under the supervision of Friedrich Ahlert (1787–1833) and his successor Ernst Friedrich Zwirner (1802–61). Both men were associates of Schinkel. For the completion, Zwirner drafted the basic plan in consultation with Schinkel, who advocated a very modest completion, in an effort to control costs for the Prussian government, which had a long history of frugality and restraint with respect to the construction of public buildings and monuments. The major tasks were the completion of the partially built towers on the west side of the building as well as the construction of the elevations of the nave and transept. The published medieval drawings contained detailed work on the western facade, including the great towers, but they completely lacked drafts for the transept and the entire southern facade. Zwirner finished the first set of plans in 1833, but the actual work of construction, which Zwirner supervised until his death, did not begin until much later. (A groundbreaking ceremony took place in October 1842.) The delay occurred in part, certainly, because of conflicts about the proposed nature of the completion. Zwirner based his design of the west face on the medieval plans, but it was "less gothic" because the emphasis on horizontal lines departed from the verticality of the original drawings.[18] For the nave and transept Schinkel had suggested further departures from Gothic styles. The nave was to be covered only by a flat roof, and neither an internal vaulted ceiling nor flying buttresses were foreseen. Other architectural details, especially on the facade, would have been cast in a neo-Gothic style that incorporated some classicistic features, the historical style that Schinkel preferred for his own buildings. (Schinkel did admire Gothic architecture and designed some buildings in a neo-Gothic style based on North German "brick gothic.") Zwirner, who wished to preserve as much as possible of the original plans, opposed the flat roof, and, with the help of the then Prussian crown prince (later Friedrich Willhelm IV, a religious-Romantic historicist with respect to the arts), determined that a peaked roof, interior vault, and buttresses would be constructed. In its support of Zwirner, the Prussian royal family was undoubtedly moved by political as well as aesthetic considerations. The predominantly Catholic population of the Rhineland had opposed the annexation of its territory and viewed the predominantly Protestant heartland of Prussia hundreds of miles to the east with suspicion and aversion. Throughout the nineteenth century, there was almost constant tension between the central Prussian administration and Rhenish political bodies and the powerful Catholic Church that peaked later in the century during the "Kulturkampf" led by Bismarck against the power of the Catholic Church in Germany and in Rome. In the 1830s and 1840s, the project to restore and complete the cathedral was drawn into the broader political-religious conflict.[19] Schinkel's ideas for the completion met with heated local resistance, and Zwirner's plans also faced opposition, because they were considered to contain too many departures from authentic Gothic style. A new figure now emerged and became both a leader of the Rhenish cathedral faction and a leading advocate for historic authenticity in architecture: August Reichensperger (1805–95), a native of Koblenz, who was a prominent attorney and judge, a member of the Prussian State Parliament and, after unification, a member of the German Imperial Parliament (Reichstag), representing the oppositional Catholic Center Party. Reichensperger, a passionate amateur architectural historian, published an essay on the cathedral in 1834 and a book on *The Christian-Germanic Architecture and Its Relationship to the Present* in 1845.[20] He criticized the restoration that had been supervised by Ahlert, notably the work on the choir and the facade, including the existing flying buttresses, objecting to the many departures from the original plans and the tendency to simplification, and he warned against the completed restorative work as a model for the future completion. On the other hand, he argued that the completed plans, which were not by a single master architect, included relatively little detail and also that the completed original structure, which took centuries to complete, contained many departures from the plans that had survived. Hence, neither the original plans nor the original existing structure (before the restoration had begun) could be regarded as reliable models for a building in authentic Gothic style. Reichensperger urged that Zwirner and his associates study German and foreign (French) Gothic churches that were completed in their own era; it cannot be determined whether this lead was followed. Reichensperger's passionate appeal for an authentic Gothic style was founded not only on his historicist aesthetics but also on his belief that only in this form could the cathedral fulfill its historic mission: to be a true expression and symbol of Rhenish-Catholic tradition and, secondarily, to embody the notion of an ideal Christian Germany that embraced and superseded specific denominations. Yet Reichensperger was a pragmatist. His objections were directed toward details, not the entire plan, and, in the 1840s, along with Boisserée, he defended Zwirner against attacks by fellow members of the Cathedral Building Society (Dombauverein), an organization founded in 1842 for the dual purpose of raising money for the construction and defending local interests against Prussian central authority.

After a grandiose ceremony in 1842 that was attended by the king of Prussia, the construction began with the nave and transept and the construction of a temporary wooden roof; work on the completion of the towers and west facade commenced only in 1863. A photographic image (fig. 10.2) taken from the east bank of the Rhine River shows the state of construction in 1856. The construction was concluded in 1880.[21] Modern construction techniques were used, notably the use of an iron framework for the permanent roof and the towers. With respect to decorative elements such as windows and sculptural work, one can clearly distinguish between work finished in the original phase of construction and the nineteenth-century completion, and not only because of the age of the materials. The Cologne Cathedral is an unmistakably neo-Gothic building, but despite Reichensperger's fears, it has fulfilled the symbolic and cultural functions that he envisioned for it.[22]

૭૦

An initiative simultaneous with and parallel to the cathedral project, albeit on a much smaller scale, focused on a valuable collection of paintings left to the city of Cologne in the estate of Ferdinand Franz Wallraf. Wallraf began to acquire art in the 1780s and intensified his collecting during the French occupation of the Rhineland in order to protect art from destruction or confiscation by French troops. By 1816, Wallraf had accumulated 1600 paintings from different time periods and national schools; many of them were in very bad condition. Schinkel inspected the collection in 1816 and sent a memorandum to Berlin in which he recommended that the paintings be restored and exhibited. No action was taken for ten years; only in 1826 did M. J. de Noël, a member of the Cologne municipal administration and the director of the municipal museum bearing Wallraf's name (Städtisches Wallrafsches Museum) receive a commission from the museum board to supervise the restoration of

Figure 10.2. Panorama along the Rhine c. 1856. Wikimedia Commons.

334 of the paintings. In 1828, Noël hired the art conservator Anton Lorent of Ghent, with the charge, "to restore the original condition" of the paintings.[23] Lorent and his successors worked on the project for thirty-three years; paintings were cleaned, restored, and completed. Many of the works were "panel paintings" on wood, a common genre before the sixteenth century; their paint was transferred to canvas, a standard technique of preservation in the nineteenth century. The completion and transfer of paintings certainly departed from the specification of "original condition"; they are analogous to musical arrangements.

Similar projects were being undertaken in museums all over Europe. Not surprisingly, they were accompanied by lively debates about the goals and techniques of restoration. In 1820, for example, the Dutch painter Stanislaus Pereira was harshly criticized in the *Kölnische Zeitung* for his use of smoke to clean paintings in Wallraf's collection. He was said to have caused great damage to the paintings, but he continued to receive commissions in other parts of Germany in the 1820s and 1830s.[24] In Dresden, circa 1815, Ferdinand August Hartmann, a professor at the Saxon Academy of the Arts, wrote an essay on "The cleaning and restoration of damaged paintings." The essay was never published and I was unable to obtain access to it,[25] but Hartmann's ideas have been transmitted indirectly: through a report submitted by Goethe to the director of the art collections in Dresden, Georg Friedrich von Friesen. The cosigner and probable actual author was Johann Heinrich Meyer, a prominent art historian, member of the ducal administration in Weimar, and a friend and artistic adviser to Goethe. Hartmann proposed a very nonaggressive (*sanft*) restoration technique that allowed some dirt to remain on the paintings so that harsh cleaning agents would not be necessary. Hartmann's position on the question of whether to strive for a restoration of the original condition or to permit the effects of the aging process was praised in the memo. Hartmann opposed the principle that "good, old paintings appear as if they were new, because the so-called patina is lost through aggressive washing and supposed cleaning of light parts [of the painting] and with this [loss] also the delicate, light glaze over the entire painting, with which the master finishes the work and brings all of its parts into harmony."[26]

Hartmann's recommendations about restoration are diametrically opposed to the viewpoints and practices that obtained in Cologne. His argument that the painting "should not appear as if it were new" is motivated by the same historical perspective that underlies Rochlitz's reservations about arrangements of Handel oratorios and Mendelssohn's reforms. But when considering the analogies between them, we must recognize their limitations, problems, and paradoxes. If the patina of a painting or cracks in a cathedral wall are "left in peace" (Schleiermacher), their admirer is not moved toward their creator, who created works that were fresh and new, without any accretions of time. The artist is left in peace only when his art, in its present (in our case nineteenth-century) form is disturbed; that is when a restoration (more or less) successfully restores the original form of the work, eliminating the manifestations of its aging process. The paradox is that only by making a painting "new," can it be made "aged" in the sense of its original condition. However, the agedness of a painting or a building reveals itself not only through differences in materials, style, and form, but rather also through all the changes (ivy growing up a wall) that the work has experienced during the centuries of its "life" and that are often attractive to the modern eye. For this reason, nostalgic Romantics built artificial ruins, in addition to imitating old architectural styles for new buildings. And for this reason, prominent restorations such as the Sistine Chapel and Leonardo's *The Last Supper* in Milan have been attacked with great vehemence and passion. In the case of music, the chronologically "new," in our case the nineteenth-century performance practice based on arrangements, must be relinquished, in order to attain (theoretically, at least) the historic "old." One other difference between the media is significant: historic music (and literature) is less "permanent" than the historic visual arts because they are subject to ever new editions and new performances. Once a restoration (of whichever kind) of a painting, sculpture, or building has been completed, the work remains in its new state for a considerable length of time.

ဢ

The translator of foreign-language literary texts and the collector/publisher of older texts in the native language faced problems similar to those of the restorer of paintings and other forms of visual art. Like Schleiermacher, many prominent German literary figures and intellectuals undertook translations and also wrote on the problems of translation. This development contributed to the increasing cultural significance of translation; "Weltliteratur" (world literature) as propagated by Goethe and Herder could make a vital contribution to cultural education ("Bildung").[27] Schleiermacher's essay on translation was, nevertheless, the only systematic attempt in its time to present a theory of translation. Its conceptual basis is, naturally enough, in large measure based on his hermeneutics: no one is more directly confronted with the problem of "Verstehen" (understanding) than the translator of a text. Because of these difficulties, two contrasting approaches to translation have developed, according to Schleiermacher: the "paraphrase," which contains explanatory commentary embedded in the text; and the "Nachbildung," whose conventional translations (imitation, facsimile, reproduction) actually imply the opposite of what Schleiermacher intended: a free translation that does not seek to retain the original Gestalt of the text. But, in Schleiermacher's view, neither of these is the "actual" translation, which is achieved only when the translation makes clear to the reader that the original text is, indeed, foreign and remote, linguistically and culturally.[28] Hence a translation must be "estranged" (*verfremdet*); it must not be in colloquial modern German; it must not move the author to the reader; the reader must try to approach the author. The "Germanization" (*Eindeutschung*) of a text makes it "null and void" (*nichtig und leer*). August Wilhelm Schlegel and Novalis shared this view; they characterized modernizing translations in colloquial German as a "travesty."[29] From our perspective, with our contemporary ideas about authenticity (which include an awareness of the problematic nature of the concept and its limitations), their position seems legitimate. But, as Andreas Huyssen has shown, this stance can produce translations that are difficult to understand and lack literary elegance. Huyssen gives a drastic example, a passage from Plato's discussion of love in the *Symposium* (Gastmahl) as translated by Schleiermacher. With its prolix sentence structure, (over)use of gerunds and indirect discourse, the German, appropriately enough, simply cannot be rendered faithfully in English translation, so it is given in the "original" German translation from the Greek:

> Sage mir nur soviel, ob die Liebe das, dessen Liebe sie ist, begehrt oder nicht?—Allerdings, habe er gesagt.—Und ob sie wohl schon habend, was sie begehrt und liebt, es begehrt und liebt, oder es nicht habend?—Nicht habend, wie es ja scheint, habe er gesagt.[30]

> [Just tell me this, if love desires that, whose love it is, or not? Certainly, he said. And if it already having, that which it desires and loves, it desires and loves, or not having. Not having, as it appears, he said.]

Huyssen rejects the translation as "un-German" and inimical to good language and notes that Schleiermacher was often criticized for his "translator's German"

("Übersetzerdeutsch" is his invective). Nevertheless, Huyssen sympathizes with Schleiermacher, who himself was aware of the dangers in attempting this kind of translation, and argues that the validity of Schleiermacher's theoretical positions should not be measured only with the yardstick of his translations.

Schleiermacher's theory and practice broke decisively with the methodologies of the eighteenth century, when it was common practice for a translator to make changes and additions to a text, and to write commentaries on the original and the revisions in the translation, each of these according to the translator's own sensibilities and his estimation of public expectations. Lessing, for example, defined part of his task as translator to be the correction of deficiencies that he discovered in texts. On the other hand, according to Mark Zybura, the Romantic translator, such as Ludwig Tieck, saw himself in the service of the original author; he placed the author and his work in the foreground; and refrained from the kinds of interventions frequent in "enlightened" translations of the previous generation.[31]

To the extent that a translation of a verbal text represents an adaptation or arrangement of an original text, it is legitimate to view it as analogous to an arrangement of a musical text. But one must consider several caveats: (1) the differences in materials and form in these media; (2) the difficulties of establishing legitimate and rigorously conceived analogies between them; and (3) the varying degrees of difficulty that the translated text and the arranged music present to their translators and arrangers (and their readers and listeners). In music the difficulty approaches that of a foreign-language text only when the musical text (the score) cannot be read without transcription—pre-sixteenth-century European music and music that is not based on European pitch and notation systems. In both these cases, the first task is to prepare a legible, comprehensible text. Schleiermacher's advocacy of "estrangement" in translation could have provided a potent theoretical argument against the principles underlying arrangements of early music, but there is no evidence that Mendelssohn was in any way influenced by Schleiermacher's perspective. An undocumented conversation at the Mendelssohn home in Berlin?

A closer literary analogy with musical arrangements and efforts for authenticity may be found in the work of the two great early nineteenth-century projects of collecting and publishing historical German texts: *Des Knaben Wunderhorn* by Achim von Arnim and Clemens Brentano, and the *Kinder- und Hausmärchen* by the Grimm brothers. (The fact that both collections were devoted to "folk" art does not undermine the analogy to Handel's "art" music.) With the exception of the relatively few translations of French texts and inclusion of texts in German regional dialects, both collections focused on already comprehensible German-language texts. These collections had a very powerful influence (not least in music) and have been celebrated since their appearance, but in the past several decades literary philologists have provided a more refined, differentiated view of their goals and their results, which often contradict the long prevailing view of "authentic" transmissions of "authentic" folk literature. When von Arnim and Brentano began their project in 1805, they agreed that they would limit their collecting to medieval song texts. These would be published in a "modernized form,"[32] that is, in an adaptation of the original. They soon expanded their field to include more recent and even contemporary texts, which they found in manuscript codices, and books, journals, and single-sheet publications (or "fliegende Blätter"). They received texts from individuals who knew about their work and also transcribed the words of songs that were recited or sung to them. In choosing their texts, they were less concerned about the authenticity of source and transmission than their own aesthetic criteria: personal artistic preferences outweighed philology. And they were sometimes less than honest in identifying their sources; several song texts were given as orally transmitted, in order to conceal revisions in texts that they had found in published sources.[33] Plans to publish their own texts and to include settings by Friedrich Reichardt were dropped. But von Armin and Brentano were as much poets as they were collector-publishers: every one of the 723 texts that were published in the original edition (1802–5) was revised.

The decision to revise the texts led to differences of opinion about method, and these differences produced tension and even bitterness between the two men. One essential question that they faced is closely related to the issues concerning historical music and to artistic and architectural preservation and restoration: if and how the age of a text should be transmitted in the revised text. Arnim criticized Brentano for "artificially creating old age, through which the songs assumed a false patina and a unified style that had never existed." Brentano, in turn, found fault with the "undisciplined mixing of old and new" in the texts that von Arnim prepared.[34] This reminds us of Ebelin's critique of Krause's arrangement of *Das Alexanderfest*. Another controversial point concerned the contents of the songs and their literary style. In one extreme case, Armin refined the style of a rather coarse text and wrote a new final strophe without consulting Brentano, who had sent him a fair copy of the original. Brentano learned of this intervention only when reading the published edition. According to Heinz Rölleke, Brentano was, in general, more concerned about the preservation of the original quality of the texts. But Rölleke, who is the leading expert on the collection and its origins, concludes that the "folk song" was transformed into "elevated poetry," as the collector-arrangers (he calls them "Bearbeiter") indulged their own poetic fantasy.[35] Hence, authenticity was never a primary goal of the project. This hardly mattered in the early reception of the collection: no less an authority than Goethe heartily praised the adaptation, including the presence of newly written material, in a discussion of the first volume (*Jenaische Allgemeine Literatur-Zeitung*, 1806).

Following the appearance of the last volume of *Des Knaben Wunderhorn* in 1805, Arnim and Brentano considered a similar project devoted to fairy tales, in part because their public call for such a publication had fallen on deaf ears.

Soon thereafter, the Grimm brothers, Jacob and Wilhelm, whom Brentano had known since 1802, began to collect fairy tales; the first phase of their work took place in the years 1807–10. Although Brentano's encouragement had been instrumental for them, they had reservations about his and Arnim's methods.[36] But the Grimms were prepared to work with them, and even to make available the texts they had found. However, after their friendship to Brentano cooled in 1811, Arnim helped convince them that they should prepare their own edition. The most intensive phase of collecting occurred in the years 1810 through 1814 and the volumes appeared in the years 1812 through 1815. The Grimms included tales based on printed sources, but they made more extensive use of texts in manuscript sources (including tales submitted in letters) and transcribed many more orally transmitted texts than Brentano and von Armin had done for the *Wunderhorn*.[37] With the exception of the twenty tales in dialect ("Dialektmärchen," as they were identified in the collection), all the stories appeared in High German. Recent research has established that almost all of the tales for which manuscript or printed sources could be determined were heavily revised. Only the dialect tales escaped heavy revision and, tellingly, it was these relatively authentic texts that were not well received by some critics. The revisions took several forms: conflation of several sources, significant changes in language, including more precise formulations and a higher literary style, the translation of foreign-language words into German (many of the fairy tales were based on originally French texts), and the substitution of the imperfect tense for the present tenses (presumably to create a linguistic patina).[38] In later editions, Wilhelm Grimm purged numerous texts of social-critical themes and eliminated obscenities and sexual language, in part as a reaction to Arnim's criticism that these stories were not suitable for children. The status of the orally transmitted tales is more difficult to trace. Rölleke, also an authority on the fairy tales, argues that the versions that were recited or sent to the Grimms themselves constitute a refinement of the originals, because their source was a secondary one: bourgeois women with good educations, who spoke or wrote in a "middle" style that was higher than the language they heard from the primary source, their own domestic servants.[39] And the brothers might well have gone further in revising these tales, because the collection on the whole established a "new literary genre, the Grimmian book fairy tale [Grimmsche Buchmärchen]." Although the brothers might have believed that they were discovering and disseminating the "real, old fairy tale in the folk style," they actually created texts in a style that is as far removed from the original folk tale as the "Wunderhorn" songs are from the true folk song.[40]

ଓ

The Grimms' fairytales—in their refined *Hochdeutsch*—were favored over several contemporary collections of fairy tales in their original dialect and character. The success of both collections in this discussion reveals the German Bildungsbürgertum's aesthetic preferences as well as their indifference to or ignorance of questions of authenticity. The editors did not leave their "authors" in peace as much as possible; they moved their authors to their readers. Mendelssohn, of course, attempted to do exactly the opposite, but his lead was not followed by his contemporaries, despite the fact that his Handel performances were popular successes. It is impossible to say whether the success of the Handel revival on the whole depended on the performance of arrangements that brought the music closer to and more familiar to its public audience. This was certainly an argument made by supporters of arrangements, in addition to justifiable pragmatic considerations, such as the lack of scores and instruments. Mendelssohn himself denied the necessity of arrangements for the modern listener; he wrote, just after the critique of arrangements, in his letter to Horsley: "And yet the public cannot be alleged as the reason for it, for they like truly, what they call old music and the room is always crowded when there is something of Handels [sic] to be heard."[41] However, Gottfried Wilhelm Fink's carefully worded apologia for Mendelssohn's performance of Israel in Egypt in Leipzig in 1836,[42] and Heinrich Dorn's strongly polemical attack on arrangements of historical works[43] only confirm the strength of the prevailing practice, which continued well into the twentieth century.

Authenticity was a matter of greater significance in architecture, the visual arts, and literature than in music in Mendelssohn's lifetime, but in these areas as well, the attitude that the great works of the past required not only preservation (which includes the publication of texts in modern editions) and restoration but also improvement was widespread. This point of view is understandable; historicism was in its early stages and Enlightenment and post-Enlightenment (Hegelian) theories of progress, although challenged by historicism, were still strong. It is striking that Mendelsohn evoked the notion of progress, but dialectically, in a way that was opposed to Hegelian theory, in reference to his performance-practice reforms. He wrote, in January 1838, to the conductor Ernst Heinrich Wilhelm Verkenius in Cologne about his plans for the Lower Rhine Festival of that year: "This kind of progress is very important to me, even though it hardly seems to be recognized. At any rate, it is my primary interest [in performing historic music]."[44] Mendelssohn, a genius, was simply ahead of his time. His achievements emerge with particular clarity when they are considered in their cultural context, the discussion of which reveals both the potential for an increased understanding of intracultural dynamics and the complexity of considering broad and complex aesthetic issues from a holistic perspective embracing different forms of art.

Appendix 10.1

Excerpts of Mendelssohn's Preface to His Edition of Handel's *Israel in Egypt*

Preface by the Editor
(Excerpts)

The Council of the Handel Society having done me the honour to request me to edit "Israel in Egypt," an Oratorio which I have always viewed as one of the greatest and most lasting musical works, I think it my first duty, to lay before the Society the Score as Handel wrote it, without introducing the least alteration, and without mixing up any notes or remarks of my own with those of Handel. In the next place, as there is no doubt that he introduced many things at the performance of his works that were not written down, and which even now, when his music is performed, are supplied by a sort of tradition, according to the fancy of the Conductor and the Organist, it becomes my second duty to offer an opinion in all such cases; but I think it of paramount importance that all my remarks should be kept strictly separate from the Original Score, and that the latter should be given in its entire purity, in order to afford to every one an opportunity of resorting to Handel himself, and not to obtrude any suggestions of mine upon those who may differ from me in opinion.

The whole of the Score (excepting my Organ Part and Pianoforte Arrangement, which are distinguished by being printed in small notes) is therefore printed according to Handel's manuscript in the Queen's Library. I have neither allowed myself to deviate from his authority in describing the movements in the Score, nor in the figuring of the Bass, because he has done so frequently himself in his manuscripts (for instance, the Chorus "The people shall hear" affords a striking instance of the accuracy with which he occasionally did it). These remarks of mine which I had to offer are therefore only to be found in the Pianoforte Arrangement, and those which are contained in the Score are written by Handel himself.

There are a few instances in this manuscript where Handel evidently omitted an accidental, or wrote a different note in one part from that which he gave to the other. The Council decided that I should alter such notes, and the places where this has been done are the following:

[There follows a *Revisionsbericht* with a list (including page and measure numbers) detailing the alterations as well as a description of other notable features in Handel's manuscript.]

I have now only to add a few remarks concerning the Organ Part and Pianoforte Arrangement; for both of which I am responsible. As for the Organ

Part, I have written it down in the manner in which I would play it, were I called upon to do so at a performance of the Oratorio. These works ought of course never to be performed without an Organ, as they are done in Germany, where additional wind instruments are introduced to make up for the defect. In England the Organist plays usually ad libitum from the Score, as it seems to have been the custom in Handel's time, whether he played himself, or merely conducted and had an Organist under his control. Now as the task of placing the chords in the fittest manner to bring out all the points to the greatest advantage, in fact of introducing, as it were, a new part to Compositions like Handel's, is of extreme difficulty, I have thought it useful to write down an Organ Part expressly for those who might not prefer to play one of their own. I must leave it to the Organist to choose the stops according to the strength and number of the Chorus singers, to the nature of his instrument, etc., but I have indicated six gradations of strength: PP, P, MF, F, FF, FFF; meaning by the last the whole power of the full Organ, and by the first one soft stop of eight feet alone. Whenever the word *Bassi* appears in the Organ part, I want the Organ *not to play at all*, (the notes being written merely to enable the Organist to follow the performance); and where the word *Organo* comes after it, the Organist is to resume playing. There are also two Violoncello parts for the accompaniment of the Recitatives to be found in the Organ Part; I have written them likewise, in order to indicate to the performers (should they not choose to follow their own fancy) the manner in which I would place the chords. The description of movements, metronomes, pianos and fortes, etc., which I would introduce had I to conduct the Oratorio, are to be found in the *Pianoforte Arrangement*. Whoever wishes to adopt them, can easily insert them in the Original Score, and he who prefers any other is not misled so as to take my directions for those which Handel wrote himself.

Felix Mendelssohn-Bartholdy
London, July 4, 1844

Source: George Frederic Handel, *Israel in Egypt: An Oratorio Composed in the Year 1738,* ed. Felix Mendelssohn-Bartholdy, vol. 5 of *The Works of Handel, Printed for the Members of the Handel Society* (London: Cramer, Beale and Co., 1845), ii–v.

Notes

This essay is based on the paper "Mendelssohns 'authentischer' Händel im Kontext: Zum Umgang mit alter Musik, Kunst und Literatur in der ersten Hälfte des 19. Jahrhunderts," which I presented at the conference, "Mendelssohn und das Rheinland" at the University of Koblenz, October 29–31, 2009. The paper was published in the report on the conference, *Mendelssohn und das Rheinland: Bericht über das Internationale Symposium Koblenz 29.-31.10.2009,* ed. Petra Weber-Bockholdt (Munich: Wilhelm Fink Verlag, 2011), 79–96. I am grateful to Petra

Weber-Bockholdt for her permission to publish the text in its present form. The original spoken character of the talk has been, as in the published German version, for the most part retained.

1   *Epigraph.* The German original reads: "Entweder der Übersetzer läßt den Schriftsteller möglichst in Ruhe, und bewegt den Leser ihm entgegen. Oder er läßt den Leser möglichst in Ruhe, und bewegt den Schriftsteller ihm entgegen." The translations are by the author unless otherwise indicated. Schleiermacher first read the text as a lecture at the Royal Academy of Sciences in Berlin on June 24, 1813; he was working on a translation of Plato at this time. It was first published in *Sämtliche Werke, Dritte Abteilung: Zur Philosphie*, vol. 2 (Berlin, 1838), 207–45. It is considered to be the most important theoretical discussion of translation in the nineteenth century. See Jekatherina Lebedewa, "Die vollkommene Übersetzung bleibt Utopie," *Ruperto Carola*, March 2007, http://www.uni-heidelberg.de/presse/ruca/ruca07-3/wort.html.

      Susanna Grossman-Vendrey, *Felix Mendelssohn und die Musik der Vergangenheit* (Regensburg: Bosse, 1969); Glenn Stanley, "Mozarts *Messias* und Mendelssohns *Israel in Ägytpen*. Zur Frühgeschichte der Aufführungspraxis historischer Musik," in *Bericht des Internationalen Gewandhaus Symposiums Leipzig Oktober 1992* (Leipzig, 1993), 112–21; Ralf Wehner, "Mendelssohn and the Performance of Handel's Vocal Works," in *Mendelssohn in Performance*, ed. Sieghart Reichwald (Bloomington: Indiana University Press, 2008), 147–70.

2   Carl Dahlhaus, *Nineteenth-Century Music*, trans. J. Bradford Robinson (Berkeley: University of California Press, 1989), 182.

3   See Letter 654 in *Felix Mendelssohn Bartholdy: Sämtliche Briefe*, vol. 3: *August 1832 bis Juli 1834*, ed. Uta Wald (Kassel: Bärenreiter, 2010), 104. English is the original language of the letter.

4   See Alain Gehring, "Händels 'Solmon' in der Bearbeitung von Felix Mendelssohn Bartholdy (1835)," *Die Musikforschung* 65 (2012): 313–37.

5   See Anselm Hartinger, "Between Tradition and Innovation: Mendelssohn as Music Director and His Performances of Bach in Leipzig," in *Mendelssohn Perspectives*, ed. Nicole Grimes and Angela R. Mace (Farnham: Ashgate, 2012), 145–62, esp. 151–57.

6   The Westminster concerts were, however, not representative of English practice in general (personal communication from Reinhard Strohm), but they were the most prominent Handel performances in England after the composer's death. English music critics criticized the German-Austrian practice of arranging Handel with a larger wind ensemble, although Charles Burney had reported on similar practices in eighteenth-century England, and, by the 1830s, English opinion began to shift in favor of arrangements. See Howard Smither, "Messiah and Progress in Victorian England," in *Early Music* 13 (1985): 339–49.

7   See Clive Brown, A *Portrait of Mendelssohn* (New Haven, CT: Yale University Press, 2003), 41–43.

8   The German text was prepared by Karl Wilhelm Ramler. See Annette Monheim, "Händel auf dem Weg nach Wien. Die Rezeption Händels in Florenz, Berlin und Wien zwischen 1759 und 1800," in *Beethoven und die Rezeption der Alten Musik. Die hohe Schule der Überlieferung. Kongreßbericht Internationales Beethoven Symposium, Bonn 12–13 Oktober 2000*, ed. Hans-Werner Küthe (Bonn: Beethoven-Haus, 2002), 147–87.

9   "Versuch einer auserlesenen Bibliothek," in *Unterhaltungen* 10 (1770): 303–22, 504–34. Cited in Monheim, "Händel auf dem Weg nach Wien."

10   *Jenaische Allgemeine Literaturzeitung* 2 (1804), cols. 01–06 and 609–14. The original German reads: "Sieht man auf das Ganze, so haben nur wenige nicht verloren und

zwar, theils, wie ein alter Grauer Rittersaal auch durch den angenehmsten Tünch verliert, theils, weil sie nun mehr herausgehoben und an sich interessanter, die beabsichtigte größtmögliche Wirkung der von Händel allein reich ausgeführten Chöre schwächen, wie anziehende Nebenparthien und Seitenlichter den Effect der Hauptgruppe eines Gemäldes."

11 Cited from Anton Friedrich Justus Thibaut, Über Reinheit der Tonkunst, 2nd ed. (Heidelberg: Mohr, 1851), 166.

12 *Berliner Allgemeine musikalische Zeitung* 1 (1824), cols. 427–29 and 435–39.

13 See, for example, James Garrat, "Mendelssohn's Babel: Romanticism and the Poetics of Translation," *Music and Letters* 80 (1999): 23–49. Garrat focuses on Mendelssohn's own compositions.

14 See Gertrud Klevinghaus, "Die Vollendung des Kölner Doms im Spiegel deutscher Publikationen der Zeit von 1800 bis 1842" (PhD diss., University of Saarland, 1971).

15 "Briefe auf einer Reise durch die Rheinlande, Rheingegend, die Schweiz und einem Teil von Frankreich (1802–1804)," in *Poetisches Tagebuch für das Jahr 1806*, ed. Friedrich Schlegel (Berlin: Johann Friedrich Unger, 1806).

16 Georg Moller, *Facsimile der Original-Zeichnung des Doms zu Cöln* (Darmstadt, 1818). In 1818 Moller persuaded the Grand Duke of Hessen-Darmstadt to decree the first German law concerning the protection and preservation of historical monuments (Denkmalschutz).

17 Sulpiz Boisserée, *Ansichten, Risse und einzelne Teile des Domes von Köln* (Stuttgart: Boisserée and Cotta, 1821–31; *Geschichte und Beschreibung des Doms von Köln* (Stuttgart: Cotta, 1823). See also Boisserée, *Der Briefwechsel mit Moller, Schinkel und Zwirner* (Cologne: Greven, 2008).

18 See Angelika Leyendecker, "Der Kölner Dom und die Sakralarchitektur," in *Der Kölner Dom im Jahrhundert seiner Vollendung*, vol. 2, *Essays*, ed. Hugo Borger (Cologne: Historische Museen Köln, 1980), 227.

19 See Michael J. Lewis, *The Politics of the German Gothic Revival: August Reichensperger* (Cambridge, MA: MIT Press, 1993), 1–87.

20 August Reichensperger, *Einige Worte über den Dombau zu Cöln* (Koblenz: J. Hölscher, 1834), and *Die christlich-germanische Baukunst und ihr Verhältnis zur Gegenwart* (Trier: Verlag der Fr. Lintz'schen Buchhandlung, 1845).

21 The celebrations included a grand procession through the city, but many residents of Cologne avoided the ceremony at the site of the cathedral to protest the presence of Kaiser Wilhelm I, who had recently banished the Archbishop of Cologne in the struggle over Papal and German Catholic influence in the civil life of Germany.

22 Hugo Borger, "Aus dem Lebenslauf des Kölner Domes," in Borger, *Der Kölner Dom im Jahrhundert einer Vollendung*, 2:15. Borger uses the formulation "die neue Gotik" positively; new construction techniques made possible a more delicate style that has "its own artistic value."

23 Cited in Petra Mandt, "Gemälderestaurierungen am Wallraf-Richartz Museum in den Jahren 1824–1890. Ein Beitrag zur Restaurierungsgeschichte im 19. Jahrhundert," in *Wallraf-Richartz-Jahrbuch* 48–49 (1987): 318.

24 See Andreas Priever, "Carl Becker, das 'Verzeichnis einer Anzahl schätzbarer Kunstwerke' und die Anfänge der Gemäldeinventarisation in der preußischen Provinz Westfalen," in *Westfälische Zeitschrift* 155 (2005): 312–13.

25 The manuscript is in the Goethe- und Schillerarchiv Weimar, Schriften zur Kunst 1816–32, Zweite Abteilung (Bildende Kunst VI). Several requests to the archive for information or a copy of the manuscript were not answered.

26   Johann Wolfgang von Goethe, *Kunsttheoretische Schriften und Übersetzungen. Schriften zur bildenden Kunst ii, Aufsätze zur bildenden Kunst (1812–1832)*, ed. Siegfried Seidel (Berlin: Aufbau-Verlag, 1974), 55–58.

27   Andreas Huyssen, *Die Frühromantische Konzeption von Übersetzung und Aneignung. Studien zur Frühromantischen Utopie einer deutschen Weltliteratur* (Zurich: Atlantis, 1969), 50–60.

28   Ibid., 58. For the full text of the essay in German, see H. J. Störig, ed., *Das Problem des Übersetzens* (Darmstadt: Wissenschaftliche Buchgesellschaft, 1963), 38–70. For a translation into English by Susan Bernofsky, see "On the Different Methods of Translating," *The Translation Studies Reader*, ed. Lawrence Venuti, 2nd ed. (New York: Routledge, 2004), 43–63.

29   Huyssen, *Konzeption*, 59.

30   Ibid., 61.

31   See Mark Zybura, *Ludwig Tieck als Übersetzer und Herausgeber. Zur frühromantischen Idee einer "Weltliteratur"* (Heidelberg: Winter, 1994), 39–40. Tieck, however, never attempted to "leave the author in peace as much as possible." His famous translations of Shakespeare are in modern, colloquial German, and Tieck has been criticized by Huyssen and other literary scholars for the lack of rigor in his philological approach to sources and the freedoms he took with the actual translations.

32   See Heinz Rölleke, ed., *Des Knaben Wunderhorn. Alte Deutsche Lieder Gesammelt von Achin von Arnim und Clemens Brentano* (Frankfurt/Main: Insel, 2000), 1200.

33   Rölleke, "Das Wunderhorn und die Heidelberger Romantik," in *Das "Wunderhorn" und die Heidelberger Romantik. Mündlichkeit, Schriftlichkeit, Performanz: Heidelberger Kolloquium der Internationalen Arnim-Gesellschaft*, ed. Walter Pape (Tübingen: Niemeyer, 2005), 7–13. Song no. 277 in volume 2, "Der Star und das Badwännelein," was identified as "having been transcribed in the weaving room of a Hessian village." It was actually a new text by Brentano on the basis of a model in a modern edition.

34   Rölleke, "Das Wunderhorn," 13.

35   Rölleke, *Des Knaben Wunderhorn*, 1206.

36   See Hans-Jörg Uther, *Handbuch zu den "Kinder-und Hausmärchen" der Brüder Grimm: Entstehung, Wirkung, Interpretation* (Berlin: de Gruyter, 2008), 486.

37   On the origins of the fairy-tale collections, see Heinz Rölleke, ed. *Kinder- und Hausmärchen, gesammelt durch die Brüder Grimm. Vollständige Ausgabe auf der Grundlage der dritten Auflage (1837)* (Frankfurt/Main: Deutscher Klassiker Verlag, 1985), 1151–68.

38   See Uther, *Handbuch*, 504–7.

39   Rölleke, *Kinder- und Hausmärchen*, 1156.

40   Ibid., 1157.

41   See Letter 654 in *Felix Mendelssohn Bartholdy: Sämtliche Briefe*, vol. 3: *August 1832 bis Juli 1834*, ed. Uta Wald (Kassel: Bärenreiter, 2010), 104.

42   *Allgemeine musikalische Zeitung* 38 (1836), cols. 1765–70.

43   "Original oder Bearbeitung," in *Allgemeine musikalische Zeitung* 46 (1844), cols. 561–66.

44   Letter no. 1863 in *Felix Mendelssohn Bartholdy: Sämtliche Briefe*, vol. 5: *Juli 1836 bis Januar 1838*, ed. Uta Wald (Kassel: Bärenreiter, 2012), 468. The original reads: "An einen solchen Fortschritt, wenn er auch im Augenblick kaum beachtet werden mag, scheint mir viel zu liegen, wenigstens hängt mein Hauptinteresse daran."

Chapter Eleven

Beyond the Ethical and Aesthetic

Reconciling Religious Art with Secular Art-Religion in Mendelssohn's "Lobgesang"

Benedict Taylor

> The ethical absolute does not rob life of its beauty; rather, it alone makes life beautiful. It gives life security and peace, for it is always calling to us: "what you are seeking is here." It protects us from all weakening sentimentality; it gives the soul health and strength.
>
> —Judge Vilhelm, *Either/Or*

> The ethical is just as boring in life as it is in learning. What a difference! Beneath the sky of the aesthetic everything is light, pleasant and fleeting; when ethics comes along everything becomes hard, angular, and unending ennui.
>
> —Johannes the Seducer, *Either/Or*

It has long been customary to use binary divisions to describe Mendelssohn or divide his oeuvre into two—more often than not with wildly contrasting evaluations attached to each part. Greg Vitercik, for instance, calling upon the imprimatur of George Bernard Shaw and Donald Tovey, speaks of "two Mendelssohns"—the "immensely talented, vigorously original" Mendelssohn of the Octet (MWV R20, op. 20), *Hebrides*, and *Midsummer Night's Dream* overtures (MWV P7 and P3, opp. 26 and 21); and a "pseudo-Mendelssohn" of the "Lobgesang" (MWV A18, op. 52), *St. Paul* (MWV A14, op. 36), and *Elijah* (MWV A25, op. 70), those "platitudinous monuments to early Victorian seriousness."[1] From a rather less judgmental perspective, John Toews has similarly characterized a dualism in Mendelssohn's work between his "secular, instrumental, 'humanist' music in which he presented himself as the heir of Haydn, Mozart, and Beethoven" and the "German Protestant tradition of sacred liturgical music."[2] In fact, for all the familiar orchestral and chamber masterpieces and the more selectively known piano works and songs, there exists beyond the two oratorios and the wings of countless doves an enormous body of liturgical and religious music few ever hear (or hear about).

What Vitercik's comment clearly delineates is the often ideological nature of this division and its rootedness in a conflict—or rather apathy—between proponents valorizing predominantly secular "aesthetic" qualities, with their affiliated emphasis on artistic progressivism and individual subjectivity, and the religious or broadly speaking "ethical" elements of Mendelssohn's music, with their corresponding appeal to intersubjective comprehensibility and social function. While such a duality is arguably at least as much an imposed extramusical construct as an accurate reflection of Mendelssohn's own music and views, the fact that this partition has long been present in Mendelssohn reception is undeniable and forms moreover a key feature in his problematic reception history. This essay examines the implications this hypothetical split in Mendelssohn's work has had for the historiography and reception of his music, focusing particularly on the "Lobgesang," a "symphony cantata" poised (for some perilously) between the sacred and secular.

∞

Historically, the seeds for this supposed division in Mendelssohn's oeuvre, and indeed the contrasting evaluations attached to each side, were present even in Mendelssohn's own day. By the later 1840s, a split in critical reception was beginning to form between a wide public regard for the large-scale civic or religiously oriented pieces such as *St. Paul*, the "Lobgesang," and *Elijah*, and the agenda pursued by more self-consciously progressive critics (such as Franz Brendel), who viewed Mendelssohn's concert overtures and instrumental music as his most signal contribution to music history. This latter outlook was aligned with a radical political ideology that saw conventional religion and social forms as outdated, and correspondingly held a belief in musical progress.[3] Not surprisingly, proponents of this viewpoint were by and large hostile to Mendelssohn. Even critics professing some type of religious affiliation disputed the correct nature of Christianity and religious art in contemporary society. Eduard Krüger, reviewing the posthumously published *Three Psalms* (MWV B35, B46, B51; op. posth. 78), in 1850, criticized the work openly for its religiosity, contending that "it is not possible to recover the sacred until our life is reformed."[4]

It is this potent fusion of political ideology with musical criticism that, as Friedhelm Krummacher has shown, passed through figures such as George Bernard Shaw, with his "despicable oratorio mongering" and "Sunday-school sentimentalities," Wilfrid Mellers and his "spurious religiosity," down to the late twentieth century.[5] By Vitercik, this unresolved mix of aesthetic and quasi-ethical grounds is clear to see. One side of Mendelssohn's output (predominantly his early instrumental music) is praised for aesthetic qualities, primarily those premised upon historically based criteria such as artistic originality; the other lambasted without further thought on apparently unrelated ethical-social grounds, although the exact problem with the latter is never really touched on. Here we see how, in common with so much of Mendelssohn's reception, a (negative) evaluation remains even though the grounds originally used to support it have long since dropped away or are no longer tenable.[6]

Such considerations may well demonstrate historical reasons for the propagation of this criticism, but tell us little about Mendelssohn's own views and music. Even less do they form a compelling argument for accepting such a viewpoint. For a start, while certain critics may assume that religion is passé or incompatible with their goals, a certain ground assumption—that conventional religion or belief in God has been somehow conclusively (or even largely) invalidated in the past two centuries—is, to put it gently, hardly proved or uncontroversial. Though one hears with monotonous regularity the truism that, at some indeterminate point in the nineteenth century, God died, and while it is undeniable that social and scientific changes in this period undercut some important traditional grounds for belief, beyond the self-justifying truth of repeated cliché, this question is in fact no closer to having been answered, and, one might justifiably say, is in any case beyond the capabilities of rational speculation to answer either way.[7] Likewise, while not all critics of Mendelssohn's religious music are overtly atheistic, they share as a rule a distrust of conventional religion, which is rarely interrogated or justified by the authors in question but stems from particular cultural-political prejudices.[8] Seldom do such arguments go beyond bald assertions of an extremely subjective cast; indeed, often their very nature is incapable of proof.[9]

In short, one may say that criticism of Mendelssohn's religiously oriented music is generally premised upon an unspoken assumption that religious belief is either mistaken or that Mendelssohn's particular form is wrong, in both cases often due to having been historically superseded. These contentions are furthermore either unprovable or now (ironically) historically no longer relevant, if indeed they ever were valid, which is questionable. In other words, the fact that Mendelssohn was a religious man who on occasion wrote religious music, broadly defined, cannot of itself be demonstrated to be "wrong." At best, it merely goes against the prejudices of certain critics that are themselves no better grounded. There is no a priori reason for accepting that religion or religious belief in the nineteenth and twentieth centuries is metaphysically erroneous, or any less problematic than nonbelief.

What is often also notable within the ideological viewpoint criticized above is a peculiar historical double standard that manifests itself in the sentimental prizing of religious music up to the age of Bach and Handel alongside the degradation of any later work, as if this earlier religiosity is somehow legitimate but all subsequent attempts are necessarily invalid. (The assumption that God and religion somehow become irrelevant around the late eighteenth century is taken as given.) Thus, the religious becomes legitimated only through being sentimentalized and aestheticized as belonging to a lost past where belief was possible—that is, permitted as an pardonable former illusion now historically superseded. A pertinent example is provided by the criticism cited from Eduard Krüger, which echoes an important earlier passage by E. T. A. Hoffmann that Carl Dahlhaus cites as key text in the emergence of art-religion: "It would probably be quite impossible today for a composer to write as Palestrina, Leo, and later Handel . . . did—as exquisitely as when Christendom still shone in its full glory; that age seems to have disappeared forever from this earth."[10] This attitude persists at some level to the present day in music criticism; ironically Mendelssohn may himself have played a significant part in this process in his defunctionalizing of Bach's religious music by taking it out of the church and into the concert hall, notwithstanding his own genuine religious convictions.

Underlying this whole discussion is the key question of the emergence in the nineteenth century of the idea of art-religion. The potential mixture of art and religion forms a complex problem and resists easy subsuming into one formula. For the purposes of the present argument one may distinguish three general categories of relationship between these two terms. Religious art (1), the use of art within the scope of traditional religion, such as the liturgical music of Machaut, Palestrina, or Bach, is fairly unproblematic in this context, and has existed for millennia.[11] Slightly more delicate is the idea of "art-religion" (2) that arose, particularly in Germany, around the turn of the nineteenth century, such as that found in the *Herzensergießungen* of Wackenroder's Art-Loving Friar, the writings of other Romantic or proto-Romantic authors such as Herder, Novalis, Tieck, and Hoffmann, and the theology of Schleiermacher. This body of thought, as Carl Dahlhaus contends, can genuinely be considered art *and* religion simultaneously. Art is believed to form a path from the human to the absolute; a transcendent medium truly imbued with religious feeling.[12]

Both these above definitions use art as the means to an indisputably religious end, even though in the latter, the nature of the religion so served is often vague or unconventional. What is more problematic here is the notion of "art-religion" that has given rise to the popular, perhaps debased image of the concept (3): the extension of art-religion (2) to the idea of art outside any question of God or religion, being seen as an end in itself, it (or its creators) deified as something quasi-divine. This cult of art, what one might even call a secular "religion of art," may be seen to grow across the nineteenth century with the cult of artistic genius, heroes and hero worship, and the increasing estrangement of Romantic art-religion from its original divine underpinning.[13] The "aesthetic" qualities outlined earlier—the demand for constant newness, originality, emotionally extreme subjective states, the "egotistical sublime"—are closely bound up with this last viewpoint, and indeed much of the reception of music since the later nineteenth century has been dominated by such criteria.[14]

While the distinctions between the definitions given above are not absolute and the three can merge into one another, it is nevertheless apparent that in the former two the category of the aesthetic serves a deeper ethical or religious end, whereas in the latter it becomes considered an end in itself.[15] In other words, we are faced with the distinction between an ultimate religious justification for art and an aesthetic conception in which constant novelty, sensual immediacy and the power of the ego of the genius-creator become in themselves paramount.[16]

It is here that the parallels between Mendelssohn's predicament and Kierkegaard, mentioned in passing by Eric Werner in his 1963 biography, become particularly pertinent. "Of his contemporaries," claims Werner, "probably Kierkegaard alone understood the dilemma with which Mendelssohn was confronted, consciously or unconsciously."[17] Werner revives here the aesthetic/ethical conceptual dualism articulated in the Danish philosopher's *Either/Or*, in which, he holds, Kierkegaard "defends Mendelssohn's ideal of value."[18] Essentially, in this early work Kierkegaard contrasts the aesthetic life—narcissistic, egotistic, desirous of constant novelty, standing outside (and to some extent against) the mores of conventional society—and the ethical life of social integration and responsibility, in which the aesthetic is integrated into a more holistic conception.[19] As so often with Kierkegaard's pseudonymous works, it is arguable that neither side is conclusively ascendant; indeed, perhaps the two viewpoints are in the last resort incompatible, though it seems likely that we are meant to find the ethical position the more sagacious option as the aesthetic leads inevitably "to despair." In his later writings (such as the following *Fear and Trembling* and *Stages on Life's Way*), Kierkegaard suggests that both the aesthetic and ethical are important and necessary stages toward a third category, the religious, in which alone can one find justification and meaningful existence.

Viewing the reception problem outlined above through these categories forms a useful way of conceptualizing the issue, though, as I will suggest, these categories eventually become blurred, combined, and transcended in Mendelssohn's music. Put very briefly, it appears that much of Mendelssohn's religiously or ethically motivated music (which falls on the genuinely religious side of art-religion) is being judged largely or indeed solely by particular aesthetic criteria drawn from the third definition (secular "aesthetic religion"), which for Mendelssohn is already transcended by a deeper religious justification.[20]

Mendelssohn's "Lobgesang," Op. 52

Sondern ich wöllt alle künste sonderlich die Musica gern sehen
im dienst, des der sie geben und geschaffen hat.

[I would rather see all the arts, in particular music,
in the service of Him who has given and created them.]

—Martin Luther, epigram to Mendelssohn's "Lobgesang," op. 52

Mendelssohn's "Lobgesang," his Symphony Cantata written for the 1840 Gutenberg celebrations, embodies this interplay between aesthetic, ethical, and religious categories, in a manner that enabled this piece to become one of Mendelssohn's most popular works and at the same time proved increasingly problematic for critics hostile to organized religion.

Most pertinent here is the comparison frequently made between Mendelssohn's work and Beethoven's Ninth Symphony, which for many critics became a clear-cut case of aesthetic failure to live up to the ideal composer-genius, whose beatification as the aesthetic avatar par excellence was already at work in the nineteenth century. (While Beethoven himself was certainly religious, albeit in a not-exactly-orthodox manner, this inopportune feature has tended to become marginalized in the eyes of reception history.) The extent to which the "Lobgesang" bears any relation to Beethoven's Ninth is admittedly slight, being confined to a broad structural similarity of three symphonic movements followed by an extended choral part (in Mendelssohn drastically longer and falling into more discrete sections), though this apparently has not stopped several generations of critics from falling over themselves in invective. But to persist with the comparison between the two—a comparison central to those critics who would have us dismiss Mendelssohn's work—the vast differences in their expressive worlds point up this conflict between particular aesthetic-ethical desires and separate ethical-religious intentions. At best, taking further the perceptive interpretations of Mark Evan Bonds and John Toews, Mendelssohn's cantata could be described as a more overtly Christian "misreading" of a Ninth Symphony that has become exegeted as the paradigm of secular aesthetic humanism.[21]

In Mendelssohn's work, the existence of a God whose nature can be revealed through traditional religion (in this case Lutheran Christianity) is a precondition, a metaphysical "given." The very start of the work presents a hymnic motive that, in Toews's words, stands as "a fully-developed, authoritative declaration, resonant with the authority of divine revelation and historical tradition"[22] (ex. 11.1). This initial theme will go on to recur throughout Mendelssohn's work as a type of motto, in a manner familiar from the composer's earlier cyclic instrumental works. Woven into the texture of the first movement and central trio of the second-movement scherzo, it is recalled in

Example 11.1. Mendelssohn, "Lobgesang," no. 1 Sinfonia, mvt. 1, opening
motto theme

the anticipatory lead-in to the first choral number, going on to form an integral part of the latter. Finally, in the closing measures of the piece, it is manifested in full choral magnificence for the revelation of the essential message
of the work: "All that has breath praise the Lord." "The whole of it, vocal and
instrumental, is founded on the[se] words," wrote Mendelssohn. "Indeed,
first the instruments praise in their own way, then the chorus and solo voices
in theirs."[23]

The motto theme hence acts in this manner as the music's alpha and
omega, an underlying divine presence that is gradually internalized through
revelation. The process of Mendelssohn's work may indeed be seen as structurally analogous to the course of Christian universal history: In the beginning there is God (the motto), existing fully formed, a first, irreducible
principle. Intimations of this glory are given within the first and second movements of the instrumental Sinfonia (the prophesies of the Old Testament or
the foretelling of John the Baptist[24]); this culminates in the first choral number with the full revelation of God's light, now verbally semanticized[25] (the
coming of Christ and giving of the Word to mankind; alternatively, in a more
explicitly Protestant reading relating to the 1840 Gutenburg celebration, the
spreading of the Word through printing). Finally, at the very end, the motto
recurs one final time in eschatological splendor, uniting the trombone statement of the work's opening with the choral version as the telos of history
(God and the Faithful).

The idea of the work can thus be seen as the gradual realization and envoic-
ing of a religion truth, an underlying core or essence underpinning humanity
and the cosmos. It is this "given" quality that immediately makes Mendelssohn's
work so different from Beethoven's Ninth Symphony—a process of creation ex
nihilo, a "search for order" from basic grounds, as humanist readings have presented it.[26] The existence of a (Christian) God in the heavens and the resulting informed presence in the cosmos is an a priori assumption—an act of faith
that can neither be proved nor disproved through reason. This is religious
belief—a set of metaphysical assumptions and values that must be shared or
at least understood in order to appreciate the work properly. (The charge that
Mendelssohn should have made the search for the Deity "harder" or whatever

is hence ludicrous and ideological in the bad sense; as a view it is itself premised upon an alternate, somewhat mutually exclusive notion of metaphysical reality, and blindly ignores the still considerable presence of religion to this day.) In other words, to judge Mendelssohn's work solely against what we have termed "aesthetic" criteria is to commit a category error, advancing an independent and mutually exclusive viewpoint that can itself be no better grounded.

As also suggested, however, the "Lobgesang" is not solely a work of religious art but a combination of aesthetic, ethical, and religious strands—as Thomas Grey argues, a fusion of the genre and institution of the symphony and choral festival, "the desire to reconcile the claims of a secular, Enlightenment heritage with the authorities of the modern church and state."[27] While the end posited is religious, the means used to get there are aesthetic. In fact, Mendelssohn's work can be seen as fusing these three categories, tracing a Kierkegaardian path through the aesthetic and ethical to an ultimately religious end.

The "Lobgesang" is of course most obviously entitled to be considered "aesthetic" through the simple fact of being a work of art—indeed, in what was for Kierkegaard the aesthetic medium par excellence, music.[28] Moreover, some material for the first three (instrumental) movements seems to have originated independently a couple of years earlier as part of a projected symphony in the Beethovenian tradition of "secular-humanist" instrumental music. Significantly, critical disapproval has rarely focused on these movements, being reserved for the later, overtly religious part of the work and the corresponding subsuming of the secular-aesthetic into this underlying sacred conception.[29]

The "ethical" properties of this work meanwhile are clearly present in the historical context of the cantata's conception as part of the national Gutenberg celebrations and generic status within the tradition of the large-scale civic choral festival, this work forming a creative contribution to what Leon Botstein has famously dubbed the "Mendelssohn Project"—the use of music as an ethical force for the integration and development of community.[30] (As Richard Taruskin remarks, no one did more for civic music in the nineteenth century than Mendelssohn, "the *de facto* president of German musical culture" in the *Vormärz* years.)[31]

The final end of the "Lobgesang," however, is unmistakably religious: a "Song of Praise" by humankind (the ethical sphere) to the divine benefactor. The work thus traces a path from the secular-humanistic aesthetic of the opening instrumental movements, through the civic ethical community of the choral sections (with their nod to humanistic progress personified in the historical figure of Johannes Gutenberg) to a sacred telos uniting mankind with God and reaffirming the divine underpinning of the universe.

Yet—and this is what makes the conception unmistakably Kierkegaardian—the deepest connection with the divine is actually reached through the subjectivity of the lone individual's relationship before God.[32] In the famous "Watchman" passage, added after the first performances in Leipzig for the

English premiere of the "Lobgesang," we are faced with a moment of doubt and despair, scarcely encountered elsewhere in the work, of startling intensity, that momentarily throws us back to the aesthetic extreme. (Naturally, one can easily guess that this passage is one of the few sections in the later stages of the piece that has long been admired by critics.) "Watchman, will the night soon pass?"—the tenor soloist repeats these words three times with ever increasing fear and urgency, as the otherwise largely placid musical language gives way to an unreciprocated questioning figure in the wind,[33] anguished diminished harmonic sonorities and an impassioned rising chromatic sequence (ex. 11.2). It is this moment of doubt that leads to the most resounding affirmation of faith, the final plateau of the last four numbers that brings the work to its conclusion. The path to God is not simply through the ethical community but is found in a deeper and truer sense through the self, a dialectic in which both the aesthetic individual and ethical society are necessary to reach the final religious level.

On closer analysis, one perceives that this fusion of individual subjectivity and religious grounding is built into the very fabric of the work, to the extent that one could claim the idea of integration to be the central constructive principle of the "Lobgesang." The music abounds in foreshadowings and reminiscences, a web of interconnecting allusions running throughout the cantata's separate parts. Most clearly this is seen by the interweaving of the motto theme, standing, as Toews has it, for divine authority, throughout the first two symphonic movements. Mendelssohn's amalgamation is made with remarkable skill; the motto does not simply appear in the "seams" of the movement (transition, closing theme, development) and paratextual spaces (introduction and coda) but its first two reappearances within the Allegro are both prepared through the gradual introduction of its characteristic dotted rhythm some measures before its explicit manifestation (mm. 57 and 121).[34]

Furthermore, the Allegro's second subject (m. 94), when finally attained in the "correct" secondary key of F major, is marked by a distinctive cycle-of-fifths progression for its second half (the bass movement $\hat{3}$–$\hat{6}$–$\hat{2}$–$\hat{5}$–$\hat{1}$–$\hat{4}$, under a more elaborate harmonic progression predominantly using sevenths), mirroring exactly the close of the motto heard at the opening and very end of the cantata. Thus, the more intimate lyricism of the second theme reveals an unexpected link to the grandeur of the motto, despite their apparent expressive polarity. In a comparable manner, this second theme itself exhibits a similarity with the continuation of the first theme (mm. 27–30) in the swaying dotted-quarter plus eighth-note rhythm, and this is highlighted by the second-subject group's second theme (m. 106), which explicitly takes up the continuation of the first subject for its material. While this first subject (aptly described by Thomas Grey as reflecting "a spirit of restless optimism, a propulsive energy" characteristic of the "Judeo-Protestant work ethic that was so much a part of Mendelssohn's upbringing")[35] is expressively quite distinct

Example 11.2. Mendelssohn, "Lobgesang," no. 6 "Stricke des Todes," mm. 77–129

Example 11.2.—(continued)

Example 11.2.—*(concluded)*

from the softer lyricism of the second subject, the two again are seen to be but two faces of the same underlying reality, as is confirmed by the overt reappearance of the dotted rising arpeggio of the first subject as the exposition's closing theme at measure 126—leading in turn to the reentry of the motto theme a few measures later.

The interweaving of motto theme and chorale into the trio of the second movement, meanwhile, has long been admired. In counterpoint to the apparent continuation of the minor-hued Allegretto material, a chorale melody enters in the woodwind, combined with a barely disguised rhythmic transformation of the similarly liturgical-like motto in the oboe, bringing what appears a ray of hope to the music. The fragments of the *poco agitato allegretto* fill in the spaces between chorale phrases, suggesting the ongoing presence of this music behind the chorale material, a spatial separation of the music into at least two distinct aesthetic levels. Yet the juxtaposition has a dynamic consequence, in that the chorale phrases grow stronger and more confident, as the gentle lament of the Allegretto appears to acquiesce to its need for spiritual consolation.[36] Upon its formal return in the ternary reprise, the G-minor music is notably altered, petering out rapidly into an indecisive *pianissimo* close that leads without break into the ensuing Adagio religioso.

If the first movement suggested a buoyant human striving that was nevertheless underpinned by a deeper religious foundation (the "Lobgesang" motto), and the Allegretto told in a gently understated manner of the dependence of mankind upon God, this Adagio forms the decisive movement to a state of subjective interiority, of dawning self-consciousness and the "feeling of absolute dependence" that in Schleiermacher's view was the quintessence of religious experience. The hymn-like primary theme, upon its initial presentation, is quite uncomplicated in its devotional simplicity; later in the movement the plain repeated notes of the third measure will be reinterpreted and deepened through increasingly sophisticated harmonic treatment. The entire movement in fact is an exemplary illustration of the successive enrichment of originally simple material upon its recall following two slightly darker intervening episodes (functioning as transitions to the second tonal area and the brief central developmental space), leading to a lyrical flowering of music in the highly modified reprise.

Commentators have long recognized the explicit foreshadowing of the lead-in to the ensuing first choral number in the transitional figuration that enters in measure 35.[37] What has often gone unnoticed is the further link between the melodic figure in measures 36–37 and a prominent motive in the duet "I waited for the Lord" (no. 5)—apparent particularly in the latter's minor-key continuation (mm. 15–16). Hence, the connection between the instrumental Adagio and the later choral duet with the theme of subjective dependence upon God is underscored. One further point of note is the commonalities between various movements apparent through the use of an initial rising arpeggio figure in the orchestra, first given as the head motive of the Allegro first subject (m. 23). This gesture recurs for the second part of no. 2, "Praise the Lord with lute and harp," and again for no. 2a, "Praise thou the Lord" (and potentially also in no. 7). Even though a rising major arpeggio is hardly an uncommon opening strategy, such general affinity marks up a structural parallelism between instrumental and choral part that is already articulated through the large-scale cyclic return of the motto theme.

The instrumental movements are moreover characterized by a harmonic-contrapuntal fluidity at a larger syntactic level that helps to undercut the formal self-sufficiency of their material. Befitting the syntax of a large-scale instrumental structure, Mendelssohn creates a musical surface untroubled by the more extreme elements of Romantic harmonic practice, yet there flows a subtler destabilizing undercurrent, manifested as early as the second measure of the Allegro's first theme (m. 24), where a mild chromaticism already infiltrates the confidence of the opening ($I–^{\#5-6}–V^4_2–o^7–V^5_6$). The harmonic style of this first movement is marked by the predilection for underarticulating larger structural cadences by chromatic slippage through augmented triads and augmented-sixth chords. Particularly apparent in this regard is the second subject, which is almost invariably approached obliquely through the augmented triadic harmony introduced at measure 24 (also mm. 82, 94, and 226), and the recapitulation, which is attained through a chromatically altered dominant that adds a seventh degree to this augmented harmony (m. 259). Allied to this tendency is the deceptive harmonic treatment given to the second subject (V/f | A♭–; A♭→V/f | F, mm. 82–94). Cadencing on the dominant of the implied dominant *minor* and proceeding instead to the generically expected dominant *major* is a traditional ploy;[38] where Mendelssohn goes further is in the interpolation between of a lengthy statement of the second theme in the false flattened mediant, which is only rectified when V/f is obtained a second time.[39]

What especially contributes to the sense of dependence on the external "Lobgesang" motto is the undercutting of the expected expositional and recapitulatory points of closure. The projected expositional close at measure 145 is undermined by the marked registral drop for the tonic chord, whereupon the introductory motto reenters. Effectively the secular sonata-form material has been unable to ensure satisfactory closure through its own means, at which point the religious reappears. The close of the recapitulation presents a comparable case, in that both potential structural cadences (mm. 338 and 367) are underarticulated, leading on consequently to the second movement and ultimately without break into the cantata and the revelation of God's Word. Thus by undercutting the structural articulation of sonata material Mendelssohn points up the dependency of this "secular" realm on the spiritual. The overall effect not only links the instrumental and choral parts together but demonstrates the former's insufficiency without the latter—the need to combine the secular and sacred, to integrate individual subjectivity, the civic and the religious.

Beyond the "Lobgesang": Aesthetic and Ethical Considerations in Mendelssohn's Music

Poetry is youth, and worldly wisdom comes with the years,
and religiousness is the relation to the eternal;
but the years make a person only more and more obtuse
if he has lost his youth and has not won the relation to the eternal.

Viewed religiously, the fortunate person, whom the whole world favours,
is just as much a suffering person, if he is religious,
as the person to whom misfortune comes from outside.

—Johannes Climacus, in Kierkegaard,
Concluding Unscientific Postscript

We have observed in the "Lobgesang" a collapsing and merger of the categories of secular and sacred and the aesthetic and ethical—a transcending of the heuristic framework suggested earlier. At a broader level across the Mendelssohn oeuvre, too, one may similarly suggest that while some works are more clearly slanted to one side of a hypothetical secular/sacred, aesthetic/ethical binary pairing, the two sides are in reality not necessarily so distinct. *Pace tantorum virorum* Shaw, Tovey, and Vitercik, *St. Paul* and the *Hebrides* do, after all, originate from the same creative mind (at much the same time), one that is not known to have been schizophrenic.

Particularly revealing on this point are the parallels with Mendelssohn's other large-scale cantata from these years, *Die erste Walpurgisnacht* (MWV D3, op. 60). Having started work in 1830, Mendelssohn was dissatisfied with the first version he produced and came to revise the work in the early 1840s. It even appears that the successful reception of the "Lobgesang" spurred the composer on to tackle the revision; in a letter written in November of 1840, five months after the cantata's premiere he speaks of "strongly thinking of taking up work" on the *Walpurgisnacht* again under the same name of "symphony-cantata" and opening now with three symphonic movements just as in the "Lobgesang."[40]

Despite these intended formal commonalities, the two are ostensibly very different in subject and message. *The First Walpurgisnacht*, a setting of a ballad by Goethe, is secular, humanist, pagan, even apparently anti-Christian and anti-establishment; the *Hymn of Praise*, on the other hand, based on Psalm texts, is religious, Christian, and seemingly socially conformist. Unsurprisingly, the former cantata is valued more highly from a secular-aesthetic perspective, and has correspondingly attained higher regard in twentieth-century scholarship. Yet, on further reflection, the differences between the two works are not as great as might be thought. Both praise the power of enlightenment and the validity of religious expression for mankind, and both combine the aesthetic, ethical, and religious, tracing a movement toward an ultimately religious end. The message of both works could be encapsulated as "Let everything praise God in its own way through the power of light and reason—but let everything praise God!" The two thus present complementary treatments of the theme of religion and enlightenment in human society. And at the very least, it is noteworthy that Mendelssohn was able to consider quite imperturbably two such contrasting pieces in close succession, which is suggestive of the multifaceted nature of his ethical and religious beliefs.

It is plausible, indeed, that the separation between the radical "Beethovenian" secular-aesthetic Mendelssohn (as epitomized in the early chamber masterpieces and overtures) and the more conservative "Bachian" ethical-religious tendency increasingly closed across Mendelssohn's career, especially after around 1835 with the death of his father, the success of *St. Paul*, his Leipzig appointment, and a little while later his marriage. Certainly the op. 44 Quartets (MWV R30, R26, and R28) attempt little of the youthful aesthetic radicalism of opus 13 (MWV R22) and opus 12 (MWV R25) with their focus on expressive intensity and starkly original form, but rather are the fruit of a deeper consideration of the purpose and ethical function of music. Thus, while the younger Mendelssohn could compose coetaneously in strikingly contrastive styles (think of the numerous sacred works in antiquated idioms he was composing in the early 1830s), increasingly from the later 1830s on the division between aesthetic, civic, and liturgical merges without ever quite sundering the relative boundaries between secular and sacred genres.[41] This may explain in part that old chestnut of a "Mendelssohn problem": the negative comparison (from the narrow "aesthetic" perspective defined above) of some of Mendelssohn's later works with (certain) early ones that reveal more readily the requisite aesthetic qualities desired by critics. Rightly or wrongly, everything is grounded for Mendelssohn in God, and this cannot help affect the nature of his ethical and aesthetic decisions. This simply differs from the values of many subsequent commentators. The purely aesthetic is not the ultimate arbiter for Mendelssohn.[42]

It may be pertinent given the approach taken in this essay to interpret this movement in Mendelssohn's life and work from an expressly Kierkegaardian perspective, namely the concept of "the choice." Werner again quotes Kierkegaard's Vilhelm on this matter: "Either, then, one has to live aesthetically, or one has to live ethically."[43] One may continue in the aesthetic life, swayed one way then another by events occurring accidentally outside oneself and putting off making any decision that will reduce the enticing realm of possibility, or one can "choose oneself," take responsibility for one's future and decisions. For Vilhelm, this does not entail necessarily abandoning the aesthetic, but raises it up to a higher level within the wider sphere of the ethical:

> In his life the ethical individual goes through stages we previously set forth as separate stages. He is going to develop in his life the personal, the civic, the religious virtues, and his life advances through his continually translating himself from one stage to another. As soon as a person thinks that one of

these stages is adequate and that he dares to concentrate on it one-sidedly, he has not chosen himself ethically but has failed to see the significance of either isolation or continuity and above all has not grasped that the truth lies in the identity of the two.[44]

Or in the words of Kierkegaard's Johannes Climacus, "To exist is an art. The subjective thinker is aesthetic enough for his life to have aesthetic content, ethical enough to regulate it, dialectical enough in thinking to master it."[45]

Mendelssohn (1809–47) and Kierkegaard (1813–55) were near contemporaries, both coming from a well-off background, Protestant, deeply religious, and dying at a young age (thirty-eight and forty-two, respectively). Kierkegaard even spent time in Berlin attending Schelling's lectures during the period that Mendelssohn was carrying out his appointment there as director of sacred music under Friedrich Wilhelm IV; both were, furthermore, critical of Hegel, indeed of all theorizing disconnected from actual life and intellectual abstraction in general. Yet Mendelssohn was able to adjust himself to life better than Kierkegaard, who exhibited an exaggerated self-torment and guilt foreign to the composer.

Sometime around the mid-1830s, Mendelssohn chose to embrace the "ethical" life, and as a result this decision had consequences for his music's direction and aims. Kierkegaard, on the other hand, never made it—indeed twice balked, first in 1841 from marriage to Regine Olsen, then in 1846 from laying down his pen and taking orders following the publication of the *Concluding Unscientific Postscript*, intended as the summa and end of his philosophical work—though continued to proselytize about it.[46] Mendelssohn, having gone through a darker period in the early 1830s, managed to embark upon a successful life and career, financially making his own way in life (rather than slowly frittering away a small fortune as with his Danish contemporary), marrying and raising a family, and establishing himself as the leading composer of the age and preeminent figure in Germanic musical life.[47]

Yet, notwithstanding the argument pursued above, one must be careful not to exaggerate in this discussion the distance of Mendelssohn's music from the "aesthetic." After all, according to Kierkegaard's Vilhelm, choosing the ethical does not necessitate renouncing the aesthetic, and the ethical nature of Mendelssohn's life is moreover not the same as the potential aesthetic quality of his music. The "aesthetic" remains relevant to Mendelssohn most transparently in the sheer beauty of his music—"the category the aesthetic always claims for itself"[48]—and his consummate, unfailing craftsmanship. It is not the case that Mendelssohn's music lacks anything in technical quality, a claim that no one would impute; neither is it deficient in beauty, which for many (especially in the eighteenth century) was the central category of aesthetic judgment. In fact one may go further and suggest that all it *sometimes* lacks are particular "aesthetic" qualities (in the narrower sense used in this article) such as constant novelty, the valorization of the self, a fairly abstruse idiom and rejection of the possibility of intersubjective communication—which are themselves just as premised upon wider ethical assumptions (in this case, a conception of society and the position of humanity that is inimical to organized religion) that are underpinned by an alternative, antithetical philosophical standpoint (that there is no God or organized religion is at least wrong; that history is a path of continuous progress) that cannot be proved. And these two contrasting worldviews, in the last resort, do not mix.[49]

&

To sum up this necessarily brief account of what is obviously a far deeper and more richly faceted topic, one simply cannot understand, let alone legitimately judge Mendelssohn's religiously oriented music from secular, "aesthetic" criteria, for in doing so we are applying tools that can have no purchase on the categories he thought of as deeper and more fundamental. The problem some secular or religiously disenfranchised critics have had with such works are based almost entirely on the music's expressive qualities and (perceived) underlying metaphysical assumptions; the clear musical quality and technical sophistication of this music is never in question. If one is only aware of this, one's appreciation of Mendelssohn's music becomes more informed, and banal criticisms of this aspect of his oeuvre fall away. One need not share the same beliefs as his, but we have to understand this difference, and appreciate his music on these terms.

Notes

1   Gregory Vitercik, *The Early Works of Felix Mendelssohn: A Study in the Romantic Sonata Style* (Philadelphia: Gordon and Breach, 1992), 2–3, citing Donald Tovey, *Essays in Musical Analysis*, 6 vols. (London, 1935–44), 4:90 (on *The Hebrides*) and George Bernard Shaw, "A Dismal Saturday," *World*, November 19, 1890 (reviewing the "Lobgesang"). See also Alexander Brent Smith's factually insecure polemic, "The Workmanship of Mendelssohn," *Music and Letters*, 4 (1923): 18–23.

2   John E. Toews, "Musical Historicism and the Transcendental Foundation of Community: Mendelssohn's *Lobgesang* and the 'Christian German' Cultural Politics of Frederick William IV," in *Rediscovering History: Culture, Politics and the Psyche*, ed. Michael S. Roth (Stanford: Stanford University Press, 1994), 184; this article is reproduced and extended in Toews's *Becoming Historical: Cultural Reformation and Public Memory in Early Nineteenth-Century Berlin* (Cambridge: Cambridge University Press, 2004), a valuable contribution to Mendelssohn scholarship.

3   See particularly Donald M. Mintz, "1848, Anti-Semitism, and the Mendelssohn Reception," in *Mendelssohn Studies*, ed. R. Larry Todd (Cambridge: Cambridge University Press, 1992), 126–48.

4   Eduard Krüger, review of Mendelssohn, *Three Psalms*, op. 78, in *Neue Berliner Musikzeitung*, January 2, 1850, reproduced in Douglass Seaton, ed., *The Mendelssohn Companion* (Westport, CT: Greenwood Press, 2001), 282–87, esp. 283.

5   Friedhelm Krummacher, "Composition as Accommodation? On Mendelssohn's Music in Relation to England," in Todd, *Mendelssohn Studies*, 80–105.

6   It hardly needs to be pointed out that the original grounds for such negative criticisms—the political change desired by Young Hegelian-aligned critics, the self-serving historical determinism of Wagner or Liszt in their role as musicians of the future, or Shaw's own brand of utopian socialism to be obtained through the superseding of God by Wagner, Ibsen, and Shaw himself—hold scant validity or relevance for present-day society.

7   Cf. Immanuel Kant, *Critique of Pure Reason*, I, Pt II, Div. II, Bk. II, Ch. III; *Prolegomena to Any Future Metaphysics*, §57; Søren Kierkegaard, *Philosophical Fragments*, III: The Absolute Paradox; Ludwig Wittgenstein, *Tractatus Logico-Philosophicus*, esp. propositions 6.1, 6.11, 6.41, 6.4312, and 6.5.

8   As Krummacher argues, "Shaw and Mellers share a distrust of religious morality as well as an antipathy towards Mendelssohn's religious music"; their criticism, in other words, is against what they conceived of as the culture and ethics of Victorian England. "The relationship is clear: false religiosity and an inauthentic archaism in Mendelssohn's music correspond to the hypocritical morality and moribund musical culture of England. . . . In combination the two express a reciprocal affinity. And the analogies are directed in such a way that the question scarcely arises how their validity may be demonstrated so that they become more than personal opinions" (Krummacher, "Composition as Accommodation," 87).

9   Note, for instance, Wilfrid Mellers's astonishingly self-assured pronouncement that "Mendelssohn betrays no interest in, let alone knowledge of, religious experience" (*Man and His Music: Romanticism and the Twentieth Century* [Fairlawn, NJ: Essential Books, 1957], 31), or similarly, if slightly more honest, Eduard Krüger's statement that "the devout can say from personal experience what differentiates the ecclesiastical from the spiritual, and we cannot demonstrate this to others" (review of Mendelssohn, *Three Psalms*, op. 78, 283). The argument that religious experience may not be demonstrable is perfectly fair, but a necessary consequence of this is that the function of criticism becomes annulled if the author is totally incapable of substantiating his or her disaffection with the religiosity of Mendelssohn's music.

10   E. T. A. Hoffmann, "Alte und neue Kirchenmusik," *Allgemeine musikalische Zeitung* 16 (August 31, September 7 and 14, 1814), cols. 577–84, 594–603, 609–19; see Carl Dahlhaus, *The Idea of Absolute Music*, trans. Roger Lustig (Chicago: University of Chicago Press, 1989), 92, translation slightly altered.

11   This should nevertheless be distinguished from Hegel's use of the term "art-religion" to characterize the religion of the ancient Greeks (*Aesthetics*).

12   Dahlhaus, *The Idea of Absolute Music*, chapters 5 and 6.

13   Friedhelm Krummacher has perceptively demarcated a potential conflict between the former two conceptions above which may have contributed to their estrangement and corresponding growth of art-religion (3): in an age in which all art that deserved the name inherently tended toward religion, religious art becomes something of a tautology ("Art-History-Religion: On Mendelssohn's Oratorios *St. Paul* and *Elijah*," in Seaton, *The Mendelssohn Companion*, 306–9).

14   Dahlhaus in particular is at pains to defend art-religion (2) from attacks against art-religion (3) in the twentieth century such as those by Stravinsky, who objected to both the sacralization of art and to the secularization of religion (*The Idea of Absolute Music*, 88).

15   This distinction might be illustrated by comparing Wagner's *Parsifal*, a work using religious topoi and symbolism for nonreligious ends, with Elgar's *The Dream of Gerontius*, a piece of undoubted religious sincerity. The distinction between the two rests significantly on the perception of authorial intention. "Bad" art qua art is furthermore not a major problem when considered from an underlying religious justification (hence, the proliferation of genuine religious kitsch).

16   Please note that I am using the term "aesthetic" here in rather a specific sense after the manner of Kierkegaard, itself drawing on Hegelian conceptual terms that some readers may find overly systematized. Of course, these so-called aesthetic criteria are themselves just as premised upon wider assumptions concerning the nature of the world and the ethical imperatives of its participants, as is implicit in the earlier discussion of ideological objections to organized religion. I will return to this point at the end of the chapter.

17   Eric Werner, *Mendelssohn: A New Image of the Composer and His Age*, trans. Dika Newlin (New York: Free Press, 1963), 500.

18   Ibid., 342.

19   For Kierkegaard, in his famous account of Mozart's *Don Giovanni* in the first part of *Either/Or* ("The Immediate Erotic Stages *or* The Musical Erotic"), music is the perfect medium for expressing the inconstancy and sensual immediacy of this "aesthetic" subject matter. While Kierkegaard's reading of Mozart's work and the potentiality of music is compelling, his idea of music is rooted in a primarily Hegelian conception (such as his denial of instrumental music's status as a self-standing art and the problem of its ontological being), which Mendelssohn surely thought unnecessarily limited. Music, for Mendelssohn, following his teacher Zelter, was not purely narcissistic sensual immediacy but was to be used to ethical ends. The idea that music is expressive of precognitive sensual immediacy may be viewed positively in light of Schleiermacher and German Idealist/Romantic thinkers, as a form of communication avoiding the pitfalls of language (and, moreover, for Schleiermacher closely connected therefore to the essence of religious experience), rather than negatively as Kierkegaard appears to do.

20   Note Henry F. Chorley's revealing contemporary verdict on *St. Paul*: the composer "has thought more of his story than himself: and this resolution of making his music *a means* and not *an end*, raises him high above" (review in the *Athenaeum* 468 [October 15, 1836], 739). Or as Kierkegaard (through the guise of Johannes Climacus) formulates the issue: "The decisive difference between the poet and the upbuilding speaker remains, namely, that the poet has no *telos* [end, goal] other than psychological truth and the art of presentation, whereas the speaker in addition has *principally* the aim of transposing everything into the upbuilding." Kierkegaard, *Concluding Unscientific Postscript to "Philosophical Fragments,"* trans. Howard V. Hong and Edna H. Hong, 2 vols. (Princeton, NJ: Princeton University Press, 1992), 1:257.

21   Mark Evan Bonds, "The Flight of Icarus: Mendelssohn's *Lobgesang*," in *After Beethoven: Imperatives of Originality in the Symphony* (Cambridge, MA: Harvard University Press, 1996), 73–108; Toews, "Musical Historicism," and *Becoming Historical*. Bonds pertinently teases out the idea that Mendelssohn's work may be seen to be addressing a problem perceived in Beethoven's symphony by many nineteenth-century musicians, Mendelssohn included.

22   Toews, "Musical Historicism," 193. On this point one might plausibly counter Mendelssohn's critics simply by playing the opening of the "Lobgesang" alongside

that of Beethoven's Ninth Symphony and comparing Mendelssohn's imitation with the purported model. This is not, of course, an exhaustive comparison, but when anyone who has listened to Mendelssohn's work encounters a critic like Gerald Abraham floundering in his own execration in describing it as "the most dismal attempt to follow the lead of Beethoven's Ninth Symphony ever conceived by human mediocrity," one has to wonder who the mediocrity conceiving the "Lobgesang" as such really was—for it was not Mendelssohn.

23 Mendelssohn, letter to Karl Klingemann, July 21, 1840, in Karl Klingemann [d.J.], ed., *Felix Mendelssohn-Bartholdys Briefwechsel mit Legationsrat Karl Klingemann* (Essen: Baedeker, 1909), 245.

24 In Protestant Germany, John the Baptist was closely associated with Johannes Gutenberg; the 1840 Leipzig Gutenberg festivities took place around June 24—*Johannistag*.

25 In Christopher Reynolds's useful formulation, the instrumental motive has become "texted" (*Motives for Allusion: Context and Content in Nineteenth-Century Music* [Cambridge, MA: Harvard University Press, 2003], 88–100).

26 See especially Maynard Solomon's influential account, "The Ninth Symphony: A Search for Order," in *Beethoven Essays* (Cambridge, MA: Harvard University Press, 1988), 3–32. It must be admitted that of all pieces, the Ninth Symphony is one of the most intractable to give a single, definitive meaning to (on this matter, see especially Ruth A. Solie, "Beethoven as Secular Humanist: Ideology and the Ninth Symphony in Nineteenth-Century Criticism," in *Explorations in Music, the Arts and Ideas: Essays in Honor of Leonard B. Meyer*, ed. Eugene Narmour and Ruth A. Solie (Stuyvesant, NY: Pendragon, 1988), 1–42; also Nicholas Cook, *Beethoven: Symphony No. 9* (Cambridge: Cambridge University Press, 1993) and Andreas Eichhorn, *Beethovens Neunte Symphonie: Die Geschichte ihrer Aufführung und Rezeption* (Kassel: Bärenreiter, 1993); however, Solomon formulates very well a prevailing humanist interpretation that synthesizes many salient features in this work's reception. (To this extent, I am more interested in pointing up the difference of the "Lobgesang" from a prevailing trend in Beethoven reception and its aesthetic-humanist ideology than whether or not the latter interpretation is actually what Beethoven may have conceived.)

27 Thomas S. Grey, "The Orchestral Music," in Seaton, *The Mendelssohn Companion*, 435. For Toews, similarly, "This extraordinary amalgam of the secular instrumental structure of the classical symphony and the vocal forms of a sacred cantata based on Biblical texts . . . combin[ed] the forms of traditional Protestant sacred music (epitomized by the revival of Bach) and classical symphony (epitomized by the cult of Beethoven) in a synthetic conception of ethical/cultural reform grounded in historical tradition and religious faith" (Toews, "Musical Historicism," 184).

28 Obviously this is an important distinction between Kierkegaard's consideration of the aesthetic and ethical life and these categories as applied to art. Art is eo ipso going to be in all likelihood "aesthetic."

29 Robert Schumann, who picked up on this hypothesis of the separate origin of the symphonic movements, appeared to demur concerning Mendelssohn's fusion of the secular-aesthetic and ethical-religious: "If we are right in supposing that the symphonic portion was composed independently of the *Lobgesang*, we should prefer to see them published separately, to the advantage of both sections of the work." Even more noteworthy is Schumann's commentary on "I waited for the Lord"— "It was like a glance into a heaven filled with the Madonna eyes of Raphael"—a

statement that really points up the difference between Mendelssohn's genuine religious belief and Schumann's vaguer, more secular Romantic "religion of art" (Schumann, "Gutenbergfest in Leipzig," *Neue Zeitschrift für Musik* 13 [July 4, 1840]: 7–8; the implied former criticism was cut for the republication in Schumann's collected writings, Robert Schumann, *Gesammelte Schriften über Musik und Musiker*, vol. 3 [Leipzig: Wigand, 1854], 245–46).

30   Leon Botstein, "The Aesthetics of Assimilation and Affirmation: Reconstructing the Career of Felix Mendelssohn," in *Mendelssohn and His World*, ed. R. Larry Todd (Princeton, NJ: Princeton University Press, 1991), 32–37. See also Michael P. Steinberg, *Listening to Reason: Culture, Subjectivity, and Nineteenth-Century Music* (Princeton, NJ: Princeton University Press, 2004), 97–122, esp. 99; James Garratt, *Music, Culture and Social Reform in the Age of Wagner* (Cambridge: Cambridge University Press, 2010), 102–16. It is this quality, of course, that endeared the piece to several generations of middle-class choral societies in Germany, Britain, and America, and correspondingly contributed to its inevitable castigation by matching generations of self-appointed aesthetic and moral guardians of society.

31   Richard Taruskin, "Nationalism: §7 after 1848," in *The New Grove Dictionary of Music and Musicians*, ed. Stanley Sadie (London: Macmillan, 2001), 17:694–95.

32   See *Fear and Trembling*, esp. "Problemata I" ("Faith is namely this paradox, that the single individual is higher than the universal . . . the single individual as the single individual can stand in an absolute relation to the absolute, and consequently the ethical is not the highest"; writing as Johannes de Silentio in *Fear and Trembling / Repetition*, trans. Howard V. and Edna H. Hong [Princeton, NJ: Princeton University Press, 1983], 55, 113); also see the *Concluding Unscientific Postscript*, pt. 2, sec. 2, chap. 1, "Becoming Subjective," and the entire argument of *The Sickness unto Death.*

33   A variant of the "Frage" topos, used earlier in Mendelssohn's, opus 9, no. 1 and op 13 (see further Ariane Jessulat, *Die Frage als musikalischer Topos: Studien zur Motivbildung in der Musik des 19. Jahrhunderts* [Sinzig: Studio Schewe, 2000]).

34   Grey pertinently questions the extent the first movement is conceivable *without* the motto theme, despite its ostensible extraneousness to the main body of the music, such is its level of integration (Grey, "The Orchestral Music," 431).

35   Ibid., 430.

36   Cf. the comparable procedure in the Adagio of Mendelssohn's Cello Sonata no. 2 (1843). The gradual emboldening of this chorale material in the woodwind also has a parallel in the lead-in to the finale of Mendelssohn's earlier "Reformation" Symphony, one of several links between the two works.

37   Bonds, along with several other scholars, also points to the clear influence of Handel's anthem "Zadok the Priest" on this passage (Bonds, "The Flight of Icarus," 87).

38   Cf. the first movement of Beethoven's Symphony no. 2.

39   This playing with the tonality of the second group is typical of Mendelssohn's mature sonata practice: see the Piano Concerto no. 1, Caprice, op. 33, no. 1; Quartet, op. 44, no. 2; and Symphony no. 3, mvt. 4.

40   Letter to Karl Klingemann, November 18, 1840, in Klingemann, *Briefwechsel*, 251; the final version of the *Walpurgisnacht* only has one instrumental introductory movement, the A-minor overture, which leads in through an inspired connective passage to the choral part of the cantata. See further John Michael Cooper, *Heathen Muse: Mendelssohn, Goethe, and the Walpurgis Night* (Rochester, NY: University of Rochester Press, 2007), esp. 89.

41 See further on this issue in the perceptive account by Thomas Christian Schmidt, *Die ästhetischen Grundlagen der Instrumentalmusik Felix Mendelssohn Bartholdys* (Stuttgart: M. und P. Verlag für Wissenschaft und Forschung, 1996), 191–96.

42 Kierkegaard explores this conflict in the *Concluding Unscientific Postscript*: "A religious poet . . . is in an awkward position. That is, such a person wants to relate himself to the religious by way of imagination, but just by doing that he ends up relating himself aesthetically to something aesthetic. . . . If the religious is truly the religious, it has passed through the ethical and has it in itself, then it cannot forget that religiously the pathos is not a matter of singing praises and celebrating or composing song books but of existing oneself. *Thus the poet-production . . . is regarded by the poet himself as the accidental, which shows that he understands himself religiously, because aesthetically the poet-production is the important thing, and the poet is the accidental*" (1:388, emphasis added; see also 390 and 590).

43 Kierkegaard (as Judge Vilhelm), *Either/Or*, part 2, ed. and trans. Howard V. and Edna H. Hong (Princeton, NJ: Princeton University Press, 1987), 168; see Werner, *Mendelssohn: A New Image*, 500.

44 Kierkegaard (as Judge Vilhelm), *Either/Or*, part 2, 262.

45 Kierkegaard (as Johannes Climacus), *Concluding Unscientific Postscript*, 1:351.

46 For instance, in 1849, Anti-Climacus writes: "From the Christian viewpoint, every poet-existence . . . is sin, the sin of writing instead of being, the sin of relating oneself in imagination to the good and true instead of being it" (Søren Kierkegaard, *The Sickness unto Death*, trans. Alistair Hannay [Harmondsworth: Penguin, 1989], 109). The argument for praxis against mere abstract thought is sustained at length in the *Concluding Unscientific Postscript*: "The development of subjectivity consists precisely in this, that he, acting, works through himself in his thinking about his own existence, consequently that he actually thinks what is thought by actualising it" (1:169; see further esp. 303, 343, and 351). More succinctly put (as Virgilius Haufniensis), "truth is for the particular individual only as he himself produces it in action" (Søren Kierkegaard, *The Concept of Anxiety*, trans. Reidar Thomte and Albert B. Anderson [Princeton, NJ: Princeton University Press, 1980], 138).

47 The propinquity of this public success to the well-worn image of the blithely contented Felix should not, however, blind us to the darker, more irascible side of his character.

48 Kierkegaard (as Judge Vilhelm), *Either/Or*, part 2, 272.

49 Cf. Alasdair Macintyre's notable argument in *After Virtue: A Study in Moral Theory* (Notre Dame, Indiana: University of Notre Dame Press, 1981). This whole issue articulates a deeper problem of particular relevance to modern Western society concerning the relationship between secularism and religion, which, when pushed to extremes, become incompatible.

Chapter Twelve

Mendelssohn's Religious Worlds

Currents and Crosscurrents of Protestantism in Nineteenth-Century Germany and Great Britain

Celia Applegate

In March 1842, one of Felix Mendelssohn's oldest friends, the historian Johann Gustav Droysen, wrote to tell him that in Kiel, Felix was the talk of the town—"das Kieler Stadtgespräch." Rehearsals were in full swing for the Kiel premiere of Mendelssohn's oratorio *Paulus* (MWV A14, op. 36). Droysen, a newly appointed professor at the university and a member both of the city's Liedertafel and Sing-Akademie, described the energy and seriousness with which the choral societies rehearsed, the distance people traveled to rehearsals, and the intense feeling of anticipation among the general public. "You will get a sense of this," he wrote, "when I tell you that Otto Jahn has written a little brochure about it, in order to make the public as *au fait* as possible. . . . It is quite unique [*einzig*] how fully your music has been embraced by this public, so serious in its Protestantism." And he continued, "my dear friend, it is your great achievement that you have come to embody in so unambiguous a way a great movement of our time and indeed to stand at the forefront of it. It is the movement of Protestant music, which has lain dormant since J. S. Bach— Händel does not belong to it—and which now lives again."[1]

Droysen's palpable excitement about the reinvigoration of Protestant music is saturated with cultural-political, as well as biographical, significance. By 1842, this son of a Protestant military chaplain and former student of the leaders

MENDELSSOHN'S RELIGIOUS WORLDS 311

of German idealism and classical learning—George Wilhelm Friedrich Hegel, August Boeckh, and Karl Lachmann—had already made a name for himself among the educated public as a brilliant young historian.[2] His biography of Alexander the Great, first published in 1833 in Berlin and never since out of print, had not only defined what he named the "Hellenic" period but had also implicitly reminded readers of Napoleon's own world-conquering efforts. The work was, in other words, a commentary, though not an explicit one, on Germany's own need for a Napoleon or an Alexander to realize its full potential, politically and culturally.[3] And it was a view strongly inflected by Droysen's Protestantism. For Droysen, as for his onetime mentor Hegel, the Prussian Protestant state was the obvious vehicle for Germany's future realization. By 1846, from his university post in Kiel, he had become actively engaged in the Schleswig-Holstein question as historian; in the revolutionary year of 1848, he served as a liberal deputy to the short-lived German parliament, where he became one of the most powerful voices for the need to rally support behind Prussian leadership of a future German nation.

By 1848, of course, Mendelssohn was dead, but in the half decade or so before his death, a decade of mounting excitement among nationalists, what he represented for men like Droysen was precisely the kind of cultural leader that Germany needed—endlessly gifted, internationally renowned, classically educated (by Droysen himself), and deeply committed to an ethical vision of Germany as the vital center of Protestantism. As a musician, Mendelssohn embodied the "perpetually creative power" that, in Droysen's view, ultimately shapes the fate of nations. "There is in human things," wrote Droysen much later, in his *Outline of the Principles of History*, "a truth, a power which the greater and more mysterious it is so much the more it challenges the mind to recognize it and to fathom [*ergründen*] it."[4] The truth and power of the "human things" to which Mendelssohn contributed lay for Droysen in threads of continuity stretching from the work of the Reformation through men such as Bach and into the present, where such work took on ever broader ramifications.

Droysen first recognized the potential importance of Mendelssohn's and his creative work in 1829, when he was twenty and Mendelssohn was nineteen. At that time, the two young men gathered several times weekly with an intimate circle of friends to imagine how together they could bring about what John Toews has characterized as the "ethical reformation" of society through art and learning.[5] For these young idealists in Berlin in the late 1820s, Mendelssohn's most significant project, and one in which they all played their part, was his revival of J. S. Bach's long-forgotten *St. Matthew Passion*, two performances of which Mendelssohn conducted in Berlin in March 1829.[6] Writing for the *Berliner Allgemeine musikalische Zeitung*, Droysen declared that Mendelssohn had revived an entire lost epoch when "on Good Friday there was complete and solemn quiet in the city, and the streets were free of traffic, the market empty, and all the bells summoned people to church . . . where all worshipped and sang together "O Haupt voll Blut und Wunden." "That," wrote Droysen in 1829, "is the essence of our Protestant confession." Bach's great work thus belonged "not to art and its history alone but much more, as art should, to the community, to the people." And he continued, "the time has come to restore this religion to where it belonged, as the central point and purpose of our lives and the life of the state."[7] For Droysen, then, the work begun in 1829 was being carried forward in such seemingly small matters as the enthusiastic rehearsals in Kiel for a performance of Mendelssohn's *Paulus* oratorio. Generalized outward in its effects to all Germans, his friend's greatness lay in his capacity to contribute to an overall reinvigoration of Protestant piety in the public and private life of the German people, making it again vital to the present.

The case of Droysen's admiration for Mendelssohn's contributions to Protestant music, suggestive though it may be, is but one of many episodes in the recasting of religious life in the century once regarded as one of inexorable secularization. Stepping back from the particularities of Droysen's Prussia, this chapter provides a general portrait of Protestantism in the Germany and England where Mendelssohn lived and made music. What was this Protestantism, or evangelical faith, that came so alive for Droysen in Berlin in 1829 and Kiel in 1842? Was it the same Protestantism whose believers welcomed *Paulus* in Düsseldorf, Liverpool, and London, or *Elijah* (MWV A25, op. 70) in Birmingham? Although building on the work of Jeffrey Sposato in emphasizing differences in the English and German receptions of *Paulus*, this account will instead emphasize common trends in the first half of the nineteenth century that worked to make religious music an essential, even unavoidable part of public life.[8]

৪০

The religious situation of Europe in the first half of the nineteenth century was as unsettled as it had ever been, though for reasons fundamentally altered from those that had fed conflicts and change in earlier centuries. Everywhere in Europe there were revolts against the official churches, Protestant and Catholic; everywhere there were new demands for freedom and equality in religious life. Everywhere there were also tensions among clericals, nonclericals, and anticlericals; among old believers, new believers, and nonbelievers; and among supporters of established churches and members of sectarian groups, more or less independent of officialdom. In short, the nineteenth century was, in the words of Hugh McLeod, "both the archetypal period of secularization and a great age of religious revival."[9] Although the period was characterized by repeated crises of faith among intellectuals and aristocrats as well as among peasants and artisans, these crises resolved themselves as often as not in favor of religion. They led to redefined religiosity and alternative expressions of religious belief, or they resulted in a redirection of intellectual and emotional attention, which is not the same phenomenon as atheism. Religion in the nineteenth century by and large ceased to serve as the foundation of a broad social unity, irrespective of class, nation, and gender. Instead it came to express the innumerable and distinctive identities of specific communities, classes and factions, among which one could count, albeit cautiously, a few modern nationstates. In Christopher Clark's estimation, the early nineteenth century was "in religion as in politics, an era of differentiation, fragmentation and conflict."[10]

Even if we look only at the loose conglomeration of states and groups that constituted Protestant Europe, we find a bewildering array of communities and churches, as complicated as in the first century after Luther's protest was lodged against the Church of Rome. The situation is hardly simpler, even if we confine our gaze to England and Germany, the two most important cultural milieus of modern Protestantism in Europe and, at the same time, the two most vexed in working out new relations between church and state as well as achieving new balances between toleration and cohesion. Traditionally, scholars have seen a fundamental difference between an outward and civic version of Protestantism in Great Britain and an inward and contemplative Protestantism of the German-speaking lands. The musical shorthand for this distinction is that between the English Handel, with his confident, even triumphant oratorios and the German Bach, inward, complicated, the joys of salvation less noisily extolled, the sorrows of life more tenderly expressed. But this comparison, when embraced by contemporaries like Droysen, does justice neither to the transnational connections between these two areas nor to the actions of lay communities nor, for our purposes, to their musical lives.[11] In both countries the first decades of the century were characterized by the recovery and reconfiguration of church establishments. This in turn reflected the fact that the embers of the great religious awakenings of the eighteenth century—Methodism, Pietism, and others—were still glowing, and prone, time and again, to flare up into flames. Finally, the social and economic transformation of Europe, although less dramatic in its effect on German-speaking lands in the early nineteenth century, had profound consequences for religious communities and practices in their efforts—or failures—to minister to the changing nature of poverty and social displacement. In Great Britain, the population increased threefold between 1750 and 1850. Population growth was not so rapid in German lands, but it was by no means negligible. For the churches in both countries, population growth made it necessary to find resources to build new churches and schools and bring in more ministers to attend to the spiritual and physical needs of more people. In sum, the political, the personal, and the practical aspects of religious life all came under increasing pressure on both sides of the English Channel.

છ

The many states of German Europe, though reduced in sheer numbers by the massive transformations of the revolutionary and Napoleonic period, remained as much of a religious patchwork as they were a political one. Prussia, the state in which Felix Mendelssohn received his upbringing, education, and early musical successes, had once been the bastion of toleration, where a politics of religious rights seemed to serve well both state interests and those of the majority Protestant population. The Edict of Potsdam in 1685 had allowed persecuted French Huguenots to settle in Prussia, and from 1731 to 1733 the state had offered asylum to the 20,000 Salzburg Lutherans expelled by their bishop-ruler. The case of the Salzburgers had been a propaganda coup of great value to the Hohenzollerns and the Prussian state, establishing them as the moral and political leaders of transconfessional, transnational Protestant unity. But after 1815 and in tense relationship to its celebrated tradition of toleration, the state embarked on a new era of unprecedented state activism in church affairs. In 1817, in the midst of celebrations of the tercentenary of Luther's ninety-five theses, the Prussian monarch Friedrich Wilhelm III announced a union between the Lutheran and Reformed branches of Protestantism. Just half a decade after key efforts to streamline the fiscal management of churches, the move may have seemed to its architects the extension both of rational state management and of religious toleration, informed perhaps by the impulse to create harmony among all religious confessions through enlightened rule. But the implementation of the union was so clumsy and the population so ill-prepared for the change that it became in practice a heavy-handed enforcement of religious uniformity.

The king's involvement also reasserted the conservative religious principles he had articulated in 1802 in a royal memorandum "On the Decay of Religiosity." Church and state were not separate entities, he had asserted, nor was the order of liturgy a matter for individual parishes to decide for themselves. The Union of 1817 thus enforced the state's interest in all aspects of church life on the basis of the conservative notion "that the state was in some sense Christian," and hence the ruler had the right to shape every aspect of Christian worship, including repeated revisions of the new liturgy.[12] The Union liturgy was Friedrich Wilhelm's own invented tradition, with its mingling of aspects of the German, Swedish, Huguenot, and Anglican orders of service and, most unexpectedly, its inclusion of modern arrangements of medieval Russian Orthodox chants. He expected everyone to adhere to it and showed an obsessive concern with uniformity both in its creation and in its enforcement. There was something recognizably Napoleonic about his approach, something resembling the wholesale imposition on a people of practices, like the Napoleonic Code, deemed good for all, and especially good for the state's ability to administer. The Union church and its liturgy were a kind of prefabricated religion and as such were intended to be imported into every city, town, and village of Prussia. Their imposition brought a centripetal force to bear against the centrifugal tendencies of nineteenth-century life and the unruly, anarchic forces of religious revival, which Friedrich Wilhelm III regarded with an instinctive aversion.

But it also brought no end of trouble in the form of resistance from religious communities who wanted to retain the old ways.[13] By changing things so drastically, the state created a community of dissenters and nonconformists, more or less in the British sense, out of people who would otherwise have retained their traditional support for established authority. At the same time, the resurgence of nonconformity and revivalism after the end of the Napoleonic wars encompassed much more than Prussia's ill-considered effort to assert a new religious uniformity. The so-called Awakening in the first decades of the century was a socially diverse movement of religious revival that swept across the Protestant north of Germany. Awakened Christians emphasized the emotional, penitential character of their faith and experienced the transition from unbelief or from merely nominal Christianity as a traumatic moment of rebirth. In contrast to the Union church agenda, it was personal and practical rather than ecclesiastical. Rulers tended to have a horror of Awakened religiosity, because it seemed to them inimical to state order. Even before resistance to the Union church exploded in the 1830s, the Prussian minister of religion, health and education was keeping a close eye on various awakened sects, assembling lists of their publications, and sending spies to their meetings.[14] Those who resisted the invented traditions of the Union church quickly fell into this category of people to be kept under surveillance.

For their part, the Union resisters sounded all of a piece with Awakened Protestants, articulating their resistance in the language of the spiritual authority of each individual soul. Through such informal bonds of affinity, resistance to the Union church became part of a larger Lutheran Awakening that had found a spiritual center in celebrations of the tercentenary of the Augsburg Confession, the key doctrinal text of Lutheranism. The tendency of nineteenth-century Awakenings, wherever one encountered them in Europe (including Great Britain) was to begin ecumenically and end up creating their own boundaries or establishments. In Germany, the most identifiable group of Awakened and resisting Protestants were a group that became known as the Old Lutherans. The Old Lutherans found their emotional core in the traditional Lutheran liturgy, including its music. At its height, the movement included more than 10,000 active separatists, most of them concentrated in Silesia, where the influence of Saxony, the heartland of traditional Lutheranism was especially strong. The Prussian king responded to their protests with outrage and incomprehension, declaring them to be malevolent agitators and persons "of limited mental capacity" under the influence of fanatics.[15]

Thus did revival, repression, and underground movements all contribute to an uneasy, turbulent communal life in wide swathes of Prussia and Saxony. Religious nonconformists also raised important questions about how and *where* one worshipped, which attracted the attention of a much broader public than those actually partisan on one side or another. After these passions had somewhat died down again, German Protestants began to seek rapprochement among their sects and state churches, beginning in the 1840s with various transregional meetings of Protestant clergy. These efforts reached a tentative resolution in 1846, a year before Mendelssohn's death, with the convening of the first general Protestant synod in Berlin. It articulated the desirability of developing a constitution of greater independence for the church, in Nicholas Hope's judgment a "wistful, but nevertheless fundamental" step away from the old dependence of the Reformation-era principle of *cuius regio, eius religio.* In so doing, Hope argued, the general synod in its own nonemphatic way achieved a permanent "disruption of the provincial mould of historic Reformation church order."[16] In such a context, works like *Paulus* and *Elijah*, not to mention the Handelian oratorios and Bach cantatas and passions, had an important, community-integrating role to play, as we shall see below.

The situation in Great Britain was no less unsettled in religious matters. Religion and political life intersected more often and more openly there than they did in the states of the German Confederation, where public life was censored and circumscribed. In the first half of the nineteenth century, people experienced, in the words of Frank Turner, one of "the most fervent religious crusades that the British nation had known since the seventeenth century, indeed, the last great effort on the part of all denominations to Christianize Britain."[17] The upsurge of religious activism went beyond the nonconformity of the Quakers, Puritans, Presbyterians, Congregationalists, and Baptists of various sorts who had been around since at least the seventeenth century. Its most powerful expression was the Methodist movement. It had grown gradually since John Wesley began preaching in fields in 1739, taking off in the years immediately after his death in 1791 and doubling in size, decade by decade, in the nineteenth century. In 1811, around the time of Mendelssohn's birth, there were about 143,000 Methodists in Great Britain; in 1850, shortly after his death, there were nearly half a million. Like Awakening movements elsewhere, Methodism reasserted the doctrines of the reformation: the Bible as the revealed word of God, the sinfulness of man, the possibility of redemption through God's grace, and justification by faith. Its appeal for common people (though not necessarily for the most poor) lay at least partially in the opportunity it provided to assert one's own personal grace against that of state-appointed ministers of all sorts.

Awakened Christians would jump up during regular services to denounce the doctrines expounded from the pulpit or sing hymns so loudly—in groups often assembled outside the church—that the vicar's droning voice could not be heard. Mass meetings and conversion experiences, renewed faith and social missionary activity—these sorts of works developed not only within the ranks of self-proclaimed Methodists or other nonconformists but also within the

Church of England itself. Ironically or not, the intensification of religious life also accompanied the accelerating decline of the exclusive Anglican confessional state. This had begun in earnest with the late eighteenth-century drive by Protestant Nonconformists to secure broader civil rights and later became fully realized in the repeal of the Test Acts and Catholic Emancipation in 1829, the year that Mendelssohn first traveled to England. In the face of these reforms—destructive for some, liberating for others—and the unrelenting pressure of Nonconformism on the Church of England, the Anglican establishment found that it had to compete as a denomination among other denominations in the religious marketplace. This was an extension of Free Trade Liberalism that none had anticipated. In the period in which Mendelssohn became thoroughly caught up in British musical life, the great explosion of popular religiosity and social, even political, activism of evangelicals served as the backdrop to the efforts of Anglicans to define themselves theologically. Such soul-searching resulted most prominently in the Oxford or Tractarian movement. W. R. Ward, in an effort to take comparative stock of the Anglo-German Protestant world, wrote that taking all these movements, reforms, and reassessments together, "the whole Protestant world [of the nineteenth century had] fragmented into mutually uncomprehending regional enterprises."[18] Hugh McLeod, in his classic study of *Religion and the People of Western Europe*, agrees: "Religion became," he argues, "a major basis for the distinctive identity of specific communities, classes, factions in a divided society."[19]

Yet this judgment may be too summary. If one takes a comparative view of the role of Protestantism in the making and integrating of nations in the nineteenth century, then the picture takes on different coloration. For Linda Colley, in her now classic study *Britons* (first published in 1992), the Protestant self-understanding of destiny and chosenness actually "forged" a nation out of the historic entities of England, Scotland, and Wales: she contends that the variations within Protestantism did not preclude its ability to function as a force for integration.[20] The high musical expression of this "forging" was, of course, the Handelian oratorio. In Germany, nationhood was a more vexed question, even when one gives all due weight to the complications posed by Welshmen, Scotsmen, and Irishmen, the latter of whom most certainly laid obstacles in the path of Protestant triumphalism. Nevertheless, in German-speaking lands as well, consciousness of a common Protestant faith and belief in the role of German Protestants as a kind of chosen people found expression in the century of nation-building. Cults of Gustavus Adolphus, Oliver Cromwell, and Johannes Gutenberg (the John-the-Baptist figure of Protestantism, thus a kind of honorary Protestant, avant la lettre) developed and flourished in Germany, and numerous celebrations of the great milestones in the triumphal forward march of Protestantism could be found even in regions where Protestants were in the minority. Well before 1871, as Kevin Cramer has shown, Gustavus Adolphus became "one of the most powerful symbols of unity in the political folklore of Germany," embodying a "vision of a unified Protestant Reich," the figurehead of an often "inchoate Protestant nationalism."[21]

Johann Gustav Droysen was among the most prominent promoters of such visions of a Protestant in-gathering that would "forge" the German nation. In the letter with which this chapter began, Droysen had written to tell Mendelssohn that his Liedertafel, an institutional form that played a significant role in the German national movement, was rehearsing Mendelssohn's "valiant *Gutenberglied*" (MWV D4). Droysen sought permission to substitute the words "Vaterland" and "deutsches Volk" in place of the syllabically similar "Gutenberg": thus did the national heroes of the past serve the future.[22] We do not have evidence of Mendelssohn's ever replying to this request; it seems unlikely he would have been thrilled by the possibility, given, for instance, his refusal to cater to popular excitement during the so-called Rhine Crisis of 1840 and compose a patriotic *Rheinlied*. "Never was a man of any country more sincerely, affectionately national," wrote his friend Henry Chorley in his reminiscences of Mendelssohn's last days; but at the same time, as another observed, he took more pleasure in the "sympathetic blending of nationalities" than in the strident claims of nationalism.[23] Still, in other ways, what Mendelssohn was doing in the realm of religious music did encourage and sustain a kind of Protestant nationalism, with or without his explicit permission or any deliberate efforts to encourage it on his part.

ॐ

We need finally, then, to consider the consequences for music of this complicated, labile historical situation in which Protestant conformity, nonconformity, sectarianism, establishmentarianism, fragmentation, and in-gathering conflicted and coexisted. In order to come up with sensible answers to such a broad question, an attention to place provides a useful guide. As the previous discussion implied, religious developments of the nineteenth century did not represent a rearguard action against the progressive forces of modernity but rather a deep transformation in the nature and expression of religious piety. Lucien Hölscher has argued that the meaning of communion changed decisively over the course of the eighteenth century, from a "judgment of conscience" that bound the community together in "rigorously enforced" church attendance, to a more metaphorical experience that had "lost its power of socio-political and physiological-spiritual integration." This "epochal caesura" in the history of piety signaled the emergence of a "modern piety" that was just as widespread but less "churched" than traditional piety.[24]

The nineteenth century, by these lights, saw belief made individual and religious experience made both more private and more ubiquitous. People expressed their religious commitments around the family dinner table and in bedtime prayers as assiduously as they did in church. More to the point, they moved a great deal of religious experience outside. Romantic paintings of the era, such as the haunting landscapes of Caspar David Friedrich with their solitary figures poised amid ruined abbeys, tumbled rock cliffs, and ancient, half-decrepit forests, expressed an affective, aesthetic imagining of religious experience in the out-of-doors. But people also ventured out from enclosed spaces to have what we might call formal religious experiences. Open-air preaching and revival meetings were the very essence of evangelicalism and awakening. And if awakened Christians did not worship in the open air, they nevertheless gathered outside of traditionally sacred spaces, in prayer meetings in the houses of believers, not to mention in the countless venues in which people expressed their religious commitment through charitable and social-reforming activities.

In Great Britain, the distinction between Church with a capital C and chapel with a small one expressed a comparable break with the past. Chapels could be anywhere and by and large escaped the controlling interest of the state, both in Great Britain and in Prussia. They could be small structures in fields; they could be integrated parts of nonconformist assembly halls; they could be rooms in private homes. At the same time, Churches with a capital C were unable to keep up with the population explosion, as noted at the beginning of this chapter. State resources were simply inadequate to build new churches or to maintain old ones. Churches were chronically understaffed: many of the complaints about the Union church in Prussia had to do with the inadequacy of the state funds earmarked to institute and support the changes in liturgical practice that Friedrich Wilhelm wanted to see happen. Church Union was, in other words, an unfunded mandate.

Both the movement out of churches and the financial difficulties of established churches affected the kind of music people heard and performed in the course of practicing their religious lives. In Prussia, the same period in which Hölscher identified the decline of institutional belief saw, in musical terms, the decline of the Lutheran cantoral position, the relegation of organist to an impoverished profession, the deterioration of the chorale, the spreading silence of the congregation, the marginalization of musical training in the Latin schools, and the virtual disappearance of the trained choir of students. The Prussian *Allgemeines Landrecht* or legal code of 1794 hastened the disintegration of traditional musical life by abolishing the corporate categories of cantor and organist. Likewise, the guilds of town musicians, which had regulated the participation of their members in sacred music, were disappearing by the end of the eighteenth century. So too went the *Kantoreien*, the societies of townsmen who sang Protestant choral music in the churches. Even before Friedrich Wilhelm III expressed his views on what church music should sound like, contemporaries were expressing considerable dismay about the lack of new compositions for church services. Even worse, what concerned observers regarded as the saucy and superficial musical taste of the secular realm seemed to be insinuating its way into church song. The ever-present insufficiency of financial support for established churches meant that the serious, excellent sacred music of the past was performed only badly, if at all, in the churches themselves.[25]

Reluctant to antagonize the hand that fed them, those concerned about this state of affairs tended to blame society as a whole rather than the governments that had allowed it to develop. In 1807, Carl Friedrich Zelter, the director of the Berlin Sing-Akademie, wrote to Karl August von Hardenberg, an important member of the Prussian cabinet of ministers, that in the current musical environment "the inferior [in art] is raised up, and the great is cast aside." He further noted that "serious, one might even say, religious" music lay "uncultivated in these modern times." Thus "nothing interesting or healing," no "edification and emotion," could be found in churches, only "much that is cold and dirty," "a bungler at the organ," and "pitiful voices, deforming and dismembering the noble, elevated chorale." Music, declared Zelter, had abandoned the church for the theater, and to the "disdain and horror of philosophers and moralists," it had become a "luxury good," plied by "flute players and dancers" in the "chambers of the wealthy."[26]

What Zelter and other musical reformers of the early nineteenth century really wanted was for the state to take a more active role in overseeing church musical affairs so as to encourage the performance and composition of "uplifting church music." What they got, a decade or so later, was the Union church liturgy. But its royally eccentric set of requirements for service music proved a bitter disappointment and certainly not the musical agenda that those hoping for a reinvigoration of the Protestant musical tradition, with J. S. Bach at its center, had envisioned. Friedrich Wilhelm III's taste, like that of his Romantic contemporaries, tended toward the music of Palestrina's era and even earlier.[27] During his exile from Prussia after the defeats of 1806, he had heard church music in the Russian military encampments and had become enamored of the male-voice, a cappella sound of the Russian Orthodox service, so reminiscent of Gregorian chant and so distant from the instrumental chamber music he is said to have detested since childhood. His new service rites of 1817, 1821, and 1822 consequently broke with contemporary church music, such as it was, as well as with the entire Protestant musical tradition that originated with Luther. He retained only fragments of the original Lutheran sung liturgy, reduced congregational participation to a mere three hymns, and called for much of the liturgy to be sung between priest and a capella male choir, with the priest facing the altar throughout. Even if they put aside their distaste for the Catholic/Orthodox ritualistic coloration of the proceeding, congregations had to deal with the fact that the king's liturgy required a small but highly trained choir that would have to be made familiar with at least some musical traditions not native to them.

It is thus no coincidence that one of the enduring images of the Old Lutheran revolt was the departure of several thousand separatists to North

America and Australia, men and women together singing Lutheran hymns as their barges passed down the Oder River on their way to Hamburg and from there to London and beyond. Mutatis mutandis, the Tractarians' solutions to similar musical problems in the established Church of Great Britain (neglect and decline, poorly trained choirs, and slovenly organists) were surprisingly like those favored by Friedrich Wilhelm III—that is to say, the search for musical traditions that reached back before the Reformation to plain chant, a restrained a cappella repertoire, and a trained choir of disciplined singers (in the English case, wearing white surplices).[28] On the Nonconformist, Awakened side of things, the importance congregations attached to hymn-singing at all times and places cannot be overstated, but this was hymn singing largely detached from the full array of musical riches that Zelter encompassed in his phrase "noble and serious sacred music." Thus none of the existing church musical establishments of the early nineteenth century, whether established or disestablished, conformist or orthodox, indoors or outdoors, were prepared to take on the work of preserving and promoting the Baroque, Classical, and contemporary repertory of composed music for trained instrumentalists and singers. For sacred music, in fact, the most important consequence of reconfessionalization—what I called above the emergence of modern piety—was that most churches had become unreliable, and often inhospitable, sources of support for composed sacred music. For those interested in something other than, something *more than* plain chant and hymnody, one had to work largely outside of established and disestablished churches. And for all his incorporation of the Lutheran chorale into his compositions, Mendelssohn was certainly one such person.[29]

The difficulty of cultivating sacred music through church institutions was at least partially responsible for Carl Friedrich Fasch's creation of the Berlin Sing-Akademie in 1791. The same difficulty led serious-minded admirers of the sacred music tradition of Protestantism—like Luise Reichardt in Hamburg or Johann Theodor Mosewius in Breslau—to follow suit, establishing various kinds of amateur choral groups to practice and occasionally perform the cantatas, oratorios, motets, and Passions of the Protestant sacred music tradition. Finally, this difficulty was why in 1804 Friedrich Schiller suggested to Zelter, who was preparing to petition the Prussian government for money to support the Sing-Akademie, that he should present the institution as the "instrument lying ready to hand" for "coming to the aid of religion": "it seems to me an extremely happy circumstance," he continued, "that the interests of art just now meet such an external want."[30] Similar difficulties led to similar responses in Great Britain. There the Sacred Harmonic Society was founded in 1832 and flourished for the next four decades as a focus for the practice and performance of the works of Handel, later Mendelssohn, and ultimately the whole range of polyphonic and instrumental sacred music from the sixteenth century to the modern times.[31] Amateur choral groups focused largely on oratorios and other genres of sacred music also used the increasingly frequent and large music festivals, some in outdoor locations, some in halls, some in churches, and in England often based in hotbeds of nonconformism like Birmingham, for the venues for premieres of new oratorios.

If we cannot give the Nonconformist or Awakened movements the credit for promoting the work of Bach, we can at least allow that their reconfigurations of religious experience made it possible for musical activists to reimagine the functions and forms of sacred music performance. Thus, family resemblances and national patterns emerge among the many musical associations and practices of Protestants in the early nineteenth century. To be sure, as Sposato has shown, there are important nuances in the degree of understanding for Mendelssohn's very German oratorios exhibited in England and in Protestant Germany, as indeed there are important nuances in the nature of the Bach revival in England and Germany and the performances of sacred music and the growing audiences for them. But in neither of these eminently, vibrantly, passionately Protestant cultures did, for instance, the Bach revival proceed under the patronage of an established Church, and only fitfully and almost accidentally did the movement gain the patronage of a Nonconformist chapel.[32] At the same time, the performance of Bach by amateur singers in a concert hall in this period did not mean that religious experience had taken the back seat to aesthetic experience. While certainly some strands of European thought and art did seem to substitute a kind of "worship" of art for experiences of transcendence, nevertheless many, if not most, performances of sacred music or of music on religious themes or models (oratorios, concert masses) fit more comfortably into a model of an outgoing transformation of religious life than one of its relative decline.

გ

Meanwhile, Felix Mendelssohn, moving among the cities of north Germany and Great Britain in these years of religious transformation and turmoil, developed his own means of navigating the crosscurrents. Düsseldorf, where he served as director of the city's musical institutions in 1833 and 1834, was an outpost of Prussian state authority in largely Catholic territory and as such a focus for the missionary activities of "awakened" Protestants. Leipzig, where he became conductor of the Gewandhaus Orchestra in 1835, was a stronghold of traditional Lutheranism (though not Old Lutheranism). Berlin, home of his youth, his parents and his siblings, and frequent site of his musical performances, was the Prussian capital in which the very definition of religious Enlightenment and religious progress was subject to the disputes among an activist king, a progressive, even at times radical university faculty, and a conflicted, divided church establishment. London had powerful Anglican and Nonconformist churches as well as all else besides; Birmingham was "famous as a bastion of radical non-conformism."[33]

His family's heritage and reputation, his father's choice of Lutheran Christianity for him, his musical training, and his extraordinary musical achievements from youth on all made his contributions to religious life in the broadest sense a matter of considerable public interest.

That these contributions might be something out of the ordinary for a composer and musician—even one so prodigiously talented—became apparent with his revival of the *St. Matthew Passion* in 1829. Without either challenging or following traditional religious practices, the performance had established a new space in public life for the musical expression of religious experience. In all the polemics that so disfigured his reputation in the second half of the nineteenth century, Mendelssohn's role in the Bach revival and his own sacred music came in for their share of criticism, scorn, and belittlement. In some criticism, one senses a kind of retrospective disquiet about the extent to which Bach, the greatest of all Christian composers, the fifth evangelist, and so on, had spent so much time outside the church premises. Still, the fact that Bach's sacred music initially spread outside church and state establishments made it more widely known across national, and indeed confessional, lines than might have otherwise been the case—indeed, made it more accessible to the culture of nationhood than a strictly Protestant Bach would have been, certainly in the period before 1871. And Mendelssohn practiced what he had preached in arguing to the musical powers-that-be that Bach should be heard in the secular hall of the Sing-Akademie. Mendelssohn's own sacred music spoke at the least to a broadly circumscribed Protestant public and even, like Bach's, could cross the fiercely defended confessional lines between Protestants and Catholics. For his own part, committed to the constant improvement of the state of music in Germany and to the invigoration of religious music through new works, he held himself apart from the political questions, including those of his friend Droysen, who saw the future of Protestantism firmly attached to the development of a Prussian-led German nation. Even if Mendelssohn had been more sympathetic to Droysen's political involvement, he did not live long enough to be drawn into the outsized admiration for Bismarck or anti-Catholic polemics that have shaped our ambivalent view of Droysen himself. For as long as Mendelssohn lived, he held to a generous and broad view of culture as a force for excellence and practiced his religion, as he did his music, in a Europe where the borders were permeable, especially for those with music in their packs.[34]

Notes

1   "Du bist jetzt das Kieler Stadtgespräch. . . . Wie Ernst wir die Sache nehmen, kannst
    Du daraus sehen, dass O. Jahn, dessen Du Dich vielleicht noch erinnerst, eine kleine Broschüre geschrieben hat, um das Publikum möglichst au fait zu setzen. . . . Es
    ist ganz einzig, wie Deine Musik gerade hier bei dem sehr protestantisch ernsten

Publikum rechten Eingang findet. O die Glücklichen! Dies habe ich in der Freude meines Herzens schreiben wollen. Und das ist eine große Errungenschaft für dich, dass Du einer bestimmten Bewegung in der Zeit auf so unzweideutige Weise entsprichst und an ihre Spitze trittst. Es ist etwas damit, dass die protestantische Musik, die seit J. S. Bach still gelegen—denn Händel gehört nicht zu ihr—endlich wieder lebendig wird." Droysen to Mendelssohn, March 7, 1842, in Carl Wehmer, ed., *"Ein tief gegründet Herz": Der Briefwechsel Felix Mendelssohn-Bartholdys mit Johann Gustav Droysen* (Heidelberg: Lambert Schneider, 1959), 77. Translations are by the author unless otherwise indicated.

2   Arnold Momigliano has called him "one of the greatest historians of any time." Arnaldo Momigliano, "J. G. Droysen between Greeks and Jews," *History and Theory* 9, no. 2 (1970): 139. For the only English-language book on Droysen, see Robert Southard, *Droysen and the Prussian School of History* (Lexington: University of Kentucky Press, 1995). The standard modern biography is Wilfried Nippel, *Johann Gustav Droysen: ein Leben zwischen Wissenschaft und Politik* (Munich: C. H. Beck, 2008).

3   Droysen was one of the progenitors of historicism, the view that to understand the artifacts of the past one must place them within their social and cultural contexts. But as John Toews has argued, Droysen did believe that "the ancient Greeks could still speak to modern Germans, that a spiritual thread connected ancient Greeks and modern Prussia, and that Greek artists and thinkers should be assimilated into contemporary German consciousness through creative transitions." John Toews, *Becoming Historical: Cultural Reformation and Public Memory in Early Nineteenth-Century Berlin* (Cambridge: Cambridge University Press, 2004), 260.

4   "In den menschlichen Dingen ein Zusammenhang, eine Wahrheit, eine Macht sei, die, je größer und geheimnissvoller sie ist, desto mehr den Geist herausfordert, sie kennen zu lernen und zu ergründen." J. G. Droysen, *Grundriss der Historik*, 3rd ed. (Leipzig: Veit und Comp., 1882), 4.

5   Toews provides sharp insight into their circle's dreams and projects in "Memory and Gender in the Remaking of Fanny Mendelssohn's Musical Identity: The Chorale in *Das Jahr*," *Musical Quarterly* 77 (1993): 727–43. Besides Droysen and Felix, the group included Felix's sister Fanny, her fiancée Wilhelm Hensel, the singer Eduard Devrient, his wife, Therese Schlesinger Devrient, the violinist Eduard Rietz, theology students Julius Schubring and E. F. A. Bauer, and, on the periphery, the music journalist Adolf Bernhard Marx.

6   Celia Applegate, *Bach in Berlin: Nation and Culture in Mendelssohn's Revival of the "St. Matthew Passion"* (Ithaca, NY: Cornell University Press, 2005).

7   Johann Gustav Droysen, "Über die Passions-Musik von Johann Sebastian Bach," reprinted from the *Berliner Konversationsblatt* in the *Berliner Allgemeine musikalische Zeitung* 6, no. 13 (March 28, 1829): 98–99.

8   Jeffrey Sposato, "Saint Elsewhere: German and English Reactions to Mendelssohn's *Paulus*," *19th-Century Music* 32, no. 1 (2008): 26–51.

9   Hugh McLeod, *Religion and the People of Western Europe* (New York: Oxford University Press, 1981), vi.

10   Christopher Clark, *Iron Kingdom: The Rise and Downfall of Prussia* (Cambridge, MA: Harvard University Press, 2006), 412.

11   While the study of Protestant religious cultures in the British Isles continues to produce rich and multifaceted research, the comparable field of study for Germany languishes, a situation exacerbated by the rapidly increasing neglect of the nineteenth century among English-speaking as well as German scholars of central

Europe. The imbalance has consequences to our overall understanding of popular Protestantism in German-speaking Europe.

12 Christopher Clark, "The 'Christian' State and the 'Jewish Citizen' in Nineteenth-Century Prussia," in *Protestants, Catholics and Jews in Germany, 1800–1914,* ed. Helmut Walser Smith (New York: Berg, 2001), 67–93.

13 Christopher Clark, "Confessional Policy and the Limits of State Action: Friedrich Wilhelm III and the Prussian Church Union 1817–40," *Historical Journal* 39, no. 4 (1996): 985–1004.

14 This *Kultusministerium* was established in the same year as the Union church and, like it, expressed the state's effort to weave tightly together the interests of the state with a culturally progressive agenda of education and social welfare.

15 Clark, "Confessional Policy," 993.

16 Nicholas Hope, *German and Scandinavian Protestantism 1700–1918* (New York: Oxford University Press, 1999), 260–61.

17 Frank W. Turner, "The Victorian Crisis of Faith and the Faith That Was Lost," in *Victorian Faith in Crisis: Essays on Continuity and Change in Nineteenth-Century Religious Belief,* ed. Richard J. Helmstadter and Bernard Lightman (Stanford, CA: Stanford University Press, 1991), 11.

18 W. R. Ward, "Faith and Fallacy: English and German Perspectives on the Nineteenth Century," in Helmstadter and Lightman, *Victorian Faith in Crisis,* 46.

19 McLeod, *Religion and the Peoples,* v.

20 Linda Colley, *Britons: The Forging of a Nation, 1707–1837,* 2nd ed. (New Haven, CT: Yale University Press, 2006).

21 Kevin Cramer, "The Cult of Gustavus Adolphus: Protestant Identity and German Nationalism," in *Protestants, Catholics and Jews,* 97. See also his study of the role of histories of the Thirty Years' War in expressing confessional solidarities among Protestants on the one hand and Catholics on the other: Kevin Cramer, *The Thirty Years War and German Memory in the Nineteenth Century* (Lincoln: University of Nebraska Press, 2010).

22 Droysen to Mendelssohn, December 31, 1841, in *"Ein tief gegründetes Herz,"* 73–74.

23 Henry Fothergill Chorley, "The Last Days of Mendelssohn," *Modern German Music* (London, 1854; repr. 1973), 2:385; Wilhelm Adolf Lampadius, *Felix Mendelssohn-Bartholdy: ein Denkmal für seine Freunde,* trans. W. L. Gage (New York, 1866), 132–33.

24 Lucien Hölscher, "The Religious Divide: Piety in Nineteenth-Century Germany," in Cramer, *Protestants, Catholics, and Jews in Germany,* 33–48. See also Lucien Hölscher, "Die Religion des Bürgers: Bürgerliche Frömmigkeit und Protestantische Kirche im 19. Jahrhundert," *Historische Zeitschrift* 250 (1990): 595–630.

25 See, for instance, G. W. F. Schlimmbach, "Ideen und Vorschläge zur Verbesserung des Kirchenmusikwesens," *Berliner Musikalische Zeitung* 1, no. 59 (1805): 231; no. 60 (1805): 235–36.

26 Zelter to Hardenberg, June 1, 1802; "Erste Denkschrift," September 28, 1803; "Zweite Denkschrift," n.d.: reprinted in Cornelia Schröder, *Carl Friedrich Zelter und die Akademie: Dokumente und Briefe zur Entstehung der Musik-Sektion in der Preußischen Akademie der* Künste (Berlin: Deutsche Akademie der Künste, 1959).

27 On the Palestrina revival, see James Garratt, *Palestrina and the German Romantic Imagination: Interpreting Historicism in Nineteenth-Century Music* (Cambridge: Cambridge University Press, 2010).

28 For the fullest account of these developments, see Bernard Rainbow, *The Choral Revival in the Anglican Church, 1839–1872* (repr., Woodbridge, UK: Boydell Press, 2001).

29   We can recall his impatience with the much ballyhooed music of the Sistine Chapel or with those who would reduce Bach to a kind of fugue-producing machine.

30   Friedrich Schiller to Carl Friedrich Zelter, July 16, 1804, in A. D. Coleridge, ed. and trans., *Goethe's Letters to Zelter, with Extracts from Those of Zelter to Goethe* (London, 1892), 23–24.

31   See *The Catalogue of the Library of the Sacred Harmonic Society*, W. H. Husk, editor and librarian, revised and augmented edition (London: Sacred Harmonic Society, 1872).

32   It is perhaps relevant that both Samuel Wesley and Samuel Sebastian Wesley, the musical line of descent from the first generation of Wesleys (John and Charles) who championed the music of Bach, should have led such scattershot and irregular religious lives, converting to Catholicism, sort of, and performing Bach in places like the Portuguese chapel in London.

33   Antje Pieper, *Music and the Making of Middle-Class Culture: A Comparative History of Nineteenth-Century Leipzig and Birmingham* (Basingstoke, Hampshire: Palgrave Macmillan, 2008), 9.

34   For further exploration of his border crossing, see Celia Applegate, "Mendelssohn on the Road: Music, Travel, and the Anglo-German Symbiosis," *The Oxford Handbook of the New Cultural History of Music*, ed. Jane Fulcher (New York: Oxford University Press, 2011), 228–44.

Contributors

Celia Applegate is William R. Kenan Jr. Professor of History at the Vanderbilt University. She has written extensively on German nationalism and national identity with particular attention to places and practices of music. She is the author of *A Nation of Provincials: The German Idea of Heimat* (1990) and *Bach in Berlin: Nation and Culture in Mendelssohn's Revival of the St. Matthew Passion* (2005), and coeditor, with Pamela Potter, of *Music and German National Identity.* She is currently president of the Central European History Society and a past president of the German Studies Association.

John Michael Cooper is professor of music and holder of the Margarett Root Brown Chair in Fine Arts at Southwestern University (Georgetown, Texas). He is the author of four books: *Historical Dictionary of Romantic Music* (2013); *Mendelssohn, Goethe, and the Walpurgisnacht: The Heathen Muse in European Culture, 1700–1850* (2007), *Mendelssohn's "Italian" Symphony* (2003), and *Felix Mendelssohn Bartholdy: A Guide to Research* (2nd ed., rev. Angela R. Mace, 2012). He also coedited *The Mendelssohns: Their Music in History* with Julie D. Prandi (2002). He has published articles, book chapters, reviews, and translations on subjects ranging from eighteenth- and nineteenth-century aesthetics to performance practice, source studies, and editorial method, discussing composers ranging from Johann Sebastian Bach and Christoph Graupner through Hector Berlioz, Anton Bruckner, Antonín Dvořák, Franz Schubert, Robert Schumann, Louis Spohr, and Richard Strauss. His numerous published editions include a two-volume facsimile edition of the complete surviving autograph sources for Mendelssohn's A-major ("Italian") Symphony and the first published edition of the revised version of that work (1997–99), the first complete version of Mendelssohn's setting of Goethe's *Die erste Walpurgisnacht* (2008), and five major works with Bärenreiter-Verlag's *Bärenreiter Urtext* series: Mendelssohn's *Three Motets* op. 69 (2006), the *a cappella* Psalm settings op. posth. 78 (2007), *St. Paul* (2008), the final (1843) version of *Die erste Walpurgisnacht* (2010), and *Der 42. Psalm (Wie der Hirsch schreit)*, op. 42 (2013). He is currently preparing an article on music in nineteenth-century utopian societies in the United States, and writing a book on music and secular religion in the long nineteenth century.

HANS DAVIDSSON is professor of organ at the Royal Danish Academy of Music in Copenhagen, Denmark. From 2001 to 2012, he served as professor of organ at the Eastman School of Music and project director of the Eastman-Rochester Organ Initiative in Rochester, New York. He served as professor of organ at the School of Music at Göteborg University from 1987–2002, as the Artistic Director of the Göteborg International Organ Academy (GIOA) from 1994–2009, and he was the founder of Göteborg Organ Art Center (GOArt). In 2007, he was appointed Professor of Organ at the Hochschule für Künste Bremen in Germany where he is also the director of the Arp Schnitger Institute of Organ and Organ Building. He performs and teaches at major festivals and academies throughout the world. He has made many recordings, including most recently the complete works of Dietrich Buxtehude on the Loft label.

WM. A. LITTLE, a specialist in German organ music of the eighteenth and nineteenth centuries, is professor of German and music emeritus at the University of Virginia. He is the editor of *Felix Mendelssohn Bartholdy: Complete Works for Organ* in five volumes (1987–90). He received the LTCL in Organ Performance from Trinity College, London, a PhD in German from the University of Michigan, an MA from Harvard, and a BA from Tufts. He taught German at Williams College and Tufts, where he was Department Chair. He moved to the University of Virginia in 1966 to chair the German Department. From 1970 to 1978, he edited the *German Quarterly*, the principal journal for German studies in the United States. He has lectured and published widely in the United States and abroad, with particular emphasis on the life and works of Felix Mendelssohn. His most recent book, *Mendelssohn and the Organ*, published by Oxford University Press in 2010, was awarded the John Ogosapian Book Prize by The Organ Historical Society (2011).

PETER MERCER-TAYLOR is associate professor of musicology and director of graduate studies at the University of Minnesota School of Music. After receiving his doctorate from the University of California, Berkeley, he taught humanities and popular culture in the interdisciplinary honors college of Valparaiso University before joining the University of Minnesota faculty in 2001. Mercer-Taylor's scholarship has been divided between the nineteenth-century German classical tradition—Felix Mendelssohn in particular—and contemporary popular music, including the work of the Bangles, Bill Staines, R.E.M, and Manfred Mann's Earth Band. Mercer-Taylor's articles have appeared in a range of journals, including *19th-Century Music*, *Popular Music*, *Musical Quarterly*, *Journal of Musicology*, and *Music Theory Spectrum*. He is the author of *The Life of Mendelssohn* (2000) and the editor of *The Cambridge Companion to Mendelssohn* (2004).

SIEGWART REICHWALD received his doctorate from Florida State University and is now professor of music history at Converse College where, in addition to teaching, he also conducts the Converse Symphony Orchestra. His book, *The Genesis of Felix Mendelssohn's Paulus* (2001), deals with the compositional process of Mendelssohn's oratorio *Paulus*. He is the author of articles on music by Mendelssohn, Brumel, and Poulenc. His principal research interests are in the music of Felix Mendelssohn, the Classic/Romantic period, and orchestral performance practice. He recently edited *Mendelssohn in Performance* (2008), a collection of essays dealing with performance practice issues in the music of Felix Mendelssohn.

GLENN STANLEY is professor of music history at the University of Connecticut. He has published extensively on Beethoven, Mendelssohn, Wagner, and German music and musical life in the nineteenth and twentieth centuries. He edited the *Cambridge Companion to Beethoven* (2000) and volumes 3 and 7 of *Beethoven Forum* and has organized international conferences on Beethoven at the University of Connecticut and at Carnegie Hall. He also writes on questions of aesthetics, methodology, and music criticism, and contributed the articles on historiography and German music criticism to the revised *New Grove Dictionary of Music and Musicians*. He has held guest professorships at the Humboldt University Berlin, the University of Salzburg, and the Free University Berlin. Recent and current work includes a study of the ideological character of Arnold Schering's work, a project on Wagner's *Faust* overture and the presence of Goethe in his thought and work, an analysis of the Archiv für Musikforschung during the Third Reich, and the reception and performance history of *Fidelio*. The essay on Fidelio will appear in volume 4 of the *Beethoven-Handbuch* (Laaber-Verlag) in 2014.

RUSSELL STINSON is the Josephine Emily Brown Professor of Music at Lyon College and organist-choirmaster at St. Paul's Episcopal Church in Batesville, Arkansas. He holds a BMus degree in organ from Stetson University and a PhD in musicology from the University of Chicago. During 2009 he was the Gerhard Herz Visiting Professor of Bach Studies at the University of Louisville. Stinson also serves on the editorial board of *Bach Perspectives*, a series published by the American Bach Society. His research in European archives has been supported by grants from the International Research and Exchanges Board, the Deutscher Akademischer Austauschdienst, and the American Bach Society. His numerous publications on the music of J. S. Bach include books on the *Orgelbüchlein* and the Great Eighteen organ chorales. His latest monograph, *J. S. Bach at His Royal Instrument: Essays on His Organ Works*, was published by Oxford University Press in 2012. Most recently, Stinson has authored the "Notes" to the *Oxford Bach Books for Organ*, a forthcoming five-volume edition of Bach's organ works edited by Anne Marsden Thomas. His current research project is Richard Wagner's reception of Bach's music.

BENEDICT TAYLOR is Chancellor's Fellow in the Reid School of Music, University of Edinburgh. A graduate of St Catharine's College, Cambridge, he subsequently held fellowships at Heidelberg, Princeton, and Berlin before going to Oxford in 2011 as Stipendiary Lecturer in Music at Magdalen and Senior Research Fellow of New College. He is the author of *Mendelssohn, Time and Memory: The Romantic Conception of Cyclic Form* (2011) and has published on a range of nineteenth- and twentieth-century music. His article "Cyclic Form, Time and Memory in Mendelssohn's A minor Quartet, Op. 13" (*Musical Quarterly*, 2010) was the recipient of the Jerome Roche Prize from the Royal Musical Association for a distinguished article by a young scholar. Taylor's most recent book, *The Melody of Time*, a study of music and temporality from Beethoven to Elgar, is forthcoming from Oxford University Press in 2015, alongside an edited collection of essays on Mendelssohn for Ashgate's The Early Romantic Composers series.

NICHOLAS THISTLETHWAITE is a leading authority on the history and use of the organ in England. In addition to writing *The Making of the Victorian Organ* (1990) and coediting *The Cambridge Guide to the Organ* (1999), he has published many other monographs, articles, and reviews relating to organs, organists, church music and liturgy. He was a teaching member of the Music Faculty of the University of Cambridge for some years, and has served on various public and voluntary bodies in the UK, including the Cathedral Fabric Commission for England and the British Institute for Organ Studies (of which he was Secretary and subsequently Chairman). Thistlethwaite is a member of the Association of Independent Organ Advisers. His projects as organ consultant include a new organ for St. John's College, Cambridge; the reconstruction of the Hill organs in Birmingham Town Hall and Eton College Chapel; and the restoration of historic instruments in Buckingham Palace, St. Ann Limehouse, and Reading Town Hall. Current projects (2014) include the restoration of the Richard Bridge organ (1734) in Christ Church Spitalfields and the Lincoln organ (1821) in Thaxted Parish Church. Dr. Thistlethwaite is also an Anglican priest, and is Sub Dean and Precentor of Guildford Cathedral.

JÜRGEN THYM has been at the Eastman School of Music (University of Rochester) for more than forty years. Now a professor emeritus of musicology (and still teaching), he has published on text-music relations in the Lieder of Schubert, Mendelssohn, Schumann, Brahms, Wolf, Weill and others (coauthoring several essays with the late Ann C. Fehn), in journals such as *Archiv für Musikwissenschaft*, *Ars Lyrica*, *American Choral Review*, *Comparative Literature*, *Fontes Artis Musicae*, *Journal of Musicological Research*, *Journal of the American Liszt Society*, and *Notes*. He edited the anthology *100 Years of Eichendorff Songs* (1983), coedited several volumes in the Arnold Schoenberg Collected Works Edition (with Nikos Kokkinis, 1984–94), and was cotranslator of music theory treatises by Kirnberger (*Die Kunst des reinen Satzes in der Musik*, with David Beach, 1982) and Schenker (*Kontrapunkt*, 2 vols., with John Rothgeb, 1987). His most recent accomplishments are *Luca Lombardi: Construction of Freedom*, a translation and edition of the composer's selected writings (2006), and *Of Poetry and Song: Approaches to the Nineteenth-Century Lied* (2010). From 1982 to 2000, Thym was the chair of musicology at the Eastman School of Music.

R. LARRY TODD is the author of *Mendelssohn: A Life in Music* (Oxford University Press), named best biography of 2003 by the Association of American Publishers, and described in the *New York Review of Books* as "likely to be the standard biography for a long time to come" (a German translation appeared from Reclam/Carus Verlag as *Felix Mendelssohn Bartholdy: Sein Leben, seine Musik*). Arts and Sciences Professor of Music and former chair of the music department at Duke University, where he has taught for three decades, Todd has published widely on nineteenth-century music with a focus on Mendelssohn and his sister Fanny Hensel, as well as essays on Haydn, Robert and Clara Schumann, Liszt, Brahms, Richard Strauss, and Webern. He is a former fellow of the John Hope Franklin Humanities Institute and recipient of fellowships from the Guggenheim Foundation and National Humanities Center. His biography of Fanny Hensel, titled *Fanny Hensel, the Other Mendelssohn* (2010), was awarded the Nicholas Slonimsky Award from ASCAP. He serves as general editor of the Routledge Studies in Musical Genres and of the Master Musician Series for Oxford University Press and has recently released a recording with Nancy Green of the complete cello music of Mendelssohn and Fanny Hensel (JRI Recordings).

CHRISTOPH WOLFF recently retired as Adams University Professor at Harvard University. Born and educated in Germany, he studied organ and historical keyboard instruments, musicology and art history at the Universities of Berlin, Erlangen, and Freiburg, taking a performance diploma in 1963 and the DPhil in 1966. He taught the history of music at Erlangen, Toronto, Princeton, and Columbia Universities before joining the Harvard faculty in 1976 as professor of music; William Powell Mason Professor of Music, 1985–2002; and Adams University Professor, 2002–12. At Harvard he served as chair of the music department (1980–88, '90–91), acting director of the University Library (1991–92), and dean of the Graduate School of Arts and Sciences (1992–2000). Recipient of various international prizes, several honorary degrees, he holds an honorary professorship at the University of Freiburg and memberships in the American Academy of Arts and Sciences, the American Philosophical Society, and the Sächsische Akademie der Wissenschaften. He served as director of the Bach-Archiv in Leipzig from 2001 to 2013 and concurrently also as president of the *Répertoire International des Sources Musicales*. He published widely on the history of music from the fifteenth to the twentieth centuries, notably on Bach and Mozart. His latest book, *Mozart at the Gateway to His Fortune: Serving the Emperor, 1788–1791*, was published in 2012.

Index